Dictionary
of Proverbs
and their origins

Linda Flavell completed a first degree in modern languages and has
subsequent qualifications in both secondary and primary teaching.
She has worked as an English teacher both in England and overseas,
and more recently as a librarian in secondary schools and as a writer.
She has written three simplified readers for overseas students and
co-authored, with her husband, *Current English Usage* for Papermac
and several dictionaries of etymologies for Kyle Cathie.

Roger Flavell's Master's thesis was on the nature of idiomaticity and
his doctoral research on idioms and their teaching in several European
languages. On taking up a post as Lecturer in Education at the Institute
of Education, University of London, he travelled very widely in pursuit
of his principal interests in education and training language teachers. In
more recent years, he was concerned with education and international
development, and with online education. He also worked as an
independent educational consultant. He died in December 2005, just
after completing the work on the revised edition of *Dictionary of Idioms*.

DICTIONARY
OF PROVERBS
AND THEIR ORIGINS

Linda and Roger Flavell

Kyle Cathie Ltd

First published in Great Britain in 1993 by
Kyle Cathie Limited
122 Arlington Road
London NW1 7HP
general.enquiries@kyle-cathie.com
www.kylecathie.com

Published in paperback 1994

Reprinted 6 times

This completely revised and updated edition published 2008

10 9 8 7 6 5 4 3 2 1

ISBN 978 1 85626 736 6

© 1993, 2008 by Linda and Roger Flavell

A Cataloguing in Publication record for this title is available
from the British Library.

Printed and bound in Great Britain by Cox & Wyman

· Introduction ·

A proverb has three characteristics: few words, good sense,
and a fine image
(Moses Ibn Ezra, SHIRAT YISRAEL, 1924)

Proverbs have been in use for thousands of years. A major early collection is the BOOK OF PROVERBS in the Old Testament of the Bible. This is, in fact, a collection of collections, which reached its final edited form in about the fifth century BC although, according to scholars, many of its individual sayings date from at least the seventh century BC. Proverbs have always had a strong hold on cultures throughout the world. Each language has its own treasuries of folk sayings. For British collections, see AN ACCUMULATION OF WISDOM (page 120); and for one of the greatest and most influential collections, see ERASMUS'S ADAGIA (page 34).

Why is it that proverbs have exercised such a fascination over the millennia? Moses Ibn Ezra's definition above provides an explanation. Above all, proverbs offer good sense. They are guidelines for life, based on collective folk wisdom. Such riches are eagerly sought after at any stage in mankind's development. Proverbs are also pithily, even wittily, and always memorably phrased, the result of a refining process that often takes them through various versions before they reach their polished final form (see A MATTER OF FORM, page 100). Many people have tried to define a proverb; some of their efforts are gathered in WHAT IS A PROVERB? (page 14). This book responds to the interest in proverbs by providing information both for reference purposes and for the browser.

Browsing

It may be Ezra's *fine image* of the language, it may be fascination with customs of past ages, it may be a love of life and wisdom – whatever the attraction to books on proverbs, we have taken great pains to please the browser.

In this revised edition of *Dictionary of Proverbs and their Origins*, we have omitted those proverbs that have fallen from the language and included some new sayings that have come into popular use. The entries have been selected because they have a tale to tell. There are many more that could have been included, but we hope that we have provided a satisfying cross section of the vast range of proverbs that occurs in English, even if we cannot claim it be a comprehensive list.

The etymology (or etymologies, since there are sometimes alternative accounts) tries to go back to the earliest origins. We endeavour to give dates, although it is often impossible to do this with any confidence. As proverbs are passed down in the oral tradition from generation to generation, the first written record (even if we can specify *that* with any certainty) is likely to be a poor indication of the saying's actual origin. This is an important reservation to bear in mind when, for brevity in an entry, we say something like 'This is the earliest use'. Sometimes *The wit of one* reflects the previous *wisdom of many*, as with Shakespeare's *Neither a BORROWER nor a lender be*, or Pope's *To err is human, to FORGIVE divine* – both expressions that were in common use long before they were immortalised by these writers.

We have done our utmost to be precise about the dates of quotations in order to show the development of the sayings in form, meaning and use. There are real difficulties with many works, and in each case we have chosen what seems to be an appropriate solution. For example, we have followed the Oxford English Dictionary dates for Shakespeare's plays; given the last edition (1536) that Erasmus himself produced of his *Adagia*; used one date for the *Canterbury Tales*, even though they were written over a period of fourteen years or so, and so on.

Proverbs often come from worlds that are far removed from our contemporary civilisation. Where necessary, we have offered information on the context of the saying within the entry itself or within one of the boxes or essays throughout the book. For example, there is an explanation of sixteenth-century sleeping arrangements in *As you make your BED so you must lie in it* and of the growth of printing in *The PEN is mightier than the sword*. On occasions we have gone beyond the general cultural context to events surroundings the use of proverbs. For a tale of skulduggery in the highest places, follow the sad story of Sir Thomas Overbury and the dubious activities of James I in *No NEWS is good news* and *BEAUTY is only skin deep*.

The essays and boxes strategically situated throughout the book (usually near entries on a connected theme) are of various kinds – cultural, linguistic or just plain curious. They are designed to reflect the riches and diversity of proverb lore.

Reference

Each saying dealt with in the body of the book is listed alphabetically in relation to a key word within it. As proverbs are whole sentences, there is necessarily a choice to be made regarding the main word. We have exercised our judgement as to which is the key word (normally a noun or a verb) but, in case our intuitions do not coincide with the reader's, we have provided an index of all the important words in each saying at the back of the book.

The proverb itself is followed by a definition, giving the contemporary meaning. This is often necessary because the sense, after a long history of slowly changing use, may not be entirely clear. Common variants are also included. Occasional notes on formality and informality, connotations, grammatical peculiarities and so on are found under *Usage* at the end of an entry.

Each entry contains at least two contemporary quotations showing the proverb in present-day use. These are listed in chronological order and come from a wide range of newspapers, magazines, periodicals and literary works.

The bibliography is there both to show our sources and to provide a point of extended reference. It is only a selective list. To have included all the thousands of sources we referred to would have made the bibliography unmanageable. In the text of the book we often refer to an author just by the name (e.g. Walsh). Full details are in the bibliography. If there is the possibility of confusion because the author has more than one entry, the name is followed by the date of publication of the relevant book.

Our task in producing this revised edition has been greatly helped by the internet, which has given us access to information and texts not easily available to us before. Our thanks are due to the various libraries we consulted extensively for the first edition: our local library in Sussex, the University of London Library and, above all, the British Library, without which it would not have been possible to write a book like this. Our indebtedness is even greater to scholars who have preceded us in the field. The subject of proverbs has benefited from the herculaen labours of many. V. S. Lean, for example, devoted over fifty years of his life to his monumental collection of 1902–4. We would particularly like to acknowledge our appreciation of the pioneering work of William Shepard Walsh, whose aims, approach and spirit are very much our own. We stand in awe of the erudition, scholarship and diligence of Burton Egbert Stevenson. We are grateful for the comprehensive bibliographical endeavours of Wolfgang Mieder. We hope that where we have followed their lead they will indeed recognise that *IMITATION is the sincerest form of flattery*.

Inevitably we will have made mistakes, for which we bear sole responsibility. We would welcome readers' comments and corrections.

In short, our aim has been to inform and entertain, to provide a balance of reference material and a rich and varied diet for the curious; we have striven for scholarly accuracy without falling into academic pedantry. Now it is for you to judge for, after all, *The proof of the PUDDING is in the eating*.

How to find a proverb
Each proverb is listed under a key word. For example: *An APPLE a day keeps the doctor away* is under *apple*. However, there is often a choice of keyword, so the index at the back of the book lists all the significant words within an expression. You could look up *apple, day* or *doctor* and immediately be guided to the right page. To make cross-references to other entries easy to find, the keyword used appears in SMALL CAPITALS: for example, *An APPLE a day keeps the doctor away* or *Out of SIGHT, out of mind*.

Linda Flavell, YORK, NOVEMBER 2007

MAIN ESSAYS

· A ·

ABSENCE

absence makes the heart grow fonder
our feeling for those we love increases when we are apart from them

This is a line from the song ISLE OF BEAUTY by songwriter and dramatist Thomas Haynes Bayly, published posthumously in 1850:

Absence makes the heart grow fonder:
Isle of Beauty, fare thee well!

Although it was Bayly who popularised the words, they are not of his inspiration, being originally the first line of an anonymous poem in POETICAL RAPSODY (1602), a miscellany compiled by Francis Davison.

    The sentiment that yearning for a loved one grows stronger through absence is endorsed in literature. In Shakespeare's MERCHANT OF VENICE (1600), Portia confesses *I dote upon his very absence*; in FAMILIAR LETTERS (1619), James Howell discloses that *Distance sometimes endears friendship, and absence sweeteneth it*; La Rochefoucauld quotes a French proverb which says that *Friends agree best at a distance* (MAXIMES, 1665), while French memoire writer Roger de Bussy-Rabutin writes that *Absence is to love what wind is to fire; it puts out the little, it kindles the great* (MAXIMES D'AMOUR, 1666).

    Of course, the other side of the coin is *Out of SIGHT, out of mind*. Psychologists say that many people are lazy about personal relationships and find it quite easy to put them aside when separated. However, for those who are parted from a loved one and concerned that absence might not be having its intensifying effect, Charles Lamb in his DISSERTATION ON A ROAST PIG (1823) offers this advice: *Presents, I often say, endear absents.*

I spent so much time on the road this year that it was difficult to achieve the right balance in my life,' she says. 'I don't believe that absence makes the heart grow fonder, but as a couple, Tom and I are really strong, and it's been a test that we've survived.
DAILY TELEGRAPH, 24 OCTOBER 2003

*This summer, I'm taking a sabbatical and heading off for Georgia, USA. And guess what? Hubby's coming too. But for the first time in eight years, we'll be teaching at different schools. They say **absence makes the heart grow fonder**? I'll let you know.*
TIMES EDUCATIONAL SUPPLEMENT, 9 JULY 2004

ACCIDENTS

accidents will happen in the best regulated families
not even well ordered lives are immune from mishap or calamity

Variant: Accidents will happen even in the best circles

The line *Accidents, accidents will happen* appears in the eighteenth-century farce THE DEUCE IS IN HIM (1763), written by George Colman the elder. The modern ear is probably more accustomed to *Accidents will happen* than to the longer, nineteenth-century proverb alluded to by Sir Walter Scott in PEVEREL OF THE PEAK (1823): *Nay, my lady,... such things will befall in the best regulated families.*

In the first half of the twentieth century, the proverb became a favourite of popular crime writers when a skeleton in the family cupboard, came to light.

*...I will never understand why you are so easily willing to give our basic freedoms away in the name of safety. Face it, we are human and **accidents will happen** no matter what you try to do to prevent them. We cannot protect everyone from everything. I have said before that educational programs to persuade people to wear seat belts are the answer, not more legislation.*
KENTUCKY POST,
30 NOVEMBER 2001

*Although New Delhi's underground railway is being built, the capital's transport strategy is to build more highways. The skyline is strewn with flyovers and half-built elevated sections; the traffic clogs up the capital's roads most hours of the day. **Accidents will happen** and the chances in Delhi of a prang are higher than almost anywhere in the world.*
GUARDIAN, 14 AUGUST 2004

Usage: The abbreviated proverbial form *accidents will happen...* is often left hanging in the air as a comment on any situation. The tone implicit can range from the commiserating through to the delighted.

ACTIONS

actions speak louder than words

what people do reveals more about them than what they say

An abundance of proverbial literature, some of it dating back to ancient times, exhorts the reader to relate his words to his deeds. *Deeds are fruits, words are but leaves*, declares Thomas Draxe (BIBLIOTHECA, 1633). The Bible's message *By their fruits ye shall know them* (MATTHEW 7:20) supports his analogy, exhorting us to judge people on the quality of their lives rather than the persuasiveness of their speech. Another old saying on a horticultural theme compares a person whose words are more in evidence than his actions to a garden, as recounted by James Howell in ENGLISH PROVERBS (1659):

*A man of words and not of deeds
Is like a garden full of weeds.*

The Roman poet Ovid is quite blunt about the criterion for assessing others. No need of words, trust deeds, he urges (FASTI, c. AD 8). George Herbert concurs, citing *The effect speaks, the tongue need not* (JACULA PRUDENTUM, 1640). This would seem to be a precursor of our present-day proverb *Actions speak louder than words* which, though relatively recent in coinage, dating back to the early twentieth century, expresses the ancient wisdom that the way a person conducts his life proclaims his character better than any words can.

*Actions speak louder than words.
How many times have we heard that expression? Why is that old adage still around? Because we have been raised, as a people in the United States of America, to take people on their word...We take for granted that people are telling the truth. On the other hand, when we see their actions, we are astounded. They do just the opposite of what they say.*
COLUMBUS TIMES, 2 JUNE 2004

Manners are all about respect for yourself and for others; treat people with the same courtesy you would like them to show you, remembering always that actions speak louder than words.

INDEPENDENT, 17 NOVEMBER 2005

See also *HANDSOME is as handsome does; FINE words butter no parsnips*

APPEARANCES

appearances are deceptive

outward demeanour can be misleading; internal reality is often different from external looks

Variant: Appearances are deceiving

Giovanni Torriano records *Appearance often deceives* in his monumental reference book of Italian proverbs PIAZZA UNIVERSALE (1666), and Tobias Smollett has *Appearances are very deceitful* in his translation of the French novel GIL BLAS (1750).

The proverb was well established in English by the mid-nineteenth century but the wisdom behind it is ancient. In his fable THE WOLF IN SHEEP'S CLOTHING (c. 570 BC) Aesop tells of a wolf who pulls a sheepskin over his back and joins a flock so that he can enjoy a meal when the fancy takes him. Appearances are indeed deceptive.

Walsh quotes the interesting entry of Judge Haliburton (1796–1865) in his MAXIMS OF AN OLD STAGER to illustrate the proverb: *Always judge your fellow-passengers to be the opposite of what they appear to be. For instance, a military man is not quarrelsome, for no man doubts his courage, but a snob is. A clergyman is not over strait-laced, for his piety is not questioned, but a cheat is. A lawyer is not apt to be argumentative, but an actor is. A woman that is all smiles and graces is a vixen at heart; snakes fascinate. A stranger that is obsequious and over-civil without apparent cause is treacherous; cats that*

purr are apt to bite and scratch. Pride is one thing, assumption is another; the latter must always get the cold shoulder, for whoever shows it is no gentleman: men never affect to be what they are, but what they are not. The only man who really is what he appears to be is – a gentleman.

The January sky is thronged with brilliant stars, and further enlivened this year by Jupiter and Saturn. It's easy to imagine these luminous objects are the main ingredients of the universe. But appearances are deceptive. Astronomers have discovered that most of the matter and energy in the universe are invisible. They are not just beyond human vision, but they cannot even be seen by the most powerful telescopes. Until now, that is.

INDEPENDENT, 21 DECEMBER 2001

Jeans-clad, a hanky to her cold-ridden nose and her eyes glued to children's cartoons on telly, at first sight Tamzin Outhwaite is the antithesis of a leading lady. But appearances are deceptive. Tamzin is one of TV's most popular actresses, as well as a successful model and, by the most conservative estimate, a self-made millionaire.

EVENING STANDARD, 23 JANUARY 2004

See also *Never judge by APPEARANCES; BEAUTY is only skin deep; All that glitters is not GOLD; The cowl does not make the MONK*

never judge by appearances

outward demeanour should never be used as a criterion for assessment of character

Variant: Don't judge by appearances

Why should one *never judge by appearances*? Because, to quote another proverb, *APPEARANCES are deceptive*. Not surprisingly, this thought finds expression in both Old and New Testaments. When the prophet Samuel

WHAT IS A PROVERB?
Proverbs have been part of the fabric of language for so long and encapsulate such a store of wisdom in so few words that writers have, again and again, attempted to pinpoint their power in an equally pithy definition (see the introduction on page 5):

The wisdom of the street

Daughters of daily experience

A short pithy saying in common and recognized use
(OXFORD ENGLISH DICTIONARY)

A concise sentence, often metaphorical or alliterative in form, which is held to express some truth ascertained by experience or observation and familiar to all
(OXFORD ENGLISH DICTIONARY)

A brief epigrammatic saying that is a popular byword
(WEBSTER'S NEW INTERNATIONAL DICTIONARY)

Proverbs are short sentences drawn from long experience
(CERVANTES, DON QUIXOTE, 1605)

The People's Voice
(JAMES HOWELL, 1594–1666)

Proverbs may not improperly be called the Philosophy of the Common People, or, according to Aristotle, the truest Reliques of old Philosophy
(HOWELL, LEXICON, PROVERBS, 1659)

Much matter decocted into a few words
(THOMAS FULLER, THE WORTHIES OF ENGLAND, 1662)

What is a proverb, but the experience and observation of several ages, gathered and summed up into one expression?
(ROBERT SOUTH, SERMONS, 1692)

Notable measures and directions for human life
(WILLIAM PENN, ADVICE TO HIS CHILDREN, 1699)

The wit of one man and the wisdom of many
(LORD JOHN RUSSELL, QUARTERLY REVIEW, 1850)

A proverb has three characteristics: few words, good sense, and a fine image
(MOSES IBN EZRA, SHIRAT YISRAEL, 1924)

searches amongst the sons of Jesse for God's intended king over Israel, he is tempted to choose the brother with the most striking appearance. God, however, rejects him, saying, *Look not on his countenance, or on the height of his stature, because I have refused him; for the Lord seeth not as man seeth, for man looketh on the outward appearance, but the Lord looketh on the heart* (I SAMUEL 16:7). God's choice is the youngest son, David. In John's gospel, when he was criticised for healing a man on the Sabbath day, Jesus commanded his followers *Judge not according to the appearance, but judge righteous judgement* (JOHN 7:24).

The same wisdom is found in other ancient texts. In his SATIRES (c. AD 120), Juvenal has *Fronti nulla fides*. This translates as 'No faith in the forehead', meaning that a man's character is not written on his face. Samuel Fielding quotes the Latin proverb in TOM JONES (1749), calling it *a true saying*.

Another Latin proverb *Vilis saepe cadus nobile nectar habet* ('A common jar often holds noble nectar') scrutinises the way a person is turned out. This is the line Hawley Franck took when he wrote the lyrics to the song MANY AN HONEST HEART MAY BEAT BENEATH A RAGGED COAT (1901):

Don't judge by appearances, but by his actions more,
You never know when you may drive a good man from your door;
Clothes don't make the man, you know, some wise person wrote,
For many an honest heart may beat beneath a ragged coat.

The generally accepted wisdom of the proverb does not go unchallenged, however. Oscar Wilde, master of ostentatious witticisms, turns the proverb on its head, declaring *it is only the shallow people who do not judge by appearances* (THE PICTURE OF DORIAN GRAY, 1891), indicating that such individuals do not have the wit or wisdom to form a shrewd opinion of what they see.

Never judge by appearances in this new economy: it's the man with the beaten up shoes who's worth £20m.
SUNDAY TELEGRAPH, 12 MARCH 2000

*I was disappointed to see Simon Hoggart falling into the common trap of assuming that if a person is not visibly crippled or using a wheelchair, he or she has no right to be described as disabled. If he were to observe me sitting on the tube, he could deduce nothing from my outward appearance of the daily painkillers, fortnightly visits to an osteopath and stringent daily exercise regime which enable me to function to some extent... Count yourself lucky, Mr Hoggart, if you are still relatively pain-free for most of the time, but please **don't judge by appearances**.*
GUARDIAN, 27 AUGUST 2001

See also *APPEARANCES are deceptive; never judge a BOOK by its cover; Fine FEATHERS make fine birds; The cowl does not make the MONK*

APPLE

an apple a day keeps the doctor away

eating an apple every day will keep you in good health

Apples were originally cultivated from wild crab-apples, which are native to Britain. During the Roman occupation, several varieties of apple were introduced and grafted on to the native stock so that, before the Norman Conquest, there was already an abundance of the fruit.

The Anglo Saxons drank apple juice and cider. Orchards were planted in monasteries and the fruit grown both for eating and cider making. When the Normans invaded in 1066, several new varieties of apple were introduced in Britain, among them the Pearmain, an excellent cider apple, and the Costard, a large variety of cooking apple. In his encyclopedia DE PROPRIETABIUS RERUM (ON THE NATURE OF THINGS, c. 1243–1247), the English monk Bartholomeus Anglicus says of the apple tree:

Malus the Appyll tree...is gracious in syght and in taste and vertuous in medecyne... some beryth sourysh fruyte and harde, and some ryght soure and some ryght swete, with a good savoure and mery.

Medieval cookbooks include recipes for apple moys, an apple sauce for serving with flesh or with fish, and for an apple muse, a rather thin dessert: *Take Appelys an sethe hem, & Serge hem thorwe a Sefe in-to a potte: thanne take Almaunde Mylke & Hony, an caste ther-to, an gratid Brede, Safroun, Saunderys, & Salt a lytil, & caste all in the potte & lete hem sethe; & loke that thou stere it wyl, & serue it forth* (from T Austin (ed), TWO FIFTEENTH-CENTURY COOKERY-BOOKS, 2000).

The apple has had special significance in many cultures and is central to several Greek, Roman, Celtic and Norse legends. In England, over the centuries, a number of charms and omens have sprung up about it. Apple pips cast into a fire or pressed to the cheek are a test of true love. Apple peel cast over the shoulder will form the initial of one's future sweetheart and a good crop of apples signifies a good year for twins.

In THE HAVEN OF HEALTH (1612), Thomas Cogan writes that *apples are thought to quench the flame of Venus* and he quotes the rhyme:

He that will not a wife wed,
Must eat a cold apple when he goeth to bed.

As Bartholomeus Anglicus stated, apples were thought to be *vertuous in medecyne*, and an apple before retiring, this time for medicinal purposes, recurs in what is called by some *an old English verse*:

Ate an apfel
avore gwain bed
makes the doctor
beg his bread.

Appearances may flatter to deceive, however. In spite of its archaic spellings, the verse has yet to be traced to a medieval manuscript. Instead, a correspondent with NOTES AND QUERIES (1866) quotes:

Eat an apple on going to bed,
And you'll keep the doctor from earning
his bread

as a Welsh folk proverb. The rhyme is later cited in William Crossing's FOLK RHYMES OF DEVON (1911) and E M Wright's RUSTIC SPEECH (1913). Some claim that *An apple a day keeps the doctor away* is an American rendering of this British proverbial wisdom. According to the RANDOM HOUSE DICTIONARY OF POPULAR PROVERBS AND SAYINGS (Gregory Y Titleman, 1996), it was first attested in the United States in 1913.

But is there any truth in the proverb? It is certainly possible to eat an apple a day, for the fruit has excellent keeping qualities if stored in a cool, dry place. Nutritionally the apple contains no harmful sodium or fat to make a doctor frown. On the contrary, recent research suggests that apples promote improved lung function, protect against harmful 'bad' cholesterol and are high in anti-oxidants and fibre, thus fighting asthma, heart disease and certain types of cancer.

It seems that our ancestors were wise indeed; a daily apple can do us nothing but good – unlike some other things we might eat. Robert Reisner records this 'anti-proverb' in GRAFFITI: TWO THOUSAND YEARS OF WALL WRITING (1971): *An apple a day keeps the doctor away, but an onion a day keeps everybody away.*

An apple a day keeps the doctor away – and it might now keep the inspectors at bay, too. A primary school in Croydon which banned junk food from its tuckshop and replaced it with fresh fruit has seen a dramatic improvement in behaviour and a rise in test scores.
TIMES EDUCATIONAL SUPPLEMENT, 10 MARCH 2000

The saying goes, 'An apple a day keeps the doctor away.' But why not a cherry? Or a plum? Probably because in the old days apples were one of the few homegrown foods you could eat fresh all winter. A cellar full of long-keepers supplied you with a daily, living package of vitamin C right up to the time when the summer fruits were ripe.
WASHINGTON POST, 19 JANUARY 2006

ART

art is long, life is short
there are so many skills (art) and so much knowledge to acquire that a lifetime is not long enough to do it all justice

Hippocrates was the most well-known and highly acclaimed physician of ancient Greece. His work consists of a collection of his own writings on the art of healing together with those of other Greek physicians. (See also *DESPERATE diseases call for desperate remedies*.) Of particular interest is the Hippocratic Oath which provides the ethical framework of modern day medical practice. In APHORISMS (c. 400 BC) Hippocrates expresses the frustration of the physician thus: *Life is short, the art long, opportunity fleeting, experience treacherous, judgment difficult.*

The influence of the phrase was advanced by Seneca, the Roman philosopher and dramatist, in his appropriately entitled DE BREVITATE VITAE ('ON THE SHORTNESS OF LIFE', c. AD 49). Seneca's original *Vita brevis est, ars longa* was recast in subsequent centuries to *Ars longa, vita brevis*, which is still quoted on occasion in Latin today.

In English, the earliest reference is in Chaucer's PARLEMENT OF FOULES (c. 1374):

> *The lyf so short, the craft so long to learn,*
> *Th'assay so hard, so sharp the*
> *conqueriynge.*

And two centuries later, in NOSCE TEIPSUM (1599), the Renaissance poet and playwright Sir John Davies encapsulates the full meaning of the proverb in these words:

> *Skill comes so slow, and life so fast doth fly,*
> *We learn so little and forget so much.*

Hippocrates was, of course, referring to medical skill but it has since pleased many writers to apply his words to their own particular craft. In *An Essay on Criticism* (1711), Pope uses them to refer to critics who, he argues, should know themselves, their abilities and their limitations. It is one of life's frustrations that any one person can only aspire to so much:

> *One science only will one genius fit;*
> *So vast is art, so narrow human wit:*
> *Not only bounded to peculiar arts,*
> *But oft' in those confin'd to single parts.*

Many other famous writers, in the nineteenth century in particular, have echoed similar themes. Goethe, Baudelaire, Longfellow and Browning all used the saying, thereby adding to its popularity.

During the twentieth century, however, the adage was often misconstrued to mean that art lives on beyond the end of the (short) life of its creator, providing a kind of immortality. This misuse has appeared so frequently that it is now recognised as a valid alternative and, indeed, is more commonly found than the original.

Art is long; life is short. This wise epigram captures the sentiment that while our lives are over in a blinking of an eye, or a little over three-score years and ten these days, paintings, poetry and music survives the creator by a good few years if it's any good.
BIRMINGHAM POST, 23 APRIL 2002

When Riefenstahl died in 2003, she was 102 years old and still famous, still defending herself. As Bach writes, 'She was the inexhaustible curator of her legend.' Whatever her place in film history, Riefenstahl's place in world history is, I imagine, unshakable... As the old Latin saying goes, **Ars longa, vita brevis –** *Art is long, life is short. The controversy over this fascinating filmmaker is unlikely to subside as long as we continue to see ourselves – our hopes and dreams, nightmares and fears – in the images that we project against the dark walls of history.*
ROCKY MOUNTAIN NEWS, 16 MARCH 2007

· B ·

BABY

don't throw the baby out with the bathwater

when making changes, be careful not to reject what is still useful along with what is no longer needed; don't throw out the good with the bad

This proverb is of German origin, a translation of *Man soll das Kind nich mit dem Bade ausschütten*. The Scottish-born historian and essayist Thomas Carlyle, who had a considerable interest in German culture, language and literature, brought it, somewhat clumsily, to British attention in an essay on slavery entitled AN OCCASIONAL DISCOURSE ON THE NIGGER QUESTION. The essay was published twice, first in an edition of FRASER'S MAGAZINE (1849), and later as a pamphlet (1853). It argues in favour of ameliorating the institution of slavery but insists that the *baby*, slavery itself, should be preserved:

The Germans say, 'you must empty-out the bathing-tub, but not the baby along with it.' Fling-out your dirty water with all zeal, and set it careering down the kennels; but try if you can keep the little child!

How to abolish the abuses of slavery, and save the precious thing in it alas, I do not pretend that this is easy, that it can be done in a day, or a single generation, or a single century: but I do surmise or perceive that it will, by straight methods or by circuitous, need to be done. […] And truly, my friends, with regard to this world-famous Nigger Question, – which perhaps is louder than it is big, after all, – I would advise you to attack it on that side. Try

against the dirty water, with an eye to save the baby! That will be a quite new point of attack; where, it seems to me, some real benefit and victory for the poor Negro, might before long be accomplished…

The German phrase itself was coined as an idiom, *das Kind mit dem Bade ausschütten* ('to throw the baby out with the bathwater'), possibly in the late fifteenth century. According to Wolfgang Mieder (DE PROVERBIO, Issue 1, 1995), it appears thus as a chapter heading in NARRENBESCHWORUNG (1512), a satirical work by Thomas Murner, and then in 1541 as an entry in a proverb collection by Sebastian Franck. Martin Luther made a proverb of the expression by changing it to *Man sol das kind nicht mit dem bad ausgiessen* ('Don't throw the baby out with the bathwater'). There is speculation that Thomas Carlyle came across the figure in a work by Goethe. The proverb did not come into use in English immediately on publication of Carlyle's essay, however. Not until the early twentieth century was it more successfully translated. George Bernard Shaw, for instance, has *We are apt to make the usual blunder of emptying the baby out with the bath* (A TREATISE ON PARENTS AND CHILDREN, 1914). The proverb is now so well established that its German origins are forgotten.

And this matters, it seems to me, because of the alarming extent to which modern citizens – in their rejection of these old, stuffy, and sometimes questionable images of national community and service – tend to **throw the baby out with the bathwater,**

WRITERS ON PROVERBS

Some writers show an exceptional fondness for using proverbs. Martin Luther (1483–1546) uses them in all his varied types of writing, from the theological through to the popular. This passage from his Lectures on Romans contains references to German proverbs and fables that would have been familiar to his readers:

Meanwhile the devil standing behind him laughs in his sleeve and says 'Primp yourself, little kitten, here comes company.' Then he gets up, goes into the choir to pray, and says; 'O little owl, how beautiful you are! Where did you get the peacock feathers?' If I did not know (to use the language of the fable) that you are an ass, I should think you were a lion – that is how you roar; but go on, wear your lion's skin; your long ears will betray you!

Some lesser-known French writers of the seventeenth century also used considerable numbers of popular sayings: Adrien de Montluc (1589–1646), Gédéon Tallement des Réaux (1619–90) and Antoine Furetière (1619–88). Their contemporary, Jean de la Fontaine (1621–95), is known for his celebrated FABLES, in which he made good use of many moral proverbial sayings:

Sur les ailes du Temps la tristesse s'envole
On the wings of Time grief flies away

C'est double plaisir de tromper le trompeur
It is twice the pleasure to deceive the deceiver

Goethe (1749–1832) showed a fondness for proverbs, and for reformulating them, which has been the subject of articles and a book-length study. Professor Wolfgang Mieder of the University of Vermont gives a thorough review of the use of proverbs in all the significant German authors.

See *Don't throw the BABY out with the bathwater*.

and reject the idea of social obligation and ritual altogether.
SCOTSMAN, 13 AUGUST 2002

*GEMINI (May 21–June 20): You may examine every flaw where money is concerned but, nevertheless, others close have worthwhile ideas. **Don't throw the baby out with the bathwater**. Conflicting opinions mean you should wait and see, as valuable advice will eventually be apparent.*
WASHINGTON POST, 29 NOVEMBER 2004

Usage: Informal

BACK

you scratch my back, and I'll scratch yours

if you help me, I'll help you

Mutuum muli scabunt ('Mules scratch each other') is a Latin saying recorded by Erasmus in ADAGIA (1536). Thomas Coryat defines it thus: *Mulus mulum scabit, by which the Ancients signified, the courtesies done unto friends, ought to be requited with reciprocal offices of friendship* (ENGLISH WITS, 1616).

John Ray puts it rather more bluntly: *Scratch my breech and I'll claw your elbow. Mutuum muli scabunt. Ka me and I'll ka thee. When undeserving persons commend one another* (ENGLISH PROVERBS, 1670).

The proverb has been variously expressed over the centuries with no particular fixed form. *You scratch my back and I'll scratch yours* seems to be from the nineteenth century.

A literary instance of mutual back scratching in the form of flattery took place between Sir Edward Bulwer and Dickens. In July 1865 both authors were present at the inauguration of the Guild of Literature and Art. Bulwer referred to Dickens as *a resplendent ornament of literature*. Dickens, in return, praised Bulwer as *the brightest ornament of the literary class*. Bulwer then pronounced Hertfordshire fortunate in welcoming such a famous man while Dickens declared that county *the envy of every other county in England* because Bulwer lived there. Dickens then went on to counter Bulwer's fulsome praise of his literary mastery by pronouncing that *when the health, life, and beauty now overflowing these halls shall have fled, crowds of people will come to see the place where our distinguished host lived and wrote*. Commenting on the occasion, the SATURDAY REVIEW called it *a wonderful match of mutual admiration and laudation* and looked forward to more back-scratching for it supposed that *a Guild of Literature and Art means an institution where, on paying your subscription punctually, you are entitled to be called by the others who have also paid their subscriptions 'a resplendent ornament', or any other complimentary name to which you have a mind.*

Journalism has been astoundingly indulgent of Blair's conspiratorial horse-trading approach to media relations: you scratch my back and I'll scratch yours – and give you a more-or-less exclusive leak.
DAILY TELEGRAPH, 3 MARCH 2002

Why do we have to have peerages? It's obvious to me it's a reward for people who have always supported the monarchy. You scratch my back, and I'll scratch yours.
BIRMINGHAM EVENING MAIL, 8 MARCH 2002

For the past three years, Terfel has managed the festival himself and has pulled in big acts including Jose Carreras, Andrea Bocelli and Elaine Paige. 'I have to do a couple of deals. You know, "you scratch my back, I'll scratch yours"', he explains in his sing-song voice.
INDEPENDENT, 28 MARCH 2006

Usage: The saying almost always has negative connotations. It might be at the level of the relatively harmless mutual congratulation of Dickens and Bulwer; it may well refer to insider dealing in the City or corrupt practices for contracts at the Town Hall.

See also *One GOOD turn deserves another*

BEAT

if you can't beat 'em, join 'em

if you can't get the better of someone, employ their tactics

Variant: If you can't lick 'em, join 'em

This is an American adage in use since at least the early 1940s. The variant *If you can't lick 'em, join 'em* is American usage only.

Big mainstream airlines, with high costs and prices, have been battered by a raft of low-cost start-ups. On the if-you-can't-lick-'em-join-'em principle, both BA and KLM have recently started their own cut-rate airlines within Europe.
WASHINGTON POST, 8 JUNE 2000

The trend for shopping on the net is being boosted as designer labels such as Burberry launch alluring websites and high-street chains improve online services. But traditional mail order hasn't gone away, and many companies are actively embracing the web, judiciously marrying online and offline shopping. Boden, the mail-order business set up in 1991 by Old Etonian Johnnie Boden, is a typical example. 'It's an 'if you can't beat 'em, join 'em' situation,' says Boden, who started the company from his flat, using friends as models.
DAILY TELEGRAPH, 20 NOVEMBER 2006

BEAUTY

beauty is in the eye of the beholder
one person's aesthetic sensibilities may differ from another's

Variant: Beauty lies in the eye of the beholder

Is beauty absolute or is it relative? If the latter, is it to be decided on the statement of one perceiver, or is more evidence needed? David Hume, the philosopher, certainly took the view that it was relative: *Beauty in things exists merely in the mind which contemplates them* (ESSAYS MORAL AND POLITICAL, 1742).

In POOR RICHARD'S ALMANACK (1741), Benjamin Franklin had expressed the same view just a year earlier in a rather more popular form:

> *Beauty, like supreme dominion,*
> *Is but supported by opinion.*

A hundred years earlier a proverb which looked to the farmyard for expression encapsulated a similar thought: *An ass is beautiful to an ass, and a pig to a pig* (John Ray, ENGLISH PROVERBS, 1670).

Over many centuries, then, a popular view has been that *beauty is in the eye of the beholder*, although this precise proverbial formulation is not recorded before the last quarter of the nineteenth century. The topic is still debated, sometimes with the highest level of aesthetic support. Henry Moore, perhaps England's greatest twentieth century sculptor, speaks with some authority: *Too many people say 'beautiful' when they really mean 'pretty'. To me, a hippopotamus is beautiful. I much prefer them to swans!*

Beauty is in the eye of the beholder...and has been for a very long time...It's the central conceit of the ancient fables of Beauty and the Beast and its now less well-known counterpart, The Loathly Lady, in which, at the conclusion, love literally transforms ugliness into beauty.
INDEPENDENT, 5 AUGUST 2000

If beauty is in the eye of the beholder, then it is not surprising that there is little consensus of opinion on the changing face of Edinburgh through its most dramatic period of development since the disastrous 1960s. The Scottish Parliament building sums it all up – an inspiration to some and a concrete monstrosity to most others, it is either loved or loathed, with little room for debate in the middle.
EDINBURGH EVENING NEWS,
24 MAY 2006

See also *One MAN'S meat is another man's poison*

beauty is only skin deep
a good-looking woman does not necessarily have an attractive character, so don't judge by appearance

The proverb was first suggested by lines in a poem by Sir Thomas Overbury entitled A WIFE, NOW THE WIDOW

OF SIR THOMAS OVERBURIE, which was written in 1613 but published posthumously in 1614:

All the carnall beauty of my wife
Is but skin-deep, but to two senses known.

The poem discusses all the desirable qualities a man should look for in a wife. Overbury was said to have written the poem for a friend in order to dissuade him from an unwise affair. Sadly, Overbury's opposition to the relationship brought about his murder. (For a full account of this piece of skulduggery, see *No NEWS is good news*.)

After the publication of Overbury's poem, however, and in the light of the scandal of his death, the Hereford poet John Davies took up the theme in a poem entitled A SELECT SECOND HUSBAND FOR SIR THOMAS OVERBURIE'S WIFE, NOW A MATCHLESSE WIDOW (1616):

Beauty's but skin-deep; nay, it is not so;
It floates but on the skin beneath the skin,
That (like pure Aire) scarce hides her
fullest flow:
It is so subtill, fading, fraile, and thin:
Were she skin-deepe, she could not
be so shallow,
To win but fooles her puritie to hallow.

But if *carnal beauty* is only skin deep, what lies beneath the surface? Contrasting the fine externals with *the loathesomeness* within, goes back at least to the early Church Fathers. Centuries later Thomas Fuller echoes their sentiments: *Beauty is but Skin deep; within is Filth and Putrefaction* (GNOMOLOGIA, 1732). Stevenson records a Leicestershire proverb noted in the form of an old jingle which has much the same message:

Beauty is but skin deep, ugly lies the bone;
Beauty dies and fades away, but ugly
holds its own.

And a Moroccan proverb has this to say about a woman's appearance – or a mother-in-law's jealousy: *My daughter-in-law is beautiful! But don't look any deeper.*

But although many recognise truth behind the proverb, others consider that its use is simply a weapon in the armoury of the plain woman and not to be taken too seriously. In ADVICE TO YOUNG MEN (1829), the English politician and journalist William Cobbett has this to say: *The less favoured part of the sex say, that 'beauty is but skin deep':... but it is very agreeable, though, for all that.*

Perhaps Mr Cobbett should be more careful how he encourages his young charges for, as the French say, *Beauty without virtue is a flower without perfume.*

The movie's message is childishly simple – **beauty is only skin deep**.... *Paltrow plays Rosemary, a girl whose obesity keeps people from seeing what a beautiful person she is – except for Jack Black's Hal, who is under a spell that lets him see only a person's inner beauty. So Hal sees Rosemary as a slim, beautiful girl; the 'real' Rosemary is Paltrow in a fat suit.*
GUARDIAN, 22 SEPTEMBER 2004

Waitrose, the upmarket chain owned by the John Lewis partnership, is launching a range of 'ugly' looking seasonal fruit at discounted prices for use in cooking. The 'class two' produce will be either visually flawed or oddly shaped, according to Waitrose, but otherwise perfect for eating... Waitrose fruit buyer Tom Richardson said: 'Supermarkets are often criticised for rejecting fruit and vegetables because they don't look picture-perfect. But this innovative new range will help our customers realise that while **beauty might be skin deep***, flavour certainly isn't.'*
INDEPENDENT, 19 JUNE 2006

See also *Never judge by APPEARANCES*; *HANDSOME is as handsome does*

BED

as you make your bed, so you must lie in it

you must accept the consequences of unwise actions and decisions

Bed for the sixteenth century cottager or servant would be no more than a palliasse stuffed with straw or leaves and a scrap of rough sheeting made of hemp. William Harrison, a social critic writing in Elizabethan times (*The Description of England* in HOLINSHED'S CHRONICLES, 1577), had this to say:

Our fathers and we ourselves have lyen full ofte upon straw pallettes, covered only with a sheet, under coverlets made of dogswain or hopharlots...and a good round logge under their heades, insteade of a boulster. If it were so that our fathers or the good man of the house had...a matteres or flock bed and thereto a sacke of chafe to rest hys heade upon, he thought himself to be as well loged as the lorde of the towne, so well were they contented. Pillowes, they sayde, were thoughte mete only for women in childebed. As for servants, if they had any sheete above them, it was well, for seldome had they any under their bodies, to keepe them from the pricking straws, that ranne oft thorow the canvas, and rased their hardened hides.

Of course, wealthy people enjoyed more comfort but, even so, the bed would have to be carefully made. It would have a woollen mattress topped by another, softer one stuffed with feathers or down and covered by an undersheet. Some beds of the period were very large, designed to accommodate several occupants. The sheets were therefore spread out and smoothed down with a bedstaff. The quality of the hemp or linen sheeting was of great importance because of the texture next to the skin. Next came the blankets, a bolster and pillows and, finally, a bedspread. Nights were guaranteed to be more restful if wormwood were tucked between mattresses to guard against fleas.

The proverb *As you make your bed, so you must lie in it* draws on these practical contemporary difficulties of getting a good night's sleep and metaphorically extends the field of application. An early form of the expression was known in the sixteenth century. Gabriel Harvey, an Elizabethan poet and scholar, refers to it in MARGINALIA (c. 1590): *Lett them ...go to there bed, as themselves shall make it.* In the following century *He that makes his bed ill, lies there* is included in two proverb collections: George Herbert's JACULA PRUDENTUM (1640), and John Ray's ENGLISH PROVERBS (1670). The proverb in the form we know it today emerged in the nineteenth century.

The same proverb exists in French, German, Danish and Spanish. The implication is that the person addressed has mismanaged their affairs and now must suffer the consequences.

*Meanwhile his [Iain Duncan Smith's] friends were reduced to arguing that the [Tory] party, **having made its bed, must lie on it**. 'Whether we think he's the right man or the wrong man, he's the man we've got,' says one loyalist Shadow cabinet minister. 'It would be madness to change him now.'*
OBSERVER, 3 NOVEMBER 2002

*OK, voters, you've had your say. Now, as my parents told me, **you made your bed, you have to sleep in it**. You re-elected many of those who have supervised the destruction of Virginia's budget.*
VIRGINIAN PILOT, 7 NOVEMBER 2003

...but there would always be, at the back of everything she said, the unspoken admonishment that as Marnie had chosen, deliberately, this bed of an English life, and marriage to an Englishman, she now had to lie on it.
JOANNA TROLLOPE,
BROTHER AND SISTER, 2004

See also *You REAP what you sow*

early to bed and early to rise, makes a man healthy, wealthy and wise

the individual who leads a regular, well-ordered life without excesses reaps the benefits

This proverb is sometimes erroneously attributed to Benjamin Franklin who included it in more than one edition of POOR RICHARD'S ALMANACK (1735 and 1758). In fact, the wisdom of the adage was already established in both England and continental Europe by the time John Fitzherbert wrote his BOKE OF HUSBANDRY in 1523. In it, Fitzherbert tells us how he learnt at school that *erly rysyng maketh a man hole in body, holer in soule, and rycher in goodes*. Nor can the familiar little rhyme be attributed to Franklin, for it appears in two seventeenth century proverb collections: John Clarke's PAROEMI-OLOGIA (1639) and John Ray's ENGLISH PROVERBS (1670).

The proverb John Fitzherbert recited in school must have been heard in many a classroom over the centuries. In the seventeenth century, its edifying message could be found between the pages of reading primers and Latin grammars. In the eighteenth century it appeared in the children's book GOODY TWO-SHOES (1766) where Ralph, the raven, refers to it as *a verse which every little good Boy and Girl should get by heart*. In the nineteenth century it was often coupled with another rhyming adage of the day:

*The cock doth crow,
To let you know,
If you be wise,
'Tis time to rise.*

The following verse, describing the dire fate of the child who does not heed the proverb's wisdom, comes from LITTLE RHYMES FOR LITTLE FOLKS (c. 1812):

*The cock crows in the morn,
To tell us to rise,
And that he who lies late
Will never be wise:
For heavy and stupid,
He can't learn his book:
So as long as he lives,
Like a Dunce he must look.*

The emphasis on early rising throughout these centuries is not surprising. The productive part of the day was when the sun was up. Only those who could afford candles stayed up beyond sunset. In the morning it was essential to rise with the dawn or dawn chorus (we still say up with the lark) and get down to work as soon as there was natural light.

Later, in the twentieth century, the proverb became a favourite with humorists. In EARLY TO BED (c. 1900), George Ade couldn't help feeling that to obey the proverb would be to miss out on something:

*Early to bed and early to rise
Will make you miss all the regular guys.*

All the regular guys are obviously taking advantage of the recent invention of electricity to light up their nocturnal activities; it was just a few years before, in 1881, that Sir William Armstrong had installed the first domestic electric light in his Northumberland home, Cragside.

By the middle of the century, the rot had clearly set in. Humorist James Thurber, in FABLES FOR OUR TIME: THE SHRIKE AND THE CHIPMUNKS (1940), points to the enlivening effects of a neon-lit night life:

> Early to rise and early to bed
> Makes a male healthy and wealthy
> and dead.

Perhaps the regular guys would feel happier with a proverb of equal wisdom, *All work and no play makes JACK a dull boy.*

That humans tend to vary in their circadian rhythms has been known for centuries. Benjamin Franklin's maxim **'Early to bed and early to rise makes a man healthy, wealthy and wise'** *recognized that some people are born to be larks (to get up and go to bed early) while others are owls (late risers and late to bed). Larks are 'morning people' – productive and communicative from the time their eyes open – while owls are grouchy and groggy until midday. Franklin's maxim has, however, largely been disproved by researchers. A paper in the British Medical Journal in 1998 based on nearly 1,300 people found that far from being the poorer bird, owls tended to be richer and were more likely to have their own cars than larks. There was no real difference in death rates between the two. According to Dr Chris Martyn, one of the authors of the paper, the idea of industrious, prosperous larks probably dates from before artificial light, when people needed to get up early to make the most of daylight. 'I'm an owl by nature, so I was pleased with our findings because I was fed up with larks claiming moral superiority for getting up early.'*
OBSERVER, 2 JULY 2000

At Camp David, there will be no schmoozing with rock stars or late-night talkathons about centre-Left politics in the 21st century. Mr Bush is **early to bed, early to rise**.
DAILY TELEGRAPH, 23 FEBRUARY 2001

Early to bed, early to rise
So why are a significant number of UK schools cutting back on post-lunch lessons? The most common reason given is to improve the quality of learning. The old adage about early rising being the key to wisdom still holds sway with most teachers, whose experience tells them pupils study more effectively and are better behaved in the morning. As the day wears on, students tend to lose focus, and afternoon lessons are often significantly less productive.
TIMES EDUCATIONAL SUPPLEMENT,
11 FEBRUARY 2005

See also *The early BIRD catches the worm*

BEES

a swarm of bees in May is worth a load of hay

activity at the proper season produces good fruit; lateness reduces the yields

Earliest written records of the proverb date back to the mid-seventeenth century but it must have been a pearl of country household management long before. Honey was the main ingredient used to sweeten food, so the productivity of the bees was of prime importance. No farmhouse would have been without a cluster of plaited straw hives. The repair of the hives, the wellbeing of the bees and collecting the honey were all the responsibility of the busy housewife. Some of the honey would be kept for her own household's use; the surplus would be sold.

The unknown author of REFORMED COMMONWEALTH OF BEES (1655) records the rhyme thus: *...a swarm of bees in May is worth a cow and a bottle [bale] of hay, whereas a swarm in July is not worth a fly.*

A correspondent in NOTES AND QUERIES (1864) gives this fuller version:

> *A swarm of bees in May*
> *Is worth a load of hay.*
> *A swarm of bees in June*
> *Is worth a silver spoon.*
> *A swarm of bees in July*
> *Is not worth a butterfly.*

But why should a swarm in May be so valuable? In past centuries, keepers would kill their bees every autumn. By then the early bees had produced their honey and destroying them was the only way to extract the harvest from the straw hives. There were plenty of wild bees and, with luck, a new swarm could be had the following May. The proverb is still known even though the modern understanding of bee space, and the invention of hives with moveable frames that allow the honey to be harvested without disturbing the bees mean it is no longer valid. Strong stocks of bees can now be kept through the winter and there is no need for the modern beekeeper to pray for a swarm in May.

*According to the old rhyme, a swarm of bees in June is worth a silver spoon, but **a swarm of bees in May is worth a load of hay**. In other words: the earlier, the better. But this May was so foully wet and cold that few colonies built up enough to swarm, and it remains to be seen whether June will be any better.*
INDEPENDENT, 3 JUNE 2000

*An old English rhyme insists that '**A swarm of bees in May is worth a load of hay** / A swarm of bees in June is worth a silver spoon / A swarm of bees in July is not worth a fly.' But the implication that spring honey is better than late-summer honey is either a fanciful myth or harks back to a time when wildflowers grew unmolested by herbicides; these days, the oilseed rape which covers much of the countryside in spring produces a sickly sweet, cabbage-y tasting honey disdained by connoisseurs.*
OBSERVER, 13 AUGUST 2000

BEGGARS

beggars can't be choosers
a person in need should gratefully accept what is offered rather than complain that it is not exactly what is wanted

The problem of vagabondage in the sixteenth century was dire. Town populations, especially that of London, were increasing rapidly as hungry vagrants flooded in to find work or make a living begging and stealing. An old rhyme, thought by one eminent historian to describe the vagrancy of the period, sets the scene:

> *Hark, hark,*
> *The dogs do bark,*
> *The beggars are coming to town;*
> *Some in rags,*
> *And some in jags,*
> *And one in a velvet gown.*

Apart from society's natural misfits, other factors contributed to the growing problem of homelessness. Much of the misery was caused by agrarian change. During the late fifteenth century the old feudal system, where the medieval villein was cared for by his lord, gradually gave way under economic pressure. The sixteenth century saw a steady increase in population and subsequent rise in the demand for food. Landlords, realising that larger units could be farmed more profitably, sometimes squeezed out their small tenants. There was also new wealth to be made by enclosing cultivated land and grazing sheep, a much less labour intensive industry than arable farming. Characters in John Hales's DISCOURSE OF THE COMMON WEAL OF THIS REALM OF ENGLAND (1549) complain: *...these enclosures do undo us all...all is taken up for pastures either for sheep or for grazing of cattle. So that I have known of late a dozen ploughs within less compass than six miles about me had down within these seven years, and where forty persons had their livings, now one man and his shepherd hath all.*

A further factor influencing the increase in vagrancy was a reduction in warfare. Fewer wars, at home and abroad, set large numbers of retainers at liberty with little chance of finding alternative employment. The dissolution of the monasteries under Henry VIII further exacerbated the crisis by removing the very institutions which supported the dispossessed with alms.

In spite of these obvious social and economic difficulties, popular and state opinion worked on the assumption that there was enough employment for those with a mind to do it, and that vagrancy had its roots in idleness. Distinctions, however, were made between the 'impotent poor', the aged and crippled who might expect to survive on charitable alms supplied by their own parishes, and the 'sturdy beggars' who received brutal treatment; hence the proverb *A sturdy beggar should have a stout naysayer.*

Beggars can't be choosers emerges against this background. Its tone is uncompromising. John Heywood records it as: *Folke saie alwaie, beggers should be no choosers* (PROVERBS, 1546), and the form *Beggars must not be choosers* was current from the sixteenth until the twentieth century.

*December, and its penchant for snow and ice, may not be the most opportune time to test a two-seat soft-top convertible, but hey, **beggars can't be choosers**. When select*

vehicles come around for evaluation, an auto journalist just grabs what's available, especially if it's one of the more talked about cars in recent months, like the all-new rear-drive 2006 Pontiac Solstice.
EVENING STANDARD MAGAZINE,
ARLINGTON HEIGHTS DAILY HERALD,
22 DECEMBER 2005

St Martin-in-the-Fields is in the heart of the theatre district and it's an ideal place to grab a quick bite before the curtain goes up. My wife and I were off to see The Old Country, *the newly revived Alan Bennett play at Trafalgar Studios, and we had no difficulty squeezing in two courses and a glass of wine in less than an hour... We each finished with a small tub of Ben & Jerry's – not as good as Häagen-Dazs, but **beggars can't be choosers**.*
EVENING STANDARD MAGAZINE,
31 OCTOBER 2006

See also *Never look a gift HORSE in the mouth*

BIRD

a bird in the hand is worth two in the bush

a small, certain gain is of greater value than a larger, speculative one; don't trade a certainty for an uncertainty

The general wisdom of the proverb is ancient. It was taught by Aesop in the sixth century BC in fables such as THE LION AND THE HARE and THE FISHERMAN AND THE LITTLE FISH. In THE NIGHTINGALE AND THE HAWK the nightingale, who has fallen prey to the hawk, protests that she will make a meagre meal. The hawk, however, refuses to release her, saying that he would be foolish to let go of a bird he already holds in his talons simply to hunt another.

In the early Middle Ages the proverb was known in a popular Latin form coined from an existing expression, but in the fifteenth century it was recorded in English: *Betyr ys a byrd in the hond than tweye in the wode* (HARLEIAN MS, c. 1470). *Wood* or *forest* gradually gave way to *bush* in the following century, around the time of a well-known tale concerning Henry VIII's jester, Will Somers. Lord Surrey had given the jester a kingfisher from his aviary. Shortly afterwards, Lord Northampton asked Lord Surrey for this fine bird as a gift for a lady friend. Upset at having to refuse Lord Northampton's request, Lord Surrey assured him that Will Somers would surely give the kingfisher up on the promise of two birds on some future occasion. The jester was not so easily taken in. 'Sirrah' he is reputed to have said to the messenger, 'tell your master that I am much obliged for his liberal offer of two for one, but that I prefer one bird in hand to two in the bush.'

The proverb, in one form or another, is found throughout Europe from Sweden to Romania: the Romanians say *Better a bird in the hand than a thousand on the house*; the French, *A bird in the hand is better than two in the hedge*; and the Italians have a number of variants, amongst them, *Better a sparrow in the pan than a hundred chickens in the priest's yard*.

Another European adage, dating back to at least the early seventeenth century, bears the same message but explains the context in which *A bird in the hand is worth two in the bush* was coined. *A Sparrow in Hand is worth a Pheasant that flyeth by*, recorded in Thomas Fuller's GNOMOLOGIA of 1732, is no longer used in England, though still heard, for instance, in France. It compares the greater value of a tiny, captive sparrow with the dubious worth of a much larger bird on the wing. The larger bird might be a goose, a crane, a pigeon, a heron or a bittern, depending on the language.

The proverb reflects the hunting interests and eating habits of past centuries when swans, cranes, herons or peacocks made acceptable meat for the dinner table. THE BOKE OF KERVYNGE, published by Wynjyn de Worde in 1508, gives these directions: *...lift a swan, sauce a capon, frusshe a chicken, spoyle a hen, unbrace a mallard, dismember a heron, display a crane, disfigure a peacock, unjoint a bittern, untach a curlew, allay a pheasant, wing a partridge, wing a quail, mince a plover and thigh a pigeon and other small birds.*

Many of us were raised with the adage, '*A bird in the hand is worth two in the bush.' That thinking can subtly drive us to making premature or shortsighted decisions. If you find yourself in a situation where you have an offer on the table that is not really a good fit for you, ask yourself the following questions: Can I negotiate an extended decision period to flush out other possible offers? If there are no other strong prospects at this time, is my marketability strong enough to wait for a better fit? What personal or family influences are pressuring me to accept an offer that doesn't quite feel right?* SYRACUSE POST-STANDARD, 4 DECEMBER 2002

There are few places where the saying '*a bird in the hand is worth two in the bush' is more relevant than in the stock market. When picking stocks, investment managers continually face the dilemma of whether they should sacrifice short-term value for longer-term growth.* DAILY TELEGRAPH, 5 MARCH 2005

See also *MEDIEVAL LATIN*, page 214

birds of a feather flock together
people with a lot in common seek out each other's company

Some birds are, of course, solitary but those which habitually gather together to fly or feed do so with their own kind. THE WISDOM OF BEN SIRA or ECCLESIASTICUS (c. 180–175 BC), an apocryphal text which was widely known, has *Birds dwell with their kind*, and this may have been the origin of the adage. The proverb has been current in English since the second half of the sixteenth century.

Although it sometimes means that people with similar backgrounds or interests move in the same circles, the proverb is more often used to register disapproval of another group or individual. Thus in NONSUCH PROFESSOR (1660), Thomas Secker uses the expression to warn against keeping bad company: *We say, 'That birds of a feather will flock together.' To be too intimate with sinners is to intimate that we are sinners.* And in PELHAM (1828), Lord Lytton describes the London underworld in the same terms: *It is literally true in the systematised roguery of London, that birds of a feather flock together.*

Over the years it has been home to the Wrens, Rooks and Partridges who have all made their nests in the tiny riverside cottage. But No 1 The Laurels, in the heart of Cockermouth, Cumbria, is not a hotspot for ornithologists – each family that has lived there since it was built nearly 90 years ago has shared its surname with that of a bird. Neighbour Laura Grisdale remembers when the house was built in 1911 by a builder whose name was, by coincidence, Wren. Soon after two sisters, also called Wren, moved in. When the Wrens moved out, the Ravens moved in. Then the Rooks, then the Partridges. Miss Grisdale, now 94, said: 'It really is the most amazing series of coincidences I have ever known. I know that **birds of a feather flock together***, but for there to be so many is astonishing.'*
ELECTRONIC TELEGRAPH, 14 MARCH 2000

Birds of a feather flock together, as the saying goes, and that's certainly true of the

L.A. flock that holds the most golden eggs. A look at the city's wealthiest shows that not only are many of them connected through business activities, but many pal around socially as well.
LOS ANGELES BUSINESS JOURNAL, 21 MAY 2001

'Bob used to come to our house sometimes at night, and he and my father would drink whiskey and poitín together,' she says. 'My father would say to him, "Where have you been?" He'd say, "I've been visiting relations." My father would laugh. I always felt it was some sort of code. He was creepy. They were **birds of a feather***.' Her father was eventually jailed for seven years.*
GUARDIAN, 25 MARCH 2006

Usage: The modern sense is often that wrongdoers seek out others of their own kind

See also *A man is known by the COMPANY he keeps*

the early bird catches the worm
the first in line gets the pick of the opportunities; to delay in taking action may end in disappointment

Written records of this proverb date back to the early seventeenth century. The adage urges us to seize opportunities early if we want the reward – rather like the young woman in this music hall song by T W Connor (1900):

> She was a dear little dicky bird,
> 'Chip, chip, chip,' she went,
> Sweetly she sang to me
> Till all my money was spent;
> Then she went off song –
> We parted on fighting terms,
> She was one of the early birds,
> And I was one of the worms.

But the bird's perspective is not the only one from which to see things. J G

Saxe challenges the accepted wisdom and looks at life from a worm's-eye view instead. The worm, he argues, was punished for early rising (EARLY RISING, 1860). Similarly, Walsh quotes a joke book of the same period:

A father exhorting his son to rise early in the morning reminded him of the old adage, 'It's the early bird that picks up the worm.'

'Ah,' replied the son, 'but the worm gets up earlier than the bird.'

*In pigeon racing, **the early bird catches the worm**. Some fanciers are up before dawn, mixing medicines, putting out feed and plotting. They are plotting how to grow stronger birds. They are plotting how to win races. In Little Belgium, nobody takes winning a race for granted.*
ST PETERSBURG TIMES, 4 JUNE 2002

*Don't think you can turn up halfway through the parade on Monday and still hope to grab a good look at the action. Unless you're 7ft tall. Or have X-ray vision. Or can jump ten feet in the air, thus enabling you to peer over the heads of the four-deep crowd in front of you. They say **the early bird catches the worm**, but in this case, the early bird gets to look at the parade in all its glory. We hear worms aren't that tasty anyway.*
THIS IS LONDON, 15 AUGUST 2003

See also *Early to BED and early to rise, makes a man healthy, wealthy and wise*

BITTEN

once bitten, twice shy
we learn from experience to avoid things which have caused us trouble and pain in the past

The proverb does not appear to have a long history. In MR SPONGE'S SPORTING TOUR (1853), Robert Smith Surtees, an author of humorous

sporting stories, writes: *Jawleyford had been bit once, and he was not going to give Mr Sponge a second chance.* Was Surtees alluding to an adage already established in popular parlance? Or was he remembering his Shakespeare: *What, wouldst thou have a serpent sting thee twice* (MERCHANT OF VENICE, 1596)? The proverb, or allusions to it, do not appear again until it is recorded in G F Northall's FOLK-PHRASES (1894).

There is, however, a rich stock of proverbs which preach the same lesson. *The burnt child dreads the fire* has been in French and then English since the thirteenth century. And an old German proverb says *He who has burned his tongue doesn't forget to blow on his soup.*

According to Trench (LESSONS IN PROVERBS, 1853), a similar French proverb, *A scalded dog fears cold water*, carries an even stronger message; that those who have experienced great pain or difficulty will not only draw back from the instrument of that pain in the future but will be fearful even where there is no cause.

Other languages have like proverbs:
A dog which has been beaten with a stick fears its own shadow (Italian)
Whom a serpent has bitten a lizard alarms (African)
One bitten by a serpent is afraid of a rope's end (Jewish)
The man who has received a beating with a firebrand runs away at the sight of a firefly (Singhalese)
And an old English proverb teaches:
Hang a Dog on a Crabtree, and he'll never love Verjuice (crab-apple liquor).

Once bitten, twice shy. That's how Maggie DiStefano felt after a run-in with a decorator who left much to be desired... But her big new getaway place in Southampton was being built, and it needed designing – fast. 'I was so nervous about using another decorator,' she says.
HOUSE BEAUTIFUL, 1 JULY 2004

*Dancing with the Russian bear can be dangerous to your wealth. Nobody knows this better than Lord Browne of Madingley, chief executive of BP. He's already lost one fortune through the encounter. **Once bitten, twice shy**, you might have thought, but on the basis that Russia was becoming one of the biggest oil and gas producers in the world and BP therefore couldn't afford not to be there, Lord Browne hopped straight back into bed with the very same oligarchs who had ripped him off first time around.*
INDEPENDENT, 20 SEPTEMBER 2006

BLACK

there's a black sheep in every family

every family has one rogue member who is disapproved of for not fitting into the general mould of family life

Variant: There's a black sheep in every flock

Black sheep have had a bad press since the sixteenth century, when they were accused of being *perylous* beasts and quite capable of giving a nasty nip, as detailed by Thomas Bastard in CHRESTOLEROS (1598):

> *Till now I thought the prouerbe did but iest,*
> *Which said a blacke sheepe was a biting beast.*

In Shropshire there was, apparently, a superstition that if a black lamb were born into a flock, bad luck would dog the shepherd. A ewe giving birth to black twins would bring certain disaster.

An economic factor also contributed to the unfortunate animal's unpopularity with shepherds: the fleece of a black sheep could not be dyed and was therefore worthless.

The term *black sheep* was applied idiomatically some time in the eighteenth century to a person who falls foul of the accepted standards of his fellows. In his play THE MAN OF THE WORLD (1792), Thomas Macklin writes *You are a black sheep: and I'll mark you*. The proverb, found in literature from the nineteenth century onwards, was originally *There's a black sheep in every flock (or fold)*. Its scope of application today is largely, though not exclusively, to the family, hence its more frequent contemporary form.

*'There have been no cases initiated against police officers for such crimes,' Stanchenko said. 'There are **black sheep in every family**, but it is very difficult to prove that money has been stolen, isn't it? And how can we know that these were really police officers,' he added. 'It's easy to buy a police uniform and identification.'*
ST PETERSBURG TIMES,
28 DECEMBER 2001

*Although he managed to find some acting work after the course, the role he knew best was a drink and drug addict. He lived up to the tag of **black sheep of the family** with a string of binges which led to aggression and several arrests.*
DAILY MAIL, 7 JULY 2004

*Something of a misfit ('the nominal **black sheep of the family**'), he was expelled from (or rebelled over) a series of schools.*
DAILY TELEGRAPH, 19 MARCH 2005

Usage: The 'crime' of which the black sheep stands accused can consist in, for instance, the adoption of an alternative lifestyle, or it can be a genuine matter of concern for the Courts. In any event, the nonconformity, the deviation, the rejection of standard values are all disapproved of.

BLIND

if the blind lead the blind, both shall fall into the ditch

when a person lacking in understanding or expertise attempts to guide another like himself, both will suffer serious consequences

There are numerous variants of this phrase in the ancient world: Homer (c. 850 BC) has *the vile leading the vile*; Varro (c. 50 BC) *the old leading the old*; and Horace introduces the blind man: *It is as if a blind man sought to show the way* (EPISTLES, c. 20 BC).

In the New Testament, Jesus uses this same metaphor to criticise the Pharisees who were blind to the truth and leading the people astray: *They be blind leaders of the blind. And if the blind lead the blind, both shall fall into the ditch* (MATTHEW 15:14). This verse, and another in LUKE 6:39, is the source of our present-day proverb. The earliest rendering in English is found in the ANGLO-SAXON GOSPEL of AD 995: *Se blinda gyf he blinde laet, hig feallath begen on aenne pytt.* Erasmus included the saying in his ADAGIA (1500), and it later appears in John Heywood's collection of proverbs (1546): *Where the blynd leadth the blynd, both fall in the dike.*

Thereafter the adage is frequently found in both literature and proverb collections but its influence goes beyond the written word. There is also an artistic heritage. The proverb has been illustrated by many famous painters: Hieronymus Bosch (c. 1450–1516), Pieter Brueghel the Elder (c. 1520–1569), Pieter Brueghel the Younger (1564–1638), and Jan Verbeeck (c. 1569–1619).

Suddenly, nine months after the tragedy in New York [the attack on the World Trade Center], the FBI is to be transformed. It will expend more effort on stopping terrorists than chasing bank robbers. It will hire more agents. It will even let some of the hated CIA into its offices (when the blind lead the blind, both fall into the pit). It will try to find some Arab-speaking agents. How can anyone seriously believe that those gumshoes who hunted down bank robbers and drug lords are now going to turn into counterspies, especially without the most modern computers and with supervisors more interested in protecting their careers than hunting down terrorists? CHICAGO SUN-TIMES, 9 JUNE 2002

It may be described as the blind leading the blind, but a top high street chain is trying to help men buy lingerie gifts by introducing extra male staff to help. CARDIFF WESTERN MAIL, 14 DECEMBER 2005

Usage: Often the full proverb is simply alluded to in a comment such as: *It's a case of the blind leading the blind.*

in the country of the blind, the one-eyed man is king

a man of even limited ability is at a great advantage in the company of those less able

H G Wells alludes to this proverb in THE COUNTRY OF THE BLIND (1911), a short story about a valley inhabited by a blind community closed to those who can see. John Wyndham then draws on this tradition in his science fiction novel THE DAY OF THE TRIFFIDS (1951), which tells the story of Bill Masen, who finds himself one of the few people in the world still able to see after a meteorite shower. Because of his gift of sight he becomes a leader in the fight against the Triffids, animate vegetable hybrids threatening to take over the world. The novel attributes the origin of this proverb to *a classical gentleman called Fullonius* who said '*Caecorum in patria luscus rex imperat omnis*' but Fullonius is

ERASMUS'S ADAGIA

In the proverbs of the ancient world, Erasmus wrote, *is all its wisdom enshrined.*

Desiderius Erasmus (1466–1536) was one of the greatest classical scholars of his age. Born in Rotterdam, he was educated in monastic schools and, in 1492, was ordained as a priest and took monastic vows. His mastery of Latin and a growing regard for his intellectual abilities persuaded the Catholic Church to allow him to study in Paris. Erasmus subsequently travelled widely throughout Europe, establishing himself as an independent scholar. He had strong links with England, and from 1511–15 was the Lady Margaret Reader in Greek at Cambridge University.

Erasmus's scholarship was prodigious and immensely influential. Often, however, Erasmus would turn from the labours of the day to work on his collection of Greek and Latin proverbs, an enterprise that occupied him for over 36 years.

The very first edition, the COLLECTANEA ADAGIORUM, was published in 1500 and contained 818 sayings. The second edition, the ADAGIORUM CHILIADES published in Venice in 1508, contained 3,260 entries as well as commentary in the form of brief essays inspired by the adages themselves. The collection grew in the various later editions in Erasmus's lifetime (1515, 1517–8, 1520, 1526, 1528, 1533 and 1536), mostly published in Basle.

Many of the ancient adages recorded by Erasmus have become familiar nuggets of wisdom, and a number of these proverbs are included in this book:

You scratch my BACK, and I'll scratch yours
If the BLIND lead the blind, both shall fall into the ditch
In the country of the BLIND, the one-eyed man is king
The COBBLER should stick to his last
There's many a slip 'twixt CUP and lip
DESPERATE diseases call for desperate remedies
Every man for himself, and the DEVIL take the hindmost
Talk of the DEVIL and he will appear
Every DOG has his day
FESTINA lente (Make haste slowly)
GOD helps those who help themselves
IGNORANCE is bliss
Little strokes fell great OAKS
A rolling STONE gathers no moss

better known as the Dutch humanist Gulielmus Gnapheus. His five-act play COMEDY OF ACOLASTUS, written in Latin verse, was published in Antwerp in 1529. John Palsgrave translated it into English in 1540.

But although the COMEDY OF ACOLASTUS was well known and influential in England and elsewhere in Europe, the Latin proverb had already been cited and translated into English by Erasmus in the 1523 edition of his ADAGIA.

It is also time to develop a vision and strategy outside the regulatory scope or fold. This is why opportunities like the London Financial Academy, backed by London

*Metropolitan University, are so important. I shall still keep my hand in on training and competence, but I am trying to widen the overall view. This is a large endeavour, but it is important to keep your eyes on the horizon. It is often said that **in the country of the blind the one-eyed man is king**. The two-eyed man can have a field day.*
FINANCIAL ADVISER, 29 JANUARY 2004

...I'm enjoying myself immensely. I spend some time each week preparing myself for the beginner's class, going through the lesson and making sure I understand it, before standing out in front and trying to look as if I know it all... The advanced class is, surprisingly, easier for me to handle. It's a smaller class and I make no pretence of being better than the other students, who would soon catch me out if I did. I am just the one who decides what the lesson will be this week. Both classes seem to be making good progress, and I think I would feel disappointed if, one day, the mayor's wife returned and wanted to take the classes again. Another saying comes to mind. 'In the country of the blind, the one-eyed man is king.'
DAILY TELEGRAPH, 8 FEBRUARY 2004

there are none so blind as those who will not see
it is pointless reasoning with a person who does not want to listen to sense

Variant: There are none so deaf as those who will not hear

In PROVERBS (1546) John Heywood cites the following rhyme which expresses the age-old frustration felt towards someone who refuses to face up to facts:

Who is so defe, or so blynde as is hee That wilfully will nother hear nor see?

Shortly afterwards the deaf and the blind part company permanently so that the proverb grumbles about either

those who are blind to reason or deaf to it but never both together. Thomas Ingeland laments in DISOBEDIENT CHILD (c. 1560) *None is so deaf as who will not hear*, and Andrew Boorde in his BREVIARY OF HEALTHE (1547) complains *Who is blynder than he yt wyl nat se*.

*[Dave Johnson] added: 'I appreciate that the association is constantly reminding the powers that be about workload and bureaucracy. However, members in Wigan remind me that **there is none so deaf that do not want to hear**.'*
GUARDIAN, 31 MAY 2001

The 'naked rambler' was back behind bars last night only hours after being given his freedom...Gough broke down in the witness box, saying he did not intend to offend anyone but wanted to prove to society that the naked human form was acceptable in public. He was admonished after being found guilty of breach of the peace and breaching three bail orders. Roderick Urquhart, prosecuting, told the sheriff: 'There are none so blind as those who will not see.'
DAILY TELEGRAPH, 4 OCTOBER 2003

BLOOD

blood is thicker than water
the family relationship is stronger than any other

In Europe during the twelfth and thirteenth centuries, a cycle of folk tales about sly Reynard the Fox became popular. The earliest German version, REINECKE FUCH, written by an Alsatian monk Heinrich der Glichezaer around 1180, has this line: *Kin-blood is not spoiled by water*. The same theme was taken up by English priest John Lydgate in his TROY BOOK (1412):

For naturally blood will be of kind Drawn-to blood, where he may it find.

However, it is not until the seventeenth century, when John Ray includes it in his proverb collection (1670), that the adage appears in its concise modern form.

The comparison between *blood* and *water* is not an easy one to understand. One suggestion is that blood appears to be of a thicker consistency, suggesting commitment. Another theory is that when blood and water are spilt the former leaves a stain whereas water will evaporate leaving no sign. Blood ties endure, then, while other relationships, such as friendships, acquaintances or business connections, can disappear without a trace.

Although it is mostly used to refer to the immediate family, the proverb has been used to cement relationships on a national level. The 'special relationship' present-day politicians claim is shared between Britain and the United States was very much in evidence in the nineteenth century. In 1859 US Commodore Josiah Tattnall went to the assistance of the British Navy, who were engaged in a skirmish with the Chinese. In his dispatch to US Navy headquarters the Commodore quoted the proverb as his reason for taking supportive action.

Not everyone, however, finds the proverb rings true. Family feuds which last to the grave are not unheard of, and sometimes family ties are felt more strongly on one side than the other. An old Jewish proverb which compares the strength of paternal and filial feeling says *One father can support ten children; ten children cannot support one father*. There are times, too, when an alternative allegiance can prove to be a tighter bond than blood: *If any survived they had grown rich and lost touch with their poor relations; for money is thicker than blood* (George Orwell, KEEP THE ASPIDISTRA FLYING, 1936). And

then, of course, some people just prefer water, as Aldous Huxley wrote in the NINTH PHILOSOPHER'S SONG (1920):

> *Blood, as all men know, than*
> *water's thicker,*
> *But water's wider, thank the Lord,*
> *than blood.*

Q. So can adults do anything to make sure that their children will grow up liking, not hating, each other?
A. Speak very positively about what it means to be a brother or sister, and how valuable family life is…Remind them that **blood is thicker than water** *and there are always people in the family they can turn to.*
DAILY MAIL, 17 MAY 2002

Victoria Beckham is said to be seething about the 'biography-style' book her father-in-law is writing about his famous son…You'd have thought, **blood being thicker than water**, *that family members might refrain from spilling the beans.*
DAILY MIRROR, 27 JULY 2005

BOOK

never judge a book by its cover
the external appearance is not a reliable guide to the quality of what lies within

Variants: You can't judge a book by its cover; don't judge a book by its cover

If you want to know what a book has to say, whether the information it contains is reliable or the story engaging, you need to read it. Similarly, you have to get to know a person to judge their character. Judgment based on outward appearance does not give a true impression. The proverb is of American origin, from at least the early twentieth century, when book covers were plain and no real guide to the pages' contents. Nowadays, of course, publishers put great effort into making their wares attractive so that they stand out on the shelves. Even so, the proverb is still true; the real test of the book is in the reading.

The proverb has been in British English since around the middle of the twentieth century.

You can't judge a book by its cover.
But he's tall, handsome, plays rugby, is a biology student at Oxford University, is well-bred AND mum and dad are not only respectable – but loaded. All in all, if I was Charlotte Church's mum, I would say of new boyfriend Ed Foy: 'Now that's more like it, love.'
PEOPLE, 25 JANUARY 2004

*Everyone knows **you mustn't judge a book by its cover**, but no one can deny appearance is important and a clear, fresh appearance brings confidence along with an inner beauty.*
ADVERTISEMENT FOR
BOOTS FADE OUT FACE CREAMS IN
GOOD HOUSEKEEPING, MAY 2006

See also *Never judge by APPEARANCES*

BORROWER

neither a borrower nor a lender be
the best way to stay on good terms with one's friends is to avoid getting involved in financial dealings with them

The proverb in the form we know it is from Shakespeare's HAMLET (1602). Laertes is about to leave Denmark to study in Paris. As he bids farewell, his father Polonius gives him a few final words of advice, amongst which are:

Neither a borrower nor a lender be;
For loan oft loses both itself and friend,
And borrowing dulls the edge of husbandry.

Polonius's wisdom is not new. Shakespeare is having fun with his garrulous character, and much of this wordy speech is composed of aphorisms. When the First Quarto appeared in print in 1603, these nuggets were enclosed in inverted commas, indicating that they were existing sayings that the audience would have known already.

*There remained just one problem. How would he pay for the photographs? He could hardly ask Brown for money, for his studymate often lectured him on the evils of debt. '**Neither a borrower nor a lender be!**' Brown would proclaim as he collected ginger beer bottles from neglected corners of the faggery for return to the tuck shop at a halfpenny a time.*
GUARDIAN, 28 SEPTEMBER 2005

Neither a borrower nor a lender be?
Try telling that to the institutions that offer personal loans on extremely competitive terms... And try telling it to the customers. Some 6.5 million personal loans are approved every year, each worth an average of £7,500. And with Christmas approaching, it's a fairly safe bet that many more loans will be taken out to pay for gifts, food and drink over the festive season.
INDEPENDENT, 13 NOVEMBER 2006

BOTH

you can't have it both ways
you can't benefit from two courses of action, adopt two policies, espouse two beliefs, etc that are mutually incompatible

The proverb is a common synonym for *You can't have your CAKE and eat it.* George Bernard Shaw has *You can't have anything both ways at once* (FANNY'S

FIRST PLAY, 1922), which may have been the original turn of phrase, the modern version dating from at least the early 1940s.

You can't have it both ways, fellows. I'm talking to the anti-tax referendum crowd. The folks who not only support a 'no' vote on taxes in November but who oppose holding the referendum at all. You can't hog-tie politicians with no-tax pledges when they are running for office and later criticize them for tossing tax decisions back to the voters.
VIRGINIAN PILOT, 27 JULY 2002

*Straw has now discovered the hard way that the Government **can't have it both ways**. It can't cosy up to Condi and the Pentagon warmongers, while also prostrating itself before Muslim constituencies in the hope of electoral favour.*
DAILY MAIL, 1 APRIL 2006

Usage: Informal. An idiomatic alternative phrase is *to want it both ways*.

BOYS

boys will be boys

don't be surprised when young boys behave with the mischievous and immature conduct characteristic of their age

A Latin proverb *Pueri sunt pueri, pueri puerilia tractant* ('Children are children and do childish things') is the root of the adage. William Robertson records *Children will do like children* in his full large and general phrasebook PHRASEOLOGIA GENERALIS (1681). The following century Isaac Bickerstaffe used *Young fellows will be young fellows* in his comic opera LOVE IN A VILLAGE (1762).

This shift in wording focuses on young men and is a comment on the different social expectations of girls' and boys' behaviour. The present-day wording dates from around the middle of the nineteenth century, when there is a sudden flurry of literary uses, among them Lord Lytton's THE CAXTONS (1849):

'I was a miser,' repeated the Captain, with emphasis. 'I began the habit first when my son was but a child. I thought him high-spirited, and with a taste for extravagance. 'Well,' said I to myself, 'I will save for him; boys will be boys.' Then, afterwards, when he was no more a child (at least he began to have the vices of a man), I said to myself, 'Patience! he may reform still; if not, I will save money, that I may have power over his self-interest, since I have none over his heart. I will bribe him into honor!'
Boys will be boys, but how school officials handle troublesome adolescent behavior is the question.
BOSTON HERALD, 26 SEPTEMBER 2003

*It can happen in even the best ordered of homes; **boys will be boys** even if the father of one them is the country's most senior politician and is spearheading a nationwide campaign against alcohol-fuelled yobbish behaviour. The chagrin of Jack McConnell, Scotland's First Minister, was almost palpable yesterday when it emerged that his son Mark and some of his friends had taken advantage of the fact that mum and dad were away. As parents know, in such circumstances all hell can then break out.*
DAILY TELEGRAPH, 4 NOVEMBER 2006

Usage: Remark explaining, even excusing, boisterous behaviour in boys. Often said by indulgent, complaisant parents. May also be used rather scathingly by women of their boyfriends or husbands.

BREAD

half a loaf is better than no bread

we should be thankful for what we do have or receive rather than complain about what we don't; a gift should not be despised because it is smaller than was hoped for

In use since at least the sixteenth century, the adage is recorded by John Heywood in his PROVERBS (1546):

Throw no gyft agayne at the geuers head;
For better is halfe a lofe than no bread.

The proverb was coined in an age when poverty was very real (see *BEGGARS can't be choosers*) and literally meant that some food is better than no food at all.

In the eighteenth century, Hannah More wrote pamphlets and ballads preaching morality and the political status quo to the lower class. One of her ballads was entitled THE RIOT; OR HALF A LOAF IS BETTER THAN NO BREAD (1795), and was written at a time of civil unrest. The ballad opens:

Come, neighbours, no longer be patient
and quiet
Come let us go kick up a bit of a riot;
I am hungry, my lads, but I've little to eat,
So we'll pull down the mills, and seize all
the meat...

But the general message is that such action is futile and that the government is not responsible for the weather and the resulting bad harvests; half a loaf is, indeed, better than no bread.

The proverb was often quoted to or by those suffering need and deprivation. Mrs Gaskell's novel MARY BARTON (1848) exposes the acute poverty of the workforce at the Manchester mills at that time. One of the characters has this to say:

'You see my folly is this, Mary. I would take what I could get; I think half a loaf is better than no bread. I would work for low wages rather than sit idle and starve. But, comes the Trades' Union, and says, 'Well, if you take the half-loaf, we'll worry you out of your life. Will you be clemmed, or will you be worried?' Now clemming is a quiet death, and worrying isn't, so I choose clemming, and come into th' Union. But I'd wish they'd leave me free, if I am a fool.'

These days, riots and hunger marches are rare and the proverb is no longer meant literally. Instead, it carries a more general message that we should be thankful for what we get, even if we had hoped for more.

Seventeenth and eighteenth century collections of proverbs by John Ray, John Clarke and Thomas Fuller record a number of similar sayings: *Better a louse (mouse) in the pot than no flesh at all; Half an egg is better than an empty shell; Better are small Fish than an empty Dish* but *Half a loaf is better than no bread* alone survives. A French version is *Faute de grives, on mange des merles* ('If there's a lack of cranes, we can eat blackbirds'), a reference to eating habits in the Middle Ages and later (see *A BIRD in the hand is worth two in the bush*).

*Nothing is to be gained by waiting for a comprehensive agreement before the Assembly can begin to function again, albeit in scrutiny mode...It would be better in everyone's interests to get something up and working as soon as possible, rather than wait until there was total, final and absolute agreement, until every 'i' was dotted and every 't' was crossed. At this point, another cliche is useful: **Half a loaf is better than no bread**. Everyone in Northern Ireland can understand that. Even if we only have the Assembly operating in scrutiny mode, it is better than the present dangerous political vacuum.*
BELFAST NEWS LETTER, 17 MARCH 2005

I am sorry not to have been able to give a better review to Madame Bovary's Ovaries. **Half a loaf is better than no bread,** *and it is a very good thing that popular books setting human nature in its biological, evolutionary context are being published, even if the only approach they may take is the upbeat, Tooby-Cosmidesean one that approaches Mother Nature's red teeth and claws with dentifrice and clippers.*
NATIONAL REVIEW, 20 JUNE 2005

BREVITY

brevity is the soul of wit
a witty remark is by its nature best expressed in short and pithy form

Exhortations to brevity are age-old and universal. In one form or another, Terence, Plautus, Pliny, Martial, Horace, Erasmus, Gracián and La Fontaine have commented on the value of conciseness. The proverb in its contemporary form is familiar through Shakespeare's use of it in HAMLET (1602), where a worried Polonius tells Claudius and Gertrude why he thinks Hamlet is behaving so strangely:

*Therefore, since brevity is the soul of wit
And tediousness the limb and outward flourishes,
I will be brief. Your noble son is mad.*

Here *wit* means 'understanding, reasoning' (we still refer to the *wit and wisdom* of man); Polonius means that he is less likely to be misunderstood if he comes directly to the point.

Today *wit* is more likely to be understood as the art of making telling remarks in a lively and amusing way. The best wisecracks are often one-liners: *Brevity is the soul of lingerie* (attributed to Dorothy Parker). They can be very funny or acerbically critical. Theatre critics are noted in this second category for remarks such as:

'House Beautiful' is play lousy
(Dorothy Parker)

It opened at 8.40 sharp and closed at 10.40 dull (Heywood Broun)

It is the sort of play that gives failures a bad name (Walter Kerr)

However, the proverb more properly refers to a weightier comment that is concisely and memorably expressed:

I can resist everything except temptation
(Oscar Wilde)

*God has made man in his own image –
man has retaliated* (Pascal)

To acknowledge you were wrong yesterday is simply to let the world know that you are wiser today than you were then
(Jonathan Swift)

Many a man aims at nothing and hits it with remarkable precision
(Archbishop Richard Whately)

*If **brevity is the soul of wit**, why does comedian Marcus Brigstocke make ten minutes seem like an eternity? In that time Groucho Marx would have fired off a hundred pithy one-liners and even Jim Davidson could have raised a smile. Yet poor Brigstocke, given ten minutes of prime-time television, seems fit only to squander it.*
MIRROR, 26 SEPTEMBER 2001

*If **brevity is the soul of wit**, no wonder we have so many stupid movies.Filmmakers don't know when enough is enough. It used to be that cinematic diarrhea was most common during the Christmas season. Somewhere along the way Hollywood began equating long with important, and since the holiday season was heavy with Oscar-hopeful titles, we got used to sitting through long movies...But things have gotten out of hand. Now summer movies – so-called 'light' entertainment – are clocking in at more than 160 minutes, and I have to protest.*
BERGEN COUNTY RECORD, 18 JULY 2006

BRICKS

you can't make bricks without straw

nothing can be accomplished without the right materials for the job

The proverb comes from the Bible. The children of Israel were slaves in the land of Egypt, where they worked hard making bricks for their Egyptian overlords. The bricks were made of clay mixed with straw to bind it and then baked in the sun. EXODUS, Chapter 5, tells how Moses went to Pharaoh to ask if the Israelites might go on a three-day pilgrimage into the desert to offer a sacrifice to the Lord. Pharaoh, already concerned about the size of the Israelite population in his country, was alarmed that they had found the courage to come to ask for time off. He issued a command that the Israelites were to be kept even busier. From that time on straw would no longer be supplied. The Israelites would have to go out and gather their own, and still make their daily tally of bricks. Not surprisingly, they found this an impossible task.

Allusion to this story has been current since at least the first quarter of the seventeenth century. In the eighteenth century, John Pinney, a plantation owner on the Caribbean island of Nevis between 1762 and 1818, used the proverb to make this comment on the slave trade: *It is impossible for a man to make sugar without the assistance of Negroes as to make bricks without straw.*

You can't make bricks without straw. As I wrote the other day, Scotland's problem is lack of talent. There's nothing under the kilt.
EVENING STANDARD,
5 NOVEMBER 2004

...the judge said the argument was not strong enough to uphold, ruling that 'it is, to use a tired old metaphor, an attempt to make bricks without straw.'
SCOTSMAN, 6 MARCH 2006

BRIDGE

don't cross a bridge until you come to it

don't deal with anticipated problems until they become realities; don't look for problems

In THE GOLDEN LEGEND (1851), Longfellow called this *a proverb old, and of excellent wit*, though written evidence earlier than the nineteenth century is wanting. It may well be a variant of a much older saying recorded in Heywood's PROVERBS (1546): *Ye would be ouer the style er ye come at it.* In Henry Porter's THE TWO ANGRIE WOMEN (1599), this appears as: *You must not leape ouer the stile before you come to it.*

A decision on what to do with Luna the killer whale, a juvenile from a U.S.-based pod who's been going it alone in remote Canadian waters, could come as early as next week...How would U.S. officials respond to a decision to try to reunite the whale with his family in U.S. waters? 'I guess we'll cross that bridge when we come to it,' said spokesman Brian Gorman with the regional National Marine Fisheries Service office in Seattle.
COLUMBIAN, 18 SEPTEMBER 2003

Don't cross a bridge until you come to it. Try to take one day at a time.
COVENTRY EVENING TELEGRAPH,
9 AUGUST 2006

Usage: Recent usage has turned the proverb into an idiomatic phrase, *to cross a bridge when one comes to it*, meaning 'to deal with an anticipated problem if and when it arises'.

> ### THE WISDOM OF PROVERBS
> How well accepted is the wisdom of proverbs? One small piece of evidence is from Germany. A scholar there reported the results of a test carried out in 1964. Out of 24 proverbs, *Es is nicht alles Gold, was glänzt* ('Not all that glitters is gold') came top, yet even so only 69 per cent of respondents believed it to be an acceptable truth.

See also *Sufficient into the DAY is the evil thereof; TOMORROW is another day*

BROKEN

if it ain't broke, don't fix it
don't try to improve on something that is working perfectly well

Variant: If it isn't broken, don't fix it

It seems to be a universal human instinct to meddle with something that is working perfectly well in order to make it work better. The consequences are usually dire. This is a very modern saying, popular in America and the United Kingdom since it was used by Bert Lance in the May 1977 issue of NATION'S BUSINESS. At the time, Lance was Director of the Federal Office of Management and Budget for President Carter.

The proverb has been particularly popular as a source for comment on anything from government to business and to sport, occasioning some clever witticisms: *If it ain't broke, don't fix it – unless you're a consultant* (Winton G Rossiter).

Naturally, there have been efforts to smarten the saying up by correcting the grammar. *If it isn't broken, don't fix it* is used by those who feel uncomfortable with the colloquial expression,

particularly if the written or spoken context is properly expressed. Such grammatical correctness doesn't go down well with everyone, however:

'If it ain't broke, don't fix it,' though a faux-folk saying only a few decades old, is surely preferable to the sanitized version some killjoys are spreading: 'If it's not broken, don't fix it' sounds like business boilerplate, not horse sense.
BOSTON GLOBE, 5 MARCH 2006

If it isn't broken, don't fix it. The well-known saying has become Steve Wind's personal mantra of late. Wind is one of about 50 people who live around a stretch of open land on Sleepy Hollow's west side. There, children play and neighbors gather to chat. And they want to keep it that way. Wind presented a petition signed by all of his neighbors to the village board this week urging members to leave the spot out of any new open space plans.
ARLINGTON HEIGHTS DAILY HERALD, 22 FEBRUARY 2002

Sir Jimmy Young sensationally quit the BBC yesterday rather than be sidelined… Last night a host of famous fans expressed their dismay at Sir Jimmy's departure… Former Tory cabinet minister David Mellor said: 'Maybe the BBC should remember the adage, "If it ain't broke, don't fix it."'
DAILY MAIL, 7 NOVEMBER 2002

See also *Let sleeping DOGS lie; Leave WELL alone*

BROOM

a new broom sweeps clean
a person appointed to a new position of responsibility will set out on an enthusiastic programme of reform

Stevenson records a tradition which traces the origin of this proverb to the intense trading rivalry between Britain and the Netherlands in the seventeenth century. During the first Dutch war of 1652, the scornful Dutch admiral Van Tromp is said to have bound a broom to his flagship's mast. He would, he declared, sweep the British off the seas. In reply, the English navy, led by Robert Blake, tied a horsewhip to their flagship. As it was, the Dutch ships were routed. There may be truth in the story but the expression, besides having equivalents in other European languages that show a medieval Latin origin, had already been recorded by John Heywood in PROVERBS by the middle of the preceding century: *The greene new brome sweepeth cleene*.

The true origin is much more mundane. Brooms in the Middle Ages were bundles of green stems lashed to a long handle. (The *Cytisus scoparius* bush takes its common name, *broom*, from its usefulness here.) It was not long, however, before the green stems became worn and stubbed with use and less springy as the twigs dried out. The Italian expression, *A new broom is good for three days*, illustrates its limited life.

This said, one wonders if the English had much use for brooms at all. Erasmus was just one of the foreign visitors who complained about the hygiene in most ordinary households. There were, of course, no carpets. Instead the floors were strewn with rushes, which it was customary to renew when a visitor was expected, hence the sixteenth century proverb of welcome: *Strew green rushes for the stranger*. Perhaps Erasmus would have been happier if the old floorcovering had been removed before his welcoming layer was added, for he writes: *The floors are made of clay and are covered with layers of rushes, constantly replenished, so that the bottom layer remains for twenty years, harbouring spittle, vomit, the urine of dogs and men, the dregs of beer, the remains of fish, and other nameless filth* (P S and H M Allen, eds, OPUS EPISTOLARUM DESIDERII ERASMI ROTERODAMI, OUP 1906–47). Clearly *Cleanliness is next to GODLINESS* was not much considered by the ordinary English citizen.

A new broom sweeps clean and we expect just that of the new Bush administration. And while we can tolerate some touchstones with the earlier father Bush administration, the plan of action cannot be sacrificed to cronyism and partisanship.
DIESEL PROGRESS NORTH AMERICAN EDITION, 1 JANUARY 2001

Proof that a new broom sweeps clean was underlined yesterday when Crispin Davis, the chief executive of Reed Elsevier for 16 months, presided over better-than-expected 2000 results. Rarely can a company so wrought with internal wrangling and bereft of direction have been turned round so quickly.
INDEPENDENT, 23 FEBRUARY 2001

See also *MEDIEVAL LATIN*, page 214

BUSHEL

don't hide your light under a bushel
don't hide your talents or merits away through modesty or shyness

The proverb is a biblical one and can be found in MATTHEW 5:15. In the Sermon on the Mount, Jesus encourages his disciples to bear witness to their faith, telling them that *they are the light of the world*. He goes on to explain that a lamp is of no value if it is placed under a bushel (a tub big enough to contain a bushel of grain). Its proper place is on a lampstand. If his disciples are to influence those about them by word and example, they must not hide away but mix with others and act out their faith.

ANIMALS
Until the nineteenth century most of the British population lived from the land. They observed the creatures about them, both domesticated and wild, and drew lessons from their behaviour to apply to their own. From the shepherd, for instance, we learn that:

• *There is a BLACK sheep in every flock*
• *A pet lamb makes a cross ram*
• *One foolish sheep will lead the flock*
• *Shear your sheep when elder blossoms peep.*

The herdsman would know that:

• *Many a good cow hath a bad calf*
• *Milk the cow that stands still*
• *A lowing cow soon forgets her calf (excess grief does not last long).*

Observation of the pig scavenging freely in the village street would show that:

• *Pigs grow fat where lambs would starve*

• *A pretty pig makes an ugly sow*
• *Pigs might fly, but they are most unlikely birds*
• *You can't make a silk PURSE out of a sow's ear.*

Until the nineteenth century, oxen were often used for ploughing:

• *An old ox ploughs a straight furrow*
• *A man must plough with such oxen as he hath.*

Cats were kept as mousers:

• *Cats in mittens catch no mice*
• *That which comes of a cat will catch mice*
• *Cats that drive the mice away are as good as they that catch them*
    While the CAT is away, the mice will play

but other traits in their behaviour were also recognised:

• *The cat loves fish but she is loath to wet her feet*

Early versions of the Bible translate the correct *lamp* as *candle*. Sixteenth century uses of the proverb, therefore, speak of *hiding a candle under a bushel*. Interestingly, this continued until about the beginning of the twentieth century, by which time candles were no longer the main source of lighting.

Talented pensioners in a Midland town were today urged: 'Don't hide your light under a bushel'. Tamworth Borough Council is calling on budding singers, comedians and magicians in the town to take part in the country's biggest talent competition for the over 60s.
BIRMINGHAM EVENING MAIL,
10 JANUARY 2002

We tend to follow the examples that others set. However much we think of ourselves as autonomous individuals, our actions are profoundly influenced by our perceptions of how other people act in the same circumstances. So don't hide your light under a bushel. Whether it's ditching the holiday in Ibiza for a cottage in Cornwall, spurning Tesco for the farmers' market or insulating your loft and cutting your heating bills, your stories of personal action can make a real difference.
INDEPENDENT, 13 DECEMBER 2006

• *The more you rub a cat on the rump, the higher she sets her tail*
• *Honest is the cat when the meat is out of reach*
• *An old cat laps as much as a young kitlin.*

Dogs were kept to guard a house:

• *A dog is a lion when he is at home*
• *Why keep a DOG and bark yourself?*
• *Let sleeping DOGS lie*

or to hunt:

• *The hindmost dog may catch the hare*
• *You cannot run with the hare and hunt with the hounds*

and will do anything for a meal:

• *If you wish a dog to follow you, feed him.*

All in all they lead a dog's life:

• *A dog's life, hunger and ease.*
Aesop, writing in the sixth century BC, often made foxes the subject of his fables. He depicted them as sly, cunning creatures, a reputation which is reflected in European proverbs:

• *An old fox need learn no craft*
• *The fox may grow grey but never good*
• *He that will get the better of a fox must rise early (French)*
• *Foxes prey furthest from their earths*
• *A fox should not be of the jury at a goose trial*
• *An old fox is shy of a trap.*

And last, but not least, the birds and the bees have something to teach us all:

• *Birds in their little nests agree*
• *It is a foolish bird that soils its own nest*
• *You cannot catch old birds with chaff*
• *Every bee's honey is sweet*
• *What is not good for the swarm is not good for the bees (Latin)*
• *Old bees yield no honey*
• *Bees that have honey in their mouths have stings in their tails.*

Usage: *Bushel* is a rather dated word, and it gives a somewhat antiquated flavour to the whole saying. The scope of application is now far wider than Christian witness to the world. It may refer to any hidden virtues that are undervalued.

BYGONES

let bygones be bygones

we should forget and forgive past grievances and start again

This proverb is based on a recurrent phrase from Homer's ILIAD (c. 850 BC): *These things will we let be, as past and done.* John Heywood echoes Homer's words, imploring forgiveness in his PROVERBS (1546):

God taketh me as I am, and not as I was,
Take you me so to, and let all things
past pas.

The word *bygones*, used to describe events, usually offences, from the past, first appeared in the mid-sixteenth century. By the time Samuel Rutherford wrote his LETTERS in 1636 it had been assimilated into a fixed proverb expressing the gist of Homer's phrase: *Pray…that bygones betwixt me and my Lord may be bygones.*

*Canon Vincent Whelan, a priest travelling with the [war] veterans, recounted a trip that they had taken the previous day to the adjacent German and CWGC cemeteries at Saint-Desir-de-Lisieux. 'Quite by chance, we arrived at just the same time as two busloads of German veterans and families of people buried in their cemetery. I said prayers over their graves, particularly over the graves of two men whose families were visiting at the same time. Everyone, British and German, was very moved and we all welcomed the chance to **let bygones be bygones**.'*
DAILY TELEGRAPH, 2 JUNE 2004

*It's been a few days since their season-ending loss to Johnstown, but a controversial third-period call is still eating at some members of the Reading Royals. 'For me, it's really aggravating to have gone through that,' Captain Chris Bala said on Tuesday afternoon. 'At some point, we'll have **to let bygones be bygones**. But right now it's really hard to deal with.'*
READING EAGLE, 11 APRIL 2007

See also *FORGIVE and forget*

· C ·

CAKE

you can't have your cake and eat it

you can't benefit from two incompatible plans, actions, etc at the same time

Variant: You can't eat your cake and have it

This proverb was first recorded by John Heywood in his collection of PROVERBS in the middle of the sixteenth century as *Wolde you bothe eate your cake, and haue your cake?*, and has made frequent appearances in the literature of every century since. This age-old tendency to want absolutely everything and on one's own terms is not peculiarly British but crosses national frontiers; the French say *You can't have the cloth and keep the money*, and the Italians ask *Do you want to eat your cake and still have it in your pocket?*

The proverb as it was originally recorded by Heywood shares the same logical reasoning as the French and Italian ones, and was current until at least the middle of the twentieth century. Nowadays, however, the less logical form *You can't have your cake and eat it* is more frequently found.

You can't have your cake and eat it.
You can buy a share which gives a regular dividend income or one with a chance of making your money grow. But you can't have one which offers both.
MIRROR, 4 AUGUST 2004

*When it comes to health, **you can't have your cake and eat it**; students who ignore their diet are storing up health problems for later life.*
EVENING STANDARD,
7 SEPTEMBER 2004

See also *You can't have it BOTH ways*

CAP

if the cap fits, wear it

if you find the words of blame or criticism apply to you, then accept them

The expression originally spoke of the fool's cap, headgear decorated with bells which was worn by jesters. In Nicholas Breton's PASQUIL'S FOOLSCAP (1600) we read: *Where you finde a head fit for this Cappe, either bestowe it upon him in charity, or send him where he may haue them for his money.*

Fools were entertainers who, from medieval times, held permanent positions at court or in the households of distinguished noblemen. Shakespeare's KING LEAR (1605) depicts a fool who delivers penetrating insights in a jesting fashion. The popularity of the jester dwindled in the seventeenth century and Swift's epitaph on the Earl of Suffolk's fool, written in 1728, must be a tribute to one of the last of his kind:

> *Here lies the Earl of Suffolk's fool,*
> *Men called him Dicky Pearce;*
> *His folly served to make folks laugh,*
> *When wit and mirth were scarce.*

> Poor Dick alas! is dead and gone,
> What signifies to cry?
> Dickys enough are still behind.
> To laugh at by and by.

Mention of the fool's cap remained in the proverb until well into the eighteenth century, fools and jesters being in living memory. Thomas Fuller records the saying in GNOMOLOGIA (1732): *If any Fool finds the Cap fit him, let him wear it.* But by the middle of that century direct reference to the fool's cap was being dropped, and the proverb finds its way into Samuel Richardson's novel CLARISSA (1748) without it: *If indeed thou findest... that the cap fits thy own head, why than... e'en take and clap it on.*

Have broadcasters developed an itchy conscience about how they cover the arts? Judging by some defensive publicity campaigns, both BBC and Channel 4 feel they have a case to answer. Many people, myself included, received a 28-page glossy booklet from the BBC listing prestigious arts programmes in 2002, and inviting us to judge for ourselves whether the BBC was 'failing' – as some, apparently, alleged – 'to make programmes of range and distinction'. Of course, if the BBC were doing its job in these fields, it would not need such a pamphlet.

Similarly, at a lunch sponsored by Channel 4 at the recent Canada House Conference on The Arts on Television, each seat bore a smaller leaflet titled, Who Said There's No Arts on Television? Well, who did?

The French have a phrase for it: 'Qui s'excuse, s'accuse.' Or, in the English vernacular, 'If the cap fits, wear it.'
EVENING STANDARD, 28 MARCH 2003

Asked whether the film might offend Jewish viewers now, [Mel Gibson] remarked only that 'It's not meant to. I think it's meant to just tell the truth. I want to be as

truthful as possible. But when you look at the reasons Christ came, he was crucified, he died for all mankind and he suffered for all mankind. So that, really, anyone who transgresses has to look at their own part or look at their own culpability.' In other words, if the cap fits, wear it.
INDEPENDENT, 27 FEBRUARY 2004

Usage: By using the phrase, the speaker points to a logical – usually unpalatable – conclusion that the listener should draw. The proverb is often reduced to *If the cap fits...*, the rest being understood.

CARPE DIEM

carpe diem

'sieze the day', make the most of today's opportunities while they last

The proverb comes from a line in one of the ODES (23 BC) written by the Roman poet Horace: *Seize the present; trust the future as little as you may.* It is commonly found in both Latin and its English translation. The theme of making the most of life's fleeting opportunities is common to literature. In the seventeenth century, for instance, it was the subject of Robert Herrick's TO THE VIRGINS (see *Gather ye ROSEBUDS while ye may*), and of Andrew Marvell's poem TO HIS COY MISTRESS, where the poet tries to persuade his coy mistress to sleep with him while she is still youthful and before the grave claims her:

> *...Let us roll all our strength and all*
> *Our sweetness up into one ball,*
> *And tear our pleasures with rough strife*
> *Thorough the iron gates of life:*
> *Thus, though we cannot make our sun*
> *Stand still, yet we will make him run.*

In the twentieth century, CARPE DIEM was the title of a poem by American poet Robert Frost (1874–1963). The American heavy metal band Metallica has a song CARPE DIEM BABY (1997), while the Kellogg company has used the words 'Seize the day' to launch a healthy breakfast cereal.

Williams stands his class in front of a photo of a year group and asks them to imagine what words of wisdom these accomplished professionals – all now long since dead – might pass on to them from across the years. As the class leans forward to try to imagine what their predecessors might say, Williams whispers the words: 'carpe diem' – seize the day. That phrase captures a major theme of the film: take advantage of life's opportunities and realize your full potential.
CMA MANAGEMENT, 1 APRIL 2002

Valedictorian Katherine Capella gave her fellow graduates three challenges – not to let high school be the best four years of their lives; always make a unique contribution; and seize the day.
SYRACUSE POST-STANDARD,
27 JUNE 2002

Ever since I studied Horace at University, I've followed his words 'carpe diem', or 'seize the day'. I instantly thought that was how I wanted to live my life. I interpret carpe diem as meaning to make the most of every day, as you never know if you're going to have a tomorrow. My attitude has always been, when an opportunity is there, grab it…For me, this motto also means enjoying the day and being grateful for it. I have colleagues on both sides of the House of Commons who seem to live from one reshuffle to the next, but that's completely pointless – you should be living for now.
ANN WIDDECOMBE IN GOOD HOUSEKEEPING, NOVEMBER 2006

See also *Make HAY while the sun shines*; *Strike while the IRON'S hot*; *Gather ye ROSEBUDS while ye may*; *TIME and tide wait for no man*; *There's no TIME like the present*; *Never put off till TOMORROW what you can do today*

For other proverbs commonly quoted in either Latin or English, see under: *CAVEAT emptor*; *FESTINA lente*; *Great OAKS from little acorns grow*; *TIME flies*

CAT

a cat has nine lives
used of a person whose fortunes revive time after time, who gets plenty of second chances

Cats are agile creatures who, when they fall, land nimbly upon their four legs because of an innate reflex to right themselves in the air. An old proverb likened people whose fortunes always turned out favourably to a cat for this very reason: *He's like a cat, fling him which way you will he'll light on 's legs* (John Ray, ENGLISH PROVERBS, 1678). Today we would say *He always falls on his feet*. This agility has made the cat appear resilient in life-threatening situations, so that the animal is said to have nine lives.

The tradition, however, is not European but an ancient Indian one. It is contained in the FABLES OF PILPAY (or BIDPAI), an ancient collection of Sanskrit stories. These had widespread influence on European folklore through an eighth century Arabic translation, subsequent renderings into various Continental languages and, in 1570, a translation into English.

THE GREEDY AND AMBITIOUS CAT tells the story of a cat who lives on the edge of starvation with its owner, an old woman. One day she sees another cat. This one, however, is not skinny but fat and sleek. Surprised at this, the lean cat asks her new acquaintance how she comes to look so well and is told that there is plenty of food to be had at the king's house at dinner time. The lean cat resolves to accompany her sleek companion to this house of plenty the following day. Unfortunately, that very day, the servants had been ordered to rid the house of cats – many were in the habit of going there because of the rich pickings to be had. Nevertheless, the lean cat entered and, spying a dish of meat, dragged it unobserved under the dresser. Here she gorged herself on her prize until a servant noticed her and threw his knife at her, wounding her in the breast:

However, as it has been the providence of Nature to give this creature nine lives instead of one, poor Puss made a shift to crawl away, after she had for some time shammed dead: but, in her flight, observing the blood come streaming from her wound, 'Well,' said she, 'let me but escape this accident, and if ever I quit my old hold and my own mice for all the rarities in the King's kitchen, may I lose all my nine lives at once.'

The earliest known written record of the proverb in English says that women share the cat's remarkable fortune: *A woman hath nyne lyues like a cat* (John Heywood, PROVERBS, 1546).

Indeed, this comparison remained current well into the eighteenth century and, even in the twentieth century, was used by Noël Coward to describe a woman who has lived to a very old age, despite many setbacks with her health (FUTURE INDEFINITE, 1954): *She joked about her illness and said that she was a cat with nine lives, eight of which had been lived to the full; the next attack, she said in her charming deep voice, would be the grand*

final and similarly by James Byrom in OR BE HE DEAD (1958): *I'm like a cat with nine lives; each one lasts ten years, and I've just had my eighth. I'm going to live to be ninety, you'll see. I'm not too old to have some fun!*

Other literary references just make mention of the cat's nine lives. In Shakespeare's ROMEO AND JULIET (1591), Mercutio, incensed that Romeo refuses to stand up to his enemy Tybalt, himself picks a quarrel with Tybalt. When Tybalt asks him *What would thou have with me?* Mercutio replies, *Good King of Cats, nothing but one of your nine lives.*

The cat is not totally invincible, however. Even she must take heed lest care, curiosity or a murderous hand dispatch her prematurely: see *Care killed a CAT, Curiosity killed the CAT, There's more than one way to kill a CAT than by choking it with cream.*

*If, as the proverb has it, **a cat has nine lives** and Peter Mandelson were a cat, he has just lost another life. The episode of the Hindujas' passports is a messy one* INDEPENDENT, 24 JANUARY 2001

Australian motorcycle racing's bad boy, Anthony Gobert, returns to Phillip Island this weekend after struggling with depression and admitting he almost squandered his career. A naturally talented rider, he has been undermined by weight problems and excessive partying and last April was sacked from the American AMA Superbike Championship.
'I know I've said it many times before and people will be wondering how long I go before something else happens, but truly I know this is my last chance,' Gobert said. 'They reckon a cat has nine lives and I think I must be up to about number ten in my career so far.'
AAP SPORTS NEWS, 29 MARCH 2005

a cat may look at a king
even the lowliest have rights

Both French and German have variants of this proverb and each has a story behind it. The French version *Un chien regarde bien un évêque* (Even a dog may look at a bishop) is said to be a reference to a sixth century decree that forbade bishops from keeping dogs in case the animals should bite those coming to seek counsel. The German equivalent *Darf loch the Katze den Kaiser ansehen* (Even a cat may look at an Emperor) claims to stem from an incident in which Maximilian I visited the shop of a man who made wood-cuts. During the entire visit the craftsman's cat lounged upon the table, staring at the Emperor in a suspicious fashion.

The fact that two European languages have equivalent proverbs with different stories to tell casts doubt upon the veracity of the tales. English retains no anecdote to account for the origin of its particular version, which was recorded by John Heywood in 1546. The proverb is simply a colourful way of saying that, in the presence of their superiors, even those of lowly rank have certain rights.

*For everyone is an artist, merely by virtue of drawing breath: and so **a cat may look at a king**.*
NEW CRITERION, 1 SEPTEMBER 2000

It's worth noting, then, that early in the history of photography a series of judicial decisions could well have changed the course of that art: courts were asked whether the photographer, amateur or professional, required permission before he could capture and print an image. Was the photographer stealing from the person or building whose photograph he shot, pirating something of private and certifiable value? Those early decisions went in favor of the pirates...the photographer should be free to capture an image without compensating the source.

*The world that meets our eye through the lens of a camera was judged to be, with minor exceptions, a sort of public commons, where **a cat may look at a king**.*
HARPER'S MAGAZINE, 1 FEBRUARY 2007

Usage: Those using the expression see it as an assertion of rights; those so addressed, from a different perspective, may interpret it as insolent. Now rather dated.

there's more than one way to skin a cat
there is more than one way of achieving one's aim; there's more than one way of doing something

The proverb was first recorded in John Ray's ENGLISH PROVERBS (1678). There is scant evidence of its use in English literature but the American journalist Seba Smith used it in JOHN SMITH'S LETTERS (1839) and in WAY DOWN EAST; or, PORTRAITURES OF YANKEE LIFE (1854): *'This is a money digging world of ours; and, as it is said, 'there are more ways than one to skin a cat,' so are there more ways than one of digging for money'.* Later, Mark Twain made use of the saying in A CONNECTICUT YANKEE IN KING ARTHUR'S COURT (1889).

There are several British variants involving both cats and dogs. Ray records *There are more ways to kill a dog than hanging* (ENGLISH PROVERBS, 1678). In WESTWARD HO! (1855), Charles Kingsley has *There are more ways of killing a cat than choking it with cream*, a version that is still current (see the quotation that follows).

Another variant suggests choking the cat with butter rather than cream, while yet another says *there are more ways of killing a dog than choking him with pudding*. (The *pudding* here would be a black pudding or blood sausage.) These, together with the appearance in Ray's proverb collection, show that

There's more than one way to skin a cat did not originate in the southern states of the US, where it has been said to refer to the preparation of catfish for the table.

There is more than one way to skin a cat, as the saying goes. Likewise, there is more than one way to educate children... Each year scores of educators are realizing that the one-size-fits-all philosophy of public education does not necessarily support successful learning environments...
WASHINGTON TIMES,
23 MARCH 2001

Curry powder is a handy weapon in the wife's armoury. If himself has been a little peach and in a good mood, the spices I use are mild and gentle. But if he's been awkward or stubborn, he comes home to a vindaloo. As the beads of perspiration drip endlessly down his crimson face, he'll turn to me with bulging eyes and remark that the curry is a 'bit on the hot side'. I wear a look of innocence, tell him that it's the same as usual, and ponder on the expression, 'There's more ways of killing a cat than choking it with cream'.
LIVERPOOL DAILY POST,
8 NOVEMBER 2003

But there is more than one way to skin a cat and the same set of data can be interpreted in different ways. When two or more medics are gathered together you can guarantee to have a score of opinions.
INDEPENDENT, 2 FEBRUARY 2004

when the cat's away, the mice will play

the followers of a leader will take advantage of his absence for their own ends

The African wildcat was domesticated in ancient Egypt to protect grain stores from rodents, and the European cat is descended from this stock. It is impossible to say exactly when the domestic cat came to Britain but the Welsh king Howell the Good (c. 880–950) passed legislation making it illegal to kill or harm a cat. According to an article in the RSPCA magazine, ANIMALS in 1979, in AD 948 the price of a young kitten in the kingdom was one penny but went up to two pence once a kitten had caught its first mouse.

Thomas Heywood, in his play A WOMAN KILL'D WITH KINDNESS (1607), calls *When the cat's away, the mouse may play* an old proverb, and indeed it is. A manuscript dating back to around 1470 tells us that *the mouse is lord when there is no cat* and R Hill's COMMONPLACE-BOOK (c. 1530) has *The mowse goth a-brode, wher the cat is not lorde*.

It is also a proverb common to many European languages. French, for instance, has *When the cat runs on the roofs, the mice dance on the floors*, and German has *Cat outside the house, repose for the mouse. When the cat is not in the house, the mice dance* is common to French, Spanish and Italian. Indeed, *When the Catte is not at home, the Myce daunce* was quoted in J Sandford's HOURS OF RECREATION (1576).

HELP ME, I'M A DAD
When mother's away the children will play... *up. Tim Dowling is still recovering.*
DAILY TELEGRAPH, 17 JUNE 2000

When the cat is away, the mice will play. *In this case, however, the mouse is John Scaduto, a teenager so fond of pranks he doesn't care if the cat is right there! Naturally John holds the record for disciplinary demerits in his school.*
NEW STRAITS TIMES, 29 JULY 2001

*Legend has it that a country is never better
governed than when its rulers are otherwise
engaged. People go about their business
untrammelled by rules and regulations.
They do their own thing. **When the cat is
away the mice can play**.*
EVENING STANDARD,
27 SEPTEMBER 2001

CAVEAT

caveat emptor

a purchaser should satisfy himself
that whatever he is buying is sound
as he is responsible for its condition
unless it is protected by a guarantee
or warranty

Caveat emptor is a Latin law maxim
which translates into English as *Let the
buyer beware*. Both the Latin and the
English translations are current. The
full form of the maxim is *Caveat emptor,
quia ignorare non debuit quod ius alineum
emit* ('Let the buyer beware, for he
ought not to be ignorant of the nature
of the property which he is buying
from another').

Formerly a buyer was totally bound
by a contract with the seller. The law
was amended by Chief Justice Tindal
(1776–1846), who declared:

*If a man purchases goods of a tradesman
without in any way relying upon the skill
and judgment of the vendor, the latter is not
responsible for their turning out contrary to
his expectation; but if the tradesman be
informed, at the time the order is given, of
the purpose for which the article is wanted,
the buyer relying upon the seller's judgment,
the latter impliedly warrants that the things
furnished shall be reasonably fit and proper
for the purposes for which it is required.*

This was an important influence on
our present day consumer law. An
anecdote from Reuter, published in
THE TIMES OF MALTA (4 April
1993), shows how important it is to
inspect merchandise for quality:

*For several days a new delivery of Syrian-
made shoes took the Ukrainian city of
Ivano-Frankivsk by storm, snapped up by
men with an eye to fashion and elegance.
Then the soles began peeling away, the
colours ran and finally they simply fell
apart. Itar-Tass news agency said local
investigators found the stylish footwear,
imported and sold off at a handsome profit
by a small private company, had been
made for corpses at Syrian funerals.*

*Dissenting Man Utd supporters were
conspicuous by their absence when their
club was originally floated as a public
company – an act which effectively
underwrote their successes in the 1990s
– so to complain now is typical of these
people, who bought into the capitalist
dream and then start to whinge when
the chickens come home to roost. **Caveat
emptor**, and no sympathy.*
GUARDIAN, 16 MAY 2005

*All along, this column repeated the best
piece of consumer advice ever uttered in
Latin – **caveat emptor!***
WASHINGTON POST, 4 JUNE 2006

*Latin for 'let the buyer beware', **caveat
emptor** is a legal principle that applies to
the sale of property. It means the onus is
on the buyer to ascertain the quality and
condition of a property before proceeding
with its purchase.*
GUARDIAN UNLIMITED, 4 MAY 2007

Usage: This saying carries the simple
message 'Watch out!'

For other proverbs commonly quoted
in Latin or English, see under *CARPE
diem*; *FESTINA lente*; *Great OAKS from
little acorns grow*; *TIME flies*

CHANGE

plus ça change, plus c'est la même chose

change all boils down to the same thing in the end

This French saying, which translates as *The more things change the more they stay the same*, was coined by French critic, journalist and novelist Jean-Baptiste Alphonse Karr in an 1849 issue of his satirical monthly journal LES GUÊPES (THE WASPS). The more governments change, the more they resemble each other. It is a sentiment that has found a home on this side of the Channel as well. The weary comment is now applicable not just to governments and their policies but much more widely, as the newspaper quotation below shows.

Does any of this sound familiar: a prime minister hated by his party; an invasion of an Asian country which only serves to make a bad situation worse and ends in ignominious retreat; attacks on the royal family in the gutter press; a Tory party brought low by a chronic lack of loyalty and the inability to find an effective leader; an 'Irish problem' that defies solution; a French railway system that is 'very much better than ours'; a prolonged spell of warm weather in winter, giving rise to fears of permanent climate change; a moral panic about teenage pregnancies; attacks on members of the royal family for going hunting; a queen who is alleged to dislike her eldest son, referring to him as 'a stupid boy'; a consort whose diplomatic skills and intelligence are wedded to marital fidelity so perfect that he never even looks at his wife's 'handsome Ladies and Maids of Honour'? As one reads these wonderfully evocative diaries of the second quarter of the 19th century [The Diaries of Charles Greville], again and again one finds oneself murmuring 'plus ça change, plus c'est la même chose'.
DAILY TELEGRAPH, 1 FEBRUARY 2005

These days the proverb appears in either French or translation. It is sometimes cut short to *Plus ça change...* the rest of the comment being understood.

As they say in France: 'Plus ça change, plus c'est la même chose.' The more things change, the more they stay the same. This is particularly apposite for Merchant-Ivory's film Le Divorce, which sees cinema's evergreen producer/director partnership throw off the corsets and stiff collars for a modern flit with Americans in Paris. Yet for all their modernity, the characters are as bound by codes of dress and as restricted by protocol as any in the duo's famous period films.
MAIL ON SUNDAY,
21 SEPTEMBER 2003

Variant: The more things change, the more they stay the same

For other proverbs quoted in French, see *NOBLESSE oblige*; *RÉCULER pour mieux sauter*

CHARITY

charity begins at home

look after your own interests first

Noël Coward, in his song WE MUST ALL BE VERY KIND TO AUNTIE JESSIE (1920), gives a tongue-in-cheek interpretation of this proverb, with lyrics about a family aunt who has *'never been a Mother or a Wife'* but who shouldn't be teased:

> *Though unpleasant to behold*
> *She's a heart of purest gold*
> *And Charity you know begins at home.*

The proverb is, in fact, biblical in inspiration. In his first letter to Timothy, St Paul writes that children should provide first for their widowed parent before extending their help to others in the Church: *But if any widow have children or nephews, let them learn first to show piety at home, and to requite their parents...But if any provide not for his own, and specially for those of his own house, he hath denied the faith, and is worse than an infidel* (1 TIMOTHY 5:4 and 8).

An early use comes in William Langland's PIERS PLOWMAN (1362): *Help thi kynne, Christ bit [biddeth], for ther beyginneth charitie,* and John Wycliffe's essay OF PRELATES (c. 1380) has: *Charite schuld begyne at hem-self.*

The thought was later explained more fully: *Charity begins, but doth not end, at home* (Thomas Fuller, THE APPEAL OF INJURED INNOCENCE, 1659). We should all care first for our own families, and then extend our help to others. Our children, well provided for and observing our charity outside the home, will then adopt the same attitude. There is a similar proverb in Italian: *Fa buona a te e tuoi / E poi a gli altri se te puoi* ('Do good to yourself and yours, and then to others if you are able').

Today, however, we are familiar only with *Charity begins at home,* and the original positive moral exhortation now has a rather cynical, selfish sense. It is often used to justify some act of obvious self-interest.

*Cocker's **charity begins at home**... 'The video is a parody of Band Aid's Do They Know It's Christmas,' he [Jarvis Cocker] said... 'Instead of the celebs who sang on Band Aid, we've got Kylie Minogue and Robbie Williams impersonators. It'll be just like a charity record, except we're not giving anything to charity.'*
DAILY TELEGRAPH, 24 JANUARY 2002

*I and several of my friends and families have stopped playing the Lottery after all the cash awarded to asylum seekers and their campaigners. Does [the Community Fund chief executive] not realise that **charity begins at home** and we have*

some of the poorest children in Europe living in deprived inner cities that could do with the help?
LIVERPOOL DAILY POST,
10 OCTOBER 2002

charity covers a multitude of sins

acts of charity salve the conscience of those plagued by guilt; acts of charity hide the flaws in a person's character

The proverb is a biblical one. PETER 4:8 reads: *And above all things have fervent charity among yourselves: for charity shall cover the multitude of sins.* Charity here, of course, is Christian love. Peter is saying that deep love and commitment amongst a group of believers freely forgives the wrongs of others and heals dissent.

Charity has had another long-standing sense of 'good works' or of 'financial help to worthy causes'. That is by far and away its predominant meaning today, and is the way that the proverb has been understood over the last one hundred years or so.

*Campbell's 'privacy law' would **cover up a multitude of sins.***
MAIL ON SUNDAY, COLUMN HEADLINE,
9 MAY 2004

*Human nature is never perfect but is it not written that **charity covers a multitude of sins**? Alderman Drinkwater may not plead guilty to a multitude of sins, but his generous dealings have laid up a fine balance on the credit side of his balance.*
COVENTRY EVENING TELEGRAPH,
27 SEPTEMBER 2004

CHICKENS

don't count your chickens before they are hatched

don't be overconfident and assume success before you know the outcome of a venture

Records of the proverb's use in English date back to the second half of the sixteenth century but its origins lie in the fables of Aesop written in the sixth century BC.

THE MILKMAID AND THE PAIL tells of a young girl on her way home after milking, carrying her pail of milk on her head. As she walked along, she began to daydream about what she would do with the milk. First she would make cream and, with that, butter to sell. This would bring enough to buy some eggs which would hatch into chickens. The chickens would lay still more eggs and, before long, she would have a prosperous business. When prices were high, she would sell some of the birds and buy herself a beautiful dress. This would bring her to the notice of the young men in the town but she would ignore their advances with a toss of her curls. At this, the milkmaid tossed her head and the pail of milk fell to the ground. Such are the disappointments of those who *count their chickens before they are hatched*.

It is understood, however, that the appointment of the former professional footballer, the original front-runner, is not yet a done deal. 'Palios's credentials are probably better than those of Littlewood but certain issues remain unresolved,' one FA insider said last night. 'It would be dangerous to count your chickens before they hatch.'
DAILY TELEGRAPH, 10 MAY 2003

A year later, after finally rehabilitating the knee, he broke his leg during a

preseason game. The performance bonuses he expected stopped. And Grossman, who has always expected success, learned a valuable lesson. 'Don't count your chickens before they hatch.'
MIAMI HERALD, 5 NOVEMBER 2006

Usage: Often abbreviated to *Don't count your chickens...* spoken in a warning tone.

See also *There's many a slip 'twixt* CUP *and lip*; *First catch your* HARE

CHILD

spare the rod and spoil the child

a child who is not disciplined when he deserves it will become a spoilt brat

Variant: Spare the rod, spoil the child

The adage is from a verse in the Old Testament book of PROVERBS (13:24) which reads: *He that spareth his rod hateth his son: but he that loveth him chasteneth him betimes*. Throughout the Middle Ages, writers referred to the first part of the verse as a wise saying of Solomon. It was not until the seventeenth century that the verse was adapted and the modern proverb coined. Of course, the rod means just that; a smack on the hand or buttocks with a cane. Now that corporal punishment is widely frowned upon, however, the proverb is used less as a wise saw and more as an encapsulation of the philosophy of those parents who are still in favour of smacking their children.

The Chinese have a similar approach to discipline. William Scarborough cites *The bamboo stick produces obedient children* in his COLLECTION OF CHINESE PROVERBS (1875), but the Latin comic poet Terence is also in favour of gentleness. *It is better to bind your children to you by respect and gentleness*, he says, *than by fear* (ADELPHOE, 160 BC).

The concept of 'spare the rod and spoil the child' isn't fashionable any more. Psychologists say youngsters need tenderness and understanding. Battering kids into terrified submission certainly is not the way to handle them – but there's a big difference between brutality and a touch of stern chastisement.
MIRROR, 30 APRIL 2001

Opinion polls show a substantial majority of the public still wedded to the idea that dispensing a sharp blow to a misbehaving child is both an inalienable parental right and effective discipline. The government seems to share this common sense philosophy of 'spare the rod and spoil the child': Tony Blair and David Blunkett have both admitted smacking their children.
GUARDIAN, 12 SEPTEMBER 2001

See also *You've got to be CRUEL to be kind*

the child is father of the man
the child's character gives insight into the kind of man he will grow up to be

The proverb comes from MY HEART LEAPS UP (1802), a poem by Wordsworth:

> *My heart leaps up when I behold*
> *A rainbow in the sky:*
> *So was it when my life began,*
> *So is it now I am a man,*
> *So be it when I shall grow old*
> *Or let me die!*
> *The Child is Father of the Man:*
> *And I could wish my days to be*
> *Bound each to each by natural piety.*

The thought had been expressed by other illustrious poets before Wordsworth. These words, for instance, are Dryden's from THE HIND AND THE PANTHER (1687):

> *By education most have been misled,*
> *So they believe, because they so were bred.*

The priest continues what the nurse began,
And thus the child imposes on the man.

and these Milton's in PARADISE REGAINED (1671):

> *The childhood shows the man*
> *As morning shows the day.*

but Wordsworth's concise rendition encapsulated the thought and became proverbial.

*I spent five years of my life as a Home Office minister making decisions on more than 1,000 murder files. I looked at them carefully, and it was clear that some of our worst murderers revealed their viciousness when very young, either by attacking other kids or by tormenting animals. **The child is the father of the man**.*
PEOPLE, 1 JULY 2001

Reflections on the childhood of former HIH [insurance company] director, Rodney Adler, recall the saying 'the child is the father of the man'. As a boy, Adler was popular for his quick wit and lack of respect for authority, and made a name for himself in business for refusing to live by the rules. His success as a businessman could be characterised as being more to do with confidence than actual substance.
AUSTRALASIAN BUSINESS INTELLIGENCE, 13 DECEMBER 2002

CHILDREN

children should be seen and not heard
children may be present but not obtrusively noisy

This proverb is commonly thought of as being of Victorian origin but, although it may have gained renewed attention from the strict Victorian family, it is much older than that. Aristophanes's play THE CLOUDS, written in 423 BC, cites the expression and calls it an *old rule*. In medieval England it was not children but chattering young girls who were compelled to look decorous and remain silent: *For hyt ys an old Englysch sawe: 'A mayde schud be seen, but not herd'* (John Mirk, MIRK'S FESTIAL, c. 1450).

Swift quotes this older form of the proverb in his POLITE CONVERSATION of 1738 but by 1866 the shift from maidens to children has taken place for we find E J Hardy coming to their defence and roundly declaring *'Little people should be seen and not heard' is a stupid saying* (HOW TO BE HAPPY THOUGH MARRIED). Nowadays the proverb is quoted by exasperated parents but not even heard above the din their offspring are making. Harry Graham in his RUTHLESS RHYMES FOR HEARTLESS HOMES (1899) shows the extent to which the distracted parent might go:

> *Father heard the children scream,*
> *So he threw them in the stream,*
> *Saying as he drowned the third,*
> *'Children should be seen, not heard!'*

Children should be seen and not heard *– but the old adage could be a thing of the past with the appointment of a Scottish commissioner for youngsters. An inquiry into the creation of a children's ombudsman, an advocate for the rights of the young, is already under way and the Scottish Executive seems in favour.*
DAILY MAIL, 22 MAY 2001

*Some **children should be seen and not heard**. And Charlotte Church is one of them. Yup, the Cardiff songstress is at it again with her careless comments.*
DAILY POST, 11 JANUARY 2002

Usage: In these progressive days the expression has a patronising tone to it when used to address unruly youngsters. It would be more

commonly heard today as an unavailing and unfulfilled longing of parents bombarded with the blare of pop culture and insolence.

See also *SPEAK when you're spoken to*

CLOUD

every cloud has a silver lining
every difficult or depressing circumstance has its hidden consolations; there is always a reason for hope in the most desperate situations

The far side of the darkest cloud reflects the moonlight and gleams silver, a sign of hope. The proverb has its origins in John Milton's masque COMUS (1634):

> *Was I deceiv'd, or did a sable cloud*
> *Turn forth her silver lining on the night?*

but it was Dickens who, over two centuries later, brought the lines to popular attention with his reference to the earlier work in the mouth of the cheerfully irresponsible Mr Skimpole: *I turn my silver lining outward like Milton's cloud* (BLEAK HOUSE, 1852). After Dickens, others made mention of silver-lined clouds but W S Gilbert's reference in THE MIKADO (1885) comes close to the present day proverb: *Don't let's be downhearted. There's a silver lining to every cloud*.

In the grim years of the First World War people sang to encourage themselves. By now the silvery cloud was far removed from its august origins: it had become a proverb that was on the tip of the popular tongue, finding its way into one of the best-remembered wartime songs, Ivor Novello and Lena Guilbert Ford's KEEP THE HOME FIRES BURNING (1915):

Turn the dark cloud inside out,
Till the boys come home.

And in another popular song written by
Jerome Kern and Bud DeSylva shortly
after the Great War, looking for a silver
lining remained a remedy for keeping
those weary of life's troubles cheerful
and finding *the sunny side of life.*

'I've spent 27 years in prison, 25 in
*solitary confinement. **But every cloud has***
a silver lining. *The love of my life is*
visiting on Sunday.'
MAIL ON SUNDAY, 4 MARCH 2001

*'**But my big cloud has had some***
wonderful silver linings. *I've got a life that*
allows me to travel, a fantastic job and I can
afford to go on holidays because we don't
have children...and if I knew my cancer
wasn't coming back, I'd even go so far as to
say I was pleased to have had it, because it
has taught me so much about myself.'
GOOD HOUSEKEEPING, JULY 2001

I lost 100lbs following my illness and have
*dropped four dress sizes. **Every cloud has***
a silver lining.
GUARDIAN, 6 JULY 2004

Usage: The proverb that had such
grand literary beginnings has now
become a rather trite cliché but, if it
has suffered from overuse, it is because
it answers the universal need for a ray
of hope in adversity.

See also *HOPE springs eternal in the*
human breast; The darkest HOUR is
that before the dawn; TOMORROW is
another day

COAT

cut your coat according to
your cloth

trim your expenditure according to the
money or income you have available

Sumptuary legislation, devised to
restrict extravagant expenditure on
food, entertainment and clothing, was
common in ancient Greece and Rome
and, later, in medieval Europe. The
Tudors, who were concerned to
maintain the boundaries of social
status, continued to pass sumptuary
laws. Some of these laid down the type
of cloth, the colour and the style of
clothing that different social ranks
were permitted to wear. The laws
prevented merchants from passing
themselves off as members of the
nobility, and marked out the humbler
ranks of society. Our contemporary
proverb may have been influenced by
this background, with persons of
inferior rank being tempted to buy
quantity and quality of cloth beyond
their social station and their means.
John Heywood records *I shall cut my*
cote after my cloth (PROVERBS, 1546)
and Lyly, writing in 1580, has *Cut thy*
coat according to thy cloth (EUPHUES
AND HIS ENGLAND).

The proverb preaches the wisdom
of living within one's financial means
or, sometimes more generally, within
the constraints of circumstance.
Charles Dickens's character Mr
Micawber, in DAVID COPPERFIELD
(1849), was well aware of the
advantages of financial prudence,
despite being unable to practise what
he preached:

'My other piece of advice, Copperfield,' said
Mr Micawber, 'you know. Annual income
twenty pounds, annual expenditure nineteen
six, result happiness. Annual income twenty
pounds, annual expenditure twenty pounds
ought and six, result misery. The blossom is

blighted, the leaf is withered, the God of day goes down upon the dreary scene, and – and in short you are forever floored. As I am!'

I am weary of non-stop moaning from working mothers about the cost of child care and how there should be greater subsidies and that two incomes are needed to support a family. I am on a pension which just takes me into the tax bracket and I strongly object to paying tax to support their much higher standard of living. The saying crosses my mind 'cut your coat according to your cloth'.
GUARDIAN, 19 MARCH 2005

You can always make do on whatever money you have. 'You just cut your coat according to your cloth,' says Chris.
SUNDAY MIRROR, 1 OCTOBER 2006

COBBLER

the cobbler should stick to his last

you should concern yourself only with employment that you know something about

Variants: Let the cobbler stick to his last; The shoemaker should stick to his last

The origin of the proverb is said to be in an anecdote told about Apelles, the famous Greek painter of the fourth century BC. The story goes that Apelles was wont to display his work to public view while he hung around, undetected, listening to their comments. One day a passing cobbler criticised a shoe latchet in one of the pictures. Apelles obliged by correcting the fault. The cobbler passed by again the next day and noticed the correction. Emboldened by his success he ventured to comment upon the way the thigh was painted but Apelles, who was hiding behind the picture, called out, *The shoemaker should not go beyond his last*. Erasmus alludes to

the Latin expression *Ne sutor ultra crepidam* (Let the cobbler not go beyond his last) in his ADAGIA (1536).

William Hazlitt created the word *ultracrepidarian*, based on Erasmus's citation, to refer to a critic who is ignorant or presumptuous. He first used it in 1819 of William Gifford who, before being helped with his education, was an apprentice shoemaker. The proverb itself is recorded in English literature from the sixteenth century.

...after an hour and a half of A-level English teaching in a sixth-form college, I gave up...the students put me right off in my very first teaching practice experience...so I quit and, like the wise shoemaker, returned to my last. Thank God I had found out in time...
TIMES EDUCATIONAL SUPPLEMENT, 18 JANUARY 2002

Killing one's child is not Munchausen's syndrome by proxy, if such a thing exists. The cobbler should stick to his last. Physicians should stick to theirs, and leave psychology to psychologists.
DAILY TELEGRAPH, 3 JULY 2003

COMPANY

a man is known by the company he keeps

you can tell what a person is like by the kind of friends he associates with

Variant: You can tell a man by the company he keeps

Written records of the proverb in English date back to the beginning of the seventeenth century: *As a man is, so is his company* (Arthur Dent, THE PLAINE MAN'S PATH-WAY TO HEAVEN, 1601). The proverb is common to many other European languages, which all have close variants.

Lord Chesterfield claims that *Tell me who you live with and I will tell you who you are* is a Spanish proverb, and indeed the Spanish author Cervantes uses *Tell me what company you keep, and I'll tell you what you are* in DON QUIXOTE (1615). On the other hand, the sixteenth century Italian diplomat, Stefano Guazzo, refers to the proverb twice in his CIVILE CONVERSAZIONE (1574): *Tel me with whom thou doest goe, and I shall know what thou doest*, he refers to as 'this common proverb', while *wee are alwayes taken for suche as those are, with whom we are conversant* he calls 'that common rule'. The French, Portuguese and Dutch also share the proverb. This diversity is reflected in English: the saying does not settle into the familiar form *A man is known by the company he keeps* until the nineteenth century.

An anonymous poem, apparently a parody of an earlier song ONE COLD MORNING IN DECEMBER (c. 1875), explains the proverb in a humorous vein:

> *One evening in October,*
> *When I was far from sober,*
> *And dragging home a load with*
> *manly pride,*
> *My feet began to stutter*
> *So I laid down in the gutter*
> *And a pig came up and parked right by*
> *my side.*
> *Then I warbled, 'It's fair weather*
> *When good fellows get together',*
> *Till a lady by was heard to say:*
> *'You can tell a man who boozes*
> *By the company he chooses!'*
> *Then the pig got up and slowly*
> *walked away.*

But the wisdom is ancient. Greek playwright Euripides, writing in the fifth century BC, says *Every man is like the company he is wont to keep* (PHOENISSAE) and Aesop tells fables which make this same point. THE ASS AND THE PURCHASER (c. 570 BC)

tells of a man who wanted to try out an ass before deciding whether or not to buy it. He took it home and led it to the stable where he kept his other asses. Straightaway it sought out the laziest animal there. *'My mind is made up,'* the man declared. *'It is easy to judge this ass's temperament by the companion he chooses.'*

A Moroccan proverb also illustrates the point with the behaviour of an ass. *If you let your ass mix with other asses*, it says, *you will teach it to moan, to bray and to leave the straight road*. The Egyptians, proud of their great river, say that *Even the water of the Nile loses its sweetness when it mingles with that of the sea*. Hebrew reminds us that *Dry wood sets green wood alight*, while an English alternative states that *Bad company is the ruin of a good character*.

A wealth of advice, spanning the centuries, encourages actively seeking out good company and shunning bad. Earl Rivers's translation of the SEYINGES OF [H]OMER provides a summary: *Acompanye the[e] with good people and thou shalt be on[e] of them; acompanye the[e] with badde & thou shalt be on[e] of thoos* (DICTES AND SAYENGES OF THE PHILOSOPHIRS, 1477).

Q: There are several corrupt politicians in the government you set up after the October 2002 elections in Pakistan. They include several already convicted by your accountability bureau. There's a saying that **a man is known by the company he keeps**. *How does keeping such politicians in the government reflect on you?*
UNITED PRESS INTERNATIONAL,
30 JUNE 2003

You can tell a man by the company he keeps. So goes the old saying. It is particularly true in the world of politics... William Hague, who would have been a great Tory leader given time, failed to make impact. One of the reasons was the appalling PR advice he was receiving from

his spin doctor, Amanda Platell. This lady had too much influence, and made enemies within the media. The wrong company...
BIRMINGHAM EVENING MAIL,
2 JULY 2003

COMPARISONS

comparisons are odious

comparing (usually one person to another) upsets and offends

This is an old and much-used proverb common to many European languages. Its use in French can be traced back at least as far as the thirteenth century. The earliest known English records, however, are in John Lydgate's DEBATE BETWEEN THE HORS, SHEPE AND GHOOS (c. 1430): *Odyous of olde been comparisonis*, and then in John Fortescue's DE LAUDIBUS LEGUM ANGLIAE (1471), where the author uses the proverb in his comparison of English common and civil law.

Shakespeare employs the saying to humorous effect in MUCH ADO ABOUT NOTHING (1599). Dogberry the constable, in awe of nobility, tries to speak in an educated fashion but often chooses the wrong word to convey his meaning; *Comparisons are odorous,* he declares.

Francis Hawkins, writing in the seventeenth century, has this to say about comparing one person to another: *Take heed that thou make no comparisons, and if any body happen to be praised for some brave act, or virtue, praise not another for the same virtue in his presence, for every comparison is odious* (YOUTH'S BEHAVIOUR, 1663). Sydney Smith (1771–1845) needed no such warnings: he was the very essence of tact and gallantry. On one occasion he met two attractive ladies of his acquaintance, Mrs Tighe and Mrs Cuff. *'Ah, ladies, there you are,'* he greeted them. *'The cuff that everyone would wear and the tie that no one would loose.'*

Comparisons are odious, but unavoidable here. For my money, Ben Power's version, directed by Rupert Goold at Northampton, is the grabbier of the two. While David Farr's adaptation in Bristol has an admirably austere, cerebral intensity, it rarely sets the pulse racing.
DAILY TELEGRAPH, 5 FEBRUARY 2004

In the unsaddling enclosure, the rapturous reception accorded to Arkle mixed awe and affection, an emotional cocktail which by then was served up every time he ran. But within 14 months of that extraordinary afternoon he had run his last race, hobbling over the Kempton line after being caught in the dying strides of the King George by Dormant, a horse whom a fit Arkle would have picked up and carried. Comparisons are odious. But 40 years on, Arkle is still unarguably the presiding spirit of steeplechasing...
GUARDIAN, 5 NOVEMBER 2005

COOKS

too many cooks spoil the broth

when too many people are involved in a project the result will be confusion

There is the proverb, the more cooks the worse pottage says George Gascoigne in his Life of Carew (1575). Large sixteenth century households, consisting of the family, their retinue and guests, had many cooks and scullion boys, each with his own particular job to do. Any cook who insisted on interfering with another's dish would neglect his own and perhaps be guilty of over-spicing his colleague's. Even in more modest establishments, food is easily spoilt if everyone who passes through adds a little more of this and that. A Dutch proverb concurs: *Too many cooks make the porridge too salt.*

The proverb in its modern form was current by the seventeenth century. It was used by the eccentric Huguenot painter and architect Sir Balthazar Gerbier in PRINCIPLES OF BUILDING, written in 1662.

*Undaunted, she suggested adding another couple of potatoes, then wondered if a bit more milk shouldn't be added to the rice pudding. I could **almost feel the broth spoiling** as I fulfilled my menial task of opening tins of baked beans.*
GOOD HOUSEKEEPING, FEBRUARY 2000

*It's been said that **too many cooks spoil the broth**. I believe that, and I also believe our state's child support system has so many cooks there's no broth left for the children who need help...Custodial parents who have had to use the child support system often feel they are getting the runaround. There are so many 'cooks' involved in the process that if any one missteps, the system breaks down. And the very structure of the current system makes accountability impossible.*
ARLINGTON HEIGHTS DAILY HERALD, 29 APRIL 2002

*The media has made much of the incompetence of civil servants in dealing with the construction of the new Scottish Parliament building, and questions should be asked as to the sudden lapse in their performance. The Scottish Office has had long experience in the financial management of large road projects...If civil servants could manage such projects then, why did the system collapse? Then there was a maximum of six ministers; now there are 20, with more than 100 MSPs. Perhaps **too many cooks do spoil the broth**.*
SCOTSMAN, 20 SEPTEMBER 2004

Usage: The proverb is not, of course, restricted to the kitchen. It can be used of any situation where more than the appropriate number for the particular task get involved and make a contribution that cancels out the efforts of others.

CRADLE

the hand that rocks the cradle rules the world
a mother's influence is greatest of all

The proverb comes from a well-known poem, THE HAND THAT RULES THE WORLD (1865), by the American lawyer and poet William Ross Wallace. The poem extols the role of motherhood. Each of its four verses ends with the line *For the hand that rocks the cradle is the hand that rules the world*. The third verse will suffice to give the flavour of the rest:

> *Woman, how divine your mission*
> *Here upon our natal sod!*
> *Keep, oh, keep the young heart open*
> *Always to the breath of God!*
> *All true trophies of the ages*
> *Are from mother-love impearled;*
> *For the hand that rocks the cradle*
> *Is the hand that rules the world*

Recognition of a mother's influence being paramount in a child's early years finds expression in several European languages, perhaps most memorably in Spanish: *What is sucked in with the mother's milk runs out with the shroud*.

Walsh gives two anecdotes that illustrate the proverb in reverse. The first goes back to Themistocles, the brilliant Athenian leader, who claimed his son was the most powerful person in Greece: *For the Athenians govern Greece, I the Athenians, my wife me, and my son my wife*.

The second is from the PERCY ANECDOTES (Reuben and Sholto Percy, 1823): *A nobleman accosted a lame school-master and asked him his name. 'I am R T,' was the answer, 'and the master of this parish.' 'Why, how so?' 'I am the master of the children of the parish, the children are masters of the mothers, the mothers are the rulers of the fathers, and consequently I am the master of the whole parish.'*

It is hardly surprising that humorists have found potent themes such as the exercise of power and the relationship between man and woman as perfect targets for their wit. American short story writer O Henry begins with a play on words in his title THE HAND THAT RILES THE WORLD (in GENTLE GRAFTER, 1907) and proceeds to poke fun at his unscrupulous and misogynistic male characters who are then outwitted by a beautiful woman.

*They say **the hand that rocks the cradle rules the world**. Everyone understands the unarguable truth of these words – that the person who most influences the next generation has the power to shape the future.*
BIRMINGHAM EVENING MAIL,
10 SEPTEMBER 2001

*The **hand that rocks the cradle rules the world**, as the old saying has it. I employed a series of live-in nannies for more than ten years, and it's only in the 18 months since the last one left that I've realised this truth. Put another woman at the heart of your family, and there's a risk she'll become a cuckoo in the nest.*
DAILY MAIL, 2 FEBRUARY 2006

Usage: *The hand that rocks the cradle* in this abbreviated form is often used as a synonym of 'mother'.

CROWD

two's company, three's a crowd
the presence of a third person prevents intimacy

Variant: Two's company, three is none

One's too few, three's too many is quoted by John Ray in ENGLISH PROVERBS (1678). In the nineteenth century, William Carew Hazlitt records the same saying as: *Two is company, three is none* (ENGLISH PROVERBS, 1869). More than one source has pointed out that the proverb was particularly suited to courting couples both then and now; *Two's company, three's a chaperon*, writes playwright Philip Moeller (MADAME SAND, 1917) but Oscar Wilde insists; *In married life three is company and two none* (THE IMPORTANCE OF BEING EARNEST, 1895).

Discretion is a Lancashire virtue. A correspondent of NOTES AND QUERIES (1871) describes how the saying would be used in that county as an excuse to avoid playing gooseberry. *When a lover meets his intended with her companion*, he says, *the latter will say, 'Two are company, but three are none', and pass on another road*. The popular variant *Two's company, three's a crowd* dates from the early 1940s.

*As Hughes puts it: 'I think we just started to turn on each other, but almost by giving each other the cold shoulder, going out getting drunk on our own or with other people, not with each other, not sharing the things that we might otherwise have shared. Three is a weird number: you know, **two's company, three's a crowd**, and I'm under no illusions about the key relationship in this band being between Tim and Tom, and that's fine.*
GUARDIAN, 9 JUNE 2006

*Two American women are getting themselves mugs of coffee as I arrive, before they repair to the sofa with their guidebooks. They have a slightly territorial air about them. It's as if **two's company, three's a crowd**, thank you very much. I get the message.*
DAILY MAIL, 19 MAY 2007

CRUEL

you've got to be cruel to be kind
strict discipline is sometimes necessary for long-term benefit

Catherine de Medici, who was born into one of the most influential families in Italy, married into the French royal family at the age of 14. According to R C Trench (ON THE LESSONS IN PROVERBS, 1853), she would have been conversant with the Italian proverb *Sometimes clemency is cruelty and cruelty is clemency*. And she certainly knew by heart the words of Bishop Corneille Muis in his Sermon (c. 1550), *Against rebels it is cruelty to be humane, and humanity to be cruel*, for she is said to have quoted them to her son King Charles IX on the eve of the St Bartholomew's Day massacre on 24 August 1572. Catherine and the king took the decision to assassinate prominent Huguenot leaders before they could avenge a failed attack on the Protestant Admiral de Coligny. This sparked a Parisian uprising of terrible brutality in which Protestant men, women and children were hunted down by the Catholic population and murdered, the death toll reaching the thousands.

The linguistic history of the proverb is much less dramatic. Sophocles was the first to make the association between *cruelty* and *clemency*: *You prove most cruel, meaning to be kind* (TRACHINIAE, c. 409 BC). In English, Shakespeare introduced the thought in a precursor of our contemporary expression: *I must be cruel, only to be kind* (HAMLET, 1602).

*[Dr Christopher Green's] recommendations are of the **'cruel to be kind'** school and he appears to regard toddlers rather as unbroken horses in need of a firm hand.*
INDEPENDENT, 22 JANUARY 2001

Robinson is a working rugby man with a family dependent on his monthly pay cheque. So it is up to the Rugby Football Union to apply a compassionate amount of compensation to the humane act of putting

*Robinson out of his misery. And humane, when it comes, this termination will be. When the misery is this anguished, **it is necessary to be cruel to be kind**.*
DAILY MAIL, 13 NOVEMBER 2006

See also *Spare the rod and spoil the* CHILD

CUP

there's many a slip 'twixt cup and lip

beware of being over-confident, for many things can go wrong between the starting and finishing of a project

Variants: There's many a slip between cup and lip; There's many a slip 'twixt the cup and the lip

From the sixteenth to the eighteenth centuries, the proverb was *Many things fall* (or *happen*) *between the cup and the lip*. Then, sometime during the first quarter of the nineteenth century, the rhyme we are familiar with today, together with a more rhythmical turn of phrase, gave *There's many a slip 'tween the cup and the lip*. *Twixt* was a slightly later variation, possibly the inspiration of R H Barham in THE INGOLDSBY LEGENDS (1840).

The proverb is of ancient origin. Cato cites an early form in DE AEDILIBUS VITIO CREATIS (c. 175 BC): *I have often heard that many things may come between the mouth and the morsel*. When Erasmus included *Manye thynges fall betwene the cuppe and the mouth* in his ADAGIA (1523), he attached it to the following story. Ancaeus, helmsman of the Argo, had a fertile vineyard which was cultivated by slaves whom Ancaeus worked to the limits of their endurance. One day one of the slaves came to Ancaeus and prophesied that he would die before he got the chance to taste its wine. All went well with the vineyard. An abundant harvest was gathered and pressed to make fine wine. Ancaeus, goblet in hand, mocked the slave for his hasty prophecy. But the slave replied, *Many things happen between the cup and the lip.* As Ancaeus was about to drink, a messenger ran up shouting that the Calydonian boar was wreaking havoc in the vineyard. Ancaeus threw down his goblet and rushed to the vineyard intending to kill the boar but, instead, the enraged animal turned on him and savaged him to death.

Stevenson, however, proposes an alternative origin to this. Homer's ODYSSEY recounts the adventures of Odysseus as he travels home after a long absence at the Trojan war. A number of suitors have gathered around his beautiful wife Penelope, and Odysseus is determined to destroy them. The suitors are assembled in the great hall ready to attempt a challenge, devised by Penelope, with her hand in marriage as prize. None of them succeeds but Odysseus, disguised as a beggar, successfully performs the challenge. He then turns his bow upon Antinous, the hated leader of the suitors, whom he shoots in the throat just as he is about to drink, causing his goblet to fall to the ground.

There is nothing to stop you putting the expected gift from your partner's parents in the list of your assets, but until the money is actually received it will almost certainly be ignored by the mortgage provider and not taken into consideration. There is many a slip 'twixt cup and lip, and the provider has no certainty the money will actually be paid.
GUARDIAN, 9 MAY 2002

There's many a slip 'twixt cup and lip, and especially in this electronic age when the microphones remain switched on. It's usually the politicians who fall victim. In 1993, John Major, then Prime Minister,

famously branded three Cabinet colleagues 'bastards' and promised to 'crucify' them, unaware he was still being recorded.
SCOTLAND ON SUNDAY, 25 APRIL 2004

Usage: The most commonly used form of the proverb employs the Middle English form 'twixt, a shortening of *betwixt*, meaning 'between'. This is now used only in a very few fixed expressions – in this proverb, for instance, and in *betwixt and between*. It is interesting that use of this archaic word in the proverb seems to date from the nineteenth century.

See also *Don't count your CHICKENS before they are hatched*; *First catch your HARE*

CURE

prevention is better than cure
stopping illness before it starts is better than having to treat it later when it has taken hold; taking steps to prevent an unpleasant situation from arising is better than having to deal with it when it erupts

Variant: An ounce of prevention is worth a pound of cure

How much better and more useful it is to meet the trouble in time, rather than to seek a remedy after the damage has been done, says English jurist Henry de Bracton in DE LEGIBUS ET CONSUETUD- INIBUS ANGLIAE (ON THE LAWS AND CUSTOMS OF ENGLAND, c. 1240), thus expressing the thought behind the future proverb. In his ADAGIA (1500), Erasmus quotes from the SUIDAS (c. AD 950), a Greek lexicon-encyclopaedia: *It is far better to cure at the beginning than at the end.*

The proverb as we know it started to appear in written form in the seventeenth century. Thomas Adams quotes an early form in WORKS

(1630): *Prevention is so much better than healing*. Almost a century later, the saying is much more recognisable: *Prevention is much preferable to cure* (Thomas Fuller, GNOMOLOGIA, 1732). And when Dickens uses it in MARTIN CHUZZLEWIT (1844), the proverb appears in its modern form.

Modern medical practitioners seek to follow the wisdom behind this proverb through preventative medicine and dentistry. Illness is distressing and treatment often unpleasant or painful. How much better to take steps to avoid being ill at all. Our forebears had the added incentive of avoiding all sorts of grim and excruciating cures. Some were rooted in superstition and folk medicine: in Elizabethan times tumours were treated by rubbing them with a dead man's hand and those suffering from the ague were recommended to swallow a good-sized live spider in treacle. Others were not unlike present-day practice but pity the Georgian dental patient who, without the aid of anaesthetic, sat while his aching teeth were seared with a red-hot rod to kill the nerve before being filled with molten lead. Extraction by the blacksmith might be preferred.

Prevention is better than cure. That is one of the reasons doctors are always on their patients' backs about diet, drinking, stopping smoking, starting exercise and the need for hygiene in everything.
GLASGOW DAILY RECORD,
19 FEBRUARY 2004

*The old saying **prevention is better than cure** applies to long haul travel blues. A few simple things can improve, and make a world of difference to, how you feel and how you recover from long haul flights.*
NZ BUSINESS, 1 FEBRUARY 2006

Usage: The proverb is not only applied to preventative medicine but can also refer to taking steps to prevent future difficulty in any sphere.

CURIOSITY

curiosity killed the cat
beware of poking your nose into the affairs of others; it may get you into trouble

Disappointingly, this proverb has no intriguing story behind it, but a quaint rhyming version of unknown origin explains why the cat died:

> *Curiosity killed the cat,*
> *Information made her fat.*

A variant is *Curiosity killed a monkey*. Both animals, it seems, have a reputation for being too inquisitive for their own good. Monkeys are quite obviously mischievous and curious but an incident reported by the British media in which a cat leapt into a washing machine and was then treated to a long cycle of washing and spinning suggests that cats are too. Unlike the unfortunate animal in the proverb, which had obviously come to the end of her nine lives, the cat which made the news headlines lived to tell the tale.

References in literature date from the beginning of the twentieth century. Some suggest an American origin: the American short story writer O Henry alludes to it in SCHOOLS AND SCHOOLS (1909): *Curiosity can do more things than kill a cat; and if emotions, well recognized as feminine, are inimical to feline life, then jealousy would soon leave the whole world catless.*

Curiosity killed the cat, but it's never hurt a single cruise passenger. If you'd rather learn than lounge around, enrichment programs can turn your cruise vacation into a truly educational experience.
CRUISE TRAVEL, 1 JANUARY 2001

She wanted to know why things happened. She wanted to know why people did the

things they did. She was curious. And what, she wondered, was wrong with that? **Curiosity killed the cat**, she suddenly thought, and immediately regretted the thought.
ALEXANDER MCCALL SMITH,
THE SUNDAY PHILOSOPHY CLUB, 2004

Don't even try to pull one over on me today. I learned a long time ago not to believe anything anyone tells me on April 1, better known as April Fools' Day. Being a journalist, I'm naturally pretty skeptical, but I'm also curious. That mixture of skepticism and curiosity can be volatile at times, as a degree of gullibility is inherent in curiosity. What is it they say about **curiosity killed the cat**? Well, I ain't going to let curiosity kill the journalist – today, anyway. Today, my lie detector is full tilt. Skepticism is my watchword.
SUN HERALD, 1 APRIL 2005

The old saying might be **'curiosity killed the cat'** but I think that is wrong. Curiosity is what prompts most questions. Curious minds want to know what is behind tasks being done. People want to understand the purposes for which they are conducting their lives. A mind without curiosity is like a mind on drugs: lifeless, dull and basically dumbed out. Like the television commercial says: A mind is a terrible thing to waste.
ABERDEEN AMERICAN NEWS,
12 MAY 2006

CURSES

curses, like chickens, come home to roost
speaking badly of someone will rebound ultimately to one's own detriment

English literature has several vivid similes to illustrate the notion that curses rebound and harm the very person who uttered them. The unknown author of ARDEN OF FEVERSHAM (1592) says: Curses are like arrowes shot upright, Which falling down light on the shuter's head. There are echoes of this in Sir Walter Scott's OLD MORTALITY (1816): I have heard a good man say, that a curse was like a stone flung up to the heavens, and maist like to return on the head that sent it.

Chaucer comes close to the modern proverb in his CANTERBURY TALES: And ofte tyme swich cursinge wrongfully retorneth agayn to him that curseth, as a brid that retorneth agayn to his owene nest (THE PARSON'S TALE, c. 1386). But the earliest known record of the present day saying comes in Robert Southey's CURSE OF KEHAMA (1809): Curses are like young chickens; they always come home to roost. Scholars of the period claimed it to be of Arabic or Turkish origin.

The proverb has become rather dated since the first half of the twentieth century. However, it has spawned the saying Chickens come home to roost, which carries the more general sense that a person's errors or indiscretions always recoil upon them in the end, and this expression is widely used.

The **chickens come home to roost** in Coronation Street for wide boys Mike (Johnny Briggs) and Danny Baldwin (Bradley Walsh). In a row, Mike reveals to his 'nephew' that he is really his father – devastating...
GLASGOW SUNDAY MAIL,
23 OCTOBER 2005

John Reid's hope that British soldiers get out of Afghanistan 'without a shot fired' was a tragic piece of spin. Fifteen killed in 48 hours is a terrible toll. The Taliban is resurgent and the Army says troops are stretched.
Reid has a history of moving departments before **the chickens come home to roost**.

A Premier Brown should insist he stay at the Home Office and be judged on what he does, not on what he says.
DAILY MIRROR, 6 SEPTEMBER 2006

CUSTOMER

the customer is always right
always defer to the client

Variant: The customer always knows best

The customer is always right is one of the most well-known business maxims. Sources debate whether it was coined by Marshall Field, founder of a very successful department store in Chicago in the late 1800s, or by American-born entrepreneur Harry Gordon Selfridge, who established the famous Selfridges store on Oxford Street, London, in 1909. Perhaps the confusion comes from the fact that Selfridge worked for Marshall Field for many years until 1901.

Records of the phrase as a business principle date from the early twentieth century. A piece in the Kansas City Star (January 1911) has this to say about a certain George Scott who had just set up a small country store: *Scott has done in the country what Marshall Field did in Chicago, Wannamaker did in New York and Selfridge in London. In his*

DAVID TENIERS THE YOUNGER
Belvoir Castle in Leicestershire houses a remarkable work by the Flemish artist David Teniers the Younger (1610–90) who, in a single painting entitled THE PROVERBS (1646–7), succeeded in illustrating 45 Dutch proverbs. There is, however, another claimant for the most proverbs in one picture. A French print of 1570 illustrates some 71 expressions.

---

store he follows the Field rule and assumes that the customer is always right.

A piece in the Indianapolis Star, written a year later (12 June 1912), also attributes the saying to Field: *One secret of Marshall Field's success was the motto he enforced, 'Remember that the customer is always right.'*

Of course, neither Field nor Selfridge believed the motto to be literally true; on the contrary, many customers are wrong. Both men, however, wanted their staff to put customers first and treat them with deference. This is better understood when a longer version of the expression is used: *Right or wrong, the customer is always right*.

In the 1990s, in order to get a similar customer service message through to company staff, American firms surrounded their employees with motivational plaques:

It takes months to find a customer, seconds to lose one.
Rule 1. If we don't take care of our customers, somebody else will.
A customer is the most important visitor on our premises. He is not dependent on us – we are dependent on him. He is not an outsider in our business – he is a part of it. We are not doing him a favor by serving him... he is doing us a favor by giving us the opportunity to do so.
We shall strive for excellence in all endeavors. We shall set our goals to achieve total customer satisfaction and to deliver defect free premium value products on time, with service second to none.

It seems, however, that the inspiration behind the maxim *The customer is always right* may have been Swiss rather than American. The reverse saying *Le client n'a jamais tort* ('The customer is never wrong') was attributed to the 'king of hoteliers and hotelier to kings' César Ritz in 1908.

*Tesco adheres to the maxim that **the customer is always right**. The spokesman said yesterday: 'Customers want organic, they want lots of it and it's our job to make sure they get it.'*
DAILY TELEGRAPH, 19 JUNE 2001

***The customer is always right**, said a judge who testified Wednesday in his $54 million lawsuit against a dry cleaner who lost his pants.*

Administrative law judge Roy L. Pearson argued that he is acting in the interest of all city residents against poor business practices. Attorneys for the dry cleaner call his claim 'outlandish.'
OAKLAND TRIBUNE, 14 JUNE 2007

See also BUSINESS MATTERS, page 164

· D ·

DAY

sufficient unto the day is the evil thereof

be concerned with today's problems rather than worry about tomorrow's in advance

This is a biblical proverb. In his Sermon on the Mount, Jesus preaches on anxiety. He tells his listeners not to worry but to trust God for their needs, for he who feeds the birds of the air and clothes the lilies of the field knows what these are before they ask. Rather than fretting about and storing up belongings, they are to live a life which pleases God and so they will find that their needs are faithfully met. In concluding, Jesus says: *Take, therefore, no thought for the morrow; for the morrow shall take thought for the things of itself. Sufficient unto the day is the evil thereof* (MATTHEW 6:34).

The proverb is now used in the sense of living one day at a time and refusing to give way to anxieties about tomorrow – sound advice, for *TOMORROW is another day* when today's problems might well appear in a better light. As the little jingle says: *Today is the tomorrow you worried about yesterday, and all is well.*

*...Schiffrin makes a very good case for the proposal that concentrating on numbers and profit margins at the expense of quality is doing literally incalculable damage to the culture. I am sometimes inclined to mutter that **sufficient unto the day is the evil thereof**, taking a darkly Thatcherite line on the literary marketplace...*
GUARDIAN, 5 JANUARY 2002

*'I think football was an escape from another kind of life, and I enjoyed it so thoroughly I was always congratulating myself that I was able to find an escape so tolerable to me. To maximize my life. In Green Bay I was intoxicated with the freedom... I had no more thought of the future. **Sufficient unto the day is the evil thereof**. Let the morrow take care of itself.'*
MILWAUKEE JOURNAL SENTINEL,
14 JULY 2005

Usage: Somewhat dated. Regularly reduced to *Sufficient unto the day*.

See also *Don't cross a BRIDGE until you come to it; TOMORROW is another day*

DESPERATE

desperate diseases call for desperate remedies

an almost insurmountable difficulty calls for bold and extreme measures to overcome it

Variant: Desperate diseases demand / must have / require desperate remedies or desperate situations call for desperate measures

For extreme illnesses extreme treatments are most fitting (APHORISMS, c. 400 BC) was a maxim of the great Greek physician Hippocrates. One extreme measure might be to stand by and let a disease take its course without interfering at all. Hippocrates goes on to explain that sometimes the courage to do this is just what is needed.

Richard Taverner's selection of adages compiled by Erasmus has *Strong disease requyreth a strong medicine* (PROVERBS OR ADAGES BY DESIDERIUS ERASMUS, 1539); in EUPHUES (1579), John Lyly writes: *A desperate disease is to be committed to a desperate doctor*; and, in Shakespeare's HAMLET (1602), Claudius reminds us that *Diseases desperate grown By desperate appliance are relieved, Or not at all.* In which case, there is everything to gain and nothing to lose.

Guy Fawkes certainly thought so. He was the explosives expert brought in by a Catholic group to blow up the Protestant King James I and his Parliament on 5 November 1605. Caught red handed in the vaults beneath the Houses of Parliament, Fawkes was arrested and brought before the king. Defiant to the end he confirmed his desire to destroy the Protestant government, allegedly declaring that *a desperate disease requires a dangerous remedy.*

While Hamilton, along with most other commentators, recognizes that the movement was not unproblematic, he is clearly more taken with the 'great good' it accomplished, downplaying its iniquities with the off-handed cliche 'desperate diseases require desperate remedies.'
MICHIGAN LAW REVIEW,
1 FEBRUARY 2002

Desperate diseases demand desperate remedies is an old saying. In the case of the county's troubled Martin Luther King Hospital and its teaching affiliate, Charles Drew University of Medicine and Science, it's all too true.

There were moments...when the inefficiency, ineptitude and occasional corruption at the King-Drew Medical Center could have been remedied... Instead, the county, after years of indefensible neglect, institutional infighting and political intimidation, has finally run out of choices. Faced with the closure of the entire medical center as an alternative, the Board of Supervisors has decided to close its King-Drew trauma center, which serves about 2,000 of the hospital's 45,000 yearly emergency patients.
LOS ANGELES DAILY NEWS,
4 OCTOBER 2004

Usage: The area of application of the saying goes beyond the medical to any sort of severe problem that needs drastic action

DEVIL

better the devil you know than the devil you don't know

it is better to live with the problems one already has than to act to change them and face a set of unknown, and possibly worse, difficulties; it is better to stick to a person whose faults are known to you than move on to someone whose faults you have yet to discover

The thought is an ancient one. Plautus in TRINUMMUS (c. 194 BC) says: *Keep what you have, the known evil is best.* Aesop, writing in the sixth century BC, had already put the idea into the form of a fable, which he wrote to encourage the Athenians who, having enjoyed a democracy, had come under the power of a tyrant who had arisen from amongst them. The Athenians bewailed their servitude, though it was not severe, and Aesop cautioned them against voicing their discontent with this story... The marsh frogs wanted a king and asked Jupiter for one. Amused, the god threw a stout piece of wood into their pool. The log made such a splash that it frightened the frogs into submission. As time passed, however, the log just lay there in the mud and the frogs became used to its presence and eventually began to abuse it with insults. Then they started to call out for another king, saying the one they had was no good. This time Jupiter sent them a water snake. The snake cut swiftly through the water and started to devour the frogs one by one. The frogs, in panic, sent a message to Jupiter, asking for help. The reply came: 'Since you were unwilling to put up with the good you had, you must put up with this evil.' *Likewise*, said Aesop to the Athenians, *you must bear the evil that you have, lest a greater one befall you.*

George Pettie echoes the ancients when he writes: *You had rather keep those whom you know, though with some faults, than take those whom you know not, perchance with more faults* (PETITE PALLACE, 1576). And Shakespeare records a similar sentiment in HAMLET (1602): *The dread of something after death... makes us rather bear those ills we have, Than fly to others that we know not of.*

In the light of these more general statements, the proverb we know today was developing with two different forms. One used *devil*, one *evil*. The variation is readily understandable because of the similarities in pronunciation, spelling and meaning. Over time, *evil* lost out to *devil*. Trollope in BARCHESTER TOWERS (1857) refers to it as *an old saying*.

*In cases like these, **better the devil you know**. If your sister-in-law's imagination is so poor that she gives you pillow cases on an annual basis, what would she buy by way of a change – a crocheted lavatory-roll cover, perhaps?*
GOOD HOUSEKEEPING,
DECEMBER 2001

Transfers need to be thought through very carefully by all parties... If Nicky Butt continues in his quest for a move from Manchester United, he too will need to give *it much thought, though I suspect he is doing just that. **Better the devil you know, Nicky, than the one you don't...***
DAILY TELEGRAPH, 28 FEBRUARY 2004

Usage: The proverb is often found shortened to *Better the devil you know.*

every man for himself, and the devil take the hindmost
everyone should concentrate on taking care of himself and his own interests

This is a proverb of self-preservation. In his ADAGIA (1536), Erasmus records a phrase used by Horace, *Occupet extremum scabies*, which translates as *The itch take the hindmost* (DE ARTE POETICA, c. 20 BC). This was an allusion to a children's chasing game in which the itch, or scabies, was wished upon the child who came in last. The robust seventeenth century English wished worse than scabies upon the unfortunate individual who was unable to look after himself and lagged behind. The devil himself would take the hindmost: *What if...they run all away, and cry the Devil take the hindmost* (Beaumont and Fletcher, PHILASTER, 1608). English essayist and Liberal politician G W E Russell agrees with the Latin origin. In SOCIAL SILHOUETTES (1906) he writes: *He starts in life with a plan of absolute and calculated selfishness... His motto is* 'Extremum occupet scabies' – *the devil take the hindmost.*

In his biography of Horatio Lord Nelson (c. 1795), Robert Southey quotes Nelson using the phrase to describe the flight of terrified soldiers: *General de Vins gave up the command in the middle of the battle, pleading ill health. 'From that moment,' says Nelson, 'not a soldier stayed at his post: it was the devil take the hindmost. Many thousands ran away who had never seen the enemy; some of them thirty miles from the advanced posts.'*

The entire proverb as we know it today is used in a similar context by Mark Twain in LIFE ON THE MISSISSIPPI (1874): *By and by the Federals chased the rebels back, and here they came! tearing along, everybody for himself and Devil take the hindmost! and down under the bank they scrambled, and took shelter.*

The devil take the hindmost has one interesting restricted use in sport. It is the name of a cycle race. Riders circle a velodrome, waiting for a bell to ring. At this signal they begin to sprint, and the last one to cross the finishing line is eliminated. This continues until just one rider, the winner, is left.

...the Republicans do project a vision, centering on 'ruthless individualism,' she said. Indeed, the party has spent decades rallying support around the old proverb: 'Every man for himself, and the devil take the hindmost.'
MILWAUKEE JOURNAL SENTINEL,
21 NOVEMBER 2004

A British hurricane survivor told today how she was forced to sleep rough and loot for food after being told by American police it was 'every man for himself'.
EVENING STANDARD,
6 SEPTEMBER 2005

When couples get divorced, some wives run off with the handyman or the house painter or their husband's best friend and leave the kids behind – the devil take the hindmost.
THE WASHINGTON POST, 5 MAY 2006

Usage: The entire proverb is sometimes found, but either of the two phrases which make it up may be used separately, as was originally the case. The contemporary quotations illustrate these uses.

give the devil his due
even unpleasant characters should have their share of praise when it is deserved

This proverb is recorded from the sixteenth century. Shakespeare made use of it in two of his historical plays, HENRY IV, PART 1 (1597) and HENRY V (1599). In the latter, the Constable of France and the Duke of Orléans are talking about the Dauphin. The Duke is the Dauphin's friend and defends him against the Constable's criticism of his courage. Proverbs are weapons in their verbal duel, of which *Give the devil his due* is one. The Duke inadvertently speaks of his friend as *the devil*:

CONSTABLE:...'Tis a hooded valor, and when it appears, it will bate.
ORLÉANS: Ill will never said well.
CONSTABLE: I will cap that proverb with 'There's flattery in friendship.'
ORLÉANS: And I will take that up with 'Give the devil is due.'
CONSTABLE: Well placed; there stands your friend for the devil. Have at the very eye of that proverb with 'A pox of the devil.'
ORLÉANS: You are the better at proverbs, by how much 'A fool's bolt is soon shot.'

Give the devil his due, *Sen. Ted Kennedy is one helluva good politician – one of the best. Mr. Kennedy practices his craft in the same manner and style as the late Sen. Daniel Patrick Moynihan. He lures his philosophical opponents with his bonhomie into believing they can 'work together.' He seals the deal by making what appear to be strategic concessions to his opponents that in fact turn out to be decoys baiting a carefully laid trap.*
WASHINGTON TIMES,
1 AUGUST 2003

he should have a long spoon that sups with the devil

if you keep bad company you will need to be on your guard

Sharing a meal with someone usually means you are already on quite good terms with them, or that you want to get to know them better. If you agree to partake of the devil's hospitality, you are on dangerous ground and need to beware. A good long spoon is necessary to keep the potent contamination of the devil at a distance.

The proverb was current in the fourteenth century, Chaucer using it in his CANTERBURY TALES: *'Therfor bihoveth him a ful long spoon That shal ete with a feend,' thus herde I seye'* (THE SQUIRE'S TALE, c. 1386).

Later, Shakespeare referred to it in THE TEMPEST (1610), where Stephano says of the creature Caliban: *This is a devil, and no monster, I will leave him, I have no long spoon.*

There is an old proverb that says, 'If you're going to sup with the devil, use a long spoon.' Does the White House pantry have any long spoons? I ask because if President Bush really wants to achieve his objectives in Iraq, he may have to sup a little with Palestinian leader Yasser Arafat, Iranian leader Ali Khamenei and Syrian President Bashar Assad.
MILWAUKEE JOURNAL SENTINEL, 10 OCTOBER 2003

Now with British soldiers still embroiled in the dangerous aftermath of the war to remove Saddam, Mr Blair finds it the right moment to arm yet another dictator of proven instability. Let us hope the Prime Minister has not forgotten that when you sup with the devil you need a very long spoon.
CARDIFF WESTERN MAIL, 27 MARCH 2004

Usage: Sometimes reduced to the idiomatic *sup with the devil*, meaning 'to negotiate with unsavoury characters'.

needs must when the devil drives

used when a person is forced to take a course of action he would rather have avoided

The medieval mind was steeped in superstition and very alert to the unseen forces of evil which lurked, ever present, awaiting any opportunity to make mischief or cause a man to stumble. (See *the devil to pay*, page 76.) The proverb, originally *He needs must go that the devil drives*, is a vivid picture of a man who, though his will and better judgement warn him otherwise, has fallen prey to diabolical circumstances and is being swiftly propelled along a disastrous route.

An early written record of the proverb from John Lydgate's THE ASSEMBLY OF GODS (c. 1420) dates back to the first half of the fifteenth century:

Hit ys oft seyde by hem that yet lyues,
He must nedys go that the deuell dryues.

This original form of the expression was trimmed down and slightly altered in the seventeenth century. John Lacey has: *Needs must go when the devil drives* (THE OLD TROOP, 1672). It was streamlined still further in the nineteenth century to the familiar modern form *Needs must when the devil drives*. But usage in the second half of the twentieth century is more economical still and many people, oblivious of the satanic intervention of the devil in their affairs, will only say *Needs must*.

I was involved in the Higher English exam. You know – the one loads of kids just failed. I wasn't involved directly. I didn't sit it or set

THE DEVIL TO PAY

The devil is usually represented with horns, a tail and cloven hooves, the goat being a pagan symbol of youth, energy and sexual freedom. Jewish writers saw this figure of a goat as a symbol of uncleanliness, and the goat became a sacrificial animal upon which the sins of the people could be laid (hence the word *scapegoat*). Traditionally, the devil was an angel in the service of God. He rebelled and, being cast from Heaven, continued his insubordination by plotting to keep men from fellowship with God. Medieval churchgoers were constantly reminded of this by vivid murals painted on church walls, or by detailed carvings over the door which depicted the judgement of departed souls; those at the right hand of God were accompanied by angels into eternal bliss, those at the left hand were propelled by demons into the flames of hell as prizes of the devil. Some churches had a small door built into the north wall which was briefly opened during baptismal or communion services, so that when the devil was exorcised during the service, he could escape. Sometimes the devil would manifest himself to a terrified congregation. At the parish church in Bungay, for instance, he appeared among the Tudor worshippers as a black dog, choking two of them and viciously tearing the back of another with his talons. The striking of church spires by lightning was also recognised as satanic work. *Talk of the devil and he will appear* was sincerely meant.

People lived with an ever-present awareness of the hovering powers of evil, which conspired to blight their lives or trick them into committing evil deeds. This belief persisted until well into the second half of the seventeenth century when, in a dawning age of science and reason, a more tolerant attitude led to a less fervent and credulous religious climate.

Small wonder, then, that the devil features prominently in proverbial

---

*it (obviously) or anything like that. But my wee cousin was studying for it at an FE College. Her teacher was useless. Apparently. So she asked me to give her a hand with revision. Big mistake, I know, but **needs must when the devil drives**. Tell you what – it was demanding. It looked to be a harder exam than the one I sat years ago.*
DAILY MIRROR, 15 AUGUST 2003

*Rome was heaving. There was a three-hour queue for the Colosseum, unless you were prepared to fork out double for a guided tour. **Needs must when the devil drives**, I said stoically, counting out EUR16 per head, the devil in this case being my son's ancient history professor who reckons, quite rightly, that pretty pictures in textbooks are no substitute for the real thing.*
INDEPENDENT, 3 APRIL, 2004

Usage: The fuller form *Needs must when the devil drives* is now a little dated

speak the truth and shame the devil

be honest, resist any temptation to get out of trouble by lying

Variant: Tell the truth and shame the devil

Hugh Latimer, Bishop of Worcester, writing in the mid-sixteenth century, calls this proverb *a common saying amongst us*. For the Tudors, as for their ancestors, the devil was an ever-present, and sometimes even visible, figure (see *the devil to pay*, above). The tug against the conscience, the inner voice prompting lies rather than the literature. Some of this literature takes a warning tone, highlighting the consequences of flirting with evil – *He should have a long spoon that sups with the devil* – while some of it recognises that the devil is looking for every opportunity to exercise evil or tempt the unwary:

Needs must when the devil drives
The devil finds work for idle hands

The fifteenth century proverb, *The devil dances in an empty pocket,* refers to a destitute person's temptation to turn to crime. Coins were minted with a cross on one side. A pocket with a cross in it could not be entered by the devil: *The devil sleeps in my pocket*; *I have no cross To drive him from it* (Philip Massinger, THE BASHFUL LOVER, 1636). Other sayings recognise the power or presence of evil:

Better the devil you know
Talk of the devil and he will appear.

And still others exhort us to fight the temptation to ignore God's promptings in our lives: *The devil sick would be a monk*: said of someone who, in times of illness or difficulty, prays and makes fervent promises which are forgotten the moment pain passes. The phrase *Don't hold a candle to the devil* alludes to the Catholic and High Church custom of lighting a candle as an offering to a saint, and means 'don't support or approve of something you know to be wrong'. But anyone tempted to turn his back on his conscience can be assured of one thing, *The devil looks after his own* (early seventeenth century).

truth, were all signs that the devil was about his work, leading souls to hell. Hugh Latimer himself must have shamed the devil on many occasions for he had a reputation for plain and honest speaking. His determination to hold on to the truth cost him his life when in 1555 he was burnt at the stake for refusing to renounce his Protestant faith.

In the seventeenth century, the proverb appeared in the title of a publication said by some to have been written by the poet Samuel Butler (1612–1680): SPEAK TRUTH, AND SHAME THE DEVIL IN A DIALOGUE BETWEEN HIS CLOVEN-FOOTED HIGHNESS, OF SULPHURIOUS MEMORY, AND AN OCCASIONAL CONFORMIST. In this satirical verse dialogue, the Occasional Conformist makes all the arguments that one might expect from the devil (on how easy it is to buy men's allegiance, for example) with such persuasion that the devil finishes the piece with these ironic lines:

> *Thour't such a Master-piece in Evil,*
> *That I'll be Man, and you be Devil;*
> *Since one that can expound so well,*
> *Deserves the Government of Hell.*

More than any other institution, the press has been charged with keeping us honest and the master class of the political elite in its place. Walter Lippmann, one of the 20th century's greatest journalists, famously wrote: 'There can be no higher law in

*journalism than to **tell the truth and shame the devil**.' That seemed to have got lost somewhere as newspapers and networks, pursuing ever greater profits, gravitated toward the banal, the trivial, the juvenile.*
ROCKY MOUNTAIN NEWS, 29 MAY 2004

*Media representatives who refuse to criticize when teams play badly or their stars misbehave do no one any favours and only denigrate themselves... As my dear old Grandmother used to say, '**Speak the truth and shame the devil!**' Like so much from the past, this is good advice and sound common sense.*
DAILY TELEGRAPH WEBSITE,
1 APRIL 2007

talk of the devil and he will appear

said when a person who was being talked about makes an unexpected appearance

Variant: Speak of the devil and he will appear

The devil has nothing at all to do with the origin of this proverb. An ancient fable tells of a wolf who would appear without fail whenever he was mentioned. The ancients would cry *Lupus in fabula* ('The wolf in the fable') whenever a person they were discussing turned up unexpectedly, a practice that goes back at least to Plautus, writing in 200 BC. Erasmus quoted the proverb *Lupus in fabula* in his ADAGIA (1536) but, although other European languages use proverbs about a wolf in this same context, English does not. Instead, the devil began to figure in proverbs about the sudden appearance of a named person. John Lyly alludes to this in his play ENDIMION (1591) where Samias the page, after wishing that the brave squire Sir Tophas was with him and Dares, exclaims in the next breath *and* ecce autem, *will you see*

the devil!, for at that moment Sir Tophas himself appears.

The English say, *Talk of the Devil, and he's presently at your elbow*, says Giovanni Torriano in his PIAZZA UNIVERSALE DI PROVERBI ITALIANI (1666), a collection of proverbs given in Italian and English. Other contemporary variants are *The devil is never nearer than when we are talking of him, Talk of the devil, and he'll come or send* and *Talk of the devil, and see his horns*.

*Ashley and Claire throw a birthday party for Josh which is marred by two things. First they break the news to Fred that they're leaving Weatherfield to start a new life where Matt Ramsden can't find them. Then, **talk of the devil**, he turns up and announces he's come to take his son home.*
BIRMINGHAM SUNDAY MERCURY,
19 MARCH 2006

*Dr. Pinch thus enters the action from a realm more of fantasy than of narrative, and he stands for the fear that what one utters—by its own mere agency—might just turn into reality. As the proverb says, '**Speak of the Devil and he will appear**.'*
KENT CARTWRIGHT, STUDIES IN ENGLISH LITERATURE 1500–1900,
MARCH 2007

Usage: Usually reduced to *Talk of the devil* and used humorously.

Some authors deliberately coin new proverbs. Edgar Watson Howe (1853–1937) was one such, although many of his maxims are in fact variations of existing sayings. None the less, Howe, a journalist and publisher of the Kansas newspaper THE GLOBE, is credited at least with *Better safe than sorry*.

Thomas Chandler Haliburton (who wrote also under the pseudonym Sam Slick) offered these sayings, amongst many others:

DEVILISH WORK

Language moves on, and proverbs are falling out of use all the time. Sometimes a gem of social history is lost with them. One such is the dire reputation of medieval bakers, who were obviously in league with the devil.

Bakers were unpopular figures accused of accumulating wealth at the expense of their customers, to whom they sold underweight loaves. The punishment for this was a spell in the pillory, as a sixteenth century proverb shows: *And so late met, that I feare we parte not yeet, Quoth the Baker to the pylorie* (John Heywood, PROVERBS, 1546). The bakers' reputation did not improve in later years. They were often charged with keeping the price of bread high, hence the proverb *Three dear years will raise a baker's daughter to a portion*; the overcharged customer would indirectly finance the girl's dowry. *Tis not the smallness of the bread*, comments Ray, *but the knavery of the baker* (English PROVERBS, 1678).

The proverb *Pull devil, pull baker*, which was in use until the middle of the twentieth century, speaks of a tug-of-war of relationship. The bakers' reputation is equated with the devil's. Whichever character *pulls* there is nothing to choose between them. The proverb has its origins in a traditional puppet play of the sixteenth century, which satirised the bakers' dishonesty. The tale remained popular through the centuries for, in the nineteenth century, it was the subject of a magic lantern show. A correspondent with NOTES AND QUERIES (1856) gives details of the scenes:

Slide 1 – sets the scene with the baker's oven
Slide 2 – the baker is detected in making short weight loaves
Slide 3 – the devil enters and seizes the baker's bread and his hoard of ill-gotten wealth
Slide 4 – the baker runs after his money, grabs hold of the devil's tail and it's pull devil pull baker until the baker is pulled out of the scene
Slide 5 – the devil appears with the baker's basket strapped to his back. Inside is the baker himself who is swiftly carried into hell where the flames are hotter than in his own oven.

• *The road to a woman's heart is through her child*
• *Youth is the time for improvement*
• *The bigger the house the bigger the fool he that's in it*
• *A man that has too many irons in the fire is plaguy apt to get some of them burnt*
• *Wherever natur' does least, man does most*

See also *APPEARANCES are deceptive* and *HANDSOME is as handsome does*

the devil finds work for idle hands

if you are unoccupied you are likely to be bored and get into mischief

Variant: The devil finds work for idle hands to do

Have something to do so that the devil will always find you occupied, advised the wise St Jerome (EPISTLES, c. AD 400) and quoted by Chaucer in TALE OF MELIBEUS (c. 1386). The proverbial form of the idea recorded by James Kelly in SCOTTISH PROVERBS

(1721) and Thomas Fuller in Gnomologia (1732) was *If the devil find a man idle, he'll set him to work.* However, in 1720 Isaac Watts wrote a poem AGAINST IDLENESS (in DIVINE AND MORAL SONGS FOR CHILDREN) and put the wisdom into a poetic form to which our present-day proverb bears a closer resemblance:

> *In works of labour or of skill*
> *I would be busy too;*
> *For Satan finds some mischief still*
> *For idle hands to do.*

The work of Satan in the life of an idle person is recognised in other cultures, too. A Moroccan proverb says that *The head of an idle man is Satan's workshop.*

*This project (supported by Unicef and Brazil's Globo television network) is designed to keep the kids off the streets, to divert them away from crime. If **the devil finds work for idle hands**, he's a source of much employment here. But children are easily distracted, and initiatives such as this make a tangible difference.*
INDEPENDENT, 17 OCTOBER 2003

*I think the abbot thinks **the devil finds work for idle hands**, or whatever it is, so there's a wonderful work ethic there. People sweeping, building, grinding rock to create these Buddhas and temples.*
OBSERVER, 19 SEPTEMBER 2004

why should the devil have all the best tunes?
Christian music can properly follow secular trends; one's competitor should not be allowed to have the best of everything

This comment, which has become proverbial, has been attributed to at least three outstanding Christians: Martin Luther, Charles Wesley and William Booth. Each is said to have understood the value of popularising hymns by setting them to the music of well-known songs of the day.

In the early sixteenth century, Martin Luther introduced congregational singing into his services. He is said to have set Christian lyrics to contemporary drinking songs, but this theory has now been disproved. Luther himself composed many of the tunes, others were borrowed from the Catholic liturgy, and the 'bar form' often used to describe his music refers to a melodic pattern AAB, not a drinking establishment. There is no proof, either, that the eighteenth century evangelist Charles Wesley used popular tunes for his rousing hymns. He was simply a good hymn-writer.

William Booth, however, does fit the bill. The founder of the Salvation Army used hymns set to contemporary tunes to attract the city poor, who would never otherwise have listened to his message of salvation. The story goes that an Army officer, George Fielder, was singing his testimony for a huge crowd one evening before William Booth spoke. Later, Booth asked Fielder about the song and discovered that it had been set to the tune of 'Champagne Charlie is my Name'. After Fielder's success with his song, Booth decided to use popular music to reach the crowds on the streets, declaring *Why should the devil have all the best tunes?* And George Scott Railton, Booth's lieutenant general, had this to say in ABOUT SINGING (1874) about the songs the Army sang: *Oh, let us rescue this precious instrument from the clutches of the devil, and make it, as it may be made, a bright and lively power for good!*

What business has a bad golfer in such classy surroundings? Well, if you are a hack as well as a hacker you are often invited to inspect these hallowed acres, because golf is far too wonderful a game not

*to be shared freely among all who play.
The Salvation Army has such rousing
songs because their founder, William Booth,
dared to ask: 'Why should the devil have
all the best tunes?' Similarly, I would
question why the good golfers should have
all the best courses.*
INDEPENDENT ON SUNDAY, 8 JULY 2001

*If every child was tested for sporting
potential it would allow work to be done to
develop those skills and so establish a proper
production line of potential champions.*

*That's what they did in the old East
Germany, and it wasn't wrong. What was
wrong was doping the best to enhance their
chances even further. But even without the
drugs, a small country was able to produce
a wholly disproportionate number of medal
winners by working at it.*

*As John Wesley said: 'Why should the
devil have all the best tunes?' We should
test every child for sporting prowess just as
we do for reading and writing.*
EVENING STANDARD, 16 JULY 2004

DIRT

fling enough dirt and some
will stick

attack an opponent repeatedly and
some of the accusations will be believed

Variant: If you throw mud some of it
will stick

These days scarcely a month passes
without reports of some attempt or
other to embarrass a national figure or
a celebrity. This is no new thing,
however. A Latin saying, quoted by
Francis Bacon in DE DIGNITATE ET
AUGMENTIS SCIENTIARUM (1623),
urged *Calumniate boldly, something will
always stick*. The same expression was
also quoted by some of Bacon's
contemporaries, always with reference
to Medius, a renowned sycophant at
the court of Alexander the Great, and

who, according to Plutarch, heartily
endorsed this sort of behaviour.

Thomas Hall echoed the dubious
advice with this robust turn of phrase:
Lye lustily, some filth will stick
(FUNEBRIA FLORAE, 1660) while in
HUDIBRAS REDIVIVUS (1706)
Edward Ward explains that *scurrility* is
an approved method of besmirching a
person's reputation:

> *Scurrility's a useful trick,*
> *Approv'd by the most politic;*
> *Fling dirt enough, and some will stick.*

American usage substituted *mud* for *dirt*
and led to the coining of *mudslinging*
(the act of spreading malicious gossip
about another), a term frequently used
in a political context. We have learnt
our lesson well; the proverb is still
current, as is the practice. As American
statesman Adlai Stevenson is alleged to
have quipped, *He who slings mud, usually
loses ground* (1954).

*Speaking in the Commons, Mr Cook
claimed public figures could see their
reputations tarnished unfairly when
questioned about their personal life. 'It does
not matter what frank, open reply MPs give,
we all know that in those circumstances,
when the mud is thrown there is a
tendency for the mud to stick,' he said.*
DAILY EXPRESS, 19 JULY 2002

*'This is Jacqueline Onassis,' the voice says.
'Oh, hello!' I hear myself replying, with a
sort of desperate heartiness. The saying that
if you throw enough mud at the wall
some of it is bound to stick comes back to
me as I struggle for composure in the face of
this unlikely communication from the far side
of the Atlantic. As I try to remember which
synopsis I sent in that direction, a whole host
of embarrassments present themselves.*
DAILY TELEGRAPH, 12 DECEMBER 2004

See also *Give a DOG a bad name and
hang him*

you've got to eat a peck of dirt before you die

imperfect food hygiene is inevitable in the course of a lifetime

The *peck* in the proverb is a measurement for dry produce, although the word could also be loosely applied to mean 'a great deal', 'a heap'. No one can avoid eating a little dirt unnoticed day by day. Over a lifetime, these minuscule quantities must add up to a significant amount – as much as a peck, according to the proverb.

The earliest record of the saying comes in John Clark's PAROEMIOLOGIA (1639): *You must eat a peck of ashes ere you die.* Almost a century later Thomas Fuller includes it in GNOMOLOGIA (1732): *Every Man must eat a Peck of Dirt before he dies.*

An anecdote from the eighteenth century tells how Lord Chesterfield was dining at an inn one day and complained to the waiter that the plates were rather dirty. *'Everyone must eat a peck of dirt before he dies,'* came the reply. *'That may be true,'* replied the earl, *'but no one is obliged to eat it all at one meal.'*

*My gran used to say '**You've got to eat a peck of dirt before you die'** and I believe that. All this frenzy over cleanliness doesn't seem right. Everyone's obsessed with being free of germs. Are we going over the top?*
DAILY MIRROR, 27 MARCH 2000

*[My mother's] other advice was, '**You eat a peck of dirt before you die.'** So don't be afraid to let your kids get dirty.*
IDAHO STATESMAN, 13 MAY 2007

DIRTY

don't wash your dirty linen in public

keep your affairs private; don't discuss private feuds or scandals in public

This proverb has a French origin. Bartlett says that the French proverb, *Il faut laver son linge sale en famille* ('One should wash one's dirty linen at home') has been current since about 1720. Voltaire used it in a riposte to the Encyclopaedists, and also about some poems King Frederick II had sent to him for his comments, an act which eventually contributed to Voltaire's loss of favour at the Prussian Court. Napoleon Bonaparte made notable use of the saying in an address he gave to the French Assembly in 1815 when he returned to Paris after his short exile on Elba and temporarily restored the Empire:

What is the throne? – a bit of wood gilded and covered with velvet. I am the state – I alone am here the representative of the people. Even if I had done wrong you should not have reproached me in public – people wash their dirty linen at home. France has more need of me than I of France.

Napoleon was doubtless responsible for drawing English attention to the proverb which became current during the nineteenth century.

*It was a fashionable rabbi, Dr. Joseph Silverman of Temple Emmanuel on Fifth Avenue, who brought charges to the New York district attorney. Silverman acted on a precept acknowledged by all minorities and foreign-born Americans – "**Don't wash your dirty linen in public**. It gives the natives another excuse for looking down on you." Silverman reasoned that Asch's play was bad for Jewish public relations.*
SEATTLE POST-INTELLIGENCER,
7 APRIL 2000

*How I agreed with Sue Carroll's views on Anthea Turner. I for one won't be buying the self-promoting pile of trash that Anthea Turner laughingly calls her autobiography. It's just 'chats for cash' for herself and that wimp of a husband, Grant...Anthea, **don't wash your dirty linen in public**. Instead, do us all a favour and leave the country.*
THE MIRROR, 13 OCTOBER 2000

Usage: Informal

DISCRETION

discretion is the better part of valour

although courage is better than cowardice, one should never take unnecessary risks

The proverb in the form we know it today is traditionally considered to be a misquotation of a line from Shakespeare's KING HENRY IV, PART ONE (1597). The original line, *The better part of valour is discretion*, is spoken by Falstaff, who has just escaped almost certain death in a fight by pretending to be fatally wounded.

Although we may owe our present-day familiarity with the proverb to Shakespeare, the idea is not his alone. William Caxton in his translation of JASON (c. 1477) wrote: *Than as wyse and discrete he withdrewe him sayng that more is worth a good retrayte than a folisshe abydinge*. The proper balance between wisdom and bravery is also weighed in the classical authors Plutarch, Archilocus, Tertullian and Menander. Shakespeare, it seems, was using the character of Falstaff to embody a base human instinct for self-preservation rather than as an example of prudent courage.

The literary critic Jorgensen makes a rather different case. One part of his interesting argument is that *discretion* at that period clearly means 'strategy', as in Sidney's ARCADIA of 1584: *...by playne force there was small apparaunce of*
helping Clitophon: but some device was to be taken in hand, wherein no lesse discretion then valour was to be used. To contemporary soldiers *valour* and *discretion* were standard parts of military vocabulary, meaning together the 'sensible deployment of human courage'. Moreover, Jorgensen points out, the sense of *discretion* as *a species of lower prudence* is not listed in the OED until 1720, more than a hundred years after Shakespeare. The playwright, then, may have been portraying Falstaff not so much as self-preserving soldier but as a posturing military professional, taking a heroic pose as a master of the newest strategic approach to war.

If all this is indeed the case, it seems that later centuries have not only reordered Shakespeare's original words but also attributed to them a meaning he may not have intended.

Prince Harry may be typecast as the party-loving prince but his birthdays have lately been austere affairs.
*Mandrake blames The Sun. The prince's 21st last year came uncomfortably soon after the photographs that the rag published of him dressed in a Nazi uniform at a friend's fancy-dress party. Accordingly, he spent the big day celebrating 'quietly'... This year the ailing tabloid's decision to publish (three-year-old) photographs of the prince apparently groping his friend Natalie Pinkham has meant that courtiers at Clarence House have once again decreed that **discretion is the better part of valour**. Indeed, his 22nd on September 15 looks like it will be the dullest yet.*
DAILY TELEGRAPH, 20 AUGUST 2006

*One school of thought says Varley may decide **discretion is the better part of valour**, and walk away rather than over-pay.*
GUARDIAN, 13 JUNE 2007

Usage: Mostly used in a semi-jocular fashion

DO

do as you would be done by
treat others in the same way you would want them to treat you

Variant: Do unto others as you would have them do unto you

The proverb stems from the Golden Rule: that of treating others in the same way as one would like to be treated by them. The Golden Rule is probably most familiar to us through biblical teaching. Matthew 7:12 says: *Therefore all things whatsoever ye would that men should do to you, do ye even so to them: for this is the law and the prophets*. But it is an ancient and widespread concept. Confucius (c. 500 BC) taught it as a lifelong rule of conduct, it is a Hindu precept and is fundamental to Judaism and Christianity where, along with the command to love God with all one's being, it encapsulates the Judaeo-Christian message.

And as thee wolen that men do to thou and do thee to hem in lyk manere is found in RATIS RAVING, an instruction manual of the late fifteenth century. In the sixteenth century, the proverb itself, *Let's do as we may be done by*, appears in SIR THOMAS MORE (1590), a play by an unknown author. In the eighteenth century it was proclaimed by Lord Chesterfield as *the surest method that I know of pleasing* (LETTERS, 16 October 1747) and, more seriously, as *the plain, sure, and undisputed rule of morality and justice* (LETTERS, 27 September 1748).

It is certainly the kind of lofty moral saying that is open to re-expression: *Do unto the other feller the way he'd like to do unto you an' do it fust* (Edward N Westcott, DAVID HARUM, 1898).

When I was in the third grade, I learned the Golden Rule: 'Do unto others as you'd have them do unto you.' I loved those words. I wrote them on everything and carried them around in my school book satchel.
OPRAH WINFREY IN GOOD HOUSEKEEPING, APRIL 2006

I will be 60 this year, and have rheumatoid arthritis; one day I may need a carer, but until then I shall go on working in the profession that I enjoy, always bearing in mind that old adage 'Do as you would be done by.'
SAGA MAGAZINE, APRIL 2006

[Mr Surman] will tell the gathering in Gateshead: 'It's a question of do as you would be done by. Politeness breeds politeness. 'If you show them good manners by saying 'good morning' and 'how are you today?' you will get a good-mannered response.
DAILY MAIL, 10 APRIL 2006

Usage: The proverb has a rather elevated, moralising tone

See also *LIVE and let live*

DOG

a man's best friend is his dog
human affection may wane but a dog remains completely loyal

The faithfulness of the dog has been recognised for centuries, often to the detriment of human partnership: *Histories are more full of examples of the fidelity of dogs than of men* (Alexander Pope, LETTERS, 1737).

Wordsworth, in his aptly named poem FIDELITY (1805), told the story of a dog faithfully watching at his dead master's side in the hills of Cumberland:

> *The dog, which still was hovering nigh,*
> *Repeating the same timid cry,*
> *This dog had been through three*
> *months' space*

A dweller in that savage place.
Yes, proof was plain that, since the day
When this ill-fated traveller died,
The dog had watched about the spot,
Or by his master's side.

Lord Byron certainly knew the close relationship of a dog. His own, Boatswain, died in 1808 and is buried at Newstead Abbey. Part of the epitaph, generally attributed to Byron but probably written by his best (human) friend John Cam Hobhouse, reads:

Near this spot are deposited the remains of one who possessed Beauty without Vanity, Strength without Insolence, Courage without Ferocity, and all the Virtues of Man, without his Vices. This Praise, which would be unmeaning Flattery, if inscribed over human ashes, is but a just tribute to the Memory of Boatswain, a Dog...
The poor dog, in life the firmest friend,
The first to welcome, foremost to defend,
Whose honest heart is still his
master's own,
Who labours, fights, lives, breathes
for him alone.

Canine fidelity is equally legendary across the Atlantic. Stevenson quotes a speech given by Senator George G Vest in 1876. A farmer had shot his neighbour's dog for molesting livestock, even though the dog was well known to him as a gentle animal. The neighbour decided to prosecute. The case dragged on unresolved until Senator Vest was called in to act as counsel for the prosecution. Being unfamiliar with the case and evidence, his impromptu address was necessarily given on purely general lines but it so moved the jury that it ruled in favour of his client:

The best friend a man has in the world may turn against him and become his enemy. His son or daughter... may prove ungrateful. Those who are nearest and dearest to him... may become traitors to their faith... The one absolutely unselfish friend that man can have in this selfish world, the one that never deserts him, the one that never proves ungrateful or treacherous, is his dog.

All these expressions of loyalty have built up a universal picture of a dog's qualities, but it is difficult to pinpoint when the precise form of today's phrase was first used. And more recently, prizing canine devotion has even been judged as setting one's sights rather low. The comedian Joan Rivers put it: *It's obvious that women are smarter than men. Think about it – diamonds are a girl's best friend. A man's best friend is a dog.*

*They say **a man's best friend is his dog**: however, not every owner treats their pet in such a friendly way. On Sunday night, three ill-nourished and mange-ridden lurchers were dumped from a van in Waringsford, Dromara. Banbridge District Council's dog warden has described it as the worst case of neglect he has ever seen.*
BELFAST NEWS LETTER, 21 JULY 2001

*It is unlikely, however, that the mammoth caught flu from us. More likely, claimed Extinct, is that fleas from **man's best friend, the dog**, carried fatal diseases to creatures that had held sway for millions of years but had no immunity to canine distemper, herpes or anthrax.*
DAILY MAIL, 24 OCTOBER 2001

dog does not eat dog
one ought not to attack or take advantage of another from one's own circle

The proverb arises from the observation that, in nature, animals do not generally kill others of their own kind. Juvenal made this point in SATIRES (c. AD 120): *Wild beasts do not injure beasts spotted like themselves.*

Shakespeare remarked that bears are not naturally aggressive towards one another and, in the seventeenth century, the poet George Herbert makes the same point about wolves. Many animals will fight, of course, over territory and for a mate, though rarely to the death. In extreme circumstances, however, dog might eat dog. Thomas Fuller in his GNOMOLOGIA of 1732 cites two contemporary proverbs to this effect: *Dogs are hard drove, when they eat dogs* and *It is an hard Winter, when Dogs eat Dogs*.

David Yelland as a former editor of The Sun, is entitled to crow over the Daily Mirror's loss of circulation since the invasion of Iraq (though what became of the axiom that 'dog does not eat dog'?). All he is saying, however, is that jingoism pays.
INDEPENDENT, 11 APRIL 2003

*He then added a sentence which made former England coach David Lloyd go incandescent and break one of the golden rules in sport – that a former national coach does not criticise a successor on the basis that **dog does not eat dog**.*
BIRMINGHAM POST,
20 MARCH 2006

Usage: Contemporary often twists the proverb round to comment on a situation. Where a colleague turns viciously on another, for instance, a typical remark might be *It's a case of dog eating dog*.

See also *There is HONOUR among thieves*

every dog has his day
fortune smiles on everyone once in a lifetime

In his ADAGIA (1536), Erasmus quotes from Plutarch's MORALIA: TERRESTRIAL COMPARISONS (c. AD 95): *Even a dog gets his revenge*. Erasmus connects the proverb to the story of Euripides. Tradition has it that, whilst a guest at the Macedonian court, the Greek dramatist was savaged to death by a pack of dogs loosed upon him by two rival poets, Arrhidaeus and Crateuas. In 1539, Richard Taverner cited *A dogge hath a day* in his PROVERBES OR ADAGIES BY DESIDERIUS ERASMUS. The original sense of the Latin and early uses in English suggested that any man, however humble, would have one day in his life to avenge past wrongs. The meaning nowadays is broader; every person will have at least one moment of glory in a lifetime, be it through good fortune or revenge.

*They say **every dog has his day**, and I guess today is mine. I just found out my mean old third-grade teacher, Miss Crabtree, was wrong: A messy desk is not evidence of a messy mind.*
ROCKY MOUNTAIN NEWS,
5 NOVEMBER 2005

*When the Birmingham Six were released after 16 years in prison, Richard McIlkenny was the first to speak. 'We waited a long time for this,' he said. 'But **every dog has his day** and we will have ours.' McIlkenny and five others had always protested their innocence after being falsely convicted, in 1975, for the Birmingham pub bombings.*
INDEPENDENT ON SUNDAY, 28 MAY 2006

give a dog a bad name and hang him
ruin someone's reputation and they will never be able to re-establish themselves

Variant: As well hang a dog as give him a bad name

Dogs have not always been looked upon as loyal friends and lovable pets. Until a serum treatment was introduced in 1899, dog bites were often fatal. Stray dogs can be dangerous carriers of disease, particularly of rabies. Notable outbreaks of rabies occurred in France in the thirteenth century, in Spain in the sixteenth century, in Germany in the seventeenth century and in France, Germany, Italy and England during the first half of the eighteenth century. An old European proverb says *He that would hang his dog gives out first that he is mad*, hanging being an accepted way of ridding oneself of a troublesome or rabid animal. The proverb meant that anyone who is planning to do something unpleasant thinks up some plausible reason for doing so first.

Give a dog a bad name and hang him is first recorded in the early eighteenth century, and seems to reflect the same background as this earlier proverb, although the meaning is slightly different; if someone's reputation is sullied he is as good as hanged for he will never regain his former standing. In his SCOTTISH PROVERBS (1721), James Kelly says it is *spoken of those who rise an ill name on a man on purpose to prevent his advancement*. An Italian proverb, translated into English by John Florio in FIRSTE FRUITES (1578), is an earlier example of the same proverbial wisdom: *A man condemned is halfe beheaded*.

The criminal justice bill, now going through parliament, could allow juries in many more cases to be told about the previous convictions of defendants standing trial. It's a step too far for many lawyers and judges, who predict a whole new wave of miscarriages of justice. Police, they say, will simply 'round up the usual suspects'. It will be a case of 'give a dog a bad name and hang him.' Research shows that jurors and magistrates can be seriously prejudiced by knowing that the defendant has been convicted of similar crimes in the past.
GUARDIAN, 11 FEBRUARY 2003

David Dimbleby's reproach to Bill Clinton for the Monica Lewinsky affair in his television interview is unjustified. There is an old expression 'give a dog a bad name and hang him'… I doubt if David Dimbleby knows the scripture: 'Why, then, do you look at the speck in your brother's eye and pay no attention to the log in your own eye?' (Matthew 7:3). The scripture also says: 'Do not judge others, so that God will not judge you' (Matthew 7:1). The final assessment of Bill Clinton's life and work will be on Judgment Day when all men must stand before God and give account.
DAILY TELEGRAPH, 27 JUNE 2004

Usage: Often used today without the second part of the phrase

See also *Fling enough DIRT and some will stick*

let sleeping dogs lie
don't invite trouble by stirring up a potentially tricky situation

The allusion is to disturbing a snoozing watchdog for, as John Heywood reminds us, *It is euyll wakyng of a sleepyng dog* (PROVERBS, 1546).

Chaucer provides us with the earliest known English use of this proverb in TROILUS AND CRESEYDE (c. 1374). When the go-between Pandarus steals into Cressida's chamber at night to prepare her for a visit by Troilus, Cressida is alarmed and wants to call in some servants. Pandarus dissuades her, saying that it is never wise to wake a sleeping dog or to give people grounds for conjecture.

Shakespeare urges *Wake not a sleeping wolf* (HENRY IV PART II, 1598) and Samuel Colville in his play WHIGGS SUPPLICATION (1681) had *It's best to let a sleeping mastiff rest*, but earliest written references to the proverb in its modern form date from the beginning of the nineteenth century: *Take my advice and speer as little about him as he does about you. Best to let sleeping dogs lie* (Sir Walter Scott, REDGAUNTLET, 1824). In his HISTORIE OF SERPENTS (1607) Edward Topsell gives a very pertinent application of the proverb. *It is good therefore if you have a Wife, that is...unquiet and contentious, to let her alone,* he writes, *not to wake an angry dog.*

The saying is not unique to English, however; it is also found in other European languages. Medieval French has a use that pre-dates Chaucer by a hundred years.

This is not the motto for an active interventionist.

With memories beginning to fade of the TV documentary that detailed his bizarre lifestyle, Michael Jackson might have been wise to let sleeping dogs lie. But six months on, the eccentric superstar is clearly still determined to get his own back on journalist Martin Bashir.
DAILY MAIL, 5 SEPTEMBER 2003

I think that my wife has had one or two affairs. I haven't really confronted this before because divorce was unthinkable when the children were younger, but now they are all off at university. I am sure you will say let sleeping dogs lie, but I am consumed by the need to know.
MAIL ON SUNDAY, 19 NOVEMBER 2006

See also *If it ain't BROKE don't fix it*; *LEAVE well alone*

love me, love my dog

if you love me, you must take me as I am and be willing to put up with all my weaknesses and foibles; you must accept anything and anyone I care about

Qui me amat, amat et canem meum (He who loves me loves my dog too) is a Latin proverb quoted by the French abbot St Bernard of Clairvaux

(1090–1153) in his Sermo Primus (1150 AD). Writing at a time when dogs were not pampered pets but often disease-ridden menaces, he was illustrating the nature of true friendship: the acceptance of the whole person, faults and failings and pets included. Not surprisingly, the phrase became a proverb in French; *Qui m'aime, aime mon chien* (Whoever loves me, loves my dog). An English text by an unknown author, dating back to c. 1480 has *He that lovythe me lovythe my hound*.

In spite of his sympathetic reference to dogs, the large breed known as St Bernard was not named after St Bernard of Clairvaux but after another saint altogether, St Bernard of Menthon (923–1009).

Love me, love my dog. Part of reputation management comes down to being a consistently decent human being. That clerk you're rude to maybe – surprise! – the son of your next boss.
BC BUSINESS, 1 MARCH 2001

Love me, love my dog. That's what I said to my first girlfriend – and it worked. But after a few weeks, I realised it wasn't my dog she so adored; it was all the cool stuff that came with him.
CURVE, 1 JUNE 2005

take the hair of the dog that bit you

a remedy for a hangover which advises the sufferer to swallow another alcoholic drink the next morning

Serum to control rabies is a relatively recent discovery (see *Give a DOG a bad name and hang him*). An ancient remedy recommended that, whenever someone suffered a dog bite, a hair from the offending animal should be bound to the wound to help it to heal and to offer protection against disease. A recipe book of 1670 repeats the centuries-old advice: *Take a hair from the dog that bit you, dry it, put it into the wound, and it will heal it, be it never so sore.* The cure was still deemed good in the second half of the eighteenth century. Robert Jones recommends it in THE TREATMENT OF CANINE MADNESS (1760): *The hair of the dog that gave the wound is advised as an application to the part injured.* Procuring the important hair must have been a tricky business at times.

By the sixteenth century, the remedy for dog-bites was also being recommended for hangovers. John Heywood quotes the advice in PROVERBS (1546). Samuel Pepys found it efficacious. His diary entry for 3 April 1661 reads: *Up among my workmen, my head akeing all day from last night's debauch... At noon dined with Sir W. Batten and Pen, who would have me drink two good draughts of sack to-day, to cure me of my last night's disease, which I thought strange, but I think find it true.*

A contemporary of Pepys, William Lilly, famous for his astrological predictions and yearly almanacs, and whose advice and prophecies were derided then, much as his successor Old Moore is today, was of no more sober temperament:

But be sure, over night, if this dog you do bite,
You take it henceforth for a warning,
Soon as out of your bed, to settle your head,
With a hair of his tail in the morning.

The Monsignore poured himself more prosecco. 'A hair of the dog!' he said.
SALLEY VICKERS, MISS GARNET'S ANGEL, 2000

*I'm getting too old for all this partying and it takes me longer to recover each year. The best thing to put you back on the road to recovery is to drink loads of water. In fact, gallons of the stuff. Also avoid caffeine, as it is a diuretic and can dehydrate you. And all that advice to **take the hair of the dog** is a lot of codswallop, too.*
DAILY MAIL, 2 JANUARY 2003

Usage: The proverbial remedy is frequently shortened to *a hair of the dog*

why keep a dog and bark yourself?

why pay someone to work then do the task yourself?

There is no point in going to the expense of buying and feeding a guard dog if you are always on the look out for intruders yourself. The proverb was included in John Ray's collection of ENGLISH PROVERBS (1670): *What? Keep a dog and bark myself? That is, must I keep servants, and do my work myself?* But an earlier literary appearance was in Brian Melbancke's PHILOTIMUS (1583).

Why keep a dog and bark yourself is Nicola Smith's philosophy. Married to cordon bleu chef Yves, why would she want to do the cooking?
BIRMINGHAM POST, 11 AUGUST 2000

*Big ad agency group bosses like to claim they stay out of more mundane matters such as hirings, pitches and creative work. No more so than Sir Martin Sorrell, and when you own three of the world's biggest ad agencies...that seems a perfectly sensible thing to do. **After all, why keep a dog and bark yourself?***
DAILY TELEGRAPH, 21 MARCH 2001

Usage: Can be condescending, scorning menial tasks that others are paid to perform

you can't teach an old dog new tricks

an older person finds it hard to pick up new ideas, practices or skills

Variant: It is hard to teach an old dog new tricks

In his BOKE OF HUSBANDRY (1523), John Fitzherbert warns of the frustrations of teaching an old dog a new point of obedience: *The dogge must lerne it when he is a whelpe, or els it wyl not be; for it is harde to make an olde dogge to stoupe.* Fitzherbert's advice either became or was already proverbial, for just 23 years later John Heywood quotes it as such in his collection of PROVERBS (1546): *But it is harde to make an olde dog stoupe.* Not until the first half of the seventeenth century do *new tricks* figure in the proverb. In the 1670 edition of his ENGLISH PROVERBS, John Ray's entry includes other disparaging remarks about the elderly: *An old dog will learn no tricks. It's all one to physic the dead, as to instruct old men.*

Although he's not sure if he'll work after retirement age, Thompson has not ruled it out. He's considering taking an evening course in neurolinguistic programming. **What was that about old dogs and new tricks?**
GUARDIAN, 3 SEPTEMBER 2001

*They say **you can't teach an old dog new tricks** and as long as Donny Osmond realises that all he has to do is turn up and sing Puppy Love, he'll never have to learn any.*
BIRMINGHAM POST, 11 MARCH 2003

Usage: The expression is often an excuse for those of a certain age and older who have tried a little and failed, or who can't be bothered to try at all.

· E ·

EASIER

easier said than done

it's easier to talk about doing something than to go ahead and do it

Plautus and Livy are amongst the ancients who used this expression. Early English records date back to the fifteenth century. Heywood cites *Sooner said than done* (PROVERBS, 1546) but *Easier said than done* prevailed from the eighteenth century onwards.

You suggest removing disruptive students, reducing classroom sizes and improving students' readiness by involving parents. Duh! Much easier said than done.
VIRGINIAN PILOT, 2 JULY 2000

Interiors: Keep your cool; **Easier said than done** *in our variable climate... but Gabrielle Fagan can show you how.*
LIVERPOOL DAILY POST, 2 AUGUST 2005

EASY

easy come, easy go

anything that is come by without effort is casually lost; money that is easily come by is easily spent

The proverb teaches that money which has been gained through little effort is rapidly frittered away. Money earned through hard work is spent carefully as its value is appreciated.

The saying is a variant of an earlier proverb. *Lightly come, lightly go* was known to Chaucer and was still current in the nineteenth century. Its meaning is well expressed in John Arbuthnot's HISTORY OF JOHN BULL (1712): *A thriftless wretch, spending the goods and gear that his forefathers won with the sweat of their brows: light come, light go.* A sixteenth-century variant of this form was *Lightly gained, quickly lost,* and yet another *Quickly gained, quickly lost,* which also survived to the nineteenth century. But that century also coined its own variant; *Easy come, easy go,* wrote Samuel Warren (DIARY OF A LATE PHYSICIAN, c. 1832), *is... characteristic of rapidly acquired commercial fortunes.*

It's not all 'easy come, easy go' for Minnesota students. Important pieces of their lives, lost in substance, remain in memory, whether it be a beloved grandparent, childhood innocence or outdated Super Nintendo system.
MINNEAPOLIS STAR TRIBUNE, 8 MARCH 2004

Easy come, easy go. That's the attitude toward tax refunds from many Americans who spend the money before they receive it.
SALT LAKE CITY DESERET NEWS, 14 MARCH 2004

Usage: Applied to money itself, or to the things that money can buy. The emphasis is not so much on the means of acquisition but on its ease.

See also *A FOOL and his money are soon parted*

EAT

we must eat to live, not live to eat

we should eat to keep alive, not live to indulge our greed

Variant: Live not to eat but eat to live

The story goes that King Archelaus invited Socrates (c. 470–399 BC) to leave Athens and live a more luxurious existence at his court instead. Socrates declined the offer, replying that, as meal was cheap in Athens and water free of charge, his needs were already being met. Diogenes Laertius and Athenaeus both attribute the words *Other men live to eat, while I eat to live* to Socrates. Plutarch, however, credits the philosopher with *Bad men live that they may eat and drink, whereas good men eat and drink that they may live* (MORALIA, c. AD 95).

According to the French author Rabelais, sixteenth century monks were characterised by gluttony; *they eat not to live*, he says, *but live to eat* (PANTAGRUEL, 1545). Other writers use the proverb but manage to sound a touch smug: *Let us therefore rejoyce, that we are not in the number of those which live onelie to eate and whose hunger is bigger than their panches* (Stefano Guazzo, CIVILE CONVERSATION, 1574). Still, others give it very short shrift. There is more to life than mere existence, as Robert Burton points out: *Eat and live, as the proverb is... that only repairs man which is well concocted, not that which is devoured* (THE ANATOMY OF MELANCHOLY, 1621). American philosopher Ralph Waldo Emerson obviously enjoys his food: *Let the stoics say what they please, we do not eat for the good of living, but because the meat is savory and the appetite is keen* (ESSAYS: NATURE, 1844). Henry Fielding manages to preach this message illicitly. In his comedy L'AVARE (1668) the French playwright Molière uses the

proverb correctly but Fielding, in his translation of the play (1733), omits the all-important *not*, thus rendering it as *'We must eat to live and live to eat.'*

Those subscribing to this view may take comfort from scripture's endorsement. In ECCLESIASTES 8:15 we find: *I commended mirth, because a man hath no better thing under the sun than to eat, and to drink, and to be merry.* Owen Meredith's LUCILE of 1860 (cited by Walsh) puts everything in proportion:

> *We may live without poetry, music,*
> *and art;*
> *We may live without conscience, and live*
> *without heart;*
> *We may live without friends; we may live*
> *without books;*
> *But civilized man cannot live without cooks.*
> *He may live without books, – what is*
> *knowledge but grieving?*
> *He may live without hope, – what is hope*
> *but deceiving?*
> *He may live without love, – what is passion*
> *but pining?*
> *But where is the man that can live*
> *without dining?*

Brown says she doesn't 'waste' calories on foods that she doesn't really like, such as cheesecake and chocolate. Instead, she focuses on preparing and eating colorful fruits and vegetables, cutting out most fried foods and using healthy seasonings. Her husband is also very supportive of her eating habits. The two, says Brown, **'eat to live, not live to eat.'**
EBONY, 1 OCTOBER 2003

Obesity, it has been suggested, should be classed as a disability. Amazing. Apart from a few who have a disability which causes them to get excessively fat, for the rest of the people the word obesity needs to be linked with over-indulgent, overeating and greed. If people adjust their food intake they would not be so fat. Just **eat to live, not live to eat.**
NEWCASTLE EVENING CHRONICLE,
8 JANUARY 2007

Usage: Though doubtless sound sense, the proverb has a rather ascetic, puritanical ring to it. And in an age where being overweight is frowned upon, the proverb has had a new lease of life in newspaper and magazine articles promoting dieting and healthy eating.

See also *The EYE is bigger than the belly*; *ENOUGH is as good as a feast*

You are what you eat
your diet is reflected in your health, physique and general wellbeing

This proverb has been known in America since 1941; American dramatist Bayard Veiller uses it in BAIT FOR A TIGER and calls it a French saying. It is presently much in vogue, being regularly trotted out to support the arguments of those on the healthy eating bandwagon. In Britain the nutritionist Gillian McKeith has a TV show entitled YOU ARE WHAT YOU EAT in which she overhauls viewers' bad diets, replacing cheesecake with bananas. According to her website, Gillian McKeith's YOU ARE WHAT YOU EAT book was the most borrowed non-fiction book for 2005/06 from libraries across the UK.

The proverb, however, has been borrowed for the purpose. In PHYSIOLOGIE DU GOUT (1825) French epicure Jean Anthelme Brillat-Savarin wrote *Dis-moi ce que tu manges, je te dirai ce que tu es* (Tell me what you eat and I will tell you what you are). It is this that Bayard Veiller quotes in his play. And in 1850 the German philosopher Feuerbach, who considered that civilization was the product of man's pursuit of his everyday needs and that his outlook was moulded by this, wrote *Der Mensch ist, was er ißt* (Man is what he eats).

Nutritional experts say beauty is mainly down to what you put inside your body. Dr Sarah Schenker, of the British Nutrition Foundation, says: 'When it comes to the things we often associate with beauty, such as clear skin, the old adage 'You are what you eat' is absolutely true.'
MIRROR, 3 JULY 2003

The trend for improving health through diet is gaining popularity, giving new meaning to the phrase 'you are what you eat'. Examples of this trend can be seen from the government five-a-day initiative, to vitamin-fortified drinks or functional products that claim specific health benefits.
BUSINESS WIRE, 23 JANUARY 2006

EGGS

don't put all your eggs in one basket
don't entrust all your hopes or resources to one single venture

This is a business proverb dating from at least the turn of the seventeenth century. Eggs are fragile and easily broken. It would be unwise of any poultry farmer to put all his eggs into the same basket when taking them to market in case an accident occurred and all the income were lost. Better to spread the risk over several containers.

It is possible that the proverb came into English by way of Italian, for the earliest known citations appear in the English and Italian proverb collections of Giovanni Torriano, all published in the 1660s. English already had an equivalent expression *Don't venture all your goods in one bottom* (ship), in use since the sixteenth century. This originated as an old Greek proverb (*Don't risk all your livelihood on the narrow ships*), which came into English by way of Erasmus's ADAGIA (1550). *Don't put all your eggs in one basket* was a borrowed alternative which eventually won out.

The wisdom of the proverb has been questioned, notably by Mark Twain in PUDD'NHEAD WILSON'S CALENDAR (1893): *The fool saith, 'Put not all thy eggs in one basket' – which is but a manner of saying, 'Scatter your money and your attention'; but the wise man saith, 'Put all your eggs in one basket and WATCH THAT BASKET.'*

*She does sometimes worry about being left alone. 'One problem of not having children is that **all your love eggs are in one basket**,' she says... 'The great passion of your life is bound up in one incredibly frail human being, because we're all frail.'*
GOOD HOUSEKEEPING, MAY 2000

Don't put all your eggs in one basket. Investors are taught at stockmarket elementary school that the secret to avoiding financial disaster is to make sure they diversify their portfolios.
THE ECONOMIST, 10 MARCH 2007

you can't make an omelette without breaking eggs
nothing can be achieved without sacrifices or losses along the way

This is a translation of the French *On ne peut pas faire des omelettes sans casser les oeufs* which has been attributed to both Robespierre and Napoleon. Robespierre is said to have used the phrase to excuse the carnage of the French Revolution, and Napoleon to justify the warfare necessary to build his empire. Reliable Stevenson cites it as an epigram of Robespierre (c. 1790). Whoever coined it, the maxim attained respectability in France on being accepted into the 1878 edition of the DICTIONNAIRE DE L'ACADÉMIE. Examples of its use in English literature date from the early nineteenth century, quoted in French, and the mid-nineteenth century, translated into English.

The combined HCNO jab could produce a race of drug-free, slim non-smokers. The diet industry would be destroyed ... but you can't make an omelette without breaking eggs.
NEWCASTLE JOURNAL, 14 AUGUST 2004

You can't make an omelette without breaking eggs and you can't improve a city's infrastructure without digging up the roads.
LIVERPOOL ECHO, 22 AUGUST 2005

Usage: Often used today by a businessman, politician or military leader on announcing a decision that will call for sacrifice of jobs or lives – always someone else's

ELEPHANT

an elephant never forgets
said of someone with a prodigious memory, usually for slights and wrongs

It was the memory not of the elephant but of the camel that was renowned amongst the ancient Greeks long ago, who stated that *Camels never forget an injury*. The Greeks had a low opinion of elephants, however, regarding them as lumbering, stupid creatures. Proverbial reference to the elephant's memory is relatively recent. In REGINALD: REGINALD ON BESETTING SINS (1910), the camel is usurped by the elephant: *Women and elephants never forget an injury*. The author Hector Hugo Munro, who wrote under the pen-name Saki, was no stranger to elephants; he was born in Burma and lived there, and would have appreciated the intelligence of the animal. Saki's quip about women and elephants was later repeated by Dorothy Parker in BALLADE OF UNFORTUNATE MAMMALS (1930).

But does the elephant live up to its reputation? Well, the working elephant memorises a large number of commands given by its mahout and recognises many other animals and people, thus remembering both kindnesses and injuries. And since the animal's lifespan is 50 or 60 years these memories are usually long lived.

In a land full of the world's most majestic animals, native Africans know that old saying: 'An elephant never forgets.' But young women in Tanzania know there's also a very dedicated girl in Denver who never forgot them. After a safari visit when she was just 11, Ashley Shuler witnessed the devastating level of poverty which made a huge impression on her. Three years after that visit Ashley founded AfricAid to raise money and supplies to support young girls' education in Tanzania.
GIRLS' LIFE, 1 AUGUST 2003

*THEY say **an elephant never forgets** – and neither does the Daily Post. Our picture archive is one of the largest extant for North Wales, spanning more than a century of unbroken photo-journalism since the invention of the camera through to the digital age.*
LIVERPOOL DAILY POST, 4 MARCH 2006

Usage: Usually said of a person who does not forget injuries, but an elephantine memory could just be a good one

END

all good things must come to an end
every pleasurable activity eventually reaches an end

Variant: All good things come to an end

Every thing hath ende, everything eventually reaches a conclusion, was a proverb quoted in several of Chaucer's works in the fifteenth century. In the late sixteenth century Thomas Nashe attached a tag to the proverb, *Euery thing hath an end, and a pudding hath two*, puddings in those days being sausage-shaped. Nashe's witty variant was popular into the nineteenth century.

The word *good*, which rather changes the message of the saying, is a recent addition.

All good things must come to an end, and graduation is both a happy and a sad occasion. 'Coming down' can be a disillusioning experience if you haven't prepared for it. Enjoy your university years, but at the same time keep an eye to your future by visiting the careers office and exploring the opportunities that will be open to you afterwards. Then your graduation will be both an end and a beginning – probably the most important rite of passage of your life.
DAILY TELEGRAPH, 22 NOVEMBER 2003

*Until this week, it seemed that even Johnny Lechner had accepted the seasoned insight that **all good things must come to an end**. The 29-year-old had become a minor celebrity in the US for having been an undergraduate for 12 years; he had appeared on television talkshows and landed a book deal.*

At long last, however, the perpetual student with a flair for self publicity was due to graduate from the University of Wisconsin on Monday. Then he had a change of heart.
GUARDIAN, 12 MAY 2006

Usage: Spoken in a wistful or resigned tone when a happy time, or period of good fortune, comes to a close.

ENDS

all's well that ends well
when the outcome is happy, it makes up for any difficulty or unpleasantness that went before

This proverb, common to many European languages, immediately brings Shakespeare to mind since it is the title of one of his plays. Shakespeare, however, did not coin the expression. It was already at least 300 years old, being recorded in PROVERBS OF HENDING (c. 1300). Shakespeare merely borrowed it. His comedy (1601) tells of the young Helena and the rejection, difficulty and subterfuge she has to undergo before Bertram, her husband, willingly owns her as his wife. The ending is a happy one, making amends for all the hurt and deceit, and demonstrating the truth of the proverb that *All's well that ends well*.

All's well that ends well is a sentiment that might do well for the plot of a play, but it's a rotten way to conduct public policy.
LOS ANGELES DAILY NEWS,
20 AUGUST 2006

All's well that ends well; Shakespearean actor rescues woman from Tube tracks
EVENING STANDARD, 10 JANUARY 2007

ENOUGH

enough is enough
it is unnecessary or even harmful to do more; there is a limit to everything

Iam satis est, meaning 'now there is enough', is a phrase not uncommonly found in the writings of Roman poets and playwrights. This plea for moderation passed from Latin literature into various European languages. Italian has the rhyming *Assai basta, e troppo guasta* (Enough is enough, and too much spoils). French and Dutch concur with this sentiment. French has *Mieux vaut assez que trop* and Dutch *Genoeg is meer dan overvloed*, both phrases meaning that enough is better than too much. English is more economical; John Heywood includes *Enough is enough* in his PROVERBS (1546) and that has been the common form ever since. In English speech, it seems, enough really is enough – the rest is common sense.

Could it have occurred to the television executives, currently lamenting the drop in audience numbers for their beloved soaps, that maybe their fall in popularity could be in some way linked to the rise in the number of weekly episodes? I would guess that those people turning off have probably decided that enough is enough.
INDEPENDENT, 13 AUGUST 2002

Enough is enough. That was the demand from the Archbishop of Birmingham as he launched a ferocious onslaught on the BBC yesterday. The antagonism of the Catholic Church towards the Corporation was all too apparent as the Most Rev Vincent Nichols accused it of bias and hostility.
BIRMINGHAM POST,
30 SEPTEMBER 2003

Fun is fun, but enough's enough.
OGDEN NASH, FOR THE MOST IMPROBABLE SHE, 1938

Usage: Often uttered as a warning to stop when reasonable limits are in danger of being breached. May refer to words or actions...even enjoyable ones.

See also *ENOUGH is as good as a feast*

enough is as good as a feast
moderation is ultimately more satisfying than excess

Euripides in SUPPLIANTS (c. 421 BC) tells us that there is no virtue in gluttony and that *enough is as a feast*. The proverb was known in England in the fifteenth century, for John Lydgate uses it in THE ASSEMBLY OF GODS (c. 1420). In PROVERBS (1546) John Heywood quotes the expression in its familiar form.

When Euripides inspired the proverb, he was discussing gluttony. Although happy to accept the call for moderation in many areas, when it comes to food we tend to justify our desire to indulge. A modern variant of the proverb reflects this tendency: *Enough is as good as a feast; too much is as good as a banquet*. Author Penny Vincenzi, in this extract from GOOD HOUSEKEEPING, would endorse the modern dictum:

Enough is as good as a feast, my great aunt Daisy was wont to say to me, as I reached an ever-chubbier hand towards the chocolate biscuits. I can remember to this day the sense of outrage this induced (greater even than the removal of the biscuits); I was only about four years old at the time, but able to distinguish fact from fiction and I knew perfectly well even then that enough was nothing like as good as a feast. What was 'enough' chocolate biscuits anyway? By adult standards, it seemed to be two at most, possibly only one, and enough for what, I wanted to know? Enough to tantalise, to remind me of the taste, the texture, to give the sensation of intense pleasure, but enough? Enough! Enough chocolate biscuits (in much the same way as enough champagne, raspberry Pavlova and cheese and onion crisps) is enough to stop you wanting any more for a bit; maybe even quite a bit. That could arguably be as good as a feast, but not some neat, nannyish portion that teeters around the tastebuds and then becomes a memory.

*When as a youngster I asked for more food during World War II and there wasn't any, my mother consoled me with the reply: Never mind, **enough is as good as a feast**. I have applied her philosophy to my intake of a varied diet, alcohol and nicotine throughout my life. It has stood me in good stead.*
CARDIFF WESTERN MAIL,
2 FEBRUARY 2005

Usage: Nowadays the proverb is not always restricted to food but can also be applied to any area where excess is a danger and moderation should be called for.

See also ENOUGH *is enough* and *We must* EAT *to live, not live to eat*

EVILS

of two evils choose the lesser
when faced with challenging alternatives, choose the less damaging one

Variant: Choose the lesser of two evils

The saying has its origins in Greek philosophy. It was already proverbial in Aristotle's day: *We must choose the lesser of two evils*, as the saying is (NICOMACHEAN ETHICS, c. 335 BC). The proverb is found in French texts from the thirteenth century. Its earliest recorded use in English is in Chaucer's TROILUS AND CRISEYDE (c. 1374): *Of harmes two, the lesse is for to chese*.

According to Plutarch, a Spartan with a sense of humour used the proverb as a quip upon his marriage to a short wife. The joke was successful for it is found repeated in a seventeenth century book of CONCEITS, CLINCHES, FLASHES AND WHIMZIES (1639): *One persuaded his friend to marry a little woman, because of evils the least was to be chosen.*

But of two evils, which is the lesser? Indecisiveness was ever a human failing. An American story quoted by Walsh tells of a traveller who stopped to ask the way. He was given the choice of two roads, one long and one short, and told that it didn't matter which he chose, since either way he was bound to regret his decision and wish he had taken the other.

*Where have all the statesmen gone? The shameful state of politics has so deterred qualified persons with integrity from running for office that we no longer vote for the best candidate, but instead **choose the lesser of two evils**.*
CHICAGO SUN-TIMES, 16 MARCH 2003

*Is The Record really suggesting that we **choose the lesser of two evils** on Election Day? Do we really have to pick between a guy who is this close to the type of scandals associated with former Gov. James McGreevey and former U.S. Sen. Robert Torricelli in order to avoid voting for the guy who is nothing more than a fresh-faced son of a New Jersey political lion with no experience but who knows how to follow the party line, whether he believes it all or not?*
BERGEN COUNTY RECORD,
3 NOVEMBER 2006

Usage: The saying need not exclusively refer to high ethical dilemmas. It can be used more lightly of two strategies in sport, or even of walking to town versus waiting for an infrequent bus

EXCEPTION

the exception proves the rule
anomalies put the validity of a generalisation to the test

Variant: Exceptions prove the rule

There is no general rule without some exception, as the old proverb has it. North said so in his translation of PLUTARCH'S LIVES: ALEXANDER AND CAESAR (1579), as did Heywood, Shelton and Burton some years later, perhaps after Cicero in PRO BALBO (56 BC). Cicero was defending Cornelius Balbus, said to have been illegally granted Roman citizenship. Although agreements with some non-Roman tribes forbade them from becoming Roman citizens, this

was not the case with Balbo's people. Nevertheless, the prosecutor thought it should be assumed. Cicero argued that this was rubbish. Creating an exception simply confirms the existence of a law to the contrary.

The meaning of the word *prove* has undergone a change since the proverb was first recorded in the seventeenth century. Today we understand *prove* to mean 'confirm' or 'demonstrate' but an older sense of the word was 'test' (see also *The proof of the PUDDING is in the eating*). In the AUTHORISED VERSION of the BIBLE (1611) *prove* is often used in this way. 1 THESSALONIANS 5:21, for instance, has: *Prove all things; hold fast that which is good*. The proverb does not therefore mean that an exception shows the rule to be correct but that an exception tries out the wisdom of the rule. It may be true – or not.

Want to make a mega hit movie?…just stick 'wedding' in the title and make sure there's a happy ending. The latest to benefit from this formula: My Big Fat Greek Wedding…*has already earned $66.3m in the United States…For the same reason,* The Member of the Wedding *did not do well. Ditto Robert Altman's* A Wedding. *Both end in chaos and pass-me-the-hemlock despair. Grimness and white frocks just do not gel. J-Lo's sappy* The Wedding Planner? *Alright, smarty pants, it's **the exception that proves the rule**.*
INDEPENDENT REVIEW,
30 AUGUST 2002

*Unlike some would-be colonial powers – Germany, for example – the US never tried to join in the scramble for Africa. (Its establishment of Liberia, as a home for freed slaves, is **the exception that proves this rule**.)*
DAILY TELEGRAPH, 16 MAY 2004

EYE

an eye for an eye, and a tooth for a tooth

An eye for an eye and a tooth for a tooth is a helpful motto for those bent on revenge and seeking justification for pursuing it. The words are from the Bible and are listed amongst the penalties for slaying and injuring, which God gave to Moses along with the rest of the Law. LEVITICUS 24:20 reads: *Breach for breach, eye for eye, tooth for tooth: as he hath caused blemish in a man, so shall it be done to him again.*

Nevertheless, this law was never intended to give licence for revenge but to exact justice. Neither did it permit taking matters into one's own hands since every case was subject to public judgement.

Jesus saw the question in a different light. In the Sermon on the Mount (MATTHEW 5:38–41) he urges his listeners to fight evil with good:

Ye have heard that it hath been said, An eye for an eye, and a tooth for a tooth; But I say unto you that ye resist not evil, but whosoever shall smite then on thy right cheek, turn to him the other also. And if any man will sue thee at the law, and take away thy coat, let him have thy cloak also. And whosoever shall compel thee to go a mile, go with him two.

The intention is not to show weakness but to prove that one is free from the spirit of hate and revenge by offering more than was first demanded.

*The national cry for revenge is shameful. We Americans are presumably a people who do not believe in **an eye for an eye and a tooth for a tooth**. Yet many of our national leaders, most of the talking heads who have been babbling on television this week, and the mental defectives who repeat cliches on talk radio are demanding that we get even.*
CHICAGO SUN-TIMES, 16 SEPTEMBER 2001

*Roberto Calderoli, of the Northern League, the third biggest party in Mr Berlusconi's conservative coalition, said each country involved in the hostage crisis should expel 1,000 Iraqi and Iranian immigrants a day until the captives were released. 'The law of **an eye for an eye and a tooth for a tooth** is a cruel one, but it is the only one that criminal animals like this understand',* he said.
GUARDIAN, 16 APRIL 2004

See also *REVENGE is sweet*

the eye is bigger than the belly
the visual appeal of food makes us eat even when we have no appetite

The proverb is from the sixteenth century. John Lyly makes reference to it in EUPHUES AND HIS ENGLAND (1580): *Thou art like the Epicure, whose belly is sooner filled than his eye.*

For the Tudors the main meal of the day was taken at noon and, in reasonably prosperous households, might last for up to two hours whilst the family and their guests ploughed their way through copious amounts of food. Foreigners writing home were wont to express their amazement at how much their English counterparts could consume. The RELIQUIAE ANTIQUAE (c. 1540) reported that *Englysshemen ar callyd the grettyste fedours in the worlde.* But with a large variety of colourful dishes on offer at each meal, it is small wonder that diners tried to make room for a little of everything and found their eyes were bigger than their appetites.

Abundance at the English dining table continued into the following centuries, leading Thomas Fuller to pronounce in one of his sermons: *Gluttony is the sin of England;... our ancientest carte is for the sin of gluttony* (JOSEPH'S PARTI-COLOURED COAT, 1640). And with good reason. In his

A MATTER OF FORM

A feature of proverbs is that many of them exhibit characteristic forms or fit into set patterns. This partly explains why we so readily interpret them as proverbs. You might like to work out the patterns from the following sets of examples, and add more of your own.

- Better safe than sorry
- Better late than never
- Never say die
- Never put off till tomorrow what you can do today
- Never look a gift horse in the mouth
- Never judge by appearances
- Money talks
- Time flies
- He who hesitates is lost
- He who laughs last laughs best
- Time is money
- Seeing is believing
- Virtue is its own reward
- Honesty is the best policy
- Enough is enough
- Boys will be boys
- Nothing ventured, nothing gained
- Out of sight, out of mind
- An ounce of prevention is worth a pound of cure

diary Samuel Pepys records the menu he offered a few friends for a special dinner in 1663:

A fricassee of rabbit and chickens, a leg of mutton boiled, three carps in a dish, a great dish of a side of lamb, a dish of roasted pigeons, a dish of four lobsters, three tarts, a lamprey pit, a most rare pie, a dish of anchovies, good wine of several sorts, and all things mighty noble, and to my great content.

With such enticement to gluttony pity, then, the poor character in Dean Swift's POLITE CONVERSATION (1738) who is forced to admit defeat over a mere mouthful: *I thought I could have eaten this wing of a chicken; but my eye's bigger than my belly.* (For conspicuous consumption at medieval

feasts, see *A BIRD in the hand is worth two in the bush.*)

Our favourite media mogul Chris Evans has decided his eyes are bigger than his stomach when it comes to the restaurant business. He had set up the company ZilliChris with the London chef Aldo Zilli, but the ginger wonder's men-in-suits wanted too much of a piece of the action. Aldo, who opens his new restaurant in Notting Hill, west London tonight, told us: 'Chris pulled out of the restaurant because his accountants wanted to take too much of a percentage of the profits. I'm going it alone but we're still friends.
MIRROR, 14 AUGUST 2000

A mound of medals could transform America's latest swimming prodigy into a national icon at 18 as he tries to become

- One man's meat is another man's poison
- Practice makes perfect
- Familiarity breeds contempt
- You can't make a silk purse out of a sow's ear
- You can't get blood from a stone
- Like it or lump it
- Do or die
- Live and let live
- Live and learn
- Man proposes but God disposes
- Jack of all trades is master of none
- The spirit is willing but the flesh is weak

The sound of the proverb to the ear is very important in making it memorable, as some of the examples above show. Consider the common features of these further sets:

- Spare the rod and spoil the child
- In for a penny, in for a pound
- Where there's a will there's a way
- Waste not, want not
- Little strokes fell great oaks
- A friend in need is a friend indeed
- Every bullet has its billet
- Haste makes waste

the second individual to win seven events in a single Olympics… it is difficult to resist the temptation for Phelps, whose biggest weakness is his versatility: 'It's like a buffet – the eyes are bigger than the stomach,' Bowman said.
SAN JOSE MERCURY NEWS, 22 MAY 2004

See also *We must EAT to live, not live to eat*

what the eye doesn't see, the heart doesn't grieve over
if we are unaware of a problem, we cannot be upset by it

This proverb, recorded by John Heywood in 1546 as *That the eie seeth not, the hert rewth not* was called a common saying by George Pettie in 1576. This form persisted until well into the nineteenth century, when the variant *What the eye doesn't see, the heart doesn't grieve over* was coined. The proverb teaches quite logically that we can only be troubled by things that we know about. It is the sight of the caterpillar on the lettuce that puts us off our salad; had we unknowingly eaten it we could not have given it a thought. In his TRAVELS IN FRANCE AND ITALY (1766), Tobias Smollett recounts the tale of a young man whose heart was very much grieved upon witnessing his beloved's table manners:

I know no custom more beastly than that of using water glasses, in which polite company spirt, and squirt, and spue the filthy scourings of their gums, under the eyes of each other. I knew a lover cured of his passion, by seeing this nasty cascade discharged from the mouth of his mistress.

Turning a blind eye makes the path of true love run smooth!

*Actually, he might even have got away with this perversion: **what the eye doesn't see, the heart doesn't grieve over**. But Ross tells all to Stevie, at which point all hell breaks loose.*
MAIL ON SUNDAY, 8 FEBRUARY 2004

*When Jacey Parks cheated on her boyfriend with his best mate she thought secrecy was the best idea. '**What the eye doesn't see, the heart doesn't grieve over**,' was one of her gran's sayings. And she believed it was best that Charlie Halton never knew. For a year Jacey, 22, lived in fear that the secret would come out. But Charlie found out in the end and he was horrified – more at her deception for 12 months than her betrayal. He ended their relationship for good.*
PEOPLE, 18 NOVEMBER 2001

Usage: Often used to excuse deliberately keeping quiet about something troublesome

See also *IGNORANCE is bliss*

• F •

FAMILIARITY

familiarity breeds contempt
when one becomes used to someone or something, one's respect degenerates into disregard

Aesop's THE FOX AND THE LION (c. 570 BC) tells how a fox, upon meeting a lion for the first time, nearly died of fright and ran away. The next time he saw the lion the fox was still rather worried but stood his ground. At their third meeting, however, the fox felt no nervousness at all and dared to approach the powerful beast. Familiarity took the edge off his fear until eventually he felt none.

Another fable, THE CAMEL, (John Vernon Lord and James Michie (trs.), AESOP'S FABLES, 1989) expresses the same idea:

> *When the first men first set eyes*
> *On a camel, they were staggered by its size*
> *And ran away in fear.*
> *In time, seeing the beast seemed fairly mild,*
> *They plucked up courage to go near.*
> *Finally, when they came to realise*
> *That it was docile and their fears were idle,*
> *They used it with contempt, gave it a bridle*
> *And put it in the charge of a child.*

From here, it is only a short step to contempt. Publilius Syrus concurred. In SENTENTIAE (c. 43 BC), he writes: *Too much familiarity breeds contempt*, a statement which was echoed thereafter by Plutarch, Seneca, Martial and other ancient writers. The earliest recorded use of the expression in English is in Alanus de Insulis's SATIRES (c. 1160). The proverb has been widely used ever since.

*'Most photographers,' he explains, 'are very attached to things that are exotic, and to people who are in extreme and dramatic circumstances. But I truly believe that the ordinary is much more interesting than people make out. We are so familiar with it and **familiarity breeds contempt**, but when you go to something like a supermarket or an Argos, or a shopping mall, they are quite extraordinary places.'*
DAILY TELEGRAPH, 19 APRIL 2004

'Unfortunately for couples, I think the old saying 'familiarity breeds contempt' is all too common for a lot of us,' says Amanda. 'We wind up taking our partner for granted and forget to be as grateful as we were in the beginning for having them in our lives.'
JETSTAR ONBOARD MAGAZINE, FEBRUARY/MARCH 2006

See also *A PROPHET is not without honour save in his own country*

FATHER

like father, like son
a son is likely to exhibit the same character and behaviour as his father

Stevenson cites a fable by Aesop (sixth century BC) to illustrate the influence a parent has upon a child. A mother crab scolded her son for walking sideways, whereupon the youngster replied that he would be pleased to walk straight if she would show him how to do it.

The proverb *Like father, like son* was known in England in the fourteenth century. The Latin proverb *Qualis pater, talis filius* is quoted by Langland in PIERS PLOWMAN (1362), and in LEGEND OF GOOD WOMEN (c. 1385) Chaucer writes: *As doth the fox Renard, [so doth] the foxes sone*.

A complementary proverb exists for mothers and daughters, but there is a suggested biblical origin for this. EZEKIEL 16:44 reads: *Behold, every one that useth proverbs shall use this proverb against thee, saying, As is the mother, so is her daughter*.

*In the world of celebrity, **like father, like son** (or like mother, like daughter) is all par for the course; Martin Amis is an acclaimed novelist, as was his father Kingsley, while the career choice of photographer Mary McCartney is the same as that of her late mother, Linda.*
DAILY TELEGRAPH, 6 APRIL 2002

*I rather like zipping up my snug jacket against the cold, sticking a fleece hat on, and donning my gloves as I pedal off. I know that last bit is quite possibly stupid. When I was a kid, my dad used to drive me mad by setting off in the car and only putting on his driving gloves (you can tell how long ago that was: who wears driving gloves now?) once already down the road – convincing this young passenger that a fatal crash was imminent. But there you go: **like father, like son**. At least I don't have any passengers to scare as I balance no-handed.*
GUARDIAN, 14 DECEMBER 2006

FEATHERS

fine feathers make fine birds
expensive clothes give the wearer an appearance of respectability and breeding

Some birds are more pleasing to look at than others. The familiar simile as proud as a peacock arises from the observation that the male bird's bearing, together with the magnificent display of his plumage, gives him a haughty look. Plucked before being cooked for a medieval banquet, however, the cock bird would look as unremarkable as his dowdy hen. The Italian diplomat, Stefano Guazzo, recognised that the meanest personalities can hide behind expensive apparel. In CIVILE CONVERSATION (1574) he writes: *It may rightly be sayde of these costly clad carkases, that the feathers are more worth than the byrde*.

In the spirit of Guazzo's cynicism, the earliest uses of the proverb were often tongue in cheek. In THE SCOURGE OF FOLLY (1611), John Davies of Hereford writes:

The faire Feathers still make the faire Fowles. But some haue faire feathers that looke but like Owles.

But if John Ray (ENGLISH PROVERBS, 1670) is to be believed, the saying was not necessarily always intended to be uncomplimentary: *Fair feathers make fair fowles. Fair clothes, ornaments and dresses set off persons… God makes and apparel shapes*.

By the time Bunyan wrote PILGRIM'S PROGRESS (1678), the proverb was shifting to a more recognisable form: *They be fine feathers that make a fine bird*, and 36 years later Bernard Mandeville in THE FABLE OF THE BEES (1714) uses the exact form we know today.

***Fine feathers make fine birds** – that's something Christina Becker is learning these days. Ever since she joined the T-Mobile-Team, she's been getting a lot of attention. 'Before that', said the 28-year old, 'nobody ever even looked when I left my house in Cottbus in full gear to train'. However, since she's been wearing magenta, complete strangers keep coming up to her.*
T-MOBILE-TEAM ARTICLE,
9 FEBRUARY 2006

'Fine feathers make fine birds.' No, fine
birds make fine feathers, as well as other
fine birds. Someone never had that special
talk with their parents, huh?
DAILY IOWAN, 5 DECEMBER 2006

Fine feathers make fine birds. *Although
you look your best wearing clean and crisp
clothes, most clothes need a lot of extra
care to be shown to advantage. This will
however take only a small extra effort if you
have the right tools at hand. Braun irons
are designed to help you get that flawless
finish, quickly and easily. They will bring
out the beauty of your clothes and so
accentuate the beauty in you with the help
of powerful steam and intelligent features.*
ADVERTISEMENT FOR BRAUN IRONING
PRODUCTS, 2006

Usage: Often used ironically or
sarcastically

See also *APPEARANCES are deceptive*

FESTINA LENTE

festina lente
the best way to make good progress is
to proceed with caution

Variant: Make haste slowly

This proverb is familiar in Latin,
although its origin is Greek. According
to the Roman biographer Suetonius
and the author Aulus Gellius, the
saying was a favourite of the deified
Emperor Caesar Augustus (63 BC–AD
14), who frequently quoted it in both
conversation and letters in that
language. The Latin version, *Festina
lente*, is much discussed by Erasmus in
his ADAGIA (1508). Erasmus
considered the proverb's message so
wise that he would have had it
inscribed and carved everywhere to
bring it constantly to public attention.
A Roman coin stamped with the
device of a dolphin entwined around

an anchor was, according to Erasmus,
an illustration of the proverb, the
anchor representing steadiness and
stability to temper the dolphin's speed
and purpose. The Italian publisher and
scholar Aldus Manutius, who was
much admired by Erasmus for his
innovations in printing and for his
scholarship, began to print the device
inside his volumes. It was, Erasmus
declared, a fitting emblem; the anchor
represented   Aldus's   thoughtful
scholarship and his careful editing of
each book, and the dolphin its
swiftness of completion. *Festina lente*,
hasten slowly.

The proverb in Latin has been
current in English since the sixteenth
century. With the exception of
Chaucer, who has *He hasteth wel that
wisly can abide* (TROILUS AND
CRISEYDE c. 1385), translations into
English date from the seventeenth
century.

A contemporary twist on the maxim
was propounded by Lee Iacocca, a
former president of General Motors,
who warned that *Action should not be
confused with haste.*

*People do swing to the right later in life.
But Mr Skinner should not be too hasty in
urging miners on to their bikes to find work
as salad tossers, market researchers and
cosmetic salespersons. Though he has less
time than most MPs,* **festina lente** *must
be the watchword for Bolsover's best.*
INDEPENDENT, 21 JUNE 2002

*The Ancient Romans – well known for
building and maintaining good roads –
had a saying* **'festina lente'** *which means
hasten slowly. They knew the value of
making sure everything was right before
assigning funding for a project.*
BIRMINGHAM POST, 14 AUGUST 2004

See also *More haste, less SPEED*

For other proverbs commonly quoted in English or Latin, see under *CARPE diem*; *CAVEAT emptor*; *Great OAKS from mighty acorns grow*; *TIME flies*

FEVER

feed a cold and starve a fever

the best medicine for a cold is to eat well, for a fever to fast

Variant: Stuff a cold and starve a fever

This medical proverb, which seems to have originated sometime in the nineteenth century, is not what it appears. Originally the wording was *Stuff a cold and starve a fever*. In POLONIUS (1852), a collection of wise saws, Edward Fitzgerald says that the proverb has been *grievously misconstrued, so as to bring on the fever it was meant to prevent*. A correspondent with NOTES AND QUERIES (1881) concurs, pointing out that the saying is elliptical and that the advice should be *...[If you] stuff a cold, [you will have to] starve a fever*. This, of course, changes the wisdom of the proverb as we know it, for it suggests that anyone foolish enough to eat heartily while suffering from a cold will soon bring a fever upon himself. Other nineteenth and early twentieth century writers agree that this is indeed the proverb's message.

Modern medical advice is at odds with this view and supports the contemporary sense of the misquoted saying: a good intake of healthy food, including plenty of fruit and vegetables, is recommended for a cold, with no suggestion that a fever will result. Those who have a fever do not usually feel like eating anyway but need plenty to drink until the fever eventually 'breaks'.

Most often, the proverb is written as 'feed a cold and starve a fever.' That was the medical advice Mark Twain gave to a friend in his essay on curing a cold, published in 1864. Today the proverb is used for laughs in comic strips and greeting cards. Even Snoopy has used it to get more food in his dish by telling Charlie Brown that 'a cold just came by and said it was hungry.'
MINNEAPOLIS STAR TRIBUNE,
17 DECEMBER 2000

'Feed a cold and starve a fever' is just an old wives' tale, according to a new study which aims to separate food facts from fiction. Cold sufferers would be far better off following their usual diet, although protein, zinc and folic acid will help the immune system and drinking lots of water will help feverish sweats.
SUNDAY MIRROR, 14 APRIL 2002

FINGERS

fingers were made before forks

an explanation or excuse for not using cutlery for eating

It is said that John the Good, Duke of Burgundy, in the fourteenth century, was the proud possessor of two forks but, if he was, the novelty did not catch on. Diners continued to use their knives (carried permanently tucked into their belts and used for all sorts of purposes) or fingers to dig into the variety of communal dishes placed upon the table. In the previous century Fra Bonvicino, who had obviously been treated to stomach-churning spectacles at the monastic dinner table, had issued a few guidelines for those about to dip into the pot with their companions:

Let thy fingers be clean.
Thou must not put thy fingers into
thine ears,

Or thy hands on thy head.
The man who is eating must not be cleaning
By scraping with his finger at any foul part.

(See also Smollett's account of Continental table manners in *What the EYE doesn't see, the heart doesn't grieve over*.)

Forks were introduced to Italy by noble visitors from the Byzantine Empire. The very wealthy began to use them from the fourteenth century onwards but it was not until the sixteenth century that they were commonly used by this class. The eccentric English writer Thomas Coryat (CORYATS CRUDITIES, 1611), on his travels through Italy in the early seventeenth century, could not quite believe his eyes when he saw forks being used:

I observed a custom in all those Italian cities and towns through which I passed that is not used in any other country that I saw in my travels, neither do I think that any other nation in Christendom doth use it, but only in Italy. The Italian and also most strangers that are commorant in Italy do always at their meals use a little fork when they cut their meat. For while with their knife which they hold in one hand, they cut the meat out of the dish, they fasten their fork which they hold in their other hand upon the same dish, so that whatsoever he be that sitting in the company of any others at meal, should unadvisedly touch the dish of meat with his fingers from which all at the table do cut, he will give occasion of offence unto the company, as having transgressed the laws of good manners, in so much that for his error he shall be at the least brow-beaten, if not reprehended in words.

It was at least another 50 years before such niceties were wholeheartedly embraced by the English elite, however. And when society diners in the late seventeenth century eventually adopted the custom, there were inevitably those who would inadvertently slip back into the old ways or even just prefer them. Then, to cover their embarrassment on being noticed, they would retort, *Fingers were made before forks*.

The proverb was easily coined, being modelled on an earlier one known since at least the second half of the sixteenth century. Swift uses them both together in POLITE CONVERSATION (1738), the new with the old: *They say fingers were made before forks, and hands before knives.*

*She could handle anything from playground skirmishes to troublesome questions of lunchroom etiquette. Once, she spotted me sawing away in frustration, struggling to cut a tomato slice with my fork. When I explained my dilemma, she put a hand on my shoulder and calmly reminded me, 'Darlin', **fingers were made before forks**.'*
SOUTHERN LIVING, SEPTEMBER 2001

*Avoid excessive handling of food because bacteria are always on our bodies. Although '**fingers were made before forks**', suitable utensils should be used to serve food and, of course, everyone handling food should be scrupulous in their personal cleanliness.*
FOOD SAFETY IN ON YOUR BEHALF, ON BBC NORTHERN IRELAND WEBSITE, 27 JANUARY 2007

FOOL

a fool and his money are soon parted

a foolish person gives little thought to how he spends his money and soon finds himself without any at all

In MORE CAUTIONARY TALES (1930) Hilaire Belloc described the sad case of Peter Goole, a young man who had all the hallmarks of the fool in the proverb:

And money ran between his hands
Like water through the Ocean Sands.

The proverb appears as a maxim in Thomas Tusser's FIVE HUNDRETH POINTES OF GOOD HUSBANDRIE (1573):

> *A foole and his monie be soone at debate*
> *Which after with sorrow repents him*
> *too late.*

Fools are often helped to dispose of their income by sharp fellows who recognise spendthrift tendencies in others. Walsh tells a contemporary anecdote of the proverb in use. George Buchanan, renowned historian and wit and one-time tutor to James VI of Scotland, once made a wager with a courtier. Buchanan bet that if they both produced a piece of vulgar verse his would be the coarser. The courtier lost and Buchanan scooped up his winnings remarking, *A fool and his money are soon parted*.

I am living proof of the old saying 'a fool and his money are soon parted' after treating myself to a first-class ticket for the eight hour, bum-numbing journey to Inverness. The foolishness lies in giving a huge amount of money to Virgin Trains. When I arrived at New Street brandishing a ticket expensive enough to buy Branson's Caribbean island of Necker, there was, of course, no first-class carriage.
BIRMINGHAM SUNDAY MERCURY, 8 JULY 2001

A fool and his money are soon parted, they say, and Wayne Rooney seems to prove it. But then again, does it matter how he spends his money? To us it shouldn't, except I still find it worrying that professional players can gamble on any football matches.
EVENING STANDARD, 13 APRIL 2006

See also *EASY come, easy go*

fools rush in where angels fear to tread

imprudent people thoughtlessly and rashly tackle situations that the wise think twice about

The proverb comes from Alexander Pope's AN ESSAY ON CRITICISM (1711). Pope is discussing critics who, he says, have the audacity to voice opinions where even more enlightened readers than they would hesitate to criticise:

> *No place so sacred from such fops is barr'd,*
> *Nor is Paul's church more safe than Paul's*
> *churchyard.*
> *Nay, fly to altars; there they'll talk you*
> *dead;*
> *For fools rush in where angels fear to tread.*

Pope's line began to be quoted as a proverb in the early twentieth century, particularly in the United States. The author of POOR RICHARD JR'S ALMANACK (pub. SATURDAY EVENING POST, 1906) uses it to warn against hasty marriage: *Fools rush in where angels fear to wed* and American short story writer O Henry alludes to it in THE MOMENT OF VICTORY (1909):

> *And yet you couldn't fence him away from the girls with barbed wire. You know that kind of young fellows a kind of mixture of fools and angels – they rush in and fear to tread at the same time; but they never fail to tread when they get the chance.*

Later in the same century, again in the United States, the proverb was the subject of a popular love song FOOLS RUSH IN (1940) written by Johnny Mercer and Rube Bloom and performed by Frank Sinatra. When love is in the air, it seems that everyone is a fool.

*But as the old torch song goes, **fools rush in where angels fear to tread**. Instead of proceeding thoughtfully, the genetic industry is rushing ahead pell-mell in the commercial marketplace, developing a plethora of techniques that could be used for human germline engineering.*
WORLD WATCH, 1 JULY 2000

*After 40 years as a forecaster, he is more aware than most of the maxim '**fools rush in where angels fear to tread**'. No fool he. But in he rushed.*
In Wales, East Anglia, and the South and South-West of England, the Whitsun bank holiday on 3 June will, he says, be warm with a risk of the odd shower, but getting better for the special Jubilee bank holiday on 4 June.
EVENING STANDARD, 22 MAY 2002

you can't fool all of the people all of the time

it is possible to deceive people to different degrees, but never totally

Variant: You can't please all of the people all of the time

This piece of proverbial wisdom is part of a longer quotation: *You may fool all of the people some of the time, some of the people all of the time, but not all of the people all of the time.* But who said it? And when? In his LIBRARY OF WIT AND HUMOR (1884) the then Librarian of Congress, Ainsworth R Spofford, attributed the saying to the American showman P T Barnum. The other contender for coinage is Abraham Lincoln, who is proposed by two different sources citing two separate occasions. William P Kellogg asserts that Lincoln used the saying in an unrecorded speech given at Bloomington, Illinois on 29 May 1856, while Alexander K McClure, in his book LINCOLN'S YARNS AND STORIES (1904), claims that Lincoln

was in discussion with a caller at the White House when he said:

If you once forfeit the confidence of your fellow citizens, you can never regain their respect and esteem. It is true that you may fool all the people some of the time; you can even fool some of the people all of the time; but you can't fool all of the people all of the time.

Whoever uttered the wise words, however, was anticipated in both thought and form, as correspondents with NOTES AND QUERIES have pointed out. One of Lincoln's illustrious predecessors as President of the United States had expressed a similar idea: *You may be too cunning for one, but not for all* (Benjamin Franklin, POOR RICHARD'S ALMANACK, 1750), while the form has echoes in La Rochefoucauld's *One may be more clever than another, but not more clever than all the others* (MAXIMES, 1665). And just a few years before Lincoln's Bloomington speech, English essayist John Sterling wrote (ESSAYS AND TALES: THOUGHTS, published posthumously 1848):

There is no lie that many men will not believe; there is no man who does not believe many lies; but there is no man who believes only lies.

Perhaps ultimate credit should be given to Pliny the Younger who, around AD 10, said: *Individuals may deceive and be deceived; but no one ever deceived everybody, nor has everybody ever deceived any one* (PANEGYRICS: TRAJAN).

Mr Hague decided to apply the electrodes and bring his monster twitching back to life. It was a difficult job but he made a good effort. Mr Brown had always listed his tax cuts in the Budget speech, but left others to find the tax rises in the small print. 'He is the thief who steals your car then comes

back in the morning to return your hubcaps,' he said. 'You can't fool all of the people all of the time, but you can fool all Labour MPs on Budget day,' he went on.
GUARDIAN, 8 MARCH 2001

We have never had complaints about our portion size and would say they are much larger than most around. Our dessert list has proven to be the most popular yet, and Pinot Grigio is our best selling wine. How does the saying go? You can't please all of the people all of the time? However, we do try our very best and readers must realise that yours is only one opinion.'
NEWCASTLE JOURNAL, 2 JUNE 2006

FORGIVE

forgive and forget

do not bear a grudge but rather clear the mind of all past wrongs

I forgive and forget appears in OF JOSEPH (c. AD 40), a work by the Hellenised Jewish philosopher Philo Judeaus. Whether or not Philo's charitable sentiments were the inspiration behind the proverb is not known but the phrase certainly put in an early appearance in English literature. The unknown author of the devotional manuscript ANCREN RIWLE (c. 1200) used it in his work, and a century and a half later in PIERS PLOWMAN (1377), William Langland applied the expression to the grace of Christ:

> *So wil Cryst of his curteisye,*
> *and men crye hym mercy,*
> *bothe forgive and forgete.*

As so often happens, Shakespeare had an influence in fixing the phrase in the language, using it a total of four times in his plays. In ALL'S WELL THAT ENDS WELL (1601) there is the present-day order: *I have forgiven and forgotten all*. In KING LEAR (1605) we have the variant: *Pray you now, forget and forgive*.

Usage today has settled for the logical *forgive and forget*, in that forgiving must reasonably precede forgetting. However, as the novelist W E Norris (1847–1925) points out: *We may forgive and we may forget, but we can never forget that we have forgiven*.

'I can't stand all this raking up the past,' they say. 'We need to forgive and forget!'
JENNIFER REES LARCOMBE, JOURNEY INTO GOD'S HEART, 2006

I noticed it in Hanoi, after the Vietnam war. The Vietnamese were touchingly ready to forgive and forget. Americans, by contrast, accused the Vietnamese of concealing hundreds of their prisoners-of-war in caves.
DAILY TELEGRAPH, 24 MARCH 2006

Usage: A laudable exhortation which – perhaps because it is easier said than done – might be resented by the person to whom it is addressed

See also *Let BYGONES be bygones*

to err is human, to forgive divine

everyone makes mistakes but forgiving them is more of a challenge

The frailty of human nature has been recognised and lamented for centuries. *Being human I erred* a character in Menander's Greek comedy PHANIUM (c. 300 BC) confesses. *It is human to err* pronounced a more matter-of-fact Seneca (NATURALES QUAESTIONES c. AD 62). This Latin proverb of Greek inspiration was quoted extensively by ancient writers, and in the Latin works of the early Church fathers. St Augustine gave a Christian cast to the proverb in encouraging his readers to fight against the flesh, *It is human to err; it is devilish to remain wilfully in error* (SERMONS, c. AD 400), possibly taking his inspiration from the secular Cicero: *Any man may err, but nobody but a fool persists in error* (PHILIPPICS, 43 BC).

But it was Alexander Pope who, with remarkable insight into human nature and a genius for condensing great truth into a few telling words, gave the proverb yet another dimension and coined the wording we know today: *To err is human, to forgive divine* (AN ESSAY ON CRITICISM, 1711). There is a contrast between the tendency in man to sin and the characteristic in God to forgive. When man does forgive, it is in imitation of his maker. In a more secular age, it is perhaps not surprising that the second half of the proverb is frequently omitted today – or simply reworked after the model of this little quip: *To err is human, but to really foul things up requires a computer.*

'…You know that our present Pope has a picture of the Madonna painted above the entrance to his bedroom? Only she has the face of his mistress… Oh, yes. It is said that his table groans under the weight of so many roasted song birds that the woods around Rome are silent now, and that his children are welcomed into the house as if sin were no sin at all. But then to err is human, wouldn't you say?
SARAH DUNANT, THE BIRTH OF VENUS, 2003

'To err is human, to forgive divine!' Forgiveness is not only admirable, it's empowering. And experts say it can free you mentally, physically and spiritually.
JET, 17 APRIL 2006

See also *Even HOMER sometimes nods*

FREE

the best things in life are free
the qualities that make life worth living cannot be bought

The proverb is the title of a song written by DeSylva, Brown and Henderson for the musical GOOD NEWS. The show opened on 6 September 1927 in New York. In 1956, a film entitled THE BEST THINGS IN LIFE ARE FREE was made, based on the lives of the songwriters.

The song, which starts with the line *'The moon belongs to everyone'*, expresses the sentiment that love is priceless; it cannot be bought.

*Last night I sat looking at the beautiful sky, it was filled with the most dramatic clouds and had a deep-red glow. It was a reminder that **the best things in life are free**.*
WALES ON SUNDAY, 7 MARCH 2004

*Yes, yes. We all know that the best things in life are free – a crocus peeking through the snow, a baby's smile, and all that. But when Melanie Rogers says the **best things in life are free**, she's talking things, literally. Things you don't have to pay for. The Sandusky woman hauls in free stuff by the mailbox – shampoo, perfume, pens and pencils, calculators, candles, T-shirts, popcorn, tote bags. Photo albums, video games, shoes, CDs, mugs, water bottles, coffee, magazine subscriptions.*
TOLEDO BLADE, 29 JANUARY 2006

FRIEND

a friend in need is a friend indeed
a friend who will support you when you are in need of help is a true friend

Variant: A friend in need is a friend in deed

People have pondered the nature of true friendship since ancient times and, unsurprisingly, have concluded that the test of a relationship comes in time of difficulty. Aesop tells of two friends who were travelling together when they saw a bear. One of them quickly climbed a nearby tree; the other, seeing no chance of escape, lay down on the ground pretending to be dead. The bear began to nuzzle him, and he held his breath, for no bear will touch a corpse. At last, the bear gave up and went away, and the man's companion came down from the safety of his tree. '*What was it that the bear was whispering in your ear?*' he asked. '*The wise bear advised me not to travel in future with friends who abandon me in times of trouble,*' came the reply. Bartlett traces the proverb back as far as the playwright Plautus who, in EPIDICUS (c. 200 BC), writes: *Nothing is there dearer to a man than a friend in need.*

References to companions proving themselves in time of need are found in English literature from the twelfth century onwards. *A sug fere is his help in mod* (A safe companion one that helps in need), for instance, is recorded in the PROVERBS OF ALFRED (c. 1251), a collection of popular wisdom and instruction expressed in pithy alliterative proverbs, some of which were probably coined by Alfred the Great. And in William Caxton's fifteenth century translation of FABLES OF ESOPE (1484) we find: *The very and trewe frend is fond in the extreme need.* Just over half a century later (PROVERBS, 1546), John Heywood extends the thought, meditating upon the fickleness of friendships which he had assumed to be strong:

> *A freende is neuer knowen tyll a man haue neede.*
> *Before I had neede, my most present foes Semed my most freends, but thus the world goes.*

He was proving the truth of a French proverb which says *Prosperity gives friends, adversity proves them*, which itself goes back to the Latin maxims of Publilius Syrus in the first century BC.

During the sixteenth century, writers working in rhyme found the words *need* and *indeed* a convenient coupling when expressing the proverb. By 1678 the words were linked permanently, the proverb appearing in John Ray's collection of ENGLISH PROVERBS in its present-day form.

The proverb says: 'A friend in need is a friend indeed.' There are many who have found themselves in need,but at their time of need their so-called friends have deserted them.
DAILY POST, 13 JUNE 2003

A friend in need is a friend indeed. And if you are a friend of the Rev. J. Pat Branch, you can count on him to lend a helping hand. The longtime volunteer and coordinator for the Fellowship of Christian Cowboys has been named the 2006 recipient of the Jefferson Award for outstanding public service.
TWIN FALLS TIMES-NEWS,
9 MARCH 2006

Usage: The two variants in the form of the proverb sound alike to the ear and reflect an interesting ambiguity of sense. *Indeed* acts as an adverb, intensifying what has gone before. *In deed* means that a friend is the one that actually does something practical to help out, rather than just making encouraging noises.

FRUIT

forbidden fruit is the sweetest
if we are forbidden to do or have something, the object of our desire becomes all the more alluring

Variants: Forbidden fruit is sweet/ sweeter; Stolen fruit is the sweetest

One of the oldest references to the notion that stolen pleasures are sweetest comes in the biblical OLD TESTAMENT book of PROVERBS 9:17 (c. 350 BC): *Stolen waters are sweet and bread eaten in secret is pleasant.* In English literature, from the fifteenth to the nineteenth centuries, a variety of delights have been declared *sweetest* just because they have been stolen, and so have that extra spice: drink, fruit, venison, pleasure, apples, gold, meat and, of course, glances – *Stolen glances, sweeter for the theft* (Byron, DON JUAN, 1818). Thomas Randolph expresses the notion beautifully in SONG OF FAIRIES (c. 1635):

> *Stolen sweets are sweeter;*
> *Stolen kisses much completer,*
> *Stolen looks are nice in chapels;*
> *Stolen, stolen be your apples.*

And a down-to-earth Arabic proverb simply states that *Everything forbidden is sweet.*

As to the issue of stolen apples (as in Thomas Randal's verse) over the stolen fruit of the present-day proverb, there is a long tradition going back to Plutarch in c. AD 100 that refers to the allure of stolen apples. There is also the influence of the popular belief that Eve plucked the forbidden apple in the Garden of Eden. In fact, the book of Genesis talks only of a forbidden fruit. The proverb settled into its present-day form in the nineteenth century with *forbidden* replacing *stolen*, again probably an allusion to the forbidden fruit of the Garden of Eden.

*For years, traditional martial arts were prohibited in the Soviet Union. But, as the proverb states, **forbidden fruit is sweet**. The number of admirers of martial arts continued to grow, and naturally they desired to learn more of Chinese tradition.* WORLD AND I, 1 MAY 2000

*Instead, more Muslims here in the Fergana Valley are becoming intrigued by the group. 'The **forbidden fruit is sweeter**,' said Akhmad Madmarov, 59, an activist with the Independent Human Rights Organization of Uzbekistan. 'We know from history that any movement forbidden by the state will be the center of attention and more people will join it.'* THE WASHINGTON POST, 27 SEPTEMBER 2003

See also *The GRASS is always greener on the other side of the fence*

G

GAIN

no pain, no gain

no progress is ever made without cost

Variant: No gain without pain

This proverb has been associated with the exercise and fitness industry since the 1980s, which gives it a modern ring. It is used to suggest that it is impossible to have a perfect body without first enduring burning muscles and exhaustion but the end result is worth all the discomfort. Since then, the saying has been used as a means of encouragement in any area where unwelcome effort is demanded.

However, in spite of its modern profile, the proverb is centuries old. *Who will the fruyte that haruest yeeldes, must take the payne*, writes John Grange in THE GOLDEN APHRODITIS (1577), and the rhyming *No gaine without pain* appears shortly afterwards in Leonard Wright's DISPLAY OF DUTIE (1589). Indeed, this form of the proverb was used in 1952 by Adlai Stevenson as he accepted the nomination as the Democratic presidential candidate: *Let's talk sense to the American people. Let's tell them the truth, that there are no gains without pains.*

In a speech delivered in October 1989, future Prime Minister John Major commented on British government financial policy with the words *The harsh truth is that if the policy isn't hurting it isn't working*, a new twist on an old proverb.

*Catherine Gupta, a sports nutritionist from Littlemore, near Oxford, wants me to take a steadier approach in training than the **no gain without pain**, eyeballs-out approach suggested by Keith Wood last month.*
DAILY TELEGRAPH, 29 APRIL 2004

*A picture shows him a few days later in hospital, trying to look cheery with a broken right humerus. Ecstasy and agony are inextricably linked in the minds of those brought up with sport's '**no pain, no gain**' ethic.*
GUARDIAN, 24 MARCH 2006

GOD

God helps those who help themselves

self-help stimulates divine assistance; if you want to succeed you need to make an effort

Ancient literature holds many references to the fact that we can only expect divine help if we are prepared to play our part, too. The Greek dramatist Aeschylus (525–456 BC) expresses the thought more than once, and one of Aesop's fables, HERCULES AND THE WAGGONER (c. 570 BC), carries the same message. A waggoner was driving along a muddy track when his cart skidded into a ditch. Instead of doing something about it, the waggoner called upon the mighty Hercules for help. The god appeared and told the waggoner to put his shoulder behind the wheel and goad his oxen on. Hercules then scolded the man, forbidding him to ever call for help again unless he had first made an effort himself.

English and other European languages have coined a great number of quaint proverbs to express the idea of self-help: the French, for instance, say *God never builds us bridges, but he gives us hands*; and the Spanish *While waiting for water from heaven, don't stop irrigating*.

Similarly, many European languages have the proverb *God helps those who help themselves*. In English before the eighteenth century, the thought was variously expressed: Richard Taverner, in his PROVERBS OR ADAGES (1545) taken from the CHILIADES of Erasmus has the Latin proverb *The goddes do helpe the doers*; John Baret tells us that *God doth help those in their affaires, which are industrious* (AN ALVEARIE, 1580); and George Herbert in his JACULA PRUDENTUM (1640) has *Help thyself, and God will help thee*. Then, in POOR RICHARD'S ALMANACK of 1736, Benjamin Franklin coins or records the present-day form of the proverb.

The specialist schools movement is the Government's way of saying 'God Helps Those Who Help Themselves'. Under the drive, schools wanting to benefit from considerable amounts of extra public money must prove their worth.
BIRMINGHAM POST, 27 JULY 2005

If God helps those who help themselves, why should taxpayers be expected to do more?
BOSTON GLOBE, 4 APRIL 2007

God made the country, and man made the town
the beauty of the countryside is preferable to urban sprawl

The proverb is a line from Cowper's poem THE TASK (1785) but, since there is nothing new under the sun, the thought is not a new one. The

inspiration comes from DE RE RUSTICA (c. 35 BC), a work by the Roman scholar Varro: *Divine nature gave the country, human art built the cities*. There are also echoes of Cowper's line in Abraham Cowley's essay THE GARDEN (1656): *God the first garden made, and the first city Cain*. But Cowper's rendering is simple, quotable and memorable, and has become proverbial.

According to Alfred Ainger, Cowper's line was later extended by Tennyson: *The Borough...reminds us of a saying of Tennyson's, that if God made the country, and man made the city, then it was the devil who made the country-town* (ENGLISH MEN OF LETTERS: CRABBE, 1903).

'God made the country, and man made the town.' While pious myths of pastoral purity still appeal, no one seriously imagines the countryside as the seedbed of the arts – recall Marx's gibe about the 'idiocy' of rural life.
DAILY TELEGRAPH, 22 JANUARY 2001

The old proverb 'God made the country; man made the town; and the Devil made the little country town' certainly applies to Fedborough, the setting for Simon Brett's pacey whodunit. This imaginary Sussex town with its antique dealers, gift shops, twee tearooms and streets 'clotted with the elderly contents of coaches, and foreign language students' is fermenting beneath the postcard surface with class resentment, snobbery, grudges and general devilment.
DAILY MAIL, 15 FEBRUARY 2002

God tempers the wind to the shorn lamb
God is especially tender in his protection of the weak; God softens the trials that the defenceless have to endure

Those who do not think the proverb biblical often attribute it to Laurence

Sterne. In his SENTIMENTAL JOURNEY THROUGH FRANCE AND ITALY: MARIA (1768), Parson Yorick meets up with Maria, a character from TRISTRAM SHANDY, an earlier work. Maria is a little mad. Since their last meeting, she has roamed all over Lombardy, penniless and with no shoes on her feet. Asked how she had borne it and how she had fared, Maria can only reply, *God tempers the wind to the shorn lamb*.

The saying is, in fact, Sterne's poetic rendering of an old French proverb *Dieu mesure le froid à la brebis tondue* (recorded by Henri Estienne in 1594), which he properly puts into the mouth of a French character. A literal translation of a variant recorded by Labou in 1610 can be found in George Herbert's JACULA PRUDENTUM (1640): *To a close shorn sheep, God gives wind by measure*. Correctly, of course, only sheep and not lambs are shorn.

...a young policeman...took charge...He put rocks under the front wheels...It didn't work. The Mazda sank deeper...He drove away...A bearded Ma'ariv newspaper photographer from the Beersheva Bureau showed up and took several flash pictures of me and my car...We didn't make the Ma'ariv next day, to my disappointment. But God tempers the wind to the shorn lamb, and he visited a bit of misery on my gentle tormenter, to cheer me up. The Ma'ariv photographer also got stuck in the mud.
PALM BEACH POST, 29 JANUARY 2001

A mid-Wales couple were last night landed with a £200,000 church repairs bill following a lengthy legal battle against ecclesiastical law. Andrew and Gail Wallbank spent seven years fighting an archaic law which states they are responsible for the upkeep of a Warwickshire church...
At a High Court hearing in London yesterday to assess the extent of the couple's liability Mr Justice Lewison reached a

figure of £186,969, plus VAT, on some, but not all, items in the repair schedule...The judge said Mr Wallbank, in arguing the action against them, was 'anachronistic and unfair', had said the Church should stick to its own teaching – that 'God tempers the wind to the shorn lamb'.
LIVERPOOL DAILY POST, 6 FEBRUARY 2007

Usage: For all its poetic qualities, the proverb is not frequent today

man proposes but God disposes
people may make plans but cannot control the outcome

The ancients acknowledged the power of the gods to order puny man's plans: *Man intends one thing, Fate another.* (Publilius Syrus, SENTENTIAE, c. 43 BC) or *By many forms of artifice the gods Defeat our plans, for they are stronger far* (Euripides, FRAGMENTS, c. 440 BC).

Such a view is easily assimilated into Christian thinking with an omniscient and omnipotent God taking the place of the jealous and capricious ancient deities. Thomas à Kempis, in his DE IMITATIONE CHRISTI (c. 1420) finds the source of the Latin proverb *Homo proponit, sed Deus disponit* (Man proposes, but God disposes) in two biblical texts. PROVERBS 16:9 reads: *A man's heart deviseth his way: but the Lord directeth his steps*. And JEREMIAH 10:23 has: *O Lord, know that the way of man is not in himself, it is not in man that walketh to direct his steps*. Other authors have pointed to more passages of Scripture (PROVERBS 16:33, JAMES 4:15) on the same theme.

However, William Langland, writing some 43 years earlier, attributes the proverb to Plato, as this passage from PIERS PLOWMAN (1377) indicates:

Homo proponit, *quod a poete, and
Plato he hyght,
And* Deus disponit, *quod he, let God
done his wille.*

Nothing in Plato's work, however,
matches the wording of the proverb –
the nearest being a reference to an
ancient proverb *Human affairs are
not what a man wishes, but what he can
bring about.*

Langland's citation of the proverb
indicates just how long it has been in
circulation in England. It has an
equally long history throughout
Europe, being found from Sweden to
Italy, and quite different cultures
acknowledge the general wisdom. The
following are echoes from collections of
Chinese proverbs:

Man may plan, but Heaven executes.

*Men, without divine assistance,
Cannot move an inch of distance.*

*Man says, so! so!
Heaven says, no, no.*

*You can be what you choose to be if you
want it bad enough. Success comes with a
price. Let it not be at the expense of your
soul. Destiny is in your own hands. It must
be carefully planned and sculpted. Does
an element of 'luck' or feng-shui count?
Figure out for yourself.* **Man proposes
but God disposes!**
NEW STRAITS TIMES, 17 JANUARY 2004

*Man proposes, but God disposes. There
are, I imagine, just about 100 underclass
faculty advisers, meaning, according to my
challenged math, that the odds that any
particular entering freshman will be
assigned to any particular adviser are
about a 100 to one. When you luck out
against those odds, you know His eye is
on the sparrow.*
UNIVERSITY WIRE, 17 APRIL 2006

GODLINESS

cleanliness is next to godliness
keeping clean is second only to living
an upright life

Much importance has always been
given to personal cleanliness in Middle
Eastern countries. Herodotus, the
Greek historian writing in the fifth
century BC, informs us that it was the
practice of Egyptian priests to bathe
four times a day. He writes that the
Egyptians *set cleanliness above seemliness.*
The Jewish Talmud, a foundation upon
which Jewish law rests, insisted that
every Jewish community should
maintain a public bathhouse. The
pursuit of cleanliness and hygiene
became very much a cult of purity –
incidentally ensuring a high standard
of health. The Talmud explicitly links
the physical to the spiritual: *'Cleanliness
is next to godliness,'* it is said. *Carefulness
leads to cleanliness, cleanliness to purity,
purity to humility, humility to saintliness,
saintliness to fear of sin, fear of sin to
holiness, and holiness to immortality.* And
no excuses can be made for lapses in
purity, for a Talmudic precept states:
Poverty comes from God, but not dirt.

It is impossible to say exactly how
or when the proverb arose from these
beginnings but the notion that
cleanliness and spirituality are linked
was current in Christian thinking long
before the early seventeenth century, as
Francis Bacon tells us (OF THE
ADVANCEMENT OF LEARNING,
1605): *Cleanliness of body was ever deemed
to proceed from a due reverence to God.*
According to Thomas Fuller (THE
WORTHIES OF ENGLAND, 1655),
Sir Edward Coke concurred with this
doctrine so that he was very particular
about his own personal cleanliness:
*...and the jewel of his mind was put into a
fair case, a beautiful body, with a comely
countenance; a case which he did wipe and
keep clean, delighting in good cloaths, well*

worne, and being wont to say, that the outward neatness of our bodies might be a monitor of purity to our souls.

In similar vein, the proverb itself was used by the great evangelical John Wesley to reinforce his message (SERMONS: ON DRESS, c. 1780). Discussing the view expressed in I PETER 3:3–4 that one should not pay much attention to one's outward appearance but should concentrate on one's spiritual state, he comments: *Slovenliness is no part of religion; neither this, nor any text of Scripture, condemns neatness of apparel. Certainly this is a duty, not a sin; 'cleanliness is indeed next to godliness'.*

In Victorian England, keeping one's home clean was regarded as a moral duty which had to be performed before the Lord's Day. Cleanliness became so closely associated with purity that people assumed that those known to live in sin would necessarily have filthy houses. In the diary written in the 1870s while he was vicar of Bredwardine, Francis Kilvert expresses his astonishment at the cleanliness of one such household.

But not everyone found absolute wisdom in the proverb. Mary Baker Eddy, founder of the Christian Scientist sect, did not like to take its injunction to extremes. In SCIENCE AND HEALTH (1875) she tried to loosen the bond between cleanliness and godliness, fearing that people might imagine themselves spiritual simply by virtue of having a daily washdown, or that they might do themselves irreparable harm by exposing their bodies to too much water: *Cleanliness is next to godliness; but washing should be only for the purpose of keeping the body clean, and this can be effected without scrubbing the whole surface daily. Water is not the natural habitat of humanity.* In these days of the daily,

sometimes twice daily, bath or shower, one wonders if Mrs Eddy's concern for our bodily welfare will be proved right.

Cleanliness is next to Godliness, and these days there is little of either around. The failure of many food outlets to pass hygiene rules may sicken the appetite a little.
IRISH DAILY MIRROR, 29 JUNE 2002

It might sound like a storm in a (chipped) teacup, but this week's revelation that Laura Bush has been denigrating Hillary Clinton's housekeeping skills at the White House is, as you might expect, indicative of a larger story… Mrs Bush's message could not be clearer: Senator Clinton – a possible contender to be the first female president – is liable to make a mess of things. There are other inferences at work here, as well: if **cleanliness is next to godliness** *in Mrs Bush's world, then her predecessor is verging on the disreputable.*
DAILY TELEGRAPH, 7 APRIL 2006

GODS

whom the gods love dies young
words of comfort on a person's early death

Variant: God takes soonest those whom he loves best

The Greek historian Herodotus includes in his HISTORY (c. 445 BC) this incident told by the wise Athenian statesman Solon. A woman was anxious to go to the temple for the festival of the goddess Hera but the oxen who drew her cart could not be found, so her two young sons, Cleobis and Biton, took the yoke on their own backs and pulled her there themselves. Touched by their thoughtfulness, the mother beseeched Hera to bestow upon her sons the greatest of all blessings. When the two young men lay down to rest they never awoke. The proverb, *Whom the gods love dies young*, celebrates the virtue and blissful reward of Cleobis and Biton, and may have been coined in this form by the Greek poet Menander writing some 125 years later.

In the centuries which passed before the benefits of present-day medical understanding, early death was common and the proverb was a solace for grief. In 1553, Thomas Wilson published his ARTE OF RHETORIQUE in which he remodelled Menander's adage: *Whom God loueth best, those he taketh soonest*. Wilson's wording came to be used on many tombstones in all parts of the country. One such stone from Rainham churchyard in Kent, dated 1626, reads:

Here slepes my babe in silance, heauen's his rest,
For God takes soonest those he loueth best

Another from Morwenstow in Cornwall has:

Those whom God loves die young!
They see no evil days;
No falsehood taints their tongue,
No wickedness their ways.
Baptized, and so made sure
To win their blest abode,
What shall we pray for more?
Then die and are with God.

The following delight comes from near Hartford, Connecticut (HARPER'S MAGAZINE, AUGUST 1856):

Here lies two babies so dead as nits;
De Lord he kilt them with his ague fits.
When dey was too good to live mit me,
He took dem up to live mit He,
So he did.

But the proverb seems to brush aside those who live to a good old age yet whose life is a rich source of blessing to those it touches. Are they less worthy than those plucked in their youth? Elbert Hubbard pondered the same question and found a true answer: *Whom the gods love die young, no matter how long they live* (EPIGRAMS, 'THE PHILISTINE', 1907).

Paul Getty died too soon. There is a saying that those whom God wishes to destroy, He first makes mad. But in Paul, He was against sterner stuff. His benevolence and pleasure in his life, despite everything, was there until the end. I prefer to think of the proverb: 'Those whom the gods love die young.'
MAIL ON SUNDAY, 20 APRIL 2003

Mark Foster, 27, a talented cricketer and rugby player, was found dead at his home in Middlesbrough last Saturday...Today Mark's father David, a 58-year-old teacher living in Cambridge, spoke of the family's heartbreak.
'Now, as we say goodbye to Mark, whose life was so tragically cut short, we hope that he will be fondly remembered and spoken of kindly for many years to come. As the Greeks said, "Those whom the Gods love die young".'
MIDDLESBROUGH EVENING GAZETTE, 2 DECEMBER 2005

See also *The GOOD die young*

GOLD

all that glitters is not gold
nothing should be judged by its external appearance; superficial attractiveness does not necessarily denote solid worth

Variants: All that glisters is not gold; All is not gold that glitters

AN ACCUMULATION OF WISDOM

The last of Erasmus's editions of his great ADAGIA (see Erasmus's ADAGIA, page 34) was published in 1536, some ten years before the first collection of English proverbs: John Heywood's A DIALOGUE CONTEINING THE NUMBER IN EFFECT OF ALL THE PROVERBES IN THE ENGLISHE TONGUE (1546). Heywood subsequently produced three collections of epigrams at five-year intervals from 1550 to 1560.

From Heywood, a king's entertainer, to Fergusson, a king's minister. The latter was Moderator of the General Assembly of the Church of Scotland and at the court of King James VI. He died in 1598 but his SCOTTISH PROVERBS was not published until 1641. This was the beginning of quite a British clerical tradition of collecting proverbs (although it could be argued that this began with Erasmus, who had been an Augustinian monk and, while in England, had received the benefice of Aldington in Kent from Archbishop Warham). Thomas Draxe was an English clergyman who published in 1612 his BIBLIOTHECA SCHOLASTICA INSTRUCTISSIMA OR, A TREASURE OF ANCIENT ADAGIES, AND SENTENTIOUS PROUERBES. Next in line was Pastor John Clarke and his PAROEMIOLOGIA ANGLO-LATINA of 1639. George Herbert was another Churchman who interested himself in proverbs. His OUTLANDISH PROVERBS was published in 1640, some seven years after his death. It is best known in its 1651 edition, extended by a later editor as JACULA PRUDENTUM. Perhaps that same editor was responsible for the inspired new title – it means 'javelins of the wise'.

---

*Non teneas aurum totum quod splendet
ut aurum,
Nec pulchrum pomum quodlibet
esse bonum.*
(Do not hold to be gold everything that shines like gold, Nor every fine apple to be good.)

These words, recorded in the Winchester College Hall-book of 1401–2, are lines from the PARABOLAE of Alanus de Insulis, a French monk and poet writing in the twelfth century. That is not to say that Alanus de Insulis coined the proverb, which is common to several European languages by way of medieval Latin, merely that he expressed the thought in something like its current form.

The idea that outward appearance can be misleading was already an old one, having been thoroughly explored by the ancients: several of Aesop's fables are on the theme, including THE LEOPARD AND THE FOX (c. 570 BC), which tells us that we should *look to the mind, and not to the outward appearance*; Diogenes of Sinope discovers *In an ivory scabbard a sword of lead* (c. 400 BC); Livius Andronicus explains that *In noble trappings march ignoble men* (VIRGA, c. 235 BC) and Petronius remarks that *He sees the copper under the silver* (SATYRICON, c. AD 60).

Chaucer took inspiration from Alanus de Insulis for his Canterbury Tales. In THE CANON'S YEOMAN'S TALE (c. 1386), he writes:

*But al thing which that shyneth as the gold
Nis rat gold, as that I have herd it told;
Ne every appel that is fair at ye
Ne is nat good, what-so men clappe or crey.*

The next collections of especial note are those of James Howell (1659) and John Ray (1670). The former is strong on proverbs from other cultures and languages, resulting from his wide study and travel; the latter is well organised, with many new entries and learned notes.

The succeeding centuries brought reprints of these old works or 'new' collections that were the same old ones, but with additions. Landmarks are: James Kelly (1721) COMPLETE COLLECTION OF SCOTTISH PROVERBS; Thomas Fuller (1732) GNOMOLOGIA: ADAGIES AND PROVERBS; William Carew Hazlitt (1869) ENGLISH PROVERBS AND PROVERBIAL PHRASES; Vincent Stuckey Lean (1902–4) COLLECTANEA; George Latimer Apperson (1929) ENGLISH PROVERBS AND PROVERBIAL PHRASES

In more recent years there have been several editions of THE OXFORD DICTIONARY OF ENGLISH PROVERBS since its first publication in 1935.

In the United States of America there have been a number of works of real importance. Benjamin Franklin's POOR RICHARD'S ALMANACK flourished from 1733 to 1758. In the twentieth century undoubtedly the major work is Burton Stevenson's BOOK OF PROVERBS, MAXIMS AND FAMILIAR PHRASES of 1949. Its 3,000 pages are a master work of scholarship. More recently, decades of work carried out by the American Dialect Society have resulted in A DICTIONARY OF AMERICAN PROVERBS (1992).

Parœmiology – the study of proverbs – is fortunate to have had the benefit of the prodigious energies and intellect of so many writers through the centuries.

It was not until the second half of the eighteenth century that the word glitters entered the saying. David Garrick used it in the Prologue to Goldsmith's play SHE STOOPS TO CONQUER in 1773. Before then gold had *shone, shown a goldish hue, shone bright, glowed, glistened and glistered.*

An Italian variant of this international proverb is particularly appealing: *Every glow-worm is not a fire.*

After a dismal attempt at college Jason Florio fled London to go skateboarding and wrangle horses in Dallas, Texas. He soon found himself in the clutches of the New York fashion world, working as an assistant to some of its top photographers. But with the realisation that 'all that glisters is not gold' he took up an invitation to rejuvenate his soul in the Gambian bush...
GEOGRAPHICAL MAGAZINE,
1 JUNE 2001

Six of Zimbabwe's star footballers were on the run in Britain yesterday after failing to turn up for their flight...[Taru Simbi] predicted it would only be a matter of days before the missing footballers were found. 'The Zimbabwean community is fairly small, and does not want to be associated with people not going back home like this. I think the players will realise that all that glitters is not gold when they realise that in England you have to work hard for your money and you don't just dig gold from the streets.'
GUARDIAN, 26 SEPTEMBER 2005

See *Never judge by APPEARANCES*; *APPEARANCES are deceptive*; *Medieval Latin*, page 214

GOOD

the good die young

said to express frustration or anger that a virtuous young person has died while many wicked people live to a ripe old age

Variant: Only the good die young

Alse sone deyeth the yong as the olde is a matter-of-fact statement by the unknown author of the GESTA ROMANORUM, a medieval collection of anecdotes on themes suitable for preachers. A rather more colourful way of saying the same thing, that both young and old die, is *As soon goeth the yonge lamskyn to the market, as th'olde yewes*, a proverb dating from at least the early sixteenth century.

But in his poem THE EXCURSION (1814), Wordsworth bewails the fact that it is the young who are also virtuous who die early:

> *The good die first,*
> *And they whose hearts are dry as*
> *summer dust*
> *Burn to the socket*

The good die young is now a common proverb. A more recent turn of phrase is *Only the good die young*.

*It cannot be true that **only the good die young**, but the loss of Helen Chadwick in 1996 at the age of 42 was untimely for fans of her art as well as for the artist's family and friends. Helen had established herself as an audacious and significant figure, and this retrospective of her work, previously at the Barbican Art Gallery in London, is a salutary reminder of what we've lost.*
INDEPENDENT, 13 NOVEMBER 2004

Only the good die young, they used to say. Young heroes, poets, children – their lives cut off far too soon – have always

brought out deep sympathy and affection and often bred legends.
MIRROR, 1 OCTOBER 2005

See also *Whom the GODS love dies young*

one good turn deserves another

kindness should be reciprocal; if someone does you a particular favour take the opportunity to repay it

The principle that favours should be reciprocal is ancient: *Favour is for favour due*, writes Euripides in HELEN (c. 412 BC).

A Latin manuscript from around 1400 is our earliest record of the proverb which is later cited in the same form by John Heywood: *One good tourne askth an other* (PROVERBS, 1546). Bishop Joseph Hall found that one good turn *requires* another (CONTEMPLATIONS, 1622) but, by the first half of the seventeenth century, the proverb had settled into the present-day form.

In English this notion of mutual help was expressed in other forms, too. *Ka me, ka thee* meant 'claw me and I'll claw you', paying back kind for kind as in *You scratch my BACK and I'll scratch yours*, although *Ka me, ka thee* could refer not only to reciprocal help but also to flattery, or even injury. *If you'll be so kind to ka me one good turn, I'll be so courteous to kob you another*, write Dekker and Ford in THE WITCH OF EDMONTON (c. 1623). But John Skelton refers to a man in a more suspicious frame of mind: *Yea, sayde the hostler, ka me, ka thee; yf she dooe hurte me, I wyll displease her* (WORKS, c. 1568).

The Scottish term for this give and take, this mutual help is *giff-gaff*. It appeared in the proverbs *Giff-gaff was a good fellow* and *Giff-gaff makes good friends*. *Giffe gaffe is one good turn for another*, says John Ray (ENGLISH PROVERBS, 1670).

*George the friendly dolphin...began his impromptu visit to Lyme Regis on Friday evening. And word of his arrival spread so fast that the Dorset harbour was soon crammed with people eager to see him. George did not disappoint them, letting children of all ages swim with him. But **one good turn deserves another** – and George let everyone know he expected his tummy tickled in the shallow water.*
DAILY MIRROR, 5 AUGUST 2002

*Set in Brooklyn, the film boasts three lonely, creative heroes: snap-happy tobacconist Auggie, blocked writer Paul Benjamin, and black schoolboy Rashid. In the summer of 1990, Rashid saves Benjamin's life. **One good turn deserves another**, and another... and slowly these lives become entwined. Rashid needs a father figure; Auggie an audience; Paul plot-lines. But can the men get what they want without stealing from each other?*
INDEPENDENT ON SUNDAY,
15 JUNE 2003

See also *You scratch my BACK and I'll scratch yours*

GOOSE

what is sauce for the goose is sauce for the gander
what is good enough for one person is good enough for another in similar circumstances

The sixteenth century had a proverb *As well as for the coowe calf as for the bull*. The proverb of goose and gander is a variant first recorded by John Ray in ENGLISH PROVERBS (1670). Ray calls it a *woman's proverb* because it makes a plea for equality and fairness in the treatment of male and female alike.

The recommended sauce is the same whether one is serving a goose or a gander for dinner. Perhaps the sauce our seventeenth century forebears had

in mind was a gooseberry one. One authority claims that gooseberries are so called because, centuries ago, their fruit went into a sauce that was enjoyed with roast goose. THE OXFORD DICTIONARY OF ENGLISH ETYMOLOGY allows that a derivation from *goose* and *berry* is a possibility, although it prefers an old French origin. Whatever the origin of the word, gooseberry sauce is still served with geese and ganders today, its sharp acidity cutting through the greasier taste of the meat.

*...courts should stop sending young people to prison for a short, sharp shock. It disrupts people's lives and is less effective than non-custodial community schemes in changing the behaviour of offenders. **If this is sauce for the gosling, why not the goose?** Penal reformers have been urging ministers to apply the same approach to adults for years.*
GUARDIAN, 29 AUGUST 2001

...what is sauce for the goose is sauce for the gander and if you offer anonymity to an alleged victim, you should do the same for the accused.
NEWCASTLE JOURNAL, 1 AUGUST 2003

Usage: The early context was of the relationship between men and women. This very quickly broadened to apply to an apparent imbalance in any sphere.

GRASS

the grass is always greener on the other side of the fence
the belief that a change in one's surroundings or circumstances will get rid of one's problems or frustrations, often said of people who are always changing

Variant: The grass is always greener on the other side of the hill

This is a modern American proverb. Written references date back only to the mid-twentieth century, although the human condition it describes is as old as the hills; if only our lifestyle/family/relationship/place of work were like our friend's/neighbour's/boss's, our lives would be so much happier.

Others' lifestyles, possessions or skills may be enviable but not, perhaps, objectively desirable for after all, as the American psychologist and marriage guidance counsellor Dr James Dobson put it: *The grass may seem greener on the other side but it still needs mowing.*

The old maxim that the grass is always greener on the other side of the fence doesn't always ring true for footballers. The game's history is littered with players who have taken the leap only to find it fallow rather than fertile.
SOUTH WALES ECHO, 20 OCTOBER 2006

The grass is always greener on the other side of the fence, but for many of today's city-dwellers the supposed lifestyle advantages of rural living must seem irresistible. There is less crime in the countryside; the schools are better; there's a stronger sense of community; people have time to stop and talk to you; there are family-run small shops; it is a cleaner, better place to bring children up.
BIRMINGHAM POST, 31 MARCH 2007

See also *Forbidden FRUIT is the sweetest*

GREEKS

beware of Greeks bearing gifts
when a kindness comes from an enemy or a rival, scrutinise his motives

Variant: Fear the Greeks bearing gifts

The proverb is a line from Virgil's AENEID (19 BC) where Laocoön says: *Quidquid id est, timeo Danaos et dona ferentes* (Whatever it is, I fear the Greeks even when they bring gifts). The reference is to the Trojan horse. The Greeks had laid siege to Troy for ten years in an effort to take back the beautiful Helen of Sparta, but the city was so well fortified that it withstood every assault. Then Odysseus thought of a plan. The Greeks constructed a huge wooden horse, which they left outside the city gates before appearing to sail away. The Trojans took the horse to be a gift from the demoralised and vanquished Greeks and, in spite of Laocoön's misgivings, brought it into the city thinking it a good omen. But the horse contained soldiers who crept out under the cover of darkness to open the city gates. The Greek ships had returned at nightfall and, when the gates swung open, their troops laid the city waste. Aeneas was the only Trojan prince to escape and he became the progenitor of Rome.

Samuel Johnson used the Latin phrase *Timeo Danaos et dona ferentes* in a letter to James Boswell in 1777, and allusions to the proverbial warning have been in use ever since. The present-day saying appears in ROGET'S THESAURUS OF ENGLISH WORDS AND PHRASES (1852).

Craig Reedie is a member of the 'new broom' IOC co-ordination committee which has replaced the scandal-scourged system of Olympic city assessment. So did he beware of Greeks bearing gifts? 'Well, I was given a computer mouse mat with the Athens 2004 logo. But you can take it my conscience is clear.'
INDEPENDENT, 26 NOVEMBER 2000

Long ago it was: 'Beware of Greeks bearing gifts.' Nowadays it ought to be: 'Beware of Saudis bearing peace plans.'
SYRACUSE POST-STANDARD,
31 MAY 2002

GRIST

all is grist that comes to the mill

everything that comes one's way can be used profitably

Grist was the corn that was brought to the wind or watermill to be ground. The miller needed regular supplies of grain to keep his millstones turning and his business profitable. In the sixteenth century, the idiomatic phrase *to bring grist to the mill* meant 'to turn to advantage': *There is no lykelihoode that those thinges will bring gryst to the mill* (Golding, CALVIN ON DEUTERONOMY, 1583). The proverb *All's grist that comes to the mill* came into use later in varied forms with the meaning that everything could be put to use profitably for good or ill (Alexander Whyte, BIBLE CHAMBERS, 1896): *Your stumble, your fall, your misfortune... all is grist to the mill of the mean-minded man.*

Listeners to the series were agog wondering when the rotter would be found out and what he would do when he was. Listening figures soared and Brian Aldridge became villain or victim depending on which side of the fence you were sitting. Men, it was said, admired him, women were appalled. It was **all grist to the mill** *for The Archers, first broadcast nationally on January 1, 1951, and now by far the world's longest running radio drama.*
LIVERPOOL DAILY POST,
7 NOVEMBER 2003

A 'no' on Oct. 3 to Turkey starting negotiations to enter the European Union would have 'centuries of implications,' one influential Turkish academic, Husseyin Bagci, put it last week. It would push a wounded Turkey back into the arms of the nationalists, even perhaps the hard-line fundamentalists, and be **grist to the mill** *of those who argue that the Christian Western world will always consider itself superior to the Muslim one.*
INTERNATIONAL HERALD TRIBUNE,
16 SEPTEMBER 2005

Usage: These days the proverb is often used to express gratitude for offers of help in the sense of *EVERY little helps.*

· H ·

HANDS

many hands make light work
the more people there are to help with
a task, the faster and more easily it
is done

This is a very old proverb. The ancients
noted that more workers meant more
work done, and also that work shared
out amongst many meant less for each
to do. There are also several Latin
variants to the effect that many hands
make a great work light. In English, the
proverb appears in the DOUCE
MANUSCRIPT (c. 1350) as *Many
hondys makyn light worke*, and has been
in use ever since.

Of course, many sayings are
contradicted by an alternative piece of
proverbial advice, and this is one such.
An article in THE OBSERVER
newspaper for 11 February 1923 asks
*What is the use of saying that 'Many hands
make light work' when the same copy-book
tells you that 'Too many cooks spoil the
broth'?* They have a point.

*It is true that **many hands make light
work**. So, please contact your area organiser
today for details of how you can help...*
NEW DAY, THE LEPROSY MISSION,
JANUARY 2002

*Students soon got busy with the fires in the
small ship's galley and proved that **many
hands make light work** as they served up
a delicious meal of fish soup for starters
followed by chicken.*
NEWCASTLE EVENING CHRONICLE,
23 JANUARY 2004

HANDSOME

**handsome is as handsome
does**
the mark of a good character is deeds
not looks

Variant: Handsome is that handsome
does

The earliest known formulation is in
Chaucer's CANTERBURY TALES: *He is
gentil that dooth gentil deedis* (THE WIFE
OF BATH'S TALE, c. 1386). The
reference is to the polished bearing of a
gentleman. *Goodly is he that goodly dooth*
is quoted as *an auncient adage* by
Anthony Munday in SUNDRY
EXAMPLES (1580). In the sixteenth
century the adjective *goodly* meant 'fair
and well-proportioned', in other words
'handsome'. *Goodly* as an adverb meant
'kindly and graciously', a meaning
which *handsome* can also have, although
this use of the word is now rather old
fashioned. The proverb *He is handsome
that handsome doth* which John Ray
included in his ENGLISH PROVERBS
(1670) is, therefore, a variant of the
earlier expression and teaches that
good looks alone are a bad guide to
someone's character. Courteous, kindly
and generous behaviour is the hallmark
of a handsome nature.

In the nineteenth century, as
handsome came to be an adjective more
applicable to a man than a woman, an
attempt was made to adapt the
expression for feminine charms. *Pretty
is as pretty does* is quoted by T C
Haliburton in his collection of WISE

SAWS (1854). It did not catch on. But then women had a similar proverb to contend with already: BEAUTY is only skin deep.

*Hilleman was six-foot-one tall, with 'raccoon eyes', reading glasses on the end of his nose, and would say – but not do – outrageous things. But, as **handsome is as handsome does**, he was a deeply moral man.*
INDEPENDENT, 20 APRIL 2005

*I've always believed that '**handsome is as handsome does**'. When a child in my classroom told me that I needed a face-lift, I told the little charmer that my face was the map of my life.*
GOOD HOUSEKEEPING, MAY 2006

See also ACTIONS speak louder than words; BEAUTY is only skin deep; Alcott's moral tales, page 259

HANG

give a man enough rope and he'll hang himself
permit a suspect enough freedom and he will eventually bring about his own undoing

Variant: Give a thief enough rope and he'll hang himself

The proverb was coined centuries ago, when a more brutal attitude towards crime and punishment prevailed. Bartlett traces the saying in literature to the French satirist Rabelais who, speaking of critics, wrote: *Go hang yourselves; you shall never want rope enough* (PANTAGRUEL, 1532). The earliest known record in English is in Thomas Fuller's HISTORY OF THE HOLY WAR (1639). The variant *Give a thief enough rope and he'll hang himself* was recorded by John Ray in his ENGLISH PROVERBS of 1678 and refers to the fact that hanging was the sentence for

theft (see under *You might as well be hanged for a SHEEP as for a lamb*).

*Senator Trent Lott's comments bring to mind the old adage: **Give a man enough rope and he'll hang himself**. Looks like his comeuppance is finally here.*
WISCONSIN STATE JOURNAL, 22 DECEMBER 2002

*Police are appealing for information about the disappearance of a 3cwt bell from St Michael and All Angels' Church in Bartley Green... As the vicar said, someone must have seen something. It's not the sort of thing you could hide under your coat. Anyone approached in a Bartley Green pub by suspicious looking men looking to sell a church bell should beware. Still, **give them enough rope and they'll hang themselves**.*
THE BIRMINGHAM POST, 28 OCTOBER, 2006

HARE

first catch your hare
plan prudently and do not assume success before it has been confirmed

The proverb is an old one, recorded by Bracton in DE LEGIBUS ET CONSUETUDINIBUS ANGLIAE (c. 1250). It first referred to a stag: *It is a common saying that it is best first to catch the stag, and afterwards, when he has been caught, to skin him*. The proverb is a culinary one. Until the stag, or hare, has been caught, preparations to skin, cook and eat it are useless.

The proverb was commonly attributed to Mrs Hannah Glasse in THE ART OF COOKERY MADE PLAIN AND EASY (1747). George Brimley, for example, writing in 1853, says that Mrs Glasse's first instruction in the recipe for hare soup was *first catch your hare*. However, a correspondent in the Daily News of 20 July 1896 refuted that she had ever

NAMES ON THE MAP

The shires and towns of England have inspired numerous proverbs over the centuries. Many of them are no longer current but a study of them gives a fascinating glimpse into history.

Not surprisingly, a number of regional sayings comment on the agriculture or industry of an area. Beans were a crop that thrived on Leicestershire soil. Records from the fifteenth century state *Lesterschir, full of benys*. By the mid-seventeenth century this had become *Shake a Leicestershire man by the collar, and you shall hear the beans rattle in his belly*. In Shropshire the hiring of farmhands for the summer season often took place on May Day, giving rise to the proverb *May-day, pay-day, pack rags and go away*. In seventeenth century Lincolnshire it was said that *Hogs shite sope and cows shite fire*, a reference to the fact that the poor of that county washed their clothes with pig dung and used dried cowpats for fuel. The town of Northampton was, and still is, well known for its shoe-making industry, which arose because the town was centrally placed and surrounded on all sides by fertile grazing land, so that leather was easily obtainable. In WORTHIES OF ENGLAND (1662) Thomas Fuller refers to the proverb *Northampton stands on other men's legs*, stating that it is the place where the most and cheapest boots and stockings were bought in England.

Some places were renowned for the excellence of their produce and others were simply notorious. Sutton was well known for succulent mutton in the eighteenth and nineteenth centuries and Carshalton for beef. Other towns and villages in Surrey had a less salubrious reputation, which might surprise those who live in this prosperous part of London's commuter belt today. A proverbial jingle runs:

Sutton for mutton, Carshalton for beeves;
Epsom for whores, and Ewel for thieves.

Grose in his PROVINCIAL GLOSSARY (1787) explains it thus: *The downs near Sutton... produce delicate small sheep, and the rich meadows about Carshalton are remarkable for fattening oxen. Epsom... mineral waters... were... resorted to... particularly by ladies of easy virtue. Ewel is a poor village, about a mile from Epsom.*

The history behind other place proverbs can be somewhat grisly. A Cornish saying from the seventeenth century or earlier refers to the practice that coastal folk had of looting the wrecks of ships that foundered on the rocks: *O Master Vier, we cannot pay you your rent, for we had no grace of God this year; no shipwreck upon our coast*. While in neighbouring Devon it was proverbial that the river Dart, which was liable to swell suddenly, would claim at least one life every year: *River of Dart! O river of Dart! every year thou claimest a heart*. Devon seems to have a particularly watery reputation. An exposed stretch of its coastline is regarded as especially hazardous by sailors and fishermen alike, giving rise to the rhyme: *From Padstow Point to Lundy Light, is a watery grave from day to night*.

It is time, perhaps, to lift the spirits with some proverbial Gloucestershire kindness, an antidote for gloom and doom... until the realisation dawns that *Gloucestershire kindness* is the giving away of something that is no longer wanted or needed.

written such a thing: *The familiar words, 'First catch your hare', were never to be found in Mrs Glass's famous volume. What she really said was, Take your hare when it is cased, and make a pudding.* Since *cased* means 'skinned', the common attribution of the proverb to Mrs Glasse is quite wrong.

There is also a popular opinion that the proverb originated in Mrs Beeton's Book of Household Management (1861). This, too, is erroneous as *First catch your hare* was already proverbial by that date – a variant of the *common saying* recorded by Bracton in the thirteenth century.

Nowadays, the saying is rarely heard, unless in the context of a discussion on the works of Hannah Glasse or Isabella Beeton. However, the form of the proverb, *First catch your...*, is still alive and well, particularly in culinary contexts, the word *hare* often being replaced by a variety of other nouns, as two of the contemporary quotations below show.

Clearly, Delia's new book, with its charming cover in Cyrillic script, will not be advising Russian cooks along the lines of 'first catch your goose', (or elk?) as this is her vegetarian collection.
INDEPENDENT, 8 AUGUST 2005

First Catch Your Man; Food Notes.
DAILY MAIL, 14 FEB 2006

Jonathan Roper...has produced a comprehensive study of a rich but neglected area of English folklore, and also, in the first chapter, a survey of previous research and collecting work. However, on the principle of 'first catch your hare,' he had to begin by gathering the charms from widely scattered printed sources.
FOLKLORE, 1 DECEMBER 2006

See also *Don't count your* CHICKENS *before they are hatched*; *There's many a slip twixt* CUP *and lip*

HAY

make hay while the sun shines
take immediate advantage of an opportunity

It is not surprising that agricultural themes are evident in the vast stock of English proverbs for, until the boom in manufacturing industry, Britain was an agricultural economy and reliant upon the weather. If the hay were ready and the weather good, workers would put in extra hours to bring it in. In a changeable climate, the next day might bring heavy rain and the crop would be lost, with serious implications for the winter ahead. As Barclay wrote in SHIP OF FOOLS (1509):

Who that in July whyle Phebus is shynynge
About his hay is nat besy labourynge ...
Shall in the wynter his negligence bewayle.

The Anglican archbishop of Dublin, Richard Chenevix Trench, was also a noted philologist and poet. He commented on the very Englishness of the proverb: *Make hay while the sun shines, is truly English, and could have had its birth only under such variable skies as ours* (ON THE LESSONS IN PROVERBS, 1853). This certainly captures a popular perception. However, later philologists did not necessarily agree with him. Richard Jente demonstrated in 1937 that the expression probably reached English (its first recorded use is in John Heywood's PROVERBS of 1546) via a Latin translation of DAS NARRENSCHIFF (1494) by German satirist Sebastian Brant. Variable skies are not an exclusively English prerogative!

Whether it was the lasting shock of the plane crash, the plush comfort zone of riding the cherry-picked champions for Sheikh Mohammed's Godolphin yard, being loaded

with too many other commercial endorsements – the need all sportsmen feel to **make hay while the sun shines** *– the notion that he should be at home with his four, soon-to-be-five children, or a combination of all things, Dettori had become distracted.*
DAILY TELEGRAPH, 7 NOVEMBER 2004

U2 fans still haven't found what they're looking for – a cheap place to stay for next week's gigs. Hotels have as much as doubled prices to exploit the influx of concert-goers into Dublin next weekend. You could argue they have the right to **make hay while the sun shines***. But the danger is it will leave a sour taste in the mouth of tourists sick and tired of sky-high prices in the capital.*
MIRROR, 18 JUNE 2005

See also *CARPE diem*; *Strike while the IRON'S hot*; *Gather ye ROSEBUDS while ye may*; *TIME and tide wait for no man*; *There's no TIME like the present*; *Never put off till TOMORROW what you can do today*

HEAD

you can't put an old head on young shoulders
the young cannot be expected to have the wisdom and experience of the old

The proverb originally described a person who was young in years but old in good sense. *He carries an old mind with a youthful body* wrote the ancient Greek playwright Aeschylus in SEVEN AGAINST THEBES (467 BC). The Renaissance scholar Erasmus, however, found solemn good sense in a child irritating, and had this to say in THE PRAISE OF FOLLY (1511): *What else is childhood but silliness and foolishness? Its utter lack of sense is what we find so delightful. Everybody hates a prodigy, detests an old head on young shoulders; witness the oft repeated saying 'I hate a small child who's too wise for his years'.*

In Shakespeare's MERCHANT OF VENICE (1597), however, the *old head on young shoulders* was praised. A letter recommending the lawyer Balthazar (Portia in disguise) to the court of justice reads *I beseech you let his lack of years be no impediment to let him lack a reverend estimation, for I never knew so young a body with so old a head.*

The proverb was included in seventeenth century proverb collections, and in the nineteenth century the unknown author of the comedy THE INTRIGUES OF A DAY (1814) cites a colourful variant: *As the proverb says, a grey head is often placed on green shoulders.*

Although a young person who seems wise beyond his years might still be described as having *an old head on young shoulders*, since the twentieth century the rather negative *You can't put an old head on young shoulders* is more commonly found, a variant that was first suggested in the late eighteenth century: *There is no putting an old head on young shoulders* (Unknown, FIRST FLOOR, c. 1780).

*My mother always said, '**You can't put an old head on young shoulders,**' which is so very true. Only later in life, when I filled out job applications, did 'Last year of school completed/Degrees held' make me realize what I'd missed, but as a teenager there was no way I could have understood that.*
LOS ANGELES DAILY NEWS, 20 SEPTEMBER 2002

*Prince Harry was rather lacking in common sense when he chose to wear a Nazi uniform but he is, after all, still a young man and, as the saying goes, '**We cannot put an old head on young shoulders.**'*
SAGA MAGAZINE, APRIL 2006

two heads are better than one
it is helpful to have a second person's opinion or advice

Two have more wit than one wrote John Gower in CONFESSIO AMANTIS (c. 1390). Here wit is understood in its old sense of 'reasoning'. *Two wits are (far) better than one* was a common form of the proverb until at least the end of the sixteenth century.

John Heywood records the variant *Two heddis are better then one* in his PROVERBS (1546), and by the seventeenth century it was the preferred form.

'Two heads are better than one' was the idea behind last year's brainstorming session of the South Barrington Police Department, which developed into the First Annual Car Show to be held from 11 a.m. to 3 p.m. July 22. Sgt. Michael Deegan claims that the chief keeps prodding the department members to come up with ideas for supporting various charities.
ARLINGTON HEIGHTS DAILY HERALD, 26 JUNE 2001

*Research has found that job-sharers score highly on their ability to lead, to solve problems and to remain resilient in the face of a setback. Perhaps, more significantly, it also finds that most of them are outperforming their full-time colleagues in terms of output. A case in point is Marianne, who works in Bristol in the equal opportunities division of one of the banks. She shares her position with another woman and together they prove that **two heads are better than one**.*
GUARDIAN UNLIMITED, 6 APRIL 2000

HEART

cold hands, warm heart
the fingers may be icy but the heart is kindly. A cold exterior often disguises a warm nature

The proverb goes back to at least the nineteenth century. It is recorded in V S Lean's COLLECTANEA (1902–4), a collection of proverbs, words, folklore and superstition. Lean gives no source for the expression but does record it in French – *froides mains, chaudes amours* – which has a rather more amorous implication than the English version. The French form is also given in PROFESSOR ALPHONSE MARIETTE'S FRENCH AND ENGLISH IDIOMS AND PROVERBS (1896). The snippet of folklore is said by some to show what happens when a person falls in love, hence the little rhyme of American origin (Mody Coggin Boatright, THE BEST OF TEXAS FOLK AND FOLKLORE 1916–1954, 1998):

> *Cold hands, warm heart; warm hands cold heart.*
> *Cold hands, warm heart; cold feet no sweetheart.*

*'I'm always cold. This has nothing to do with being born in Hawaii or having lived in Australia. I just prefer the heat because I always have a chill. Even though I'm fair-skinned, I prefer the heat and sunlight. Still, **cold hands, warm heart!**'*
NICOLE KIDMAN IN MARIE CLAIRE, 1 FEBRUARY 2004

faint heart never won fair lady
courage and enterprise are needed to gain the affections of a girl

This proverb is common to other European languages. The French say *Le couard n'aura belle amie* (The coward will not win a fair lady) and Cervantes quotes the Spanish equivalent in DON QUIXOTE (1615), calling it an *old saying*. The earliest known record of the proverb in English is in John Gower's CONFESSIO AMANTIS (c. 1390) where the reference is not to a lady but to a castle:

> *Bot as men sein, wher herte is failed,*
> *Ther schal no castell ben assailed.*

Subsequent uses of the proverb speak of *fair ladies* but John Lyly in EUPHUES AND HIS ENGLAND (1580) combines the two, perhaps showing that, for a time, both were current: *Faint hart Philautus, neither winneth Castell nor Lady*. And in 1605 William Camden uses the saying in its present-day form: *Faint heart neuer wonne fair lady* (REMAINS).

The proverb possibly refers to feudal times when great landowners ruled and protected their estates from fortified castles. These castles housed retainers, fighting men pledged to their lord. Ambitious lords might extend their power and influence by laying siege to fortresses and usurping their weaker neighbours. For this a ruthless, not a faint heart, was required. Similar qualities were needed, it seems, on the battlefields of the heart.

Medieval times also saw the rise of the French cult of courtly love. This ritualised form of courtship was confined to the aristocracy and had its roots in the adoration of the Virgin, whose perfection was seen reflected in woman. Courtly love was governed by strict rules of conduct in which earthly love was honoured with all the rites accorded to divine love. In France, it was an extramarital platonic relationship at a time when marriage was usually nothing more than a business contract. In English literature, courtly love was seen more as a courtship ritual leading to marriage. A suitor needed courage to approach a lady who had become the subject of his adoration; to be scorned and rejected was the ultimate humiliation.

And here's an off-the-peg, off-the-wall romantic film for you. Hollywood in look, but in tone something else, it's about intellectually precocious, speccy, blazer-wearing 15-year-old Max Fischer who falls for one of his teachers...Unfortunately, misanthropic local steel baron, Bill Murray, is smitten, too. But faint heart never won fair lady, so soon the odd love rivals are a-rivalling with every weapon in their mismatched armouries.
EVENING STANDARD,
11 FEBRUARY 2000

He never expected to feel as strongly for Rosetta as he does and will stop at nothing to win her heart... And what his plans will mean for Frazer, who is currently in pole position having charmed the sexy young lawyer. The professional gambler is also willing to risk everything to land the woman of his dreams – so it'll be interesting to find out who comes out on top. After all, as they say, faint heart never won fair maiden, did it?
GLASGOW DAILY RECORD,
24 MARCH 2007

Usage: Often used to challenge the inhibitions of a shy suitor

See also NOTHING *ventured, nothing gained;* Throw out a SPRAT *to catch a mackerel*

HELL

hell hath no fury like a woman scorned

when rejected by a man, a woman is ferociously hostile towards him

Variant: Hell has no fury like a woman scorned

There seems to be remarkable unanimity down the ages (amongst male writers at least) that the anger of a woman who has been scorned or jilted is uniquely virulent. The Latin proverb has it that *When injured, women are generally implacable*. In English there are various similar comments until, in 1696, Colley Cibber introduces the concept of *hell: We shall find no fiend in hell can match the fury of a disappointed woman, – scorned, slighted, dismissed without a parting pang* (LOVE'S LAST SHIFT).

Just one year later, William Congreve pens the couplet that encapsulates the modern proverb (THE MOURNING BRIDE, 1697):

Heav'n has no rage, like love to hatred turn'd,
Nor Hell a fury like a woman scorned.

Surprisingly, although men continued to write about the boundless rage of a slighted woman, Congreve's words were not misquoted as a proverb until around the middle of the twentieth century.

*Dogs really do have a pathological hatred of postmen, but they aren't nearly as awkward as some householders – **hell hath no fury like** the man whose giro has not come.*
THE TIMES, 30 AUGUST 2001

*They say **hell has no fury like a woman scorned**. But when that woman is richer than the Queen, when she also happens to be your own flesh and blood and is said to be devastated at her father's betrayal, £50,000 seems a pretty measly price in exchange for a daughter's love.*
GLASGOW SUNDAY MAIL,
14 DECEMBER 2003

See also *REVENGE is sweet*

the road to hell is paved with good intentions
unless good intentions are translated into action they are useless and will never be counted to one's credit

According to a letter written by St Francis de Sales to Madame de Chantal (1605), the origin of the proverb is to be found in some words of St Bernard of Clairvaux. (See *Love me, love my DOG*.) The letter reads: *Do not be troubled by St Bernard's saying that hell is full of good intentions and desires.* St Bernard's comment was well known to seventeenth century writers both in England and abroad as frequent use in Christian sermons and writings brought it to popular notice. Thomas Adams, in one of his sermons (1629), writes: *One said, that hell is like to be full of good purposes, but heaven of good works.* George Herbert expresses the thought as *Hell is full of good meanings and wishings* (JACULA PRUDENTUM, 1640).

In LIFE OF SAMUEL JOHNSON (14 April 1775) James Boswell gives a slight variant as one of Johnson's sayings: *No saint... was more sensible of the unhappy failure of pious resolves than Johnson. He said one day,... 'Sir, hell is paved with good intentions.'* This turn of phrase may have been new to Boswell's ears but it was not Johnson's inspiration. This same reworking of St Bernard's thought had been previously used by John Wesley in his JOURNAL, 10 July 1736, and he refers to it as a *true saying*.

The modern form changes the proverb yet again. Perhaps John Ruskin was partly responsible for this. In ETHICS OF DUST (1866) he writes: *Their best intentions merely make the road smooth for them... You can't pave the bottomless pit; but you may the road to it.*

*The Office of the Deputy Prime Minister yesterday announced that it was considering broadening its age discrimination legislation to cover all goods and services. Previously, the rules were designed solely to prevent ageism at work... However, many companies offering services to older people fear they could fall foul of the law. Saga Holidays restricts its holidays to people aged 50 and above. '**The road to hell is***

paved with good intentions,' said Paul Green, a company spokesman. 'If age discrimination is taken to its logical extreme, then it could present problems for a business offering services to the over-50s.'
DAILY TELEGRAPH, 26 JANUARY 2006

The road to hell is paved with false promises, so if you tell someone you will do something, you must do it. Having known the guilt of being unreliable, making too many rash promises, I've learnt not to make them, – or do the thing straight away.
SAGA MAGAZINE, MARCH 2006

HELPS

every little helps
every contribution, no matter how small, swells the total

An amusing quotation from Flemish philologist Gabriel Meurier's TRÉSOR DES SENTENCES (1590) uses and illustrates the proverb at the same time: *Peu ayde, discoit le formy, pissanten mer en plein midy* (Every little helps, said the ant, pissing in the sea at the height of midday).

Nevertheless, the proverb does not appear in English literature until the late eighteenth century.

The proverb invites Wellerisms (see *The Wellerism*, page 215), like the one from Meurier's TRÉSOR. The popular Baptist preacher Charles Haddon Spurgeon includes the following in JOHN PLOUGHMAN'S TALK (1869): *Every little helps, as the sow said when she snapped at a gnat.*

But, as Spurgeon himself said, he was writing for the common people, and so *refined taste and dainty words have been discarded for strong proverbial expressions and homely phrases.*

Recently the British supermarket chain Tesco have seized upon *Every little helps* as their company advertising motto – perhaps little realising that, if the first and last letters are omitted from the proverb, its slogan gives a totally different message.

Every little helps when you go shopping. And it's a lesson that lenders have turned to their own advantage. Those headline-winning mortgage deals can sometimes hide a host of extra costs that boost their profits and take the shine off a 'bargain'.
MAIL ON SUNDAY, 7 AUGUST 2005

I followed Alistair Elliot's example (Your Shout, April 14) using your excellent template to request the difference between the £100 admin fee originally quoted by Cheltenham & Gloucester in August 2000 for paying off my mortgage, and the £225 I was actually charged last year. Amazingly, they responded in three days with no argument, and a cheque for the balance plus interest is in the post. *Every little helps.*
GUARDIAN, 5 MAY 2007

See also *Look after the PENNIES and the pounds will look after themselves*; *All is GRIST that comes to the mill*

HOME

an Englishman's home is his castle
an Englishman's home is a private place; no one has the right to enter without his agreement

Variant: An Englishman's house is his castle

John Ray defines this expression as *a kind of law proverb* (ENGLISH PROVERBS, 1670). For many centuries, the law of the land has said that every Englishman should have the right to absolute freedom within his own house and that no bailiff has the power to infringe this right. A man's home is therefore likened to a castle; a place where he is protected and secure. William Staunford, a judge of Common

---

PROVERBS DRIVE YOU CRAZY

Idioms are in part defined by having a literal as well as a figurative sense. You can, for example, *spill the beans* by knocking over a can of them or by divulging a secret to others. Some proverbs have a similar dual level of interpretation, a phenomenon that has not escaped psychologists and psychiatrists. In fact, it has formed the basis for a series of tests to evaluate mental health. A particularly striking case of this is *Two HEADS are better than one*, which has been written up in an article by Edward Lehman, appropriately entitled 'The Monster Test' (ARCHIVES OF GENERAL PSYCHIATRY, 1960). When patients aged between six and 16 were asked to draw a picture interpreting this proverb, some 60 per cent of psychotic children drew various types of two-headed monsters. Their work showed an inability to abstract and see beyond the literal. There has been a considerable subsequent debate in the profession between those who bring forward experimental evidence in support of Lehman's conclusions and those who point to the poor reliability of proverb tests. There exists a large bibliography of articles on the subject.

Pleas, expressed this right in LES PLEES DEL CORON (3rd ed., 1567), the first textbook of the English criminal law.

The English jurist, Sir Edward Coke, who rose to chief justice of the King's Bench and privy counsellor under James I, fiercely defended the common law even, when necessary, against the attempts of the king himself to change it by authority of divine right. In his summary of Semayne's case he wrote: *The house of everyone is to him as his castle and fortress, as well for his defence against injury and violence as for his repose.* And in the third of his INSTITUTES (influential early textbooks on modern common law, written between 1628 and 1644) he wrote: *A man's house is his castle, et domus sua cuique tutissimum refugium* (and every man's home is his safest refuge). This Latin phrase is quoted from the Roman statement of law, the Pandects on which Staunford and Coke rest their assertions of the principle that it is the law, not the massive walls of a castle, that give a man security.

It is not a long step from legal definitions and maxims to a proverb.

By Shakespeare's day there are already recorded half a dozen instances of the phrase's use, and from that time forward they have proliferated. In a detailed study, Archer Taylor (1965) points out the developing applications of the phrase from Thomas Fuller to Jack Kerouac. Fuller in his SERMONS (1642) goes beyond a strictly legal context and presses man to make his conscience his castle. Kerouac in ON THE ROAD (1957) turns the proverb into a description of domestic rather than legal freedom:

...her old man can come in any hour of the night with anybody and have talks in the kitchen and drink the beer and leave any old time. This is a man, and that's his castle. He pointed up at the tenement.

The form of the proverb also changed over the centuries. *A man's house* became *An Englishman's house*. William Pitt the Elder is reported to have used this variant as early as 1763 in a speech given in the House of Commons, but an early written use is in James and Horace Smith's HORACE IN LONDON (1813):

An Englishman's house was his castle
till now,
But castles are now and then taken.

Since the 1920s, the variant *An Englishman's home…* has crept in, such that today it is the predominant form.

The bad news, however, is that the Englishman's castle is now under attack. In a debate in the House of Lords (January 2007), Lord Beaumont of Whitley had this to say about proposed changes to the law:

'An Englishman's home is his castle' is one of the best-known and most influential maxims of English law. The rule is arguably one of the foundations of private life in England and Wales, along with the right to self-defence in the home… The saying originates from the judgment in the Semayne case, which laid down the role [sic] that no one may break into a dwelling house without proper lawful authority. For generations, this principle has been recited in numerous judgments and has been an unspoken presence in many more. It is a perfect example of how common-law rule has entered into the language and culture and shaped social conduct thereafter, to the point that it is accepted automatically and even unconsciously by all law-abiding citizens… We maintain that the Government have lost all sense of proportion by sweeping away such wisdom from the law. From 1604 to 2004, the bailiffs had to enter domestic premises peacefully. Forcible entry and the use of force against the person by bailiffs were not allowed. Now, for fines with a warrant, bailiffs can force entry without notice and, it is proposed, restrain the defaulter.

An Englishman's home is his castle – *but who will guard it while he's abroad?*
MAIL ON SUNDAY, 14 APRIL 2002

An Englishman's home is his castle, *unless of course he's got a family from hell living next door. Nuisance neighbours are a menace for thousands of law-abiding people, causing noise, harassment and stress.*
COVENTRY EVENING TELEGRAPH,
4 DECEMBER 2006

home is where the heart is
home will always hold one's affections no matter how far one may wander

The ancients, Plutarch and Cicero amongst them, were wont to write tenderly of home, and some authorities consider that this proverb was coined by Pliny. However, it receives scant attention in literature until as late as the second half of the nineteenth century when it appears in ACROSS THE CONTINENT, a contribution by an American author James J McCloskey to DAVEY CROCKETT AND OTHER PLAYS (1870). From McCloskey's use of the proverb, it is clear that it was already well established: *Well, home, they say, is where the heart is.* Later, in the early twentieth century, the American writer and publisher Elbert Green Hubbard cites the saying in A THOUSAND AND ONE EPIGRAMS (1914).

Home is where the heart is and part of that heart is a sense of family. So when adding accessories to your home, don't overlook those personal items that recall ancestors or mark the milestones in the family's life.
CINCINNATI POST, 5 AUGUST 2000

Second home is, in a sense, a contradiction in terms. If home is where the heart is, then the idea of a second heart is aberrational.
DAILY TELEGRAPH, 12 JUNE 2004

See also HOME *sweet* home; *There's no place like* HOME

home, sweet home

there is nowhere better than home, a place of ease, comfort and affection

The proverb was first the title of a well-known song by John Howard Payne (see *There's no place like HOME*), which quickly gained international acclaim and recognition. Intriguingly, the writer's immediate circumstances were very different from the romantic, emotional image conjured up by the song. Payne writes: *How often have I been in the heart of Paris, Berlin, London, or some other city, and have heard persons singing or heard organs playing 'Home, Sweet Home', without having a shilling to buy myself the next meal or a place to lay my head! The world has literally sung my song till every heart is familiar with its melody, yet I have been a wanderer from my boyhood, and, in my old age, have to submit to humiliation for my bread.*

Happily, Payne's later career was more prosperous and successful. He collaborated with Washington Irving and for 30 years had a good career as an author and adapter of plays. In 1842 he was appointed American consul in Tunis, where some ten years later he died. Thirty years on, Mr Corocoran of Washington applied to bring his remains back to his home country. As Payne was reinterred at Oak Hill Cemetery, Washington, a thousand mourners sang HOME SWEET HOME.

The phrase struck a chord in the nineteenth century heart. Along with verses from the Bible, letters of the alphabet and flowers, it is often seen on needlework samplers of the period.

*Almost **home, sweet home** for Aussies at London Olympics. Australian athletes say they're delighted that London will host the 2012 Olympics... An elated AOC president JOHN COATES says it is a very good result for Australia, as the Australian Olympic Committee has long* had a very close relationship with the British Olympic Association. He says London is a city a lot of Australians are familiar with.
AAP GENERAL NEWS, 7 JULY 2005

***Home sweet home**: [footballer] Peter Davenport will return to the ground where his career began 25 years ago.*
LIVERPOOL ECHO, 23 DECEMBER 2006

Usage: Can be rather cloyingly sentimental. Often said on return home after a trying or tiring time away

See also *There's no place like HOME; HOME is where the heart is*

there's no place like home

only in one's own home can one feel deep and warm contentment

The proverb as we know it today comes from HOME SWEET HOME, the well-known song from the musical play CLARI, THE MAID OF MILAN, which was first performed at Covent Garden in 1823. John Howard Payne (see left), a young American struggling to make a living in the London theatre, wrote the words, setting them to a tune he overheard being played through a window as he walked by:

Mid pleasures and palaces though we may roam,
Be it ever so humble, there's no place like home!
A charm from the skies seems to hallow us there,
Which, seek through the world, never is met with elsewhere.
An exile from home, splendor dazzles in vain,
Oh, give me my lowly thatched cottage again;
The birds singing gayly, that came at my call,
Give me them, and that peace of mind dearer than all.

But Payne's own inspiration is a reworking of an old, well-used proverb *Home is home (though it be never so homely)*, known since at least the seventeenth century. A related proverb *Home is homely* was recorded by John Heywood in his PROVERBS (1546). Even the title of the song may have been borrowed from Sir John Harrington's translation of Ariosto's ORLANDO FURIOSO (1591): *For home though homely twere, yet it is sweet*.

The Victorians were very fond of Payne's song, which expressed their ideal of hearth, home and family values. Nevertheless, *There's no place like home* did not immediately supplant the old proverb, for in DOMBEY AND SON (1848) Dickens still clings to the old adage: *The saying is, that home is home, be it never so homely*. The sense here of *homely* is 'ordinary, simple, unadorned', a sense which is still current in American English today, particularly in the context of plain, not very good-looking women.

*Top Irish presenter Colin Murray may be in big demand in the London showbiz world. But The Irish People's top entertainment writer, who admits he gets back to Ireland every time he's given the chance, says **there's 'really no place like home'**... Colin, who gets home every other weekend, said: 'If it wasn't for work I'd be home in a second. I love to get home every few weeks – if anything just to catch up with mates and to help me feel sane.'*
PEOPLE, 12 JANUARY 2003

*Apparently, the adage about **there being 'no place like home'** is true because Tony Stewart has been a different person this year. After NASCAR's final race last season, Stewart moved back into the Columbus, Ind., house where he lived as a youngster.*

And this season, he has a more relaxed attitude, he seems to have tamed his temper and he is second in the Nextel Cup points standings. 'That's probably one of the biggest factors that's helped me be a lot more relaxed this year is just being back home,' Stewart said.
DENVER ROCKY MOUNTAIN NEWS, 2 AUGUST 2005

See also *HOME, sweet home; HOME is where the heart is*

HOMER

even Homer sometimes nods
even the most gifted are not at their best all the time

Variant: Even Homer nods

Even the great Greek epic poet Homer could not sustain his brilliance at all times. Horace in DE ARTE POETICA (c. 20 BC) defends the master's lapses thus: *I, too, am indignant when the worthy Homer nods, but in a long work it is allowable to snatch a little sleep*. Before long *Even Homer sometimes nods* had captured popular imagination and become a common saying. There are references to it in English literature from the sixteenth century onwards.

*The news that one in five Britons is 'functionally illiterate' (a strange piece of language in itself) comes as no surprise. I'm a novelist and I find myself wandering every now and then. Or should that be wondering? Still, **even Homer nods** and I'm in the best of company: Kingsley Amis once wrote to Anita Brookner pointing out 40 grammatical mistakes in two pages of one of her novels.*
GUARDIAN UNLIMITED, 27 JUNE 2000

Even Homer nods, my old school master used to tell me – a pompous way of saying even the greatest make mistakes, and some keep on making the same ones, as Arsene Wenger proves.
EVENING STANDARD,
26 SEPTEMBER 2003

Usage: Literary and rather dated

See also *To err is human, to FORGIVE divine*

HONESTY

honesty is the best policy
truthfulness and square-dealing are sound foundations for living

Aesop's fable THE WOODMAN AND THE AXE (c. 570 BC) tells of a woodcutter who was working beside a river when he lost his axe in the water. The distressed man was sitting on the riverbank in tears when Mercury appeared and, upon hearing the sorry tale, dived into the river and brought out a gold axe. Asked if it was his, the woodman said it was not. Diving again Mercury reappeared with a silver axe, but again the man said that it was not his. When Mercury plunged into the river a third time, he brought up an iron axe, which the woodcutter claimed as his. Impressed by the man's honesty, Mercury gave him not only his own axe but the other two as well.

On hearing of the woodcutter's remarkable experience, one of his friends went off and tossed his own axe into the river. Again Mercury appeared and, responding to the man's tearfulness, plunged into the river bringing up a golden axe. As soon as he saw it the man, in great excitement, claimed it as his own but Mercury, offended by his base dishonesty, threw the golden prize back into the water and went away without even bothering to retrieve the man's own axe.

The earliest known written appearance of the proverb in English is in Edwin Sandy's EUROPAE SPECULUM of 1599, and it was in frequent use thereafter. The saying translates directly into a number of other European languages: the French, for instance say *L'honnêteté est la meilleure politique*, and Cervantes uses it in the second part of DON QUIXOTE (1615).

There is the question whether one should adopt honesty for its own sake, as a moral universal, or whether adopting it as a best policy simply turns it into a matter of self-serving expediency. Some would go even further. Honesty may generally be considered the best policy, but is it always politic? Washington Irving thinks not: *I am of the opinion that, as to nations, the old maxim that 'honesty is the best policy' is a sheer and ruinous mistake* (KNICKERBOCKER HISTORY OF NEW YORK, 1809). Realpolitik, it seems, tempers the more wholehearted endorsement given to the proverb in earlier centuries, turning an absolute into a relative mistake.

Honesty is the best policy when travelling abroad. Make sure to tell your insurer about past illnesses ahead of your trip or you risk having your claim refused by the small print.
DAILY TELEGRAPH, 10 APRIL 2004

Philosophy of life: Honesty is the best policy. Say what you mean and treat people how you would expect and want to be treated yourself.
LIVERPOOL DAILY POST,
12 FEBRUARY 2005

HONOUR

there is honour among thieves
lawbreakers subscribe to a code of practice amongst themselves

Cicero remarked that even thieves, who did not observe the laws of the land, had a code of their own to live by. The code revolved around loyalty towards others in the underworld. Publilius Syrus summarised it with more than a hint of approval when he wrote that *Even in crime loyalty is rightly displayed* (SENTENTIAE, c. 43 BC). Shakespeare took up the theme. When the companions who were to have helped him stage a highway robbery prove unreliable, Falstaff in HENRY IV, PART ONE, Act 2, scene ii (1597) is tempted to abandon the crime declaring *A plague on it when thieves cannot be true one to another* .

Essayist William Hazlitt attempts to define the nature of thieves' honour in TABLE TALK (1821): *Their honour consists in the division of the booty, not in the mode of acquiring: they do not (often) betray one another; they may be depended on in giving the alarm when any of their posts are in danger of being surprised; and they will stand together for their ill-gotten gains to the last drop of their blood.*

Many British novelists have drawn attention to the thieves' pact – Defoe, Scott and Dickens among them – and those who enjoy some kinds of modern crime fiction will know that today's thief is as honour-bound as any in ancient Rome. More realistic contemporary writing is, however, brutal in its depiction of when thieves fall out: gangster warfare, Mafia vendettas, triad feuds, etc. Honour among thieves, it seems, is in short supply.

Persistent offender Adrian Harper proved **there was no honour among thieves** *when he burgled an accomplice's flat as soon as he was granted bail.*
BIRMINGHAM EVENING MAIL,
2 JANUARY 2001

Roberts got a reduced sentence of eight years on Friday for his part in 12 robberies after going into the witness box. An Old Bailey judge told him he will be 'at serious risk of reprisal' when he is released. Roberts said: 'People talk about **honour among thieves***, but there isn't any. If you are looking at a 25-year sentence and you have the opportunity to cut it down, you would have to be very stupid not to take that opportunity.*
EVENING STANDARD, 11 MARCH 2002

Usage: The expression is a common one although it has a rather dated, Dickensian ring

See also *DOG does not eat dog*

HOPE

hope springs eternal in the human breast
to have optimistic expectations for the future is part of man's nature

The proverb is from Pope's ESSAY ON MAN (1732). The poet says that man never experiences complete happiness but is always looking forward to a brighter future:

Hope springs eternal in the human breast:
Man never is, but always to be, blest.
The soul, uneasy and confin'd from home,
Rests and expatiates in a life to come.

Pope may well have been familiar with some famous earlier contemplations on a similar theme. Pascal in his PENSÉES (1670) wrote: *Thus we never live, but we hope to live; and always disposing ourselves to be happy, it is inevitable that we never become so.*

Pope, a Roman Catholic, may also have known the work of another French preacher, Massillon, who wrote in his SERMON FOR ST BENEDICT'S DAY: We never enjoy, we always hope. A source and influence closer to home was Dryden. His play Aurengzebe was first performed in 1675. It contains the following lines:

> When I consider life, 'tis all a cheat.
> Yet, fool'd with hope, men favour the deceit;
> Trust on and think to-morrow, will repay.
> To-morrow's falser than the former day;
> Lies worse, and while it says we shall
> be blest
> With some new joys, cuts off what
> we possest.
> Strange cozenage! none would live past
> years again,
> Yet all hope pleasure in what yet remain,
> And from the dregs of life think to receive
> What the first sprightly running could
> not give.

Pope's line was taken up by Charles Dickens in OUR MUTUAL FRIEND (1865) as *Hope springs eternal in the scholastic breast*, and was much cited thereafter.

It's spring. The flowers bloom. The days grow longer. There's optimism in the air. Even as the headlines shout of war and other troubles, we feel the positive effects of the changing of the season. As many of us learned in school, hope springs eternal in the human heart.
VIRGINIAN PILOT, 11 APRIL 2004

Hope springs eternal in the human breast, especially when four influential All Blacks disappear into the bosom of the treatment room. The New Zealanders' captain, Tana Umaga, missed training yesterday after failing to recover sufficiently from the cramps that affected him towards the end of his side's humiliation of England in Dunedin at the weekend. Justin Marshall, the scrum-half, was also hors de combat, as were the flanker Richie McCaw and the wing Doug Howlett. If the tourists can get rid of the other 11 over the next few days, they might just square the series.
INDEPENDENT, 15 JUNE 2004

Usage: Often reduced to *Hope springs eternal…*, the rest being understood.

See also *Every CLOUD has a silver lining*; *The darkest HOUR is that before the dawn*; *TOMORROW is another day*

HORSE

don't change horses in midstream

if you must change your mind, choose your moment well; don't change direction or tactics in the middle of a difficult undertaking

Variant: Don't swap horses while crossing a stream

The proverb owes its popularity to US president Abraham Lincoln. Dissatisfaction with Lincoln's handling of the Civil War mounted until calls came for a change of President. In spite of this, the National Union League decided to support Lincoln's nomination for a second term. Lincoln thought it best to accept and, in a reply delivered to the League on 9 June 1864, gave his reasons for doing so:

I do not allow myself to suppose that either the convention or the League have concluded to decide that I am either the greatest or best man in America, but rather they have concluded that it is not best to swap horses while crossing the river, and have further concluded that I am not so poor a horse that they might not make a botch of it in trying to swap.

An alternative version of the same address credits an old Dutch farmer with putting the saying into Lincoln's repertoire.

Kerry said 'it's the wrong war in the wrong place at the wrong time.' What do our fighting men and women say to that? As commander in chief, President Bush 'is the

right man in the right place at the right time.' Saddam is gone and the world is safer. It is never wise to change horses in mid-stream. George W. Bush is a steadfast, compassionate conservative. John Kerry is an indecisive, undependable liberal.
ARLINGTON HEIGHTS DAILY HERALD, 31 OCTOBER 2004

Don't change horses in mid-stream, let Labour complete the job. Don't revert to the past by letting the Tories back in.
MIRROR, 5 MAY 2005

don't shut the stable door after the horse has bolted

it is no good taking precautionary measures to prevent something unpleasant happening after the event

This proverb exists in many European languages with the earliest record in a French text dating back to the late twelfth century. It does not appear in English literature until the middle of the fourteenth century. Early uses speak of shutting the stable door after the horse is *lost* or, more frequently, *stolen*. *Bolted* is a twentieth century variant.

Stevenson quotes a quaint alternative from the pen of Thomas Fuller. In WORTHIES: CHESTER (1662) Fuller writes *When the daughter is stolen, shut Pepper-gate* and explains that when the daughter of the mayor of Chester eloped she slipped through Pepper-gate, an obscure side-entrance set in the city wall, whereupon the sorrowful mayor had the gateway blocked up.

Another French proverb with the same message is *After death, the doctor*.

Management training too often attempts to shut the stable door after the horse has already bolted and is causing havoc. What is first required is a profound structural change in selecting managers and then in how they are deployed and rewarded.
DAILY TELEGRAPH, 6 MARCH 2006

The only time I try to flush out the toxins is after a night of too much red wine. As a last-ditch bid to avoid a hangover, I drink lots of water before bedtime. Talk about trying to shut the stable door after the horse has bolted.
GLASGOW SUNDAY MAIL, 6 MAY 2007

never look a gift horse in the mouth

don't find fault with something which has been offered as a present

Variant: Don't look a gift horse in the mouth

The proverb rebukes those rude and ungrateful people who insist on inspecting the gifts they receive and finding fault with their quality. When some of St Jerome's writings met with unkind criticism he chastised his critics, saying that they should never inspect the teeth of a gift horse. The carping was uncalled for since the writings had been offered out of generosity of spirit. But perhaps Jerome's critics deserve a modicum of sympathy; the scholarly saint had a reputation for being somewhat prickly and cantankerous.

Jerome's use of the expression at the turn of the fifth century may be the earliest record we have but he himself refers to it as *a common proverb*, so its history obviously goes back even further. Nor is it confined to English; the expression can be translated directly into many European languages. Italian has both this proverb and a variant *Don't worry about the colour of a gift horse*.

Never look a gift horse in the mouth alludes to the fact that a horse's age can be assessed by the number and condition of its teeth. From the time a horse's permanent teeth have all come through at about five years old, its molars are gradually being worn down until, in a very old horse, the roots are almost at the surface and some teeth may be lost altogether. The front incisors appear longer with age and protrude further to the front. A glance in the horse's mouth, therefore, would quickly determine whether the animal were a young steed or an old nag. One favourite trick amongst unscrupulous horse dealers was to file down the front teeth to make the horse look young. From the eighteenth century this practice was known as *bishoping*.

*They say **never look a gift horse in the mouth**. But if that offer is made by a bookie make sure you check every filling.*
SUNDAY MIRROR, 17 DECEMBER 2000

*You should **never look a gift horse in the mouth**, the saying goes. But that doesn't mean you can't check it out on the Internet.*

The other day, a kind soul gave me tickets to see St. John's University and Fordham University play basketball at Madison Square Garden… Anyway, in the old, pre-Internet-as-we-know-it days, I would have needed either a working knowledge of the seating situation at the Garden to know before getting there were my seats were. Not anymore. As soon as I got home, I looked up the Madison Square Garden Web site and was able to determine where I'd be sitting.
LONG ISLAND BUSINESS NEWS,
13 DECEMBER 2002

you can lead a horse to water, but you can't make him drink
you can create opportunities for a person but you can't force him to accept them

Variant: You can take/bring a horse to water, but you can't make him drink

The proverb, which speaks of taking the working horse to the trough or stream for refreshment, is first found in a manuscript dating from the late twelfth century. Later, it was included in John Heywood's PROVERBS (1546): *A man maie well bring a horse to the water, But he can not make him drinke without he will*. Samuel Johnson used a variant in a conversation with James Boswell (Boswell, LIFE OF JOHNSON, 14 July 1763). Boswell was concerned that his father intended him to become a lawyer, to which Johnson replied, *Sir, you need not be afraid of his forcing you to be a laborious practising lawyer, that is not in his power. As the proverb says, 'One man may lead a horse to water, but twenty cannot make him drink'.*

More recently, a well-known roadside restaurant chain proposed offering healthier meals as well as the usual burgers and other fast food. Asked if there would be sufficient demand the spokeswoman pointed out, *You can take a consumer to his salad but you can't necessarily make him eat* (BBC Radio 4, WOMAN'S HOUR, 7 January 1993).

Everyone has heard the saying, 'You can lead a horse to water, but you can't make him drink.' What I'm seeing is, you can send your child to school, but it's up to him to think.
PIEDMONT TRIAD NEWS AND RECORD,
23 MAY 2000

*Your son is in trouble. His lack of social contact, his moods, his withdrawal from interests – these are all classic signs of depression and do need to be taken seriously. As a first step, you could suggest that he gets in touch with an organisation that may be able to provide counselling… That said, **you can lead a** man to a support system **but you can't make him** use it.*
GOOD HOUSEKEEPING, JULY 2001

HOUR

the darkest hour is that before the dawn

when circumstances cannot get any worse, a turn for the better will not be long in coming

Variant: The darkest hour is (just) before dawn

The blackest hour of the night is the one just before the faintest traces of the coming dawn can be discerned. Applied figuratively, to someone in pain for instance, the proverb teaches that the last hour before relief comes will be worst of all but that when things are at their worst, then they will mend.

An early record in English literature comes in Thomas Fuller's A PISGAH-SIGHT OF PALESTINE (1650): *It is always darkest just before the day dawneth*.

The proverb seems to capture the universal sense of *HOPE that springs eternal in the human breast*, an optimism that is found in several synonymous adages in English as well as various other languages, as this list from Walsh shows:

When things are at their worst, they soonest mend
When bale is highest, boot is nighest
The longest day will have an end
After a storm comes a calm
By dint of going wrong, all will come right (French)
Ill is the eve of well (Italian)
It is at the narrowest part of the defile that the valley begins to open (Persian)
When the tale of bricks is doubled, Moses comes (Hebrew)

There's always a darkest moment before the dawn. Daniel's song proved a hit in clubs, but £1,000 wasn't enough for an Elton John lifestyle, and so he accepted a £200 40-hour-a-week job serving coffee at Starbucks... Just days before he was due to start, DnD rang him with the amazing news that they had sold 4,000 copies of his single in a week and big record companies like Sony and Warners were wanting to sign him for large amounts of money.
DAILY MAIL, 6 DECEMBER 2001

*You are living through the dark night of the soul at the moment, but I truly believe that **the darkest hour** is before the dawn. When things go badly wrong in our lives, it is always a sign that some good fortune is on the way. I feel you will definitely have love and romance in your life again, sooner than you would imagine.*
SUNDAY MIRROR, 7 APRIL 2002

See also *HOPE springs eternal in the human breast*; *TOMORROW is another day*

HOUSE

a house divided against itself cannot stand

any unit suffering from internal dissension will not be able to resist external pressures

The origin of the proverb is biblical. Jesus had healed many people, several of them possessed by spirits. The stir that this was causing irritated the religious authorities. The scribes came down from Jerusalem and accused Jesus of being possessed by Satan and of using satanic power to cast demons out of others. Jesus pointed out that their argument was illogical, saying in MARK 3:23–26:

How can Satan cast out Satan? And if a kingdom be divided against itself, that kingdom cannot stand. And if a house be divided against itself, that house cannot stand. And if Satan rise up against himself, and be divided, he cannot stand, but hath an end.

The biblical proverb has played a large part in the history of the United States. Thomas Paine alluded to it in COMMON SENSE (1776), a pamphlet challenging the authority of the British crown and promoting independence for the American territories:

Some writers have explained the English constitution thus: the King, say they, is one, the people another; the Peers are a house in behalf of the King, the commons in behalf of the people; but this hath all the distinctions of a house divided against itself; and though the expressions be pleasantly arranged, yet when examined they appear idle and ambiguous...

It was later used by United States senator Sam Houston who, in a speech supporting a legislative solution to a bitter conflict between the northern and southern states over slavery in 1850, declared *A nation divided against itself cannot stand*.

But the proverb was most famously employed by Abraham Lincoln in what has come to be known as his House Divided Speech. The tension between the northern and southern states continued and Lincoln, who opposed slavery, had this to say (SPEECH, Springfield, Illinois, June 16, 1858):

A house divided against itself cannot stand. I believe this government cannot endure permanently half-slave and half-free. I do not expect the Union to be dissolved – I do not expect the house to fall – but I do expect it will cease to be divided. It will become all one thing or all the other.

Lincoln was right. In 1860–1 the southern slave states seceded from the Union and on 12 April 1861 the American Civil War broke out.

The proverb now exists as a metaphor to describe disputes and controversies of all kinds.

...a house divided against itself cannot stand. Neither can a political party divided against itself long endure. A party cannot stand for two opposite things.
WASHINGTON TIMES,
20 APRIL 2003

What happened to the man who was a consensus builder? The times that we live in demand that we be united in purpose and cause. Congress and President Bush must reach out to each other in a spirit of cooperation. **A house divided against itself cannot stand**. *We need to find ways to talk with each other, not at each other, if America as a country wants to really show its strength.*
CINCINNATI POST, 23 JANUARY 2004

See also UNITED *we stand, divided we fall*

people who live in glass houses shouldn't throw stones
beware of criticising someone if you yourself are vulnerable to the same criticism

Originally, the proverb warned against throwing stones at an adversary if one's head was made of glass. In TROILUS AND CRISEYDE (c. 1374) Chaucer writes:

And forthy, who that hath a head of verre [glass],
From cast of stones wave him in the werre.

This saying, which has a Spanish equivalent, was in use up to the end of the eighteenth century. The proverb *People who live in glass houses shouldn't throw stones* is a variant of this earlier expression, and dates from at least the early seventeenth century. It was coined at a time when the use of glass in domestic architecture was increasing.

Although window glass was in occasional use during the first century AD, with the fall of the Roman Empire all types of glass production declined. During the twelfth century, stained glass for ecclesiastical purposes began to be more widely used in northern Europe but it was not until the fifteenth century that glass began to be used in domestic architecture, and then only the top of the window space would be glazed, the lower part having hinged shutters as before. By the early seventeenth century, however, technology had advanced sufficiently to allow the richer citizens the luxury of fully glazed windows, part of which could be opened for air. The poor, of course, had to content themselves with windows of horn, simple wooden shutters or hovels with no windows at all. Thomas More appreciated the difference glazed windows made and longed for good airy housing for all citizens (UTOPIA, 1516). In Amaurote, the main city of the fabulous Utopia, the houses enjoyed this benefit:

But nowe the houses be curiouslye buylded after a gorgious and gallante sorte, with three storyes one over another... They kepe the winde oute of their windows with glasse, for it is ther much used, and som here also with fine linnen cloth dipped in oyle or ambre... For by thys meanes more lighte commeth in, and the winde is better kepte oute .

In Elizabethan England when the yeomanry eventually began to aspire to glazed windows, they were still regarded as a luxury. The wills of John Tyther of Shropshire and John Butler of Surrey, both yeomen, included their glass windows among other personal effects. A person with the good fortune to live in a glazed house would be foolish indeed if he chose stones as a weapon with which to fight his neighbour.

Stevenson records a story about the Duke of Buckingham, a favourite of James I of England (James VI of Scotland). When the Scottish-born king acceded to the English throne in 1603, London was flooded with Scotsmen. The Duke mounted a campaign of harassment against them, which included hiring mobs to smash their windows. Buckingham's own London residence was popularly called the 'Glass House' because it had a great number of windows. Not surprisingly, it was not long before his victims retaliated in kind. When Buckingham complained to the king, His Majesty simply replied, '*Steenie, Steenie, those who live in glass houses should be carefu' how they fling stares.*'

Whether the story is true, and the first Stuart king is the author of the proverb variant, we will never know. All that can be said with certainty is that the present-day proverb was in use by 1640, for it is recorded by George Herbert in his JACULA PRUDENTUM.

I was amazed to see Joan Collins complaining that Baywatch star Pamela Anderson dressed like a tart. I suggest that Joan takes another look at some of the movies she made earlier in her career. **People who live in glass houses shouldn't throw stones.** *Perhaps she's just jealous of a younger woman who still clearly has her looks?*
BIRMINGHAM SUNDAY MERCURY,
8 APRIL 2001

One of Ireland's leading clerics – Diarmuid Martin, the Archbishop of Dublin – has scolded us for our 'insatiable greed'. The material obsession, he said, would only lead to 'disillusionment and despair'. I don't like to be cynical but **people who live in glass houses shouldn't throw stones.** *The Archbishop lives in a big house, known as The Palace, in Drumcondra. He also has his own private secretary to help with his busy workload.*
SUNDAY MIRROR, 31 DECEMBER 2006

See also *The POT calls the kettle black*

• I •

IGNORANCE

ignorance is bliss

upsetting news cannot dim your happiness while you remain ignorant of it

Variant: Where ignorance is bliss, 'tis folly to be wise

Sophocles, writing at the end of the fifth century BC, recognised that total ignorance of circumstances is *the sweetest life* (AJAX, c. 409 BC). From this arose two similar sayings in classical Latin, which Erasmus recorded in his ADAGIA (1536), and in his PRAISE OF FOLLY (1524 ed.) rendered as *To know nothing is the happiest life*. Thomas Gray reworked the thought in ODE ON A DISTANT PROSPECT OF ETON COLLEGE (1742), where the poet, looking out over a view of the famous public school, muses in a melancholy way upon the difficulties the future must necessarily hold for its pupils:

> *Alas! regardless of their doom*
> *The little victims play!*
> *No sense have they of ills to come*
> *Nor care beyond the day...*
> *Yet, ah! why should they know their fate,*
> *Since sorrow never comes too late,*
> *And happiness too swiftly flies?*
> *Thought would destroy their paradise!*
> *No more, – where ignorance is bliss,*
> *'Tis folly to be wise.*

The last two lines rapidly acquired proverbial status, and are still quoted in full up to the present day. However,

the saying is better known in the abbreviated form *Ignorance is bliss*, and has given rise to two idiomatic forms: *blissful ignorance* and the derived *blessed ignorance*.

Kath seemed kinda proud to be taking us home, like it was Sandringham Palace itself. Course, in those days she didn't know what lovely homes American people had, and **ignorance is bliss**.
LAURIE GRAHAM, THE FUTURE
HOMEMAKERS OF AMERICA, 2001

I know that **ignorance is never bliss**.
I'll take the grubby truth over a white lie any day.
BIG ISSUE, 18–24 JULY 2005

***Ignorance is bliss**. That has been the defence of the adulterer throughout the ages.*
BIRMINGHAM POST,
21 MARCH 2006

See also *What the EYE doesn't see, the heart doesn't grieve over*

IMITATION

imitation is the sincerest form of flattery

copying someone pays an implicit and genuine compliment to that person

Charles Caleb Colton (1780–1832) was an eccentric English writer, collector and one-time clergyman. His books of aphorisms and short essays were once enormously popular, and his LACON, OR MANY THINGS IN FEW WORDS, ADDRESSED TO THOSE

WHO THINK (1820) was reprinted several times and ran to a second volume. The elliptical *Imitation is the sincerest of flattery* is recorded in the first volume. The later addition of the word *form* to give the contemporary phrasing makes the expression clearer.

Imitation is the sincerest form of flattery, they say, and the pop industry is quicker than most to pounce on a winning trend.
COVENTRY EVENING TELEGRAPH, 7 JANUARY 2000

*Now for Rich and Brandon's home-made product. The initial surprise is that it really does taste like Coke... Having found their liquid gold, Brandon and Rich plan to sell concentrate kits to other small bars and businesses... The mega corporation remains unfazed. 'As the saying goes, **imitation is the sincerest form of flattery**,' says a Coca-Cola spokesman. 'But our product is unique. Anyone with a selection of ingredients could make a type of cola, but there can only be one Coke.'*
GUARDIAN, 28 JULY 2006

IRON

strike while the iron's hot
make the most of an opportunity; act when circumstances are favourable

The saying originates in the blacksmith's forge. There are many figurative references in ancient Greek and Latin literature to striking red-hot iron, the sense being 'seize the opportunity'. One of the Latin proverbs in Publilius Syrus's SENTEN-TIAE (c. 43 BC), for instance, reads: *You should hammer your iron when it is glowing hot.* Chaucer was aware of the figure. In TROILUS AND CRISEYDE (c. 1380), Criseyde's scheming uncle and guardian Pandarus tries to arrange a love affair between Troilus and his niece, and finds an opportune moment to further his argument:

Pandare, which that stood hir faste by,
Felte iren hoot, tyme is for to smyte.

Later, Chaucer used the proverb in a wider context, urging us to *strike while the iron is hot* when relationships are at stake: *Right so as whyl that iren is hoot, men sholden smyte, right so, men sholde wreken hir wronges whyle that they been fresshe and newe* (TALE OF MELIBEUS, c. 1386).

Indeed, from Chaucer onwards the figure is frequently found in English literature and proverb collections: Caxton informs us that *Whan the yron is well hoote, hit werketh the better* (THE FOURE SONNES OF AYMON, c. 1489); Erasmus, in his ADAGIA (1536), cites the Latin proverb *Now your iron is in the fire*, and goes on to explain that it means 'Now your iron is in the fire, get to work'; and John Heywood records it in his PROVERBS (1546), explaining its origin:

And one good lesson to this purpose I pike
From the smithis forge, whan thyron is
hot strike.

By the second half of the sixteenth century, the proverb appears in the words we are familiar with today.

*After winning one regional award already Liverpool & Ormskirk Bridal Houses are no strangers to the benefits attached to being nominated for New Business of the Year in the Daily Post Regional Business Awards... In light of its recent achievements The Liverpool Bridal Houses aim to **strike while the iron's hot** and is now looking to expand outside the region with an eye on the Isle of Man.*
DAILY POST, 15 MAY 2002

You're A Star's Mickey Harte isn't one to take success for granted. The finals to represent Ireland in the Eurovision Song Contest are three weeks away – but, Mickey has already a few plans under his belt.

*He said: 'I am planning to do a tour and release a single as well as I want to **strike while the iron's hot**.'*
SUNDAY MIRROR, 23 FEBRUARY 2003

See also *CARPE diem; make HAY while the sun shines; gather ye ROSEBUDS while ye may; TIME and tide wait for no man; there's no TIME like the present; never put off till TOMORROW what you can do today*

J

JACK

all work and no play makes Jack a dull boy

time for recreation is essential to make a balanced and interesting person

There are a number of proverbs about *Jack*. Jack was 'everyman', 'the man in the street' in past centuries, the equivalent of the present-day Joe Bloggs. Other languages have characters who represent the average man – French has *Gros Jean* and American *John Doe*. Other proverbs about Jack include *JACK of all trades is master of none* and *every Jack must have his Jill*.

An early record of *All work and no play makes Jack a dull boy* comes in James Howell's ENGLISH PROVERBS (1659). Samuel Smiles shows us the other side of the coin: *All work and no play makes Jack a dull boy; but all play and no work makes him something greatly worse* (SELF-HELP, 1859).

As we wrap up another school year, let me congratulate all the seniors who will be graduating. As you move on to the next phase of your life, I wish you well. Be passionate about what you do and remember: **all work and no play makes Jack a dull boy**, *but all play and no work makes Jack a poor boy!*
ARLINGTON HEIGHTS DAILY HERALD, 29 MAY 2001

All work and no play makes Jack a dull boy. But it's not often your boss tells you so. It may come as a shock that the Government and businesses are encouraging workers to take a stroll, have a stretch and put their feet up.
INDEPENDENT, 2 FEBRUARY 2006

See also *VARIETY is the spice of life*

Jack of all trades is master of none

to have a superficial knowledge of many skills means no real skill in any area

Variants: Jack of all trades is of no trade; Jack of all trades, master of none; Jack of all trades and master of none

The term *Jack of all trades*, to describe someone who dabbles in many skills but has no real knowledge of any, has been current since at least the beginning of the seventeenth century. Thomas Fuller cites *Jack of all trades is of no trade* in his GNOMOLOGIA (1732) and the familiar proverb *Jack of all trades and master of none* is found in Maria Edgeworth's POPULAR TALES (1800). It echoes the French proverb which states that *When one is good at everything, one is good at nothing*. Trench also quotes a graphic German proverb: *The master of one trade will support a wife and seven children: the master of seven trades will not support himself.*

There are always people who will make wide-ranging claims for themselves, yet the evidence contradicts them. The spelling and grammar (or *gramer*) of Roger Giles make one wonder about the standard of his many other accomplishments listed on this humorous eighteenth century handbill quoted by Walsh:

Roger Giles, Imperceptible Penetrator, Surgin, Paroch Clarke, &c., Romford, Essex, hinforms Ladis and Gentlemen that he cuts their teeth and draws corns without waiten a moment. Blisturs on the lowest turms, and fysics at a penny a peace. Sells godfathers cordial and strap-ile, and undertakes to keep a Ladis nales by the year and so on. Young Ladis and Gentlemen tort the heart of rideing, and the gramer language in the natest manner, also grate Kare takein to himprove there morals and spelling, sarm singin and whisseling. Teaches the jewsarp, and instructs young Ladis on the gar-tar, and plays the ho-boy. Shotish, poker and all the other ruls tort at home and abroad. Perfumery in all its branches. Sells all sorts stashionary, barth bricks and all other sorts of sweet-meats, including beeswax postage stamps and lusifers; likewise taturs, roobub, sossages and other garden stuffs, also fruits, such as hard bake, inguns, toothpicks, ile and tinware, and other eatables. Sarve, treacle, winegar, and all other hardware. Further in particular he has laid in a stock of tripe, china, epsom salts, lollipops and other pickels, such as oysters, apples and table beer, also silk, satin and hearthstones, and all kinds of kimistry, including wax-dolls, rasors, dutch cloks, and gridirons, and new laid eggs evry day by me, Roger Giles. P. S. – I lectures in joggrefy.

*Because I'm a Gemini, I start things which I don't finish. I suppose you could describe me as a **Jill of all trades and a Jack of none**...*
DAILY TELEGRAPH, 3 JANUARY 2002

*If your bankers think that your ideal client is 'someone with a lot of money', that means they think of you as a **jack-of-all-trades**. But remember, a '**jack-of-all-trades**' is '**master of none**'. I want to help transform you from a vague generality in your bankers' minds to a meaningful specific.*
BANK INVESTMENT CONSULTANT, 1 APRIL 2007

Usage: The expression is not always derogatory; in the right context and tone it could be used in the frequent short form *Jack of all trades* to describe someone competent in a range of skills.

JOB

if a job's worth doing, it's worth doing well
if you think a task merits your attention, then you should do it to the best of your ability

Variant: What is worth doing at all, is worth doing well

If a thing is worth doing, it is worth doing badly. This paradox of G K Chesterton's comes to the rescue of the perfectionist intimidated by that word *well*. If a thing is worth doing, Chesterton implies, better by far to have a go at it and risk a mediocre outcome than not to bother at all.

The proverb itself is reported to have been the favourite motto of Charles Dickens. In the Preface to LETTERS OF CHARLES DICKENS (1893), the people in the know – his sister-in-law and eldest daughter – tell us: *Dickens would take as much pains about the hanging of a picture...as... about the more serious business of his life; thus carrying out...his favourite motto of 'What is worth doing at all is worth doing well'*.

The saying, however, pre-dates the nineteenth century; Lord Chesterfield, for instance, used it in one of his letters (10 March 1746).

THE PROVERBIAL CYNIC

Several writers have taken the usually wholesome and helpful advice of a proverb and given it a cynical and witty turn. In San Francisco in 1904 Ethel Watts Mumford, Oliver Herford and Addison Mizner published THE ENTIRELY NEW CYNIC'S CALENDAR OF REVISED WISDOM for 1905. Here are a few extracts:

January
Knowledge is power – if you know it about the right person
Tell the truth and shame the – family
The wages of Gin is Debt

February
Actresses will happen in the best regulated families
Too many hooks spoil the cloth

March
He who owes nothing fears nothing
Money makes the Mayor go
There's a Pen for the wise, but alas! no Pound for the foolish

April
Wild oats make a bad autumn crop
He that is down need not fear plucking

May
Don't take the Will for the Deed – get the Deed
Nothing succeeds like – failure
Charity is the sterilized milk of human kindness

June
The gossip is not always of the swift, nor the tattle of the wrong
Advice to Parents – 'Cast not your girls before swains'

July
Only the young die good
The Doctor's Motto – A fee in the hand is worth two in the book
The wisest reflections are but Vanity

If a job's worth doing, it's worth doing well. And that's especially true of DIY. Bad workmanship could cause you or others njury and will lower the value of your 1ouse should you wish to sell.
MIRROR, 7 JULY 2001

The young teenager had been hoeing weeds in the plant nursery's far field for almost six hours. Under a hot sun, the only thing more painful than the blister on his left hand was the thought of the hours until quitting time. Bending back to the task, he spotted his boss striding toward him down the dusty tractor trail. The boss

August
The more taste, the less creed
The danger lies not in the big ears of little pitchers, but in the large mouths

September
He who fights and runs away Will live to write about the fray
A gentle lie turneth away inquiry

October
Never too old to yearn
The pension is mightier than the sword

November
A fellow failing makes us wondrous unkind
Society covers a multitude of sins
All is not bold that titters

December
The Steamer's Motto – You can't eat your cake and have it too
The more waist the less speed

There is a galaxy of writers whose fame rests on their satirical and acerbic view of life: Fred Allen, Russell Baker, Ambrose Bierce, Gordon Bowker, Leonard Louis Levinson, H L Mencken, Dorothy Parker, E B White and others. In German, Gerhard Uhlenbruck's writings are in the same tradition. In amongst their definitions, quips and witticisms are many based on proverbs. That most prolix of authors, Anon, also has a few mordant messages to his credit, as have some lesser luminaries:

A travesty is imitation without flattery
Silence is not always golden. Sometimes it's just plain yellow
Opportunity is something that goes without saying
Home is an Englishman's castle while his wife is at the pictures
Home is a place where you can scratch any place you itch (Henry Ainsley)
Tomorrow is one of the greatest labour-saving inventions of today (Vincent T Foss)
Tomorrow is always the busiest day of the week (Richard Willis)

stopped about 20 feet off and for a long minute, watched silently as the teenager hacked tiredly at the weeds. 'Give me that,' the boss finally said. Taking the hoe, he swung vigorously for a few moments, slicing the weeds cleanly. 'There,' he announced, handing the tool back to the teenager. 'That's how.

*Remember: **if a job's worth doing, it's worth doing well.**' Then he turned and walked off to his office, leaving the teenager rubbing his blistered hand and muttering under his breath.*
SYRACUSE POST-STANDARD,
8 JANUARY 2004

· K ·

KILL

kill or cure

said when medicine or surgery is so dangerous that it might kill the patient

In his essay OF FRIENDSHIP (1597), Francis Bacon, warning against taking advice from more than one friend in case their guidance conflicts, uses the analogy of a doctor who, being a specialist in one area, inadvertently harms a patient in another way: *...even as if you would call a physician, that is thought good for the cure of the disease you complain of, but is unacquainted with your body; and therefore may put you in way for a present cure, but overthroweth your health in some other kind; and so cure the disease, and kill the patient.*

Kill or cure is a proverb of last resort, its modern form dating from the twentieth century. Although it is often applied to medical matters, it can also refer to drastic action taken on behalf of any ailing plan or project, which will ultimately bring about its salvation or its demise.

*I believe in **kill or cure** so when I get a sore throat, I hit it with the strongest lozenges I can get my hands on...*
DAILY MAIL, 13 JULY 2004

*The torrid time being experienced by Panorama highlights the difficulty of keeping current affairs fresh, relevant, and attractive to viewers of a mainstream mixed-genre channel like BBC1... Changes are afoot, but whether these will **kill or cure** remains to be seen.*
GUARDIAN, 27 MARCH 2006

See also *The REMEDY is worse than the disease*

KITCHEN

if you can't stand the heat, get out of the kitchen

if the pressure is too much for you to bear, get away from it; if the demands of the job are too heavy for you, let someone else do it

The expression is attributed to Harry S Truman, US President from 1945 to 1953, who used it to describe his robust attitude to a life in politics. In his book MR CITIZEN (1960) he writes: *Some men can make decisions and some cannot. Some men fret and delay under criticism. I used to have a saying that applies here, and I note that some people have picked it up.* That expression was, of course, *If you can't stand the heat, get out of the kitchen.*

It is uncertain whether Truman was the first to use the saying. An article published in the SODA SPRINGS SUN (Idaho, July 1942) calls it a *favorite rejoinder of Senator Harry S. Truman.*

It may be, however, that the expression was simply picked up and popularised by Truman. TIME magazine (28 April 1952) has the President *quoting a favourite expression of his military jester Major General Harry Vaughan* to explain his own forthcoming retirement – *If you can't stand the heat, get out of the kitchen.*

If you can't stand the heat, get out of the kitchen. That's the phrase that springs to mind on learning more teachers in the region suffer from long-term sickness than anywhere else in the UK... If teachers can't cope with life in school they should get out. They are doing nobody any good by staying... it can't be of any benefit to the children, who are increasingly taught by supply teachers they don't know.
NEWCASTLE EVENING CHRONICLE, 10 SEPTEMBER 2004

'If you can't stand the heat, get out of the kitchen' is a tried and true saying that applies to almost any situation in which you find yourself in over your head. Essentially, it boils down to being able to keep your cool in the face of enormous pressure.
MADISON CAPITAL TIMES, 7 JUNE 2005

KNOWLEDGE

knowledge is power
the more we know, the greater the influence we have over others

In the biblical account of the Garden of Eden, God commanded Adam not to eat fruit from the tree of the knowledge of good and evil. The serpent's crafty argument to persuade Eve into eating the fruit focused on the knowledge she would gain, and on how that knowledge would make her god-like: *And the serpent said unto the woman, Ye shall not surely die; For God doth know that in the day ye eat thereof, then your eyes shall be opened, and ye shall be as God, knowing good and evil* (GENESIS 3:4–5).

Francis Bacon was well aware of the biblical dimension of knowledge and power: *The desire of power in excess caused the angels to fall: the desire of knowledge in excess caused man to fall* (ESSAYS: OF GOODNESS, 1612). In NOVUM ORGANUM (1620) he expressed the ancient relationship between knowledge and power thus: *Knowledge and human power are synonymous*. And again in MEDITATIONES SACRAE: DE HAERESIBUS (c. 1626): *Knowledge itself is power*. Bacon's near contemporary, Thomas Hobbes, developed his own view. Chapter 10 of his LEVIATHAN (1651), for example, is entitled 'Of Power, Worth, Dignity, Honour and Worthiness', and argues the case for a rather worldly-wise view of power.

The same thread of self-interest and misuse of power runs through succeeding centuries. Ethel Watts Mumford (see THE PROVERBIAL CYNIC, page 152), for instance, said: *Knowledge is power, if you know it about the right person* (1904). A recent instance is this hard, epigrammatic statement from Stanley I Benn: *The more one knows about a person, the greater one's power to destroy him*. Rabelais (c. 1495–1553) was much closer to the perspective of the Garden of Eden: *Knowledge without conscience is the ruination of the soul*.

*I have discovered in the world of the reforming smoker, **knowledge is power**. If you know everything there is to know about nicotine and you want to give it up, there is no real reason to fail...*
BIRMINGHAM POST, 4 MARCH 2000

*We used to like doctors, of course, or have some respect for them at least, but that was in the days when there was some communal respect for people who knew things we didn't. Now all such esoteric knowledge is regarded as suspect, as somehow unjust. If **knowledge is power** and power should, in a democracy, be in the hands of us all, then it follows that knowledge should be in our hands too.*
DAILY TELEGRAPH, 28 JANUARY 2001

L

LATE

better late than never

it is better to turn up (or complete a task) late than not to bother at all

It is better to be late than never to arrive, writes Dionysius of Halicarnassus around 25 BC, and Livy, in his HISTORY (c. 10 BC), has *Better late than never.* The proverb is found in many European languages, and has been in use in English for many centuries. It appears in the devotional manual ANCREN RIWLE (c. 1200) and the DOUCE MANUSCRIPT (c. 1350), as well as in Chaucer's CANTERBURY TALES (c. 1387). John Heywood, in his PROVERBS (1534), has *Better late than never to repent,* while the Baptist evangelist Charles Spurgeon, anxious lest the proverb should be used as an excuse for slackness, warns *Better late than never, but better never late* (SALT-CELLARS, 1885).

*If you want to get the news first there is only one place to look, the Daily Mirror. Over a week ago our exclusive investigation revealed thousands of builders face the dole after Northern Ireland planning chiefs cut the number of houses being built. They claimed outdated sewers across the country would collapse if new homes were built. But yesterday one of our so-called rivals at the Belfast Telegraph printed the same story. **Better late than never**, lads!*
MIRROR, 28 AUGUST 2002

*While the mayor's reforms may fall under the category of **better late than never**, they're still too late.*
CHICAGO SUN-TIMES, 24 MAY 2005

LAUGH

he who laughs last laughs longest

don't rejoice too soon – you may not come off best in the end

Variant: He laughs best who laughs last

Sir Walter Scott, writing in PEVERIL OF THE PEAK (1823), calls this *a French proverb.* It is, in fact, also found in Italian. John Ray, in his ENGLISH PROVERBS (1678), has *Better the last smile than the first laughter.* John Vanbrugh uses *He laughs best that laughs last* in his play THE COUNTRY HOUSE (1706).

The variant *He who laughs last laughs longest* was coined in the twentieth century, and is even more difficult to say than the original. The idiomatic expression *to have the last laugh* is based on the proverb.

This is for the reader whose children were always picked last in gym class. I remember the same humiliation of standing there, knowing I was 'not wanted'. So, instead of playing sports, I studied hard. Well, now I am 65, play racquetball three times a week and am in excellent health.

My message to others who, like me, were 'picked last' is this: Get the best education you possibly can, and take care of your health. Many of those boys and girls who were picked first did neither. As the saying goes, 'He who laughs last, laughs best.'
WASHINGTON POST, 8 JULY 2001

He who laughs last laughs longest and
Philip Green has had the last laugh at the
City by ignoring it completely. While the
Square Mile looks for excuses to keep him
away from the London stock market, Green
has proved that he doesn't need to go
anywhere near it.

Adding Arcadia to his existing retail
chains will make him owner of Britain's
largest private company, in turnover terms.
The man who was cold-shouldered when he
wanted to buy Marks & Spencer now has
an empire selling more womenswear than
the quoted rival, acquired for less than a
fifth of the price he would have had to pay
for Marks.
SUNDAY BUSINESS, 8 SEPTEMBER 2002

LAUGHTER

laughter is the best medicine
laughter does more than any medicine
to treat sickness or depression

The medicinal benefits of laughter
have long been recognised. Written
around the fifth century BC, the
biblical BOOK OF PROVERBS (17:22)
has *A merry heart doeth good like a
medicine, but a broken spirit drieth the
bones*. In the fourteenth century, it
became proverbial that *Lengor liueth a
glad mon then a sori* (in VERNON MS,
c. 1340). And in the prologue to his
RALPH ROISTER DOISTER (c. 1553),
Nicholas Udall writes *Mirth prolongeth
life, and causeth health*, a notion echoed
by Shakespeare in THE TAMING OF
THE SHREW (1594):

> And frame your mind to mirth and
> merriment,
> Which bars a thousand harms and
> lengthens life.

In the nineteenth century, the
American Congregationalist minister
Henry Ward Beecher wrote that *Mirth
is God's medicine*, adding that *Everybody

ought to bathe in it. Grim care, moroseness,
anxiety, – all this rust of life ought to be
scoured off by the oil of mirth* (PROVERBS
FROM PLYMOUTH PULPIT, 1887).

Then, in the 1950s, READER'S
DIGEST began a regular column
entitled *Laughter is the best medicine*. If
the DIGEST did not coin the present-
day version of the proverb, earlier
references to it are wanting.

*Derek and Susanne Foster are a bubbly
pair of jokers. Even when the Thornaby
brother and sister were both diagnosed with
breast cancer, they never lost their sense of
humour.*
'*Laughter is the best medicine*,' insists
55-year-old Susanne. 'We've always been a
family determined to let nothing get us
down. We just took it on the chin and got
on with life.'
MIDDLESBROUGH EVENING GAZETTE,
14 MARCH 2006

*They say **laughter is the best medicine**,
which is true except when you have a sore
throat. Many illnesses are stress-induced,
which is why peace and quiet is a good
remedy. But in real life the only time you
get any peace and quiet is when you're ill.
That's why, instead of 'sickies', we should
call them 'healthies'.*
GUARDIAN, 15 JULY 2006

LEARNING

a little learning is a dangerous thing
relying on a shallow understanding of
a topic where deeper knowledge is
called for will lead to problems

Variant: A little knowledge is a
dangerous thing

The proverb is a line from Alexander
Pope's poem ESSAY ON CRITICISM
(1711):

PROVERBIAL WALLPAPER

Graffiti and proverbs have a good deal in common. The relationship between them has even been the subject of academic papers. Suffice it to say that both represent the wit and wisdom of the people, and that graffiti artists often use a well-known proverb as their starting point. But the theorising spoils the fun – here are some to enjoy:

- *Laugh and the world laughs with you; snore and you sleep alone*
- *Laugh – and the world thinks you're an idiot*
- *He who laughs last doesn't get the joke*
- *A friend in need is a pest!*
- *Give a man enough hope and he'll hang himself*
- *Happiness can't buy money*
- *Every man reaps what he sows – except the amateur gardener*
- *He who finds fault in his friends has faulty friends*
- *Where there's a will – there's a greedy solicitor getting in on the act*
- *Where there's a will, there's an inheritance tax*

- *All that glitters isn't gold. All that doesn't glitter isn't either*
- *Money is the root of all evil – and a man needs roots!*
- *The money that men make lives after them*
- *He who ploughs a straight furrow is in a rut*
- *Constipation is the thief of time*
- *Diarrhoea waits for no man*
- *All's fear in love and war*
- *Beneath a rough exterior often beats a harlot of gold*
- *Chaste makes waste*
- *Familiarity breeds*
- *The devil finds work for idle glands*
- *'Tis better to have loved and lust, than never to have lust at all*
- *Two's company, three's an orgy*
- *It takes two to tangle*
- *If at first you don't succeed, try a little ardour*
- *A bird in the bed is worth two in the bushes*

Perhaps one should conclude with the old English proverb that *A wall is a fool's paper.*

A little learning is a dangerous thing;
Drink deep, or taste not the Pierian spring:
There shallow draughts intoxicate the brain,
And drinking largely sobers us again.

The poem expounds the principles of literary taste and style and discusses the rules governing literary criticism. Pope's views follow neoclassical lines, hence the reference to the Pierian spring, the dwelling place of the nine Muses, the goddesses who inspire learning in science and the arts. *A shallow draught* from this fount of inspiration makes one believe one knows a great deal; *drinking largely* makes one realise how much more there is to learn.

These days the line is widely quoted to refer to any sphere of knowledge where shallow understanding might lead one into difficulties. This is in keeping with earlier expressions of the same thought. Bacon, for example, suggests that *A little philosophy inclineth man's mind to atheism, but depth in philosophy bringeth men's minds about to religion* (OF ATHEISM, 1598), and Donne formulates the general meaning in a way that might well have become a proverb itself: *Who are a little wise the best fools be* (TRIPLE FOOL, 1633).

A little bit of knowledge can be a dangerous thing. This was particularly true in medical school exams, where examiners would attempt to trick you with subjects of which you had only a fleeting knowledge.
DAILY TELEGRAPH,
28 NOVEMBER 2005

Our modest Queen has, in all senses of the phrase, good horse sense. But she never went to school, and she would never pretend to be an intellectual. Her son Prince Charles, by contrast, is a walking embodiment of Alexander Pope's adage that 'a little learning is a dangerous thing'.
DAILY MAIL, 17 OCTOBER 2006

LEAVE

leave well alone
don't disturb or try to improve a situation which is acceptable as it is

Variants: Let well alone; Leave well enough alone

Plutarch in his MORALIA: OLD MAN IN PUBLIC AFFAIRS (c. AD 95) reminds us of a fable by Aesop which illustrates the proverb well. A hedgehog offered to remove the ticks from the coat of a fox but the fox refused the offer, reasoning that if he removed the well-fed ticks from her back their places would simply be taken up by hungry ones.

Let well alone was quoted as a saying by Terence as early as the second century BC. References to the ancient proverb are found in English from Chaucer's ENVOY TO BUKTON (c. 1386) onwards, but not until the middle of the eighteenth century do we find it quoted in the familiar form.

[Gibraltar] is also a society worth preserving: a happy, contented, prosperous, law-abiding and free place. So why not just let well alone?
MAIL ON SUNDAY, 25 NOVEMBER 2001

*A wide range of commentators urged the Bank to **leave well alone** for a while to allow its earlier increases in the cost of borrowing to take effect. Several warned of the danger of "overkill" damaging the economy.*
BIRMINGHAM POST, 6 JULY 2007

Usage: The form with *let* is more formal and less common.

See also *If it ain't BROKE, don't fix it; Let sleeping DOGS lie*

LEOPARD

a leopard can't change his spots
a person cannot change his basic nature

Variant: A leopard can't change its spots

The proverb is from the Old Testament. God, through the prophet Jeremiah, was showing his people how far short they were falling of his standards. Sin had become so deeply embedded in their character that change, without God's help, was a near impossibility. JEREMIAH 13:23 asks: *Can the Ethiopian change his skin, or the leopard his spots?*

The proverb is still used in this sense today; some undesirable traits are so ingrained that a person can no more change his behaviour than a leopard the pattern of his skin.

Jeremiah was writing in the seventh century BC, when leopards would have been familiar to herdsmen who set traps for them. They do still exist in the Sinai region but are now very rare.

Hilary's husband is lovely in many ways but flirts with women. If she complains, she's told that she's neurotic…
*The phrase that springs to mind when reading Hilary's dilemma is '**You can't make a leopard change its spots.**' But it's not true. You can make a leopard change its spots – but if you do, it's no longer very leopardy.*
INDEPENDENT, 19 JULY 2001

*The capture of IRA men in the Colombian jungle has exploded the myth that these terrorists will one day give up their guns and settle down to a life of peace. These people – and their loyalist counterparts – thrive on the power they have over people. There is an old saying that a **leopard can't change its spots** – well, it appears to be true that terrorists can't give up causing violence and mayhem.*
GLASGOW DAILY RECORD,
16 AUGUST 2001

LIGHTNING

lightning never strikes twice in the same place
one is never afflicted twice in the same way

Nowadays scientists can explain how and why lightning occurs and meteorologists give us advance warning of imminent storms. In fact, lightning strikes somewhere on the earth's surface up to 100 times a second. In ancient times, however, lightning was seen as a display of immense and terrifying power and often attributed to the wrath of the gods or evil spirits.

In Roman times it was observed that lightning never seemed to strike the bay laurel, and the Emperor Tiberius was amongst those who wore laurel on his head for protection during thunder-storms. Later bay laurel bushes were planted near houses to keep them safe. The humble house-leek, planted on a roof and left undisturbed, was another plant supposed to have protective powers. In the eighth century, Charlemagne decreed that every home in his empire should be protected by the plant. The superstition was still current eight centuries later. In NATURALL AND ARTIFICIALL CONCLUSIONS (1586), Thomas Hill wrote: *If the herb house-leek or syngren do grow on the housetop, the same house is never stricken*

with lightning or thunder. The following century Nicholas Culpeper said that *neither witch nor devil, thunder nor lightning will hurt a man where a bay tree is* (HERBAL, 1653).

By the middle of the eighteenth century, however, men were facing up to the perils of lightning in a scientific way. In the December 1753 edition of POOR RICHARD'S ALMANACK, Benjamin Franklin includes an article entitled 'How to Secure Houses, etc. from Lightning' and gives comprehensive information on the use of lightning conductors.

Superstitions about lightning, however, continue. A much more recent belief, which originated in America, is that *Lightning never strikes twice in the same place*. This weather proverb is recorded in P Hamilton Myers's THRILLING ADVENTURES OF THE PRISONER OF THE BORDER, A TALE OF 1838 (1857).

The saying has been proved untrue many times, high structures being especially vulnerable: the Empire State building in New York is struck a dozen times a year on average and the large bronze statue of William Penn on City Hall in Philadelphia is also hit several times annually. Some human beings seem to be exceptionally unlucky. Roy C Sullivan of Virginia was struck seven times during his lifetime before dying of self-inflicted gunshot wounds. But no one had told him about the bay laurel.

*Who says **lightning never strikes twice in the same place**? At Old Trafford they can tell you different – and point to the spot where it happens.*
The ghost of Massimo Taibi came back to haunt the ground yesterday. Same game, same soft shot, even the same end and, bizarrely, the same horrific mistake.
PEOPLE, 29 OCTOBER 2000

*They say **lightning never strikes twice in the same place**, but that won't stop me hoping against hope for the next few days. On Saturday, I'll be going as gambling bonkers as the rest of the country as the Grand National gets under way at Aintree. And for the 25th year on the trot, I'll be waiting for a repeat of the one genuinely X-Files moment of my life.*
LIVERPOOL ECHO, 2 APRIL 2002

LIKE

like it or lump it
the idea may not appeal to you but you will have to put up with it

Variant: If you don't like it, you can/you'll have to lump it

Lump in this context means 'to accept with bad grace something that has to be endured'. So, according to the proverb, if a plan or state of affairs is not to a person's liking there is the choice of accepting it cheerfully or putting up with it grudgingly. THE OXFORD ENGLISH DICTIONARY dates the expression from 1833, when it was used in John Neal's THE DOWN-EASTERS. Dickens, Mark Twain, Shaw and Galsworthy are amongst the authors who have used this common colloquialism since.

*Cabinet Government has been something of a joke during Tony Blair's rule. Decisions are taken by him in consultation with his unelected and unaccountable henchmen, like Alastair Campbell and Jonathan Powell. The Cabinet is then told the outcome on a **like-it-or-lump-it** basis.*
DAILY MAIL, 9 MARCH 2002

*Claudio Ranieri has admitted he cannot keep all his Chelsea players happy – but has told them they can **like it or lump it**.*
NEWCASTLE EVENING CHRONICLE, 16 SEPTEMBER 2003

Usage: Informal

LIVE

live and let live
show the tolerance towards others you would expect them to show towards you

Gerard de Malynes, writing in 1622, claims the saying is from Holland: *According to the Dutch Prouerbe... Leuen ende laeten leuen. To liue and let others liue.* There is also, however, a direct translation into Italian. The proverb may have crossed the Channel but its message travelled unheeded on the political scene. Throughout the seventeenth century, the relationship between Britain and Holland vacillated between latent hostility and uneasy peace. Three savage wars were fuelled by economic rivalry.

The title of Ian Fleming's second novel in the James Bond series, LIVE AND LET DIE (1954), is an allusion to the proverb. The book went on to become an immensely successful film in 1973.

*I don't mind if they [teenage children] snog or drink alcohol...I don't mind very much if they smoke cigarettes...I am certainly not going to keep poking my head round George's door in his converted loft to make sure that he and his friends are behaving themselves. **Live and let live**, I say.*
DAILY TELEGRAPH, 3 JANUARY 2002

*The right not to be offended replaced tolerance, respect and '**live and let live**'. Offence was deemed to be taken whenever someone decided they didn't like something and suddenly there were clear walls, policies and neutral working environments.*
BELFAST NEWS LETTER, 9 SEPTEMBER 2003

See also *DO as you would be done by; It takes all sorts to make a WORLD*

LOOK

look before you leap

think carefully before acting; beware of taking sudden, rash decisions

One of Aesop's fables, THE FOX AND THE GOAT (c. 570 BC), illustrates this old proverb and was probably instrumental in its origin. A fox tumbled into a well and was unable to climb out. A thirsty goat passed by and asked the fox if the water was sweet. The fox seized his chance and, extolling the quality of the water, encouraged the goat to join him in the well. When the goat had quenched his thirst, he began to fret as to how they would get out of the well. The fox persuaded his companion to stand against the wall so that he might climb out from on top of his shoulders, promising to pull the goat up after him. Once out of the well, however, the fox ran off, remarking that the goat was a stupid creature. 'You should not have gone down without thinking how you were going to get up,' he said.

A similar message is carried by another of Aesop's fables (c. 570 BC), that of THE TWO FROGS. When the pool in which the two frogs lived dried up in the summer heat, they left to look for another home and found a well. The foolish frog wanted to jump in but was restrained by his wise friend who pointed out the difficulty they would be in if that well dried up too.

The proverb has been in English for many centuries. The earliest record is in the DOUCE MANUSCRIPT, dating back to about 1350:

> First loke and aftirward lepe;
> Avyse the welle, or thow speke.

John Heywood counsels caution in marriage when he records the saying in PROVERBS (1534):

> Ye may learne good cheape,
> In weddyng and al thing, to looke or
> ye leape

a warning that is taken up 300 years later by Charlotte Bronte in SHIRLEY (1849): *When you feel tempted to marry,…look twice before you leap.*

Internet prices for glasses can be spectacularly low, but do **look before you leap***, warns Christopher Browne.*
OBSERVER, 12 JUNE 2005

The old adage **'look before you leap'** *has never been truer than for a company looking to export its goods or services to a new market. Doing your homework and finding out about your target market is an essential investment if you want to achieve your export goals.*
NEWCASTLE JOURNAL,
22 NOVEMBER 2006

LOVE

all's fair in love and war

no moderating rules govern a person's conduct in courtship or military matters

The assumption behind this proverb is that the end justifies the means. This has long been recognised in the theatre of war. Livy hinted at it two millennia ago: *To those to whom war is necessary it is just* (HISTORY, c. 10 BC). Courtship, too, may entail the use of any means if one is to emerge victorious and take the prize. These excesses of the heart are considered forgiveable because love has long been understood as a force which cannot be restrained: *Both might and mallice, deceyte and treacherye, all periurye, any impietie may lawfully be committed in loue, which is lawlesse* (John Lyly, EUPHUES, 1579).

The link between love and fighting for a kingdom was already established in a proverbial form by 1604: *An old saw hath bin, Faith's breach for love and kingdoms is no sin* (John Marston, THE FAWN). Later in the same century Aphra Behn writes: *Advantages are lawful in love and war* (THE EMPEROR OF THE MOON, 1677). There was also the strong contemporary influence of Cervantes's DON QUIXOTE. Publication of Part One was in 1605, and it was soon translated into English. One passage runs: *Love and war are the same thing, and stratagems and policy are as allowable in the one as in the other.* But the proverb in the form we are familiar with today did not appear until two centuries later.

Nowadays a different kind of war is being waged and the phrase is just as likely to be heard in the boardroom. As American author Christian N Bovee said: *Formerly when great fortunes were only made in war, war was a business; but now when great fortunes are only made by business, business is war.* The proverb is, in fact, elastic, a convenient excuse to justify dubious conduct in any area where self-interest reigns: *All's fair in love – an' war – an' politics* (George Ade, COUNTY CHAIRMAN, 1903).

All's fair in love and war, and man, it's a jungle out there. We come across challenges and ugly situations every day, and being nice won't get us very far. No, to prevail in the harsh reality of daily life, some subversive tactics have to be employed.
UNIVERSITY WIRE, 17 OCTOBER 2002

*They may say that **all's fair in love and war**, but now the full extent of Leanne and Danny's affair is out in the open there are lots of unhappy faces in the Rovers Return.*
GLASGOW DAILY RECORD,
26 OCTOBER 2005

Usage: Used as a comment, sometimes as an excuse, on a nasty underhand manoeuvre, perpetrated out of romantic love, out of love for one's country or for business advantage

the course of true love never did run smooth
a couple will inevitably have to overcome obstacles to and in their relationship before they can settle down together

Variant: The path of true love never runs smooth

The proverb is a quotation from Shakespeare's A MIDSUMMER NIGHT'S DREAM (1590). In Act 1, scene i, Lysander sighs:

Ay me! for aught that I could ever read,
Could ever hear by tale or history,
The course of true love never did run smooth.

His lament is heartfelt for, jokes with the young couples in the love stories he has read, his love for Hermia is fraught with difficulty. Hermia's father has ordered her to marry the young nobleman Demetrius. Under the law of Athens, she has four days in which to comply before being either put to death or confined to a nunnery.

After this, there is a prolonged silence in the literary record until 1835, when Scottish author Michael Scott uses the saying in THE CRUISE OF THE MIDGE (1835). Two years later, in PICKWICK PAPERS, Dickens reformulates it to take account of contemporary popular interest in the railways: *The course of true love is not a railway.* The expression was subsequently taken up by other writers.

*Love across the cultural divide. In this case, Romeo is a plump, 28-year-old unemployed Bangladeshi in Oldham and his Juliet is a straight-talking 18-year-old white girl. **The course of true love does not run smooth.** Notwithstanding the presence of the National Front and the 572 racially motivated crimes that took place in Oldham last year, this is a bumpy relationship at the best of times.*
THE TIMES, 24 SEPTEMBER 2001

BUSINESS MATTERS

It is hardly surprising that the massive growth in business and business studies in the twentieth and twenty-first centuries has re-invigorated older sayings: *Time is money* (Benjamin Franklin, ADVICE TO A YOUNG TRADESMAN, 1750), *Money talks* (G Torriano, ITALIAN PROVERBS, 1666). But it has also spawned many memorable new ones, of which some at least have reached proverbial status. Milton Friedman, the Nobel Prize winner, promoted: *There's no such thing as a free LUNCH*. Fred Adler, a leading American venture capitalist, put money in its place: *Happiness is a positive cash flow*. And then there's the anonymous *Buy low, sell high* and *The CUSTOMER is always right*, a maxim of disputed origin.

There are many other witty memorable sayings from the business world that have been collected together in anthologies of business quotations. This may well encourage their common currency and assimilation into the proverb stock of the language.

---

*In his three novels and two short-story collections, **the course of true love never does run smooth**. Rhodes is a master of the wrecked relationship, the fatal misunderstanding, the untimely death, the ensuing heartbreak.*
GUARDIAN, 14 APRIL 2007

love is blind

a person in love fails to recognise any faults or imperfections in the loved one

In the classical world, the god of love, known as Eros to the Greeks and Cupid to the Romans, was sometimes painted or sculpted blindfolded to illustrate the proverb that *Love is blind*. Certainly, the god was often thought of as capricious, his arrows of love piercing a heart at random and blinding the victim to the imperfections of the loved one. Shakespeare refers to this in these lines from A MIDSUMMER NIGHT'S DREAM (1590):

> *Love looks not with the eyes, but with the mind,*
> *And therefore is winged Cupid painted blind.*

Shakespeare, in fact, is fond of this proverb and quotes it in several of his plays.

The saying originated in ancient Greek literature and, like many of these ancient proverbs, came through Latin into many European languages. The earliest recorded use in English is in Chaucer's CANTERBURY TALES: THE MERCHANT'S TALE (c. 1387).

A later French proverb puts the reality more flippantly: *Love is blind; that is why he always proceeds by the sense of touch.* So does this gem: *Love is blind – and when you get married you get your eyesight back.*

---

*Proof that **love is blind** resides on the front page of this week's* Hello *magazine. The gloriously sexy Jonathan Ross is sitting with his arms wrapped around his wife, Jane Goldman, oblivious to the fact that with her tomato red hair and sullen face she looks like a Czech charlady.*
SUNDAY MIRROR, 16 APRIL 2000

***Love is blind**, of course – but usually for a reason. If Trump were witty, dashing or romantic, all would be explained. Instead The Donald, as he likes to be called, has all the character flaws of the typical tycoon: he is vain, insecure, attention-seeking and unconscionably tight.*
DAILY TELEGRAPH, 12 DECEMBER 2004

LUNCH

there's no such thing as a free lunch

you don't get something for nothing

Variant: There ain't no such thing as a free lunch

In nineteenth century America, saloon keepers would attract custom by offering free lunches on condition that at least one drink was bought. These varied from simple fare to more elaborate offerings. The cost of the lunch was unlikely to be covered by a single drink, so the saloon keeper counted on repeat orders for drinks and customer loyalty to pay for the food. An advertisement carried by the NEW YORK HERALD (4 July, 1884) for one of these lunches reads:

EADIE'S COFFEE HOUSE, 196 FULTON STREET
George Eadie respectfully intimates that having fitted up the above establishment, he will be happy to see his friends on the 4th of July. Steaks, Chops, and Scotch Mutton and Veal Pies, always on hand. Brandies, Wines, and Liquors, of the first quality. Free Lunch at 11, A.M.

The phrase *There's no such thing as a free lunch*, which is now proverbial, was coined in the 1940s in a journalistic response to US Vice President Henry Wallace's liberal views on the post-war economy. The gist of it is that there are hidden costs behind everything. Later, in 1975, the renowned economist Milton Friedman published a book entitled THERE'S NO SUCH THING AS A FREE LUNCH.

The variant *There ain't no such thing as a free lunch* often appears as the acronym TANSTAAFL.

*The Timeshare Consumers Association advises extreme caution. 'If you attempt to avoid a timeshare presentation on the holiday, you may end up paying for it in full. There are also likely to be additional costs, such as insurance and transfers. Do not sign anything.' In other words, **there is no such thing as a free holiday**.*
DAILY MAIL, 13 JULY 2002

CAN I DIET MY WAY TO A LIGHTER ECO FOOTPRINT?
*No, if you want to put some meat on the bones of your dual diet, you are going to have to make bigger adjustments. Including losing the meat. Steak from a grain-fed cow (and most of the world's cattle are now grain-fed) requires 35 calories of fossil fuel for every one calorie of meat. For the environment, you see, **there's no such thing as a free lunch**.*
OBSERVER, 8 JULY 2007

See also BUSINESS MATTERS, page 164

· M ·

MAN

manners maketh man
high standards of social behaviour establish a person's reputation and standing

Variant: Manners make the man

Written records of this old proverb go back to the fourteenth century; it appears in the DOUCE MANUSCRIPT (c. 1350). In the Middle Ages, there were ceremonies for every occasion, from the freeing of a serf to the creation of a knight, and strict codes of behaviour were laid down for each. Politeness was expected in everyday life too; guests were to be met at the gate and escorted out when they left, children were instructed to be courteous and young ladies were expected to walk rather than run and to sit with their hands demurely folded in their laps, especially when they found themselves beside a personable young man:

> If thou sit by a right goode manne,
> This lesson look thou think upon.
> Under his thigh thy knee not fit,
> Thou art full lewd, if thou does it.

Helpful guidance like this was to be found in manuals of etiquette such as the fourteenth century BOKE OF CURTASYE.

Some table manners may have changed over the centuries (see *FINGERS were made before forks*), but by no means all. This instruction on how to eat bread would pass for good manners in any classy restaurant today:

> Bite not on your bread and lay it down,
> That is no curtesy to use in town;
> But break as much as you will eat...

Some of the rules of etiquette commonly expected at feasts or dinners were laid down in guild statutes for the guidance of the members. The proverb appears in the following code devised for the guild of masons:

> Good manners maketh a man...
> Look that thine hands be clean
> And that thy knife be sharp and keen...
> If thou sit by a worthier man
> Than thyself art one,
> Suffer him first to touch the meat.
> In chamber among ladies bright,
> Hold thy tongue and spend thy sight.

Good conduct was also clearly expected of the students of New College, Oxford, whose founder, the prelate William of Wickham, had *Manners maketh man* cut into the stonework as the college motto in 1380. Indeed, so insistent was he about the importance of good behaviour that two years later he bestowed the same motto upon Winchester College. But then, as the bishop was doubtless aware, good behaviour generally springs from a considerate spirit.

Would you give up your seat on a bus or a train for a pregnant woman, asked this week's nationwide survey to mark National Pregnancy Week. The answer, disappointingly but not surprisingly, was a resounding no from the vast majority of male commuters.

They were doubtless full of the 'they wanted equality so they can have it' claptrap that ignorant ill-mannered men so often trot out. Indeed, in one instance, the only person who stood up to give a pregnant woman a seat was another pregnant woman!
Manners maketh man, *they say. Or not.*
NEWCASTLE JOURNAL,
6 SEPTEMBER 2003

Manners maketh man, *so the saying goes, and it's certainly true for this bunch of polite youngsters who have graduated with honours from Birmingham's school of etiquette. Knowing how and when to say please and thank you are habits which are too easily overlooked these days, but course organiser Rose Menns decided that the time was right to put the "cool" back into behaving properly.*
BIRMINGHAM MAIL, 2 JANUARY 2007

Usage: Fixed formulas, such as idioms and proverbs, sometimes provide the only homes for old words or grammar. The ending for *maketh* comes into this second category.

one man's meat is another man's poison
tastes differ – what one person enjoys, another will dislike

In DE RERUM NATURA (45 BC) the Roman philosopher and poet Lucretius writes: *What is food to one man may be fierce poison to others*. The proverb was in frequent use in the form we know today from at least the seventeenth century onwards.

Of course tastes differ, and people also exhibit varying sensitivity to different foods. Sufferers of coeliac disease cannot tolerate gluten, those tormented by migraine shun chocolate, and almost everyone knows someone who has an allergic reaction to some food or other. As Donald G Cooley puts it in EAT AND GET SLIM (1945): *One man's strawberries are another man's hives.*

One man's meat is another man's poison, *or so they say. And the same could be said of various sections of this newspaper, like any other. Some will read the sports pages with relish while others will avoid them like a pair of sweaty socks. Ditto the business pages, or the arts section. Some love David Banks' musings, while others would gladly shove him concreted-feet-first into the Dee. And even little old me comes in for an occasional kicking from some of you out there.*
NORTH WALES DAILY POST,
6 AUGUST 2003

Oscar Wilde once snorted that 'when I ask for a watercress sandwich, I don't mean a loaf with a field in the middle of it'. Such are the ways of cuisine, where **one man's meat is another man's poison**. *It really is all down to personal taste. I detest onions of any kind, and would rather eat the carpet than digest a meal with a trace of the accursed vegetable. My dear wife, on the other hand, would happily shovel down a plateful of boiled red onions and custard.*
LIVERPOOL DAILY POST,
26 OCTOBER 2005

Usage: The proverb can be widely applied to a difference in appreciation of films, politics, the opposite sex...in fact anything at all

See also *BEAUTY is in the eye of the beholder*

MARRIAGE

marriages are made in heaven
ideal partnerships are foreordained

Variant: Matches are made in heaven

The MIDRASH, a collection of rabbinical expositional and homiletical commentaries on the Old Testament set down in approximately AD 550, teaches that marriages are made in heaven. According to the MIDRASH, God gave Eve to Adam so that he should not be alone, and the moment they stood side by side in the Garden of Eden, God performed their wedding ceremony.

A French proverb to this effect was in circulation during the sixteenth century, and was borrowed into English: *True it is that marriages be don in heauen and performed in earth* (William Painter, THE PALACE OF PLEASURE, 1567). *Marriages are made in heaven* was coined from this by the end of that century.

An English proverb of the same period saw marriage partners not as being carefully matched by a benevolent God but being flung together, for good or ill, by destiny: *Weddyng is desteny And hangyng likewise, saith the prouerbe* (John Heywood, PROVERBS, 1546).

This negative view is reflected in the volume of harsh criticism marriage has received from literary pens over the centuries (see *MARRY in haste, repent at leisure* for a selection). It has also been a subject for humour: *Marriages are made in Heaven, and if we once set to work to repair celestial mistakes we shall have our hands full* (Henry Arthur Jones, 1851–1929). But then as Joseph Addison (1672–1719) so astutely pointed out:

No little scribbler is of wit so bare,
But has his fling at the poor wedded pair.

Marriages are made in heaven but *divorce always occurs if couples cannot agree to disagree amicably when problems arise.*
NEW STRAITS TIMES,
28 NOVEMBER 2003

Some marriages are made in heaven.
Fred and Ginger, Gilbert & George, Bogart and Bacall, Roberto Cavalli and Playboy.
INDEPENDENT, 14 JULY 2005

Usage: In these days when marital disharmony and divorce are common, the proverb is sometimes used somewhat cynically

MARRY

marry in haste, repent at leisure those who rush into marriage without thinking will have plenty of time to ponder upon their mistake after the ceremony

When he was asked whether or not a man should marry, Socrates (469–399 BC) is sagely reported to have said, *Whichever you do you will repent it* (in Diogenes Laertius, LIVES OF THE PHILOSOPHERS: SOCRATES, AD 200–250). Perhaps the French philosopher Montaigne was influenced by his cynicism, for he compared marriage to a cage where *the birds without despair to get in, and those within despair to get out* (ESSAYS, 1595). An issue of LIPPINCOTT'S MAGAZINE reiterated the thought in an anonymous rhyme from the 1830s:

Marriage is like a flaming candle-light
Placed in the window on a summer's night,
Inviting all the insects of the air
To come and singe their pretty winglets there:
Those that are out butt heads against
the pane,
Those that are in butt to get out again.

'If in doubt, don't' is the message.

Philemon, writing at the turn of the third century BC; thought the union would only bring regrets: *He who would marry is on the road to repentance* (FRAGMENTS, c. 300 BC). This wisdom is repeated in French courtly literature. The unknown author of LA CHASTELAINE DE SAINT GILLE (c. 1250) writes: *Nobody marries who doesn't repent of it*. A later French proverb, also echoed in English literature, puts it this way: *Marriage rides in the saddle, and repentance upon the croup*.

By the sixteenth century, however, it is not marriage itself but hasty marriage which brings regret in its

WHEN THERE'S AN 'R' IN THE MONTH

The British summer months from May to August (which have no 'R' in their spellings) have been the focus of considerable folk wisdom and advice. William Harrison in his DESCRIPTION OF ENGLAND (1577) writes that *Our oisters are generallie forborne in the foure hot months of the yeare, that is Maie, Iune, Iulie, and August*, adding *'which are void of the letter R'*. Two health manuals of the period, Vaughan's DIRECTIONS FOR HEALTH (1600) and Thomas Moufet's HEALTH'S IMPROVEMENT (1658), warn against eating oysters in those months which *wante the letter R*, and Henry Buttes says that oysters are *vnseasonable and vnholesome* in these months (DYETS DRY DINNER, 1599).

The advice is sound, although abstaining from an oyster feast is not strictly necessary on the grounds of health but on those of flavour: oysters spawn in this season and are not as tasty. Indeed, a seventeenth century law forbade harvesting oysters in the summer months to protect the spawning shellfish. Later Lord Chesterfield compared the cut and thrust of political life to the oyster season: *Here is no domestic news of changes and chances in the political world, which like oysters, are only in season in the R months, when the Parliament sits* (LETTERS, 1764).

According to proverbial advice, another dish to avoid in months lacking an 'R' is pork. Reasons for this are certainly health-based. Before the advent of refrigeration it was difficult to prevent the meat from spoiling and going off in hot weather and so, in order to guard against nasty bouts of food poisoning, pork was eaten only at cooler times of the year.

A Moroccan proverb follows the same guiding principle: *Eviter les mois en 'R' et vivre en plein air* ('Avoid the months with an 'R' and live in the open air'). In other words, camp out during the summer months and stay sheltered for the rest of the year.

And it seems the 'R' rule would also make the life of a fashionista easier as this advice in the *Mirror* shows:

...you should have relegated them to the back of your wardrobes. It doesn't matter how pretty they are, they won't look good with chicken-skin ankles and blue toes. Remember the golden rule and only wear them when there isn't an 'r' in the month.

---

wake. In PETITE PALLACE (1579), George Pettie warns that *Bargains made in speed are commonly repented at leisure* and English literature of the period is full of like advice. Shakespeare preaches it more than once. In MUCH ADO ABOUT NOTHING (1599), Beatrice gives the woman's perspective on the union:

Wooing, wedding, and repenting, is as a scotch jig, a measure, and a cinque-pace: the first suit is hot and hasty... the

wedding, mannerly-modest, as a measure... and then comes Repentance, and, with his bad legs, falls into the cinque-pace faster and faster, till he sink into his grave.

The proverb finds its neat expression *Marry in haste and repent at leisure* in John Ray's collection of ENGLISH PROVERBS (1670). This formulation may be Ray's translation of the Italian for, like many of our proverbs, the saying is found in a number of languages. European opinion concurs that to rush into marriage brings a lifetime of regret. Consider well before you *tie a knot with your tongue that you cannot untie with your teeth*. Gentlemen, let the French dramatist Marivaux (1688–1763) guide your thinking:

I would advise a man to pause Before he takes a wife:
In fact, I see no earthly cause He should not pause for life.

Ladies, ponder the fate of Mary Ford:

Here lies the body of Mary Ford,
Whose soul, we trust is with the Lord;
But if for hell she's changed this life,
Tis better than being John Ford's wife.

Scary Spice Mel B's 16-month marriage is over. But as she flew off to the Far East with baby Phoenix Chi last week, the split surprised few people. She wed dancer Jimmy Gulzar in September 1998, just six months after they met. With a divorce pending, the failed marriage seems to prove the old proverb **Marry in Haste, Repent at Leisure***.*
PEOPLE, 9 JANUARY 2000

He was heard with frowns and low grumbles. These, for once, were nothing to do with MPs having bolted their lunch. The indigestion was more cerebral, a suspicion that **laws passed at haste are laws repented at leisure***.*
DAILY MAIL, 20 NOVEMBER 2001

The saying '**marry in haste, repent at leisure**' *strikes true when it comes to Sir Paul McCartney and estranged wife Heather. He didn't have time to grieve properly for his first wife Linda who died of cancer before he married the much younger model.*
SUNDAY MIRROR, 28 MAY 2006

See also *MARRIAGES are made in heaven*

MASTER

no man can serve two masters
you can't give equal allegiance to two conflicting principles

Variant: No one can serve two masters

This is a biblical proverb. In MATTHEW 6:24 Jesus explains why attempting to serve two masters, in this case God and Mammon (an evil personification of wealth and avarice), is impossible: *No man can serve two masters: for either he will hate the one, and love the other; or else he will hold to the one, and despise the other.* The proverb made an early appearance in English. It is found in a collection of political songs dating from about 1330: *No man may wel serve tweie lordes.*

Scots cannot claim surprise at the shambles that is the new Parliament. It is a well-known fact that **no-one can serve two masters***, yet the Scots put the setting up and the running of their new Parliament in the hands of people who owe their loyalties to the Union and Westminster. The result is that our new Parliament has divided the Scots and not united us.*
GLASGOW DAILY RECORD,
29 SEPTEMBER 2003

Burningham created the 'confusion' that he now says keeps him from obeying the law. That is not ethical. He should not be leading the political fight against the very program that he is legally charged with putting in place... No man can serve two masters. Chairman Burningham should resign from the State Board of Education.
SALT LAKE CITY DESERT NEWS,
31 MAY 2007

MAY

ne'er cast a clout till May is out

do not remove any layers of winter clothing, or trust any improvement in the weather, until the end of May.

Variant: Ne'er cast a clout afore May is out

This could be taken as a very English proverb deriving from the unpredictability of a climate where, even as late as May, the weather might suddenly turn very chilly and make one regret leaving off one's vest.

Surprisingly, however, the origin probably lies in an old Spanish proverb quoted by Correas in his VOCABULARIO (c. 1627): *Do not leave off your coat till May*. There is a corresponding English rhyme:

Who doffs his coat on a winter's day,
will gladly put it on in May.

A French proverb explains why it is foolish to be taken in by bourgeoning May: *Mid-May, winter's tail* – even with the year so advanced a cold snap might be expected. While an old English agricultural weather proverb says that *a snowstorm in May is worth a load of hay*. A good reason to keep one's coat on.

Leave not off a Clout,
Till May be out

appeared in Thomas Fuller's GNOMOLOGIA (1732). A *clout* was a rag or cloth, and so here it means 'an article of clothing'.

May, besides being the name of the month, is also the name given to hawthorn blossom. (This meaning is found in the old English May Day rhyme *Here We Go Gathering Nuts in May*, which is a corruption of *Here We Go Gathering Knots of May*, or 'posies of May blossom'.) For this reason some authorities consider

that the proverb means 'Don't cast off any clothing until the May blossom has come into flower', but most consider that May refers to the month.

The Victorians were ever careful about their health. They thought that colds were caught by getting cold. A proverb quoted by R D Blackmore in CRIPPS CARRIER (1876) reveals why it was so important to keep on those warm winter layers even in May:

This is the worst time of year to take cold,
A May cold is a thirty-day cold.

There is evidence to suggest that the advice about not casting off clothing until May was over was taken very seriously. Different corners of the country had their own rhyming variants on the proverb. In Somerset, as cited by F T Elworthy in THE WEST SOMERSET WORD-BOOK (1886), the wisdom was:

If you would the doctor pay,
Leave your flannels off in May

On the Yorkshire coast the advice, as described by F V Robinson in WHITBY GLOSSARY (1855) was:

The wind at North and East
Was never good for man nor beast,
So never think to cast a clout
Until the month of May be out.

Another north-country saying foretold the horrors in store for those who scrubbed off the protective layers of winter grime before high summer:

If you bathe in May
You'll soon lie in the clay.

Barbecue-mad Brummies have been sent scurrying indoors as June arrived with damp, icy blasts from the Arctic. Those who

followed granny's maxim 'Ne'er cast a clout 'til May is out' and donned summer clothes for the first time yesterday were soon shivering in their short sleeves.
BIRMINGHAM EVENING MAIL,
2 JUNE 2001

I was more afraid of [the bouncers] than the drinkers, although one young thing, who had clearly forgotten to put her clothes on, raised my concerns about hypothermia later on. That old maxim, 'Ne'er cast a clout 'til May is out' came to mind, but I thought better of it and cornered swiftly off the strip and into the welcoming warmth of Louis'.
THE NEWCASTLE JOURNAL,
20 MAY 2005

Usage: Centrally heated houses and workplaces, global warming and an understanding that viruses and diseases are responsible for most illness are making these proverbs redundant. By the middle of the current century, they may well have been shelved as quaint sayings for future etymologists and collectors of proverbs to research.

MENDED

least said, soonest mended
offering long explanations for conduct that has given offence will only make the situation worse

From the sixteenth to the nineteenth centuries the proverb was commonly *Little said, soon amended*, although Thomas Cogan in JOHN BUNCLE, JUNIOR (1776) used the variant *Least said, soonest mended*, the present-day form. In SENSE AND SENSIBILITY (1811) Jane Austen uses a similar proverb, which is still current: *The less said the better*.

'Flatterer!' For the first time in her life Julia started to flirt back.

'No really. I'm serious. I won't forget our midnight walk.'
'Hardly midnight!'
'Well, dawn walk, whatever. Don't be such a schoolmarm! Look, I've never said –'
'Well don't.' Julia was crisp. 'Least said soonest mended, if you want me to be a schoolmarm...'
SALLEY VICKERS, MISS GARNET'S ANGEL, 2000

Least said, soonest mended should be Prince Edward's motto. The speech he made at the Crimestoppers Ball is the best argument I've seen in a long time for the abolition of the monarchy.
EVENING STANDARD,
22 NOVEMBER 2002

MILE

give him an inch and he'll take a mile
said of someone who takes advantage of another's kindness or generosity

Variant: Give him an inch and he'll take a yard

Stevenson traces the proverbial wisdom back to a Latin saying quoted by, amongst others, Publilius Syrus: *He that is permitted more than is right wants more than is permitted* (SENTENTIAE, c. 43 BC). The proverb's earliest known appearance in English is in John Heywood's PROVERBS (1546): *For when I gave you an inch you tooke an ell*.

An *ell*, like the *yard* which replaced it in the proverb near the turn of the twentieth century, is an old measurement of length which varied from country to country. The English ell was 45 inches (114 cm), so a person who, on being offered an inch, helped himself to an ell was overstepping the mark indeed.

Proverbs expressing the crime abound in different languages:

Give me a place to sit down, and I'll make a place to lie down (Spanish)

If you give him the length of a finger, he'll take a piece as long as your arm (French)

Call a peasant 'Brother', he'll demand you call him 'Father' (Russian)

If you let them put a calf on your back, before long they'll put on a cow (Italian)

Being taken advantage of obviously arouses strong emotions. The choice of *mile* in the current English version doubtless echoes this.

*Oscar is a male Cairn terrier cross aged six months who arrived in November, when he was brought in by an owner who could not cope with his exuberance any longer… Oscar's temperament is bright but mad, like a little hurricane. He has had no training so will need firm ground rules… He seems incredibly cute but **give him an inch and he'll take a mile**. In the wrong hands he'll turn into a very naughty boy.*
EVENING STANDARD,
12 DECEMBER 2001

*It is not difficult to imagine Broncos defensive coordinator Larry Coyer lecturing his charges in his unit's final meeting of the week: 'Gentleman, Mr. Moss can kill you a dozen different ways, and you have to be ready for all of them. **Give him an inch and he'll take a mile**. Be ready for the jump-ball catch. The one-handed circus sideline grab. And he comes back for the underthrown ball as well as anyone."*
MINNEAPOLIS STAR TRIBUNE,
20 OCTOBER 2003

a miss is as good as a mile
if you miss your goal by an inch or a mile it still counts as a failure

The proverb, found in nineteenth-century texts, is an elliptical and alliterative variant of a saying current since at least the seventeenth century:

An inch in a miss is as good as an ell. As in the proverb *give him an inch and he'll take a MILE* there is an inflationary movement from an *ell* up to a *mile*.

*It may have been a good performance but **a miss is as good as a mile** as the Giants went down to their fifth defeat in a row, now their longest losing streak since the first month of the first season over two years ago.*
BELFAST NEWS LETTER,
17 OCTOBER 2002

*The 307CC is a neat, if not beautiful, shape. It is nearly chic, although I have to say **a miss is as good as a mile**. Rather like an ageing film star with a contract requiring that she is photographed only from the waist up, the Peugeot is best seen from one angle.*
DAILY TELEGRAPH,
27 DECEMBER 2003

MILK

it's no use crying over spilt milk
what's done is done and getting upset won't change or help matters

Variant: It's no good crying over spilt milk

In his translation of AESOPE (1484) William Caxton has this to say: *The thyrd [doctrine] is that thow take no sorowe of the thynge lost whiche may not be recoured.* Milk is in this category. If the grain tub is overturned, the contents can be recovered; if a jug of milk is spilt, it can only be mopped up and is lost for ever. It is difficult to say exactly when the proverb was coined but both James Howell (1659) and John Ray (1678) record it in their collections of English proverbs as *No weeping for shed milk*. The present-day wording is from the nineteenth century.

But Mr Murdoch said there was no bitterness over the breakdown of the takeover, which deprived the media tycoon of

the biggest deal of his career. 'There's no use crying over spilt milk…. We are not going to go through life with any bitterness,' he said.
GUARDIAN, 2 NOVEMBER 2001

So what about Rotork's shares? At 525p, they are more than twice the level they reached at the bottom of the bear market in early 2003. This is of course vexing for those of us who didn't buy them then. But there is no use crying over spilt milk.
DAILY TELEGRAPH, 10 AUGUST 2005

MINDS

little things please little minds
small-minded people are easily captivated by trivia

Ovid wrote that *Little things affect little minds* in his ARS AMATORIA (c. 1 BC). In the sixteenth century, John Lyly had *Little things catch little minds* (SAPHO AND PHAO, 1584) and the Baptist preacher Charles Spurgeon cited *Little things please little minds* in JOHN PLOUGHMAN'S PICTURES (1880).

Most critics seem to love this simplistic garbage featuring long-forgotten music from the early '70s – but little things please little minds.
MIRROR, 13 FEBRUARY 2004

'Little things please little minds.' I plead guilty, I guess. Give me the little things. Sportscaster Bob Costas. The phone call from a friend who says, 'I've got two tickets to the game I can't use. You want 'em?' The wink, nod or wave from a passing athlete to a calling child…
VIRGINIAN PILOT,
18 FEBRUARY 2007

MONEY

money talks
wealth gets you special treatment and influence

Money talks has been current in literature since around the turn of the twentieth century but the idea was not new then. In CIVILE CONVERSATION (1586) Stefano Guazzo expresses a piece of proverbial wisdom current in the sixteenth and seventeenth centuries thus: *The tongue hath no force when golde speaketh*. Other writers bear testimony to the eloquence of money. Seventeenth century author Aphra Behn tells us that the language of money is international, while Henry Fielding writes that *Money will say more in one moment than the most eloquent lover can in years* (THE MISER, 1733).

Money, or rather the lack of it, can provoke a wry, envious humour. The American poet Richard Armour (1906–1989) writes:

> *That money talks I'll not deny.*
> *I heard it once – It said 'Good-bye'.*

Three-times-married Bienvenida Buck can tell you exactly what turns her on about a man – it's the size of his wallet. Money talks if you're the Spanish poor girl made good whose kiss-and-tell revelations amassed you thousands of pounds and brought down top brass in the process.
GLASGOW DAILY RECORD,
20 OCTOBER 2000

In Trenton, money talks – Big donors wield big influence
BERGEN COUNTY RECORD,
8 AUGUST 2004

the love of money is the root of all evil
the relentless pursuit of riches dulls the conscience and gives rise to selfish and evil actions

Variant: Money is the root of all evil

St Paul, writing to his disciple Timothy, urges the young man to be content once his basic needs of food and clothing have been met. Possessions, he argues, are of no use in the after-life and the pursuit of riches gives rise to harmful ambitions and hurtful lusts. *For the love of money,* he says, *is the root of all evil, leading men to flounder in their Christian faith and fall into deep unhappiness* (1 TIMOTHY 6:7–10).

St Paul's words are often misquoted as *money is the root of all evil.* The apostle, however, never condemned money. He was happy to put riches to a proper use: to relieve poverty and suffering, or to house an assembly of Christians. What Paul warned against was the accumulation of wealth for self-aggrandisement and self-indulgence.

It is not surprising that such a well-known saying on the topic of money should spawn a crop of witticisms. Mark Twain and George Bernard Shaw are both credited with the telling social comment *The lack of money is the root of all evil,* while an anonymous and down-to-earth graffito bases itself on the familiar misquotation: *Money is the root of all evil – and a man needs roots.*

We know how we handle money reflects our values and priorities. Yet for most people, this is one of the most difficult aspects of life. We as adults have been taught **the love of money is the root of all evil***. Yet society defines success, in part, as having money.*
READING EAGLE, 10 JUNE 2002

*Competent independent boards of directors are needed to devise a fair compensation system for CEOs and eliminate this bad system that promotes the love of money over people. '***The love of money is the root of all evil***.'*
CINCINNATI POST, 18 JULY 2002

MONK

the cowl does not make the monk

appearances may belie reality; external trappings are not a guarantee of what they represent

Variant: The habit does not make the monk

Monasticism flourished in the Middle Ages. At its best, it fostered learning and the arts, founded hospitals and excelled in industry. Gradually, however, as royalty and nobility alike salved their consciences with generous gifts of land and money, the monasteries grew wealthy and the light of their example dimmed. Many monks were no longer content to remain within their cloister and observe a simple way of life in accordance with their vows. By the later Middle Ages they not only kept a rich table but had ceased to labour, assuming a role of overseer to an army of servants. Nor, in many houses, was the vow of celibacy strictly observed. Chaucer gives us a fine portrait of the fourteenth century monk in his CANTERBURY TALES (c. 1387); he liked to feast on swan, wore fur-trimmed clothes, rode a fine horse and had a passion for greyhound racing and hunting.

It is not surprising, then, that this proverb should have medieval roots. The earliest (French) references date back to the thirteenth century; the first English use is *Vor the clothinge ne maketh nayght thane monek* in the AYENBITE OF INWIT (1340), a translation by Dan Michel of a French original. This borrowing clearly caught on. A similar thought is found a few years later in Thomas Usk's THE TESTAMENT OF LOVE (c. 1387): *For habit maketh no monk; ne weringe of gilte spurres maketh no knight.* Erasmus quotes the medieval Latin versions in his ADAGIA (1536).

The proverb has been a popular one through the centuries. There is always a fascination for those who make high professions and yet fail to meet the standard. In the seventeenth century George Herbert pointed out that *A holy habit cleanseth not a foul soul* (JACULA PRUDENTUM 1640) and, in the following century, Thomas Fuller observed that *A broad hat does not always cover a venerable head* (GNOMOLOGIA, 1732).

These days the national press serves as watchdog over ecclesiastical indiscretions and, in its zeal to uncover hypocrisy, is swift to publish any hint of scandal, especially of a sexual nature. And Thomas Fuller would not be surprised to know that, even in the twentieth century, broad hats were occasionally set on less than perfect heads, as this diary entry of the politician then President of the European Commission, Roy Jenkins, in Rome for the coronation of Pope John-Paul II on 22 October 1978, shows:

The Mass began at 10 o'clock and went on until 1.15… Most of the first hour was taken up by the homage of all the cardinals, and I wished I had a key to them. Emilio Colombo wasn't bad and pointed out about 14, but even his knowledge seemed far from perfect. The Duke of Norfolk, in the next row, offered pungent comments about one or two of them.

Her mother remarks that 'one must sometimes take people on trust. Appearances can be deceptive. The cowl does not make the monk'. But Cecile has not heard her, only we – the audience – have done so (and it is an important point to take in; except we must also remember that appearances can be real at the same time as being deceptive: how can we identify a monk without his cowl?)
CINEACTION, 22 JUNE 2005

In January, the former llama herder and coca grower held meetings with international *leaders wearing a traditional Bolivian alpaca chompa, which to the rest of the world looked exactly like a stripy jumper. So his relatively smart, 1980s-rocker style outfit came as something of a shock to the assembled media at last Thursday's press conference. But the habit does not make the monk, even in Latin America, and wearing a business suit doesn't mean one approves of business or capitalism.*
SUNDAY BUSINESS, 7 MAY 2006

See also *APPEARANCES are deceptive; Never judge by APPEARANCES; BEAUTY is only skin deep*

MOUNTAIN

don't make a mountain out of a molehill

don't exaggerate the size of the problem by making a trifling matter into an insuperable difficulty

French has a saying *Faire d'une mouche un éléphant* ('to make an elephant out of a fly') to express the idea of a trivial matter which has been inflated beyond all proportion. This ancient proverb was quoted by Lucian in MUSCAE LAUDATIO (AD 170), and later by Erasmus in his ADAGIA (1536).

To make a mountain out of a molehill is probably a variant. In his CATECHISM (1560) Thomas Bacon links the two sayings: *They make of a fly an elephant, and of a molehill a mountain.* This is not the earliest known example of the English proverb, however. It appears in Roper's LIFE OF MORE, written some three years earlier.

VIRGO (Aug 23–Sept 22): An obstacle could cause a permanent setback in your plans. If you feel others are controlling or censorious, a certain amount of resentment could arise. Adopt a philosophical attitude and don't make a mountain out of a molehill.
WASHINGTON POST, 13 MAY 2004

Still, a writer has to use whatever is to hand in the way of experience; he or she is in the business of making mountains out of molehills.
ALAN BENNETT,
UNTOLD STORIES, 2005

Usage: Sage counsel, perhaps, but often construed as patronising and intrusive

if the mountain will not come to Mahomet/Mohammed, Mahomet/Mohammed must go to the mountain

if things cannot be arranged in our favour we must accept the fact and follow an alternative, if less favourable, course of action

This proverb is known in English through an essay, OF BOLDNESSE (1597), written by Francis Bacon, in which he tells this story:

You shall see a Bold Fellow, many times, doe Mahomets Miracle. Mahomet made the People beleeve, that he would call an Hill to him; And from the Top of it, offer up his Praiers, for the Observers of his Law. The People assembled; Mahomet cald the Hill to come to him, againe, and againe; And when the Hill stood still, he was never a whit abashed, but said: If the Hil wil not come to Mahomet, Mahomet will go to the Hil.

The stubborn mountain was Mount Safa, which is situated near the holy city of Mecca. When the mountain did not move, Mohammed is reputed to have told the crowd that it was a sign of God's mercy towards them for, had it moved, it would surely have fallen upon them and crushed them to death.

Francis Bacon was one of the most learned men of his generation. In PROMUS (c. 1594–6), a personal collection of proverbs, words or similes for use in his own writing, he quotes in Spanish the proverb *Si no va el otero a Mahoma, vaya Mahoma al otero* ('If the hill does not go to Mohammed, let Mohammed go to the hill'). Much of Spain was, at one time, under Moorish rule, so it is quite possible that the proverb passed from Spanish into other European tongues.

As the old saying goes, if the mountain will not come to Muhammad, then Muhammad will go to the mountain. Or in this case, Willy Mason and his gig-going fans. To coincide with the release of his second album If The Ocean Gets Rough, *the US folk singer has offered his UK fans the chance of an exclusive gig – as long as they provide the setting.*
GUARDIAN, 18 JANUARY 2007

Nana battled for years, with mixed results, to adapt Western ingredients to the recipes she grew up eating back home in Tokyo… Now she need struggle no more. In a real-life case of 'if the mountain will not come to Mohammed, Mohammed will go to the mountain,' Nana has launched her own internet-based company bringing a true taste of the East to the North-East.
NEWCASTLE JOURNAL, 25 MAY 2007

MUCK

where there's muck, there's money

dirt and the creation of wealth are closely associated.

Variant: Where there's muck, there's brass

In ENGLISH PROVERBS (1678), John Ray quotes *Muck and money go together*, explaining that *Those that are slovenly and dirty usually grow rich, not they that are nice and curious in their diet, houses, and clothes*. It is generally thought, however, that Ray's comment is fanciful and that the muck referred to in the proverb is the dunghill. Ray himself cites an alternative proverb to this effect *He hath a good muck hill at his door*, together with the explanation *he is rich*.

Michael Denham quotes yet another saying that supports this: *There is an old proverb which says 'The muck-midden is the mother of the meal-ark [meal-chest]'* (DENHAM TRACTS, c. 1850).

The proverb comes from the observation that fertilizing fields with muck increases the crop yield. In his APOPHTHEGMS NEW AND OLD (1624), Francis Bacon tells of Mr Bettenham, a reader of Gray's Inn, who *used to say that riches were like muck; when it lay upon a heap, it gave but a stench and ill odour; but when it was spread upon the ground, then it was the cause of much fruit*. This metaphor had already been used by Ben Jonson in EVERY MAN OUT OF HIS HUMOUR (1599), in which Sordio says:

> *Pardon me, gentle friends, I'll make fair 'mends*
> *For my foul errors past, and twenty-fold*
> *Restore to all men, what with wrong I robb'd them:*
> *My barns and garners shall stand open still*
> *To all the poor that come, and my best grain*
> *Be made alms-bread, to feed half-famish'd mouths.*
> *Though hitherto amongst you I have lived,*
> *Like an unsavoury muck-hill to myself,*
> *Yet now my gather'd heaps being spread abroad,*
> *Shall turn to better and more fruitful uses.*

Later generations have interpreted the word *muck* differently, using it to refer to the grime of the mining and manufacturing industries. Where black smoke belched from factory chimneys, mill and pit owners were becoming rich.

That the proverb was widely used is evident from the number of regional variants it engendered:

The more muck, the more money (East Anglia)

Where there's muck there's brass (Yorkshire – *brass* being a dialect word for money)

Where there's muck ther's luck (Lancashire)

Muck's the mother of money (Cheshire)

*But let us look on the bright side. The politics of waste disposal offers manufacturing and marketing opportunities. Who will provide lockable waste bins? Shall we have offers for our waste to be moved at less than the standard fee or fine, and no questions asked? **Where there's muck there's brass**.*
INDEPENDENT, 27 APRIL 2007

*Certainly, this summer has proved that **where's there's muck, there's brass**. The warm, damp weather is good news for the rat population, which in turn is good news for Rentokil Initial. Last July was its busiest for ten years.*
GUARDIAN, 27 AUGUST 2007

Usage: Informal; particularly common in the form *Where there's muck, there's brass*

· N ·

NEWS

bad news travels fast
it does not take long for bad news to circulate

Variant: Ill news comes apace

What is news? F P Dunne defined it thus: *What's one man's news is another man's troubles* (MR DOOLEY, JOURNALIST, 1901). In other words, news is gossip about another's afflictions. This fascination we have for revelling in other people's misfortunes and hurrying to be the first to break the news to someone else is age-old.

Plutarch quotes this ancient Greek saying in MORALIA: ON CURIOSITY (c. AD 95): *How much more readily than glad events is mischance carried to the ears of men*! It was echoed in English literature from the second half of the sixteenth century. Originally, as in the Greek, the speed of bad news was contrasted with the slowness of good: *Evil news flies faster still than good* (Thomas Kyd, SPANISH TRAGEDY, 1594).

Poets and dramatists have excelled themselves in expressing the proverb in an original way. *Ill news, madam, Are swallow-wing'd, but what's good walks on crutches*, writes Philip Massinger in his play THE PICTURE (1629), and Milton has *Evil news rides post, while good news bates* (SAMSON AGONISTES, 1671). By the end of the eighteenth century, the proverb had been clipped to its present-day form *Ill news travels fast*, *ill news* becoming *bad news* during the twentieth century.

*People like my friend tell others about their bad experiences. Those people in turn are going to tell others and because **bad news travels fast**, the reputations of the hospital and the surgeon will suffer in the community. Employers who pay the bills listen to stories like this.*
MODERN HEALTHCARE,
26 SEPTEMBER 2005

Bad news travels fast, *and the gory details of John Egan's misfortunes were laid out for South China Morning Post readers, fed the story from the British Independent newspaper.*
RACING POST, 15 DECEMBER 2006

See also *No NEWS is good news*

no news is good news
without information to the contrary, it is sensible to assume that all is well

An early use of the proverb in English has a link with the tragic Sir Thomas Overbury (see *BEAUTY is only skin deep*). Overbury had a great friend at court, a lord whom he had known for several years. The poet was vehemently opposed to Rochester's burgeoning relationship with the young Countess of Essex on the grounds that, not only was she still married, but she was also immodest and would ruin his friend's career at court. Overbury's poem, A WIFE, which extolled all the virtues a man should look for in a prospective spouse, was seen as an attempt to dissuade Rochester from pursuing the Countess. Lady Essex laid a trap to discredit Overbury in the eyes of the

King, and the poet was imprisoned in the Tower of London on 22 April 1633. Here, the Countess arranged for the appointment of a new Lieutenant, and for Overbury to be supervised by a dishonest jailer. This man, with the help of a physician's wife and an apothecary, slowly poisoned the poet to death. Shortly afterwards Rochester, the new Earl of Somerset, married the divorced Lady Essex.

Some time later suspicions over the poet's death were aroused. The apothecary's servant, close to death, confessed to having taken the fatal dose of poison to the Tower. Since members of his court were implicated, King James I was forced to act. THE LOSELEY MANUSCRIPTS contain two highly secret letters in the King's own hand to the new Lieutenant of the Tower, Sir George More. The first letter dated 9 May 1616 asks him to urge Somerset to confess, in which case the King will exercise mercy. Sir George's advocacy had no effect. On 13 May, the King wrote once more to Sir George:

*Althogh I feare that the laste message I sent to youre infortunate prisoner shall not take the effecte that I wishe it shoulde, yett I can not leave of to use all meanes possible to move him to doe that quhich is both honorable for me, and his owin best. Ye shall thair fore give him assurance in my name, that if he will yett before his tryall confesse cheerlie unto the commissioners his guilteiness of this fact, I will not onlie performe quhat I promeised by my last messinger both towardis him and his wyfe, but I will enlarge it … Lett none living knowe of this, and if it take goode effect, move him to sende in haste for the commissioners, to give thaime satisfaction, but if he remaine obstinate, I desyre not that ye shoulde trouble me with an ansoure, for it is to no ende, and **no news is bettir then evill news**, and so fair well, and God blesse youre labours.*

The King's role is dubious and his motives unclear. Eventually all those involved in the crime were sentenced to death, but Somerset and his wife pleaded guilty, and were duly pardoned by the King. However, this brought no good end. As Alfred John Kempe put it in 1836, *they became indifferent to each other and lived apart in obscurity and execration. She died before her husband, of a decay so loathsome, that historians have noticed it as a manifest visitation of heaven upon her crimes.*

Although King James is often credited with originating the proverb in his letter of 13 May, it is more likely that he was quoting a saying already in existence. About 29 years later James Howell cites it as an Italian proverb, the translation of which – unlike James I's version – is almost exactly the same as our modern rendering: *I am of the Italians mind that said, Nulla nuova, buona nuova, no news, good news* (FAMILIAR LETTERS, c. 1650). By the middle of the following century the proverb was established in its present day form and has been in constant use since.

*It has been a reasonably quiet week in the world of ICT and on the basis that **no news is good news**, perhaps one should be grateful that we have not been reading about continued job losses.*
BELFAST NEWS LETTER,
22 OCTOBER 2002

*Some trades are prone to pessimism. The media, for example, are the mouthpiece of pessimism because if **no news is good news**, then all news is bad news.*
GUARDIAN, 21 JANUARY 2006

See also *Bad NEWS travels fast*

CONTRADICTIONS!

If proverbs demonstrate the wisdom of the people, then the people are frequently in two minds and do not know what they want. There are quite a number of proverbs that contradict one another:

You are never too old to learn vs *You can't teach an old DOG new tricks*
Look after the PENNIES and the pounds will look after themselves vs *Penny wise, pound foolish*
NOTHING ventured, nothing gained vs *Better safe than sorry*
Many HANDS make light work or *The more, the merrier* vs *Too many COOKS spoil the broth*
Haste makes waste or *More haste, less SPEED* vs *Strike whilst the IRON is hot*
Out of SIGHT, out of mind vs *ABSENCE makes the heart grow fonder*
LOOK before you leap vs *He who hesitates is lost*

These and other examples perhaps go to show that different people hold very different opinions. Also, the relevance of a proverb can vary in relation to the context in which it is used. Is it true that *the more* is always *the merrier*? It depends on the situation. Similarly, does *absence always make the heart grow fonder*? Again, it depends.

Proverbs appear to offer a timeless wisdom and truth, but contradictions and the way that contexts condition meaning suggest that their apparent universality is in fact a lot more relative. Building a comprehensive moral system on proverbs, therefore, seems doomed to failure. One early attempt to this end was made by Carrión in fourteenth-century Spain. However, later critics have shown his system to be full of contradictions and opposing moral adages.

NOBLESSE OBLIGE

noblesse oblige

high position brings obligations as well as privileges

This is one of a number of proverbs quoted in the language from which it is borrowed. It is the inspiration of the Duc de Lévis (1764–1830) and comes from his MAXIMES ET PRECEPTES (1808), a collection of sayings and reflections on a variety of subjects. Under the banner of equality, the exclusive rights of the French nobility were abolished during the Revolution.

However, after his coronation, Napoleon created life peers and bestowed titles upon people in prominent office, thus creating a new hierarchy. In coining *Noblesse oblige* the Duc de Lévis was pondering their role in the Empire. He concluded that elevated status carries with it certain commitments, responsibilities and a willingness to undertake for others. *Noblesse oblige* was the best maxim for the old nobility and the new.

The notion was not, however, original. Aeschylus in PROMETHEUS BOUND (470 BC) had *relationship compels* and Euripides in ALCMENE (c. 410 BC) *the nobly born must nobly meet his fate*. And during the sixteenth century, another Frenchman, the forward-thinking Guillaume Bouchet, wrote: *True nobility is acquired by living, and not by birth* (LES SÉRÉES III, 1584).

The French maxim spread across the Channel and beyond and is found in the works of several nineteenth century writers, including Matthew Arnold and Ralph Waldo Emerson:

COUNTRY LIFE

Farming was the mainstay of the economy until the mid-nineteenth century, and agricultural proverbs were legion. Many of them were weather sayings, the farmer's attempts to find climatic patterns so that he could plan his activities:

Rain from the east, two wet days at least
When the wind's in the east on Candlemas day (2 February), *there it will stick to the end of May*
A fair day in winter is the mother of a storm

Certain signs gave a more long-term view. A dry March must have brought a sigh of satisfaction to the lips of the arable farmer: *A bushel of March dust is worth a king's ransom,* and a smile of delight when April thunderstorms followed: *When April blows his horn, it's good for hay and corn.* Snow was a sign of fruitfulness: *A snow year's a rich year.* And late snow even more so: *A snowstorm in May is worth a waggonload of hay.* The Kentish weather proverb *Light Christmas, light wheatsheaf, dark Christmas, heavy wheatsheaf* meant that if there was a full moon about Christmas Day, the next year would bring a light harvest. A correspondent with NOTES AND QUERIES quoted a clerical friend who had this to say:

Old W–, now cutting my wood, tells me when he got from church yesterday, he pondered deeply the text, 'Light Christmas, light wheatsheaf,' and wondered whether he should be able to fatten a pig, for he never knew the saying to fail, in sixty years' experience.

Other proverbs guided the farmer through the farming year. On Candlemas Day, for instance, the careful farmer should still have had enough food put by to see his family and livestock through the remaining unproductive months:

A farmer should on Candlemas Day, have half his corn and half his hay.

And Candlemas was also the season for the sowing of peas and beans:

Noblesse oblige; or superior advantages bind you to larger generosity (PROGRESS OF CULTURE, 1875). The phrase continues to be widely applied to any superior role or position that carries responsibilities.

Fergie liked the attention and glamour as one of the royals. But she didn't go in much for the responsibilities. The concept of **noblesse oblige** *was not for her.*
MIRROR, 26 JUNE 2001

'It's a great Colorado story and a great American story,' says tenor Gran Wilson of Central City Opera House, the elegant little lady nestled in a mountain town high above Denver. 'It wasn't built by aristocracy or **noblesse oblige**. Cornish and Welsh miners built it – for the sheer love of beauty.'
CHRISTIAN SCIENCE MONITOR, 17 AUGUST 2001

For other proverbs quoted in French, see *Plus ça CHANGE, plus c'est la même chose; RECULER pour mieux sauter*

Sow peas and beans in the wane of the moon; who soweth them sooner, he soweth too soon.

June was the month when the harvest was set: *If you look at your corn in May, you'll come weeping away; if you look at the same in June, you'll come home in another tune.* While the shepherd was advised: *Shear your sheep in May, and shear them all the way.*

The farmer was advised to sow in plenty for his crop would inevitably attract unwelcome interest: *Sow four beans in a row, one for cowscot and one for crow, one to rot and one to grow,* otherwise it would be a case of *Little sow, little mow.*

And there was an abundance of proverbs to help the farmer remember the best conditions for the sowing and reaping of his crop:

Sow beans in the mud, and they'll grow like a wood
Sow in a slop, 'twill be heavy at top (Wheat sown in wet soil will be fruitful)
Sow wheat in dirt, and rye in dust (Wheat likes wet conditions and rye drier ones)
Oats will mow themselves
If you cut oats green, you get both king and queen (If oats are harvested before they appear fully ripe then all the grains will be preserved)
Corn is not to be gathered in the Blade, but in the Ear.

In the last analysis, though, it was all a question of economics – to grow enough for one's own needs and sell the rest for a profit at market. *Corn and horn go together* was an old English proverb meaning that the prices of cattle and corn were linked; when one was dear, so was the other (John Ray, ENGLISH PROVERBS, 1678). But proverbial economists can't agree, just like their modern-day counterparts. A correspondent with NOTES AND QUERIES (1866) quotes the contrary proverb *Up corn, down horn*, with the explanation that when corn was expensive people spent so much on bread that they could not afford beef and the price fell.

NOSE

don't cut off your nose to spite your face

beware of indulging in an act of angry or spiteful revenge which will rebound on you

Peter of Blois, one-time chief counsellor of the English king Henry II, gives the earliest citation of this saying in Latin around the end of the twelfth century. Before this, the thought of gaining revenge but at significant cost to oneself had been variously expressed. Latin authors referred to burning down their own house or their own corn, hacking their own vines, and sticking an axe into their own legs. *It is stupid*, wrote Publilius Syrus in SENTENTIAE (c. 43 BC), *to seek vengeance on a neighbour by setting one's house on fire.*

After Peter of Blois, there is a developing French tradition of cutting off one's own nose. The seventeenth-century French gossip writer Gédéon

Tallemant des Réaux, quotes it as a well-known proverb in a short biography about Henry IV: *Henry IV understood well that destroying Paris would be, as they say, to cut off his nose to spite his face* (HISTOIRETTES, c. 1657). Its earliest known citation in English comes in the CLASSICAL DICTIONARY OF THE VULGAR TONGUE (1796), in which Francis Grose comments: *He cut off his nose to be revenged of his face. Said of one who, to be revenged on his neighbour, has materially injured himself.* This same thought is nicely realised in two Chinese proverbs:

Don't thrust your fingers through your own paper lantern
Do not burn down your house even to annoy your chief wife's mother.

Don't cut off your nose to spite your face. *Emulate whatever you admire about your mom, and join her in any activities you like. If country skiing or yoga or bridge, for example, turn out to be fun, it doesn't mean you're following in her footsteps!*
GIRLS' LIFE, 1 APRIL 2001

*Gemini May 22–Jun 21: You are still not happy or comfortable concerning one close relationship. The temptation to flounce out of a situation is strong. **Don't cut off your nose to spite your face**, time and patience sees a positive outcome to whatever bugs you.*
BIRMINGHAM SUNDAY MERCURY, 8 JANUARY 2006

NOTHING

nothing ventured, nothing gained

if you aren't prepared to try or to take risks, you can't expect to meet with success

Variant: Nothing venture, nothing win/have/gain

This little bit of wisdom has been in literature since the fourteenth century.

By the sixteenth and seventeenth centuries various forms of the proverb were current:

Nought lay downe, nought take up and nought venter, nought have
(John Heywood, PROVERBS, 1546)

Nought stake, nought draw
(Anonymous, MISOGONUS, 1577)

… nought venters, nothinge gaynes
(Thomas Heywood, THE CAPTIVES, 1624)

The proverb continues to have different forms, even today. It also has close equivalents in other European languages; the French, for instance, say, *He who risks nothing, gains nothing*.

The proverbial wisdom is also variously expressed in many other languages: French and Spanish share *He who will not risk himself will never go to the Indies*, a reference to the fortunes to be made in the sugar plantations of the West Indies in the eighteenth century, where both countries had colonies; Greek refers back to the Trojan horse with *It's through trying that the Greeks took Troy* (see beware of GREEKS bearing gifts); and the Moroccans have this exchange between two beggars:

Come on! Let's try and ask for alms.
No! I'm afraid of not getting anything.

*Three single women hit the town last night in search of the perfect man. Brave ladies Lisa Rodgers, Maeve Cahalan and Catherine McDonnell took up the challenge to find a date in Dublin… Maeve, who is in her 40s, said: 'I've always believed **nothing ventured nothing gained**. But this is probably the daftest thing I've ever done.'*
MIRROR, 2 AUGUST 2002

Yes, but how easy is it to promote a sport which is played far out to sea, on a ship

which allows for almost no audience? And which is associated with pensioners?

*'**Nothing venture, nothing win**, sunshine,' says Brian, playfully boxing me on the ear. 'When we win a deck quoits gold for Britain, you'll be talking a different tune.'*
INDEPENDENT, 26 JULY 2004

See also *Faint HEART ne'er won fair lady; Throw out a SPRAT to catch a mackerel*

there's nothing new under the sun

whatever the novelty/behaviour, somewhere or other it has been seen, heard or done before

The Old Testament book of ECCLESIASTES 1:9 concludes that *There is no new thing under the sun,* and verse 10 goes on to ask *Is there any thing where of it may be said, See this is new? It hath been already of old time, which was before us.* Everything has been seen, heard and done before. Proverbial use in English dates from the early nineteenth century.

*'...originally we put the Jews in an old cannon-foundry – which disturbs me when I think of what Hitler has done later. Of course **there is nothing new under the sun**, but I wonder sometimes if with our Venetian cannon-foundry we gave him the idea for his gas-chambers?'*
SALLEY VICKERS, MISS GARNET'S ANGEL, 2000

There's nothing new under the sun, really. I mean, those super-duper devices that let students pass notes electronically in class are the same as yesterday's pen and paper.
CHICAGO SUN-TIMES, 11 DECEMBER 2000

OAKS

great oaks from little acorns grow

even that which is most impressive had a modest beginning

Variant: Mighty oaks from little acorns grow

There are many examples of the magnificent arising from the insignificant, of great things which *proceede and increase of smaul and obscure begynnynges* (Richard Eden, tr. Peter Martyr, THE DECADES OF THE NEWE WORLDS, 1555). A Chinese proverb from the sixth century BC tells us that *a journey of a thousand miles began with a single step*. The Bible, in MATTHEW 13:32, reminds us that *the minute mustard seed grows into a tree that birds delight to nest in*; and Dante describes how *From a little spark may burst a mighty flame* (DIVINA COMMEDIA, PARADISO, c. 1300). This idea is encapsulated in the Latin proverb *Magnum in parvo* ('a lot in a little'), which is still sometimes quoted in the original language today. (For other proverbs still quoted in Latin, see under *CARPE diem; CAVEAT emptor; FESTINA lente; TIME flies*).

A related idea which finds expression in Latin and Greek texts is that of the seed or shoot becoming a tree. Erasmus, a scholar of the classical world, marvels that a huge cypress tree is encased in such a small seed (SIMILIA c. 1508). It is small wonder, therefore, that the English should develop a comparison with the mighty oak with which they are so familiar. *An acorn one day proves an oak*, writes Richard Corbet (POEMS, c. 1640), a thought recorded by Thomas Fuller in GNOMOLOGIA (1732): *The greatest Oaks have been little Acorns*. But it is an American, David Everett, who gives the present-day proverb its poetic quality. In 1791 he wrote a verse for seven-year-old Ephraim H Farrar to perform at a school declamation:

> *You'd scarce expect one of my age*
> *To speak in public on the stage;*
> *And if I chance to fall below*
> *Demosthenes or Cicero,*
> *Don't view me with a critic's eye,*
> *But pass my imperfections by.*
> *Large streams from little fountains flow,*
> *Tall oaks from little acorns grow.*

Great oaks from little acorns grow and Melanie Reid hopes her modest but regular contributions into an Isa will eventually provide the deposit to buy a home of her own. DAILY TELEGRAPH, 21 MARCH 2001

*The minister added: '**Great oaks from little acorns grow**; an idea hatched or contact made at this summit may later develop into something that all our economies will benefit from.'*
BELFAST NEWS LETTER,
4 SEPTEMBER 2002

OLD

you are as old as you feel

age is all about attitude; appearance –
or the number of years lived – have
nothing to do with it

The proverb is an attempt by those of a
certain age to deny the inevitable aging
process. It has been in use since the
twentieth century and is a unisex
replacement for this distinctly sexist
adage, coined in the nineteenth century:

> *O wherefore our age be revealing?*
> *Leave that to the registry books!*
> *A man is as old as he's feeling,*
> *A woman as old as she looks.*
> (Mortimer Collins
> HOW OLD ARE YOU?, 1855)

Was there any truth in this version of
the proverb? A journalist in the
ILLUSTRATED LONDON NEWS of
25 May 1907 thought so: *The adage*
that a man is as old as he feels, and a
woman as old as she looks, may be said to
contain much inherent truth.

In spite of all the creams and
potions available today, it is usually
possible to tell a woman's age by the
condition of her skin and the shape of
her figure. Farmyard metaphors pour
scorn on any attempt she might make
to hide her advancing years. If she tries
to stay young at heart a detractor
might say *She has many good nicks in her*
horn, a cow being said to have a wrinkle
in its horn for every year of its life. If
she wears fashionable clothes she may
be accused of being *mutton dressed as*
lamb, and if she should do anything to
betray her age she is reminded that she
is *no spring chicken*. Understandably, the
aging process is resented by many
women. As the Parisian hostess and
courtesan Ninon de Lenclos
(1620–1705) wrote: *If God had to give a*
woman wrinkles, He might at least have put
them on the soles of her feet.

Some of the damage can be smoothed
over temporarily, as Helen May noted:

> *Little dabs of powder,*
> *Little smears of paint,*
> *Make a woman's wrinkles*
> *Look as if they ain't.*

But if this fails then there is nothing for
a woman to do but to lurk in the
shadows and appear constantly *in the*
dusk with a light behind her in the hope
of passing permanently for 43, as
W S Gilbert put it in TRIAL BY JURY
(1875).

Men, on the other hand, are
supposed to mellow physically with
age, achieving a distinguished but still
handsome appearance. Provided they
have no aches and pains and keep a
youthful outlook, the nineteenth
century proverb suggests that they can
laugh at the advancing years.

The experiences of those who have
gone before suggests this is not so,
however. Aches and pains are
inevitable and drag a man's mind into
old age. For Martin Luther, middle age
suddenly struck at 38: *One's thirty-*
eighth year is an evil and dangerous year,
bringing many evils and great sicknesses
(TABLE-TALK, 1521). By 43 the prime
of life is well past if Swedish writer
Esaias Tegnér is to be believed: *Today is*
my forty-third birthday. I have thus long
passed the peak of life where the waters
divide (LETTER TO M F FRANZEN,
13 November 1825). Perhaps he would
have agreed with the anonymous
comment that *middle age is when we*
can do just as much as ever – but would
rather not.

By the time a man reaches his sixties
it's uphill – or downhill – all the way.
It's only in going uphill that one realises
how fast one is going downhill, lamented
author and satirist George Du Maurier
at 62, and the poet Longfellow found
that *to be seventy years old is like climbing*

the Alps (LETTER TO G W CHILDS, 13 March 1877). In truth, a man's spirit seems to age at the same rate as his body. Dr Johnson complained to Boswell that his diseases were *an asthma and a dropsy, and what is less curable, seventy-five* (1786) and comedian Bob Hope was the voice of the lively octogenarian male: *I don't feel eighty, in fact I don't feel anything till noon, and then it's time for my nap*.

So, whether you are male or female, as old as you feel or as old as you look, you are the age you are.

Boris Becker on life after tennis:
   ***You're as old as you feel** and I feel about 72 at the moment.*
INDEPENDENT, 9 JUNE 2001

*It's good to hear that the perennially young 'Pocket Venus' Mildred Shay considers that her friends from among the Sixties pop generation are 'young' – but I suppose they would be if, like her, you are 93 years old, still 'blonde and chic' and full of beans. It may be an over-worn adage to say that **you are as old as you feel**, but this splendid lady surely proves the point.*
SAGA MAGAZINE, JULY 2005

P

PAY

you get what you pay for
paying a little more for something means better quality

This maxim of the market place is not as modern as it sounds. It was coined by the German scholastic philosopher Gabriel Biel (1425–95) in his EXPOSITIONIS CANONIS MISSAE (c. 1495). Biel had a strong grasp of economics and was forward thinking in this discipline. He considered that a fair price for a product should reflect the need for it, its availability and the effort required to produce it.

If it is true that you get what you pay for, then it is not surprising that the National Health Service scores badly in comparison with other countries' systems. According to the Organisation for Economic Co-operation and Development, Britain spends far less on its hospitals and GPs' surgeries than almost any other European nation.
DAILY TELEGRAPH, 16 JANUARY 2002

You can get what you pay for, according to people such as wine critics and car testers, who judge value for a living. But you don't typically get more when you pay more, they said; you just hope harder that you did.
MINNEAPOLIS STAR TRIBUNE,
2 SEPTEMBER 2006

PEARLS

don't cast your pearls before swine
don't lavish valuable or beautiful things upon those who are unable to appreciate their worth

The proverb comes from the Sermon on the Mount, in which Jesus says: *Give not that which is holy unto the dogs, neither cast your pearls before swine, lest they trample them under their feet and turn again and rend you* (MATTHEW 7:6). The *pearls* represent the truths of Christ's teaching. His pearls of great wisdom should not be made known indiscriminately to those so unwilling to listen that they become antagonistic.
     The proverb was plucked from the Bible and used in English literature from as early as the fourteenth century. William Langland, Shakespeare, Milton and Dickens are amongst those who have played with the proverb down the ages. The Chinese have an equivalent saying cited by Justus Doolittle in his collection of 1872: *Don't play the lute before a donkey*, and a Hindi proverb advises against *giving ginger to a monkey*. An abbreviated form of the English expression comes in an old joke:

Man, ushering woman through door before him: *Age before beauty.*
Woman: *Pearls before swine, you mean.*

Whatever you do, don't buy into the lie. Instant gratification isn't worth the potential risks and heartache casual sex brings with it. ***Don't cast your pearls before swine.***
UNIVERSITY WIRE, 16 OCTOBER 2001

It makes sense to serve good wine at parties, but it doesn't make sense to serve great wine. My point here isn't the snotty old warning against casting pearls before swine. Rather, the point is that people just don't pay close attention to wine at parties, and the better the party, the more this point holds true.
WASHINGTON POST, 1 DECEMBER 2004

Usage: If used in its basic meaning, the phrase has acquired a superior, patronising tone. Nowadays it may well be jocular.

PEN

the pen is mightier than the sword

words are more effective than weapons

The influence of the written word has grown in importance over the centuries with the increase in literacy levels and the ready availability of printed materials. Up to the end of the fifteenth century, everything was hand written and necessarily of limited distribution.

During the second half of the fifteenth century, there emerged the profession of book publisher, incorporating the trades of the type founder, printer and book seller. The power of the press began to strengthen the power of the pen.

Walsh quotes Claus Petri commenting in 1520 on the prodigious output of King Christian II of Denmark, for whom *letters did more than the sword*. The Portuguese Antonio da Fonseca in the early seventeenth century and the Frenchman Saint-Simon in 1702 both reflect upon a similar sentiment.

In seventeenth century England, Robert Burton discusses the *old saying* at some length. His ANATOMY OF MELANCHOLY (1621) explores the nature and symptoms of melancholy together with advice for their cure. Burton finds the written word a vicious weapon, capable of bringing about depression in its victims:

Scoffs, Calumnies, bitter Jests, how they cause Melancholy
It is an old saying, 'A blow with a word strikes deeper than a blow with a sword:' and many men are as much galled with a calumny, a scurrilous and bitter jest, a libel, a pasquil, satire, apologue, epigram, stage-play or the like, as with any misfortune whatsoever. Princes and potentates, that are otherwise happy, and have all at command, secure and free… are grievously vexed with these pasquilling libels, and satires: they fear a railing Aretine more than an enemy in the field, which made most princes of his time (as some relate) 'allow him a liberal pension, that he should not tax them in his satires.'

The English ballad writer Martin Parker also pointed out the danger of the pen: *More danger comes by th' quill than by the sword* (THE POET'S BLIND MAN'S BOUGH, 1641), a notion reiterated in the following century by William King: *A sword less hurt does, than a pen* (EAGLE AND ROBIN, before 1712).

So feared was the might of the written word that a publisher found guilty of circulating treasonable pamphlets might expect to be nailed to the pillory by his ears, which would later be cut off and left as a warning to others. This was a fate suffered in 1633 by William Prynne, author of a controversial book. Daniel Defoe was a staunch believer in the might of the pen and himself the author of pamphlets and satirical works. In 1703 he was fined, imprisoned and pilloried for the publication of THE SHORTEST WAY WITH THE DISSENTERS, a pamphlet which highlighted the intolerance of the established Church.

The proverb in the form we know today seems to have acquired its definitive statement in Lord Lytton's play RICHELIEU (1838):

> *Beneath the rule of men entirely great,*
> *The pen is mightier than the sword.*

As society has moved from the quill to the typewriter to the email, the saying has had to change with it. The following comes from Lee Thayer's PERSONS UNKNOWN (1941): *The typewriter is so much more to be reckoned with than the sword* and this is a headline in a LONDON EVENING STANDARD theatre review of 14 March 2006: *The pen is mightier than the email...*

Yes, indeed, we have demonstrated once again the true power of the Press and that **the pen is mightier than the sword**. *The other week, I told you about a disconsolate Brian who had battled for many months to have three dumped and wrecked cars removed from the lane at the back of his house. In desperation he came to me. The Echo highlighted the problem and within days the vehicles were shifted. This was the 'action newspaper' demonstrably in action.*
SOUTH WALES ECHO, 2 OCTOBER 2002

Some people say **the pen is mightier than the sword**, *and this man proved it. Called the 'father of American caricature,' this cartoonist used his drawings to oust corrupt officials from office, drum up support for the Union during the Civil War, and get Abraham Lincoln, Ulysses Grant, and others into the White House.*
CURRENT EVENTS, 29 OCTOBER 2004

Usage: A well-used expression, even a cliché. Often found with an alternative noun replacing *the sword*.

PENNY

a bad penny always turns up (again)

undesirable acquaintances have the habit of making unwelcome reappearances; a wayward family member will always turn up again eventually

Variant: A bad penny always comes back

The proverb refers to *bad* or 'counterfeit' money. A common trick when a counterfeit or foreign coin comes into one's possession is to attempt to pass it on to another person who, naturally, will try to do the same. Invariably the coin does the rounds until it finds its way back into the pocket from which it started out.

When the proverb was used in the early nineteenth century, it was a bad shilling which kept coming back but this was subject to devaluation in the twentieth century.

Like a bad penny, the issue of executive pay keeps on returning.
INDEPENDENT, 27 MARCH 2001

The former president is **like a bad penny;** *he will not go away. His actions and personality fit the definition of a gadfly: 'a person who is persistently critical, irritating or provocative.'*
WASHINGTON TIMES, 2 JANUARY 2005

In Neighbours, shady Sean **turns up like a bad penny** *determined to make Katya's life a misery.*
GLASGOW SUNDAY MAIL, 30 JULY 2006

in for a penny, in for a pound

once committed to a project or course of action, it is worth giving all possible resources to it

This proverb may have originated in the gambler's willingness to take a greater risk (and so reap greater reward), or in the businessman's commitment to a new venture. It is used now in much wider contexts where whole-hearted commitment is being pledged, whatever the cost.

The saying has been current since at least the end of the seventeenth century and has been used by many well-known writers including Scott, Dickens, and Somerset Maugham.

To construct their first filters they needed extruded aluminum, but the minimum order for a custom product was 1,100 pounds, far more than was immediately needed. As the old saying goes, in for a penny, in for a pound. The couple purchased the minimum quantity and stored it in their garage. They hired a student and began producing the filters using the aluminum, brass and copper.
SASK BUSINESS, 1 AUGUST 2001

Dynamic JCB duo Chris and Gavin Dolman are rising to the challenge of scaling Africa's highest mountain as they bid to reach the summit of Kilimanjaro to raise money for a national charity… Chris said: 'Gavin suffered badly with his asthma when he was younger and when he was approached by the charity to help raise some money he asked me if I was up for it. I'd run the London and Potteries marathons before for charity and said OK. When he told me we'd be trying to scale Kilimanjaro, I thought "In for a penny, in for a pound."'
BIRMINGHAM POST, 3 OCTOBER 2006

See also *You might as well be hanged for a SHEEP as for a lamb*

look after the pennies and the pounds will look after themselves

if you are careful in your management of small amounts of money, you will soon amass a larger sum

Variant: Take care of the pennies and the pounds will take care of themselves

A letter written by Lord Chesterfield to his son on 5 February 1750 attributes the adage to William Lowndes who served as Secretary of the Treasury to three monarchs (William III, Queen Anne and King George I). Mr Lowndes, whom Chesterfield had accused in an earlier letter of being miserly, lived rigorously by his maxim. It is to be hoped that he found pleasure in doing so because, since wealth cannot be taken to the grave, it was his two young grandsons who enjoyed the considerable fortune that he had amassed.

Take care of the pennies and the pounds will take care of themselves. It might be an old proverb, but it certainly holds true today. Looking after your money and planning carefully is crucial to the successful running of any business or enterprise.
GLASGOW DAILY RECORD, 24 JULY 2003

They call it the 'latte factor' – the syndrome whereby we blind ourselves to what we spend on our little skinny-with-extra-cinnamon indulgences, and then can't believe our eyes when the bank statement arrives… Back in the year 50 BC (Before Costa), the equivalent of the latte factor would have been the old grandparental adage 'look after the pennies and the pounds will look after themselves'. Sure enough, the average poundwise pensioner today can spot straight away that £2.50 is a lot of money for a cup of coffee; the rest of us, however, find this not so easy to do.
INDEPENDENT, 13 MARCH 2004

Usage: Restricted to financial contexts

See also *All is GRIST that comes to the mill; Every little HELPS*

PHYSICIAN

physician, heal thyself

before correcting or healing others, first make sure you are not suffering from the same problem yourself

Jesus chose the synagogue in Nazareth, his home town, to announce that he was the expected Messiah. When the people, dumbfounded at his audacity, started to murmur against him, Jesus said to them: *Ye will surely say to me this proverb, Physician, heal thyself, whatever we have heard done in Capernaum, do also here in thy country* (LUKE 4:23). Christ's use of the proverb in the gospel popularised it throughout Christian Europe but his words show that the saying was already familiar to his listeners.

In the sixth century BC Aesop's fable of THE WORM AND THE FOX had made the same point. It tells of a worm who boasted to a fox that it was a skilled physician. The fox pointed out that the worm was lame and asked, *How, healing others, have you not healed yourself?*

This theme was reiterated in later classical literature: in PROMETHEUS BOUND (c. 470 BC), the Athenian tragic poet Aeschylus writes: *Wretched that I am – such are the inventions I devised for mankind, yet have no cunning wherewith to rid myself of my own sufferings*; Euripedes speaks of one who was *Healer of others, full of sores himself* (FRAGMENTS, c. 420 BC); and in AD FAMILIARES, written in the half century before Christ, Cicero warns against imitating bad physicians who claim to be masters of healing but are unable to cure themselves.

Doctors have long had a reputation for not taking enough care of their own health needs, which makes the familiar phrase 'Physician, heal thyself' a doubtful prescription.
WASHINGTON TIMES, 11 FEBRUARY 2003

One day 12 years ago Dr Wesley Finegan found himself on the other side of the desk when he was told he had cancer. All too aware of the 'physician heal thyself' ironies, Dr Finegan found solace in his Christian faith and in writing about the disease, which had also claimed his wife.
BELFAST NEWS LETTER, 20 JULY 2006

PICTURE

every picture tells a story

every picture or photograph conveys an impression or message. The appearance of someone or something can reveal the true facts

Early in the novel of that name (1847), the young Jane Eyre, having been scolded and told to be seated somewhere until she can speak pleasantly, slips into the breakfast-room and chooses a book from the bookcase there, *taking care that it should be one stored with pictures*. The book is BEWICK'S HISTORY OF BRITISH BIRDS, and Jane is soon engrossed in engravings of Arctic landscapes. *Each picture told a story*, she says, allowing her imagination to run wild.

Charlotte Brontë's novel marks the earliest appearance of the phrase, but the proverb came into common usage following an advertisement for Doan's Backache Pills which first appeared in an issue of the Daily Mail dated 26 February 1904. The Edwardian advertisement, which showed a person bowed with pain, bore the legend *Every picture tells a story.*

Every picture tells a story of the picture-taker.
Some people can size up a person pretty quickly by the way they dress or the company they keep. But I think you never really know a person until you see what kind of vacation pictures they take.
CHRISTIAN SCIENCE MONITOR, 29 MARCH 2001

Every picture tells a story. What is Camilla Parker Bowles saying to Grace Jones at the Fashion Rocks extravaganza at London's Royal Albert Hall? If you can come up with an amusing caption in the speech bubble, staple, glue or tape it to a postcard and send it to...
DAILY MAIL, 24 OCTOBER 2003

PIPER

he who pays the piper calls the tune

the person who finances a project has a right to dictate how the money is spent

He who pays the piper calls the tune is recorded first in its current form in the nineteenth century. It seems to originate in *Those that dance must pay the piper*, a saying from the first half of the seventeenth century.

Country dancing on the green or in a hall was a favourite entertainment for everyone as this traditional rhyme shows:

> Much time is wasted now away,
> At pigeon-holes, and nine-pin play,
> Whilst hob-nail Dick,
> and simp'ring Frances,
> Trip it away in country dances...

People danced at festivals, which were numerous, and weddings. The music was provided by travelling musicians who were hired to play their pipes, tambours and fiddles for the merrymaking. Those who wished to dance had to pay for the music and those who paid for the music had the right to name their favourite tune.

Strolling musicians seemed to have had an unerring instinct that their services would be required, for another proverb of the period tells us that *Fiddlers, dogs and flies come to feasts uncalled*. James Kelly explains the proverb thus: *Fiddlers for money, the flies for a sip, and the dogs for a scrap* (SCOTTISH PROVERBS, 1721). An Elizabethan saying specifies what a musician would expect for his services: *Fiddler's fare: meat, drink, and money*. According to Kelly, this last proverb was later used to refer to an evening's entertainment where the guests themselves were offered *fiddler's fare* – that is food, drink and the chance to win some money at the card tables.

*Andrea Kelmanson, a consultant and former director of the National Centre for Volunteering, expressed concerns that charities receiving government money were being expected to carry out the politicians' agenda. 'I understand that **who pays the piper calls the tune**, but funders have a responsibility that just because they've got the money doesn't meant they've got all the answers. They're missing opportunities if they don't talk to those receiving funds.'*
GUARDIAN, 27 APRIL 2001

*In 2000, the Chancellor [of the Exchequer] took it on himself to criticise Magdalen College, Oxford, for refusing admission to Miss Spence, a comprehensive school pupil from Tyneside. 'Dons work desperately hard at admissions,' Mr Jenkyns writes, 'and then get traduced by Gordon Brown as incompetent or semi-criminal.' **He who pays the piper calls the tune**, Mr Brown might argue. But the original idea was that government should assist the universities, as independent institutions, by offering their students grants and loans. The dependence of tertiary education on public funding has since become so pronounced that the state feels free to indulge in micro-management, even to the extent of attempting to dictate entrance criteria. Such social engineering debauches the idea of a university.*
DAILY TELEGRAPH, 14 AUGUST 2002

PITCHER

little pitchers have big ears
be careful what you say in front of the children

Variant: Little pitchers have long/wide ears

A *pitcher* is an earthenware vessel with two long *ears*, or handles, which is generally used for storing or carrying water or other liquids. This proverb, which dates back to at least the sixteenth century, makes a play on the word ears: little children may look inattentive but, like little pitchers, their ears are long and they are quite capable of picking up titbits of information and gossip their elders would not want them to know. *Be not angry with the child. Pitchers have ears*, wrote William Shakespeare in RICHARD III (1594).

The wisdom of this adage is echoed in another: *The child says nothing but what it heard by the fire* (George Herbert, JACULA PRUDENTUM, 1640).

Obviously, a safeguard is needed should a parent be indiscreet. Benjamin Franklin has the answer: *Teach your child to hold his tongue; he'll learn fast enough to speak* (POOR RICHARD'S ALMANACK, 1734).

*Evan is a boy of eight with a loving mother and distant father. Kate and Alan love their son but haven't realized that **little pitchers have big ears**, and Evan is aware even before they are that their marriage is failing.*
PIEDMONT TRIAD NEWS AND RECORD, 2 FEBRUARY 2001

*Anyone who knows an eight-year-old knows that '**little pitchers have big ears**,' and no family secret is safe within a mile of those ears.*
WASHINGTON TIMES, 3 JUNE 2005

Usage: Somewhat dated

PLACE

a place for everything and everything in its place
keep everything neat and tidy, and life will run more smoothly

Way back in the seventeenth century George Herbert recorded the maxim *All things have their place*, adding rather weakly, *knew we how to place them* (JACULA PRUDENTUM, 1640). This indecisiveness is perhaps one of the reasons why nothing more along these lines is recorded in literature for quite some time.

By the nineteenth century, however, contemplation on tidiness is back. In an article entitled NEATNESS, published in a December 1827 edition of THE OHIO REPOSITORY, the Reverend C A Goodrich urges his reader to *Have a place for every thing, and keep every thing in its proper place*, referring to this piece of advice as an *old adage*.

From then on, written evidence of the proverb is found on both sides of the Atlantic. English author Frederick Marryat has it in MASTERMAN READY, OR THE WRECK OF THE PACIFIC (1842): *In a well-conducted man-of-war every thing is in its place, and there is a place for every thing.* The Canadian author Thomas C Haliburton uses it in NATURE (1855). On eight January 1855 Anna Matilda Whistler writes to her son, the American artist James Whistler, to say:

As I unpacked the little valise, I admired your skill in fitting the contents, which are not yet washed...I hope soon to hear of your having recd. [received] the black valise & its contents safely as despatched today... it went full. From the care you take in packing I trust you begin to think it necessary to have 'a place for every thing & every thing in its place'.

The proverb was famously used by the industrious Isabella Beeton in her BOOK OF HOUSEHOLD MANAGEMENT (1861). *Order*, she writes in Chapter 2, *is indispensable; for by it we wish to be understood that 'there should be a place for everything, and everything in its place.'* While in Chapter 4, 'An Introduction to Cookery', she says:

'A place for everything, and everything in its place,' must be her rule, in order that time may not be wasted in looking for things when they are wanted, and in order that the whole apparatus of cooking may move with the regularity and precision of a well-adjusted machine;—all must go on simultaneously.

And a few years later in THRIFT (1875), Samuel Smiles, the Scottish author and political reformer, exemplifies the brisk, businesslike approach of the self-made man. For him tidiness is the basis of sound management. *Order*, he says, *is most useful in the management of everything... Its maxim is, A place for everything and everything in its place.*

Orderliness and neatness are very Victorian values. H W Shaw puts it thus: *As a general thing, an individual who is neat in his person is neat in his morals.* (See *Cleanliness is next to GODLINESS*.)

As to how the proverb was coined, Archer Taylor (1968) hazards a theory that it comes from two simpler expressions *There is a place for everything* and *Everything in its place* that were joined to form one composite new proverb.

I've long since realised that, brilliant inventions though they are, any kind of filing cabinet, card index hanging file system could in my case be profitably replaced with an incinerator. So we adopt the converse principle of 'a place for everything and everything all over the place'.
KNOWLEDGE MANAGEMENT, MAY 2001

*However, one of the reasons the match was so enjoyable – and stand by for a piece of old-fartdom here – was that the goalkeepers wore the No 1 shirt, the left backs wore 3, the midfield play-makers, such as they were, wore 10, and the centre forward wore 9. You knew where you were. **A place for everything, and everything in its place.*** DAILY TELEGRAPH, 24 JANUARY 2007

POT

a watched pot never boils
time drags when something is eagerly expected

Variant: A watched pot is long in boiling

That commonplace kitchen object, the pot, has spawned quite a number of proverbs over the centuries. Perhaps surprisingly *A watched pot never boils*, one of the most frequent today, is not recorded before the nineteenth century, when it is used by Elizabeth Gaskill in MARY BARTON (1848). Mary E Braddon later refers to it as *that vulgar old proverb* (CLOVEN FOOT, 1880). Since then, it has lent itself to a variety of reformulations, often somewhat humorous in tone. Ogden Nash, for instance, entitles one of his poems A WATCHED EXAMPLE NEVER BOILS, and in BAMBOO BLONDE (1931) Dorothy Hughes neatly captures the frustration of waiting for a call that does not come: *A watched phone never rang.*

But is the proverb true? Two psychologists reported in 1980 on a study that they had carried out. Two groups of people were shown a pot of water on a hotplate. One group was told to say when the water began to boil; the other group was not given this instruction. After this, both groups were left for four minutes, although they were not aware of the duration of the period. Then they were asked to estimate how long the interval had been. The first group's estimated times were appreciably longer than those of the second group. The researchers concluded that *the watched pot effect* leads to heightened expectancy.

*They say **a watched pot never boils**. But if you're waiting in a courtroom for a jury to return a verdict, something has to start bubbling sooner or later. Doesn't it?*

Pot watchers suffered another setback Wednesday waiting for an outcome in the trial of Jonathan Tolliver, accused of the 1998 murder of Chicago police officer Michael Ceriale.
CHICAGO SUN-TIMES, 8 FEBRUARY 2001

*Cook with care. **A watched pot never boils**, but an unwatched pot boils over.*
GOOD HOUSEKEEPING, 1 MAY 2005

Usage: Occasionally *pan* may be substituted for *pot*

the pot calls the kettle black
used of someone who criticises failings in others that he himself possesses

An early form of this proverb in the seventeenth century was *The pot calls the kettle burnt-arse* (John Clarke, PAROEMIOLOGIA, 1639). Cooking was done over an open fire and the saying alludes to the sooty, blackened base of the cooking pots.

The proverb already existed in various forms in Spain and was possibly introduced into English by the publication there of Cervantes's DON QUIXOTE (1615) where we find: *The frying pan said to the kettle, get away blackeye*. This version is very close to an Arabic proverb, reminding us that the Moorish dominion over much of Spain from AD 711 to 1492 left a linguistic heritage behind it.

Quarrels between blackened pots and pans are common to the proverbs of several European languages, but there are also variants. German, for instance, has *One ass nicknames another Long-ears*; French has *Dirty-nosed folk always want to wipe other folks' noses*; and the Scots 'Crooked Carlin,' quoth the cripple to his wife.

*Before the Tories work themselves into a lather of indignation over [Labour] Government links with Enron, shouldn't they ask themselves whether it is ever wise for **the pot to call the kettle black**? Only this week, the party belatedly admitted that it received £25,000 from the company. Meanwhile, Conservative peer Lord Wakeham – a member of Enron's audit committee, whose job was to oversee the firm's financial results – faces a U.S. Congressional inquiry.*
DAILY MAIL, 31 JANUARY 2002

*One of Wenger's many strengths is an ability to keep a straight face while **uttering comments that would shame Mr Pot and Mr Kettle**.*
DAILY TELEGRAPH, 12 AUGUST 2002

The pot calls the kettle black as Wal-Mart hits out at Tesco size.

Business commentators and leaders have slammed Wal-Mart president Lee Scott's call for a government probe into Tesco's dominance in the UK. Although Scott's call, made in an interview with The Sunday Times last weekend, may have found favour in some quarters, many have branded Scott's comments as hypocritical given his company's position as the world's largest grocery retailer.
GROCER, 3 SEPTEMBER 2005

See also *People who live in glass HOUSES shouldn't throw stones*

POVERTY

poverty is no crime
being poor in itself is not blameworthy

Variants: poverty is no sin; poverty is not a crime

THE WELLERISM

Samuel Weller, Mr Pickwick's faithful aide in Dickens's PICKWICK PAPERS (1837), has an unusual claim to fame: he has had a type of proverb named after him; the Wellerism. These expressions all have the same basic form; quoted words are followed by a mention of the speaker, and then an allusion to context. For example, in chapter 3 of PICKWICK PAPERS (1837):

'It's over, and can't be helped, and that's one consolation, as they always say in Turkey, ven they cut the wrong man's head off.'

One kind of Wellerism involves a reference to ancient fables, in which animals often speak:

'Sour grapes,' said the fox and could not reach them.

Others date back to Anglo-Saxon times:

'Things are not well throughout the world,' said he who heard them wailing in Hell.

Some are probably genuine quotations. Blind Hugh was a noted wit of the sixteenth century: *'That I would fain see,' said blind Hugh.* This may have found more generic expression in the punning saying: *'I see,' said the blind man and picked up his hammer and saw.*

See also *Every little HELPS*.

Poverty is no sin was recorded by George Herbert in JACULA PRUDENTUM (1640). It expressed the idea already in circulation that poverty was not a vice but a difficulty (see *You may as well be hanged for a SHEEP as for a lamb*).

But while poverty itself is not a crime, it has long been recognised as engendering it. In the first century, the statesman and monk Cassiodorus wrote that *Poverty is the mother of crime* (VARIAE, c. AD 550). The Persian poet Sadi concurred, pointing out that *The needy stain the garment of chastity with sin, as those who are hungry steal bread* (GULLSTAN, c. 1258). In a letter to James Boswell (7 December 1782), Dr Samuel Johnson considered how poverty prevents even the most determined from leading blameless lives. *Poverty*, he wrote, *is a great enemy to human happiness; it certainly destroys liberty, and it makes some virtues impracticable.*

A further problem is that, while few people would subscribe to the idea that poverty is a crime, its victim is regarded with suspicion or scorned. Menander stated that *A poor man, though he speak the truth, is not believed* (FRAGMENTS, c. 330 BC).

The sin is that poverty is permitted to exist. George Bernard Shaw is to the point when he says, *What is the matter with the poor is Poverty: what is the matter with the rich is Uselessness* (MAXIMS FOR REVOLUTIONISTS, 1903). We are all to blame.

Pets can be loving, rewarding, but expensive companions. If you don't think you can afford one, don't get one. **Poverty is no crime** *– but letting animals suffer is.*
SOUTH WALES ECHO, 25 AUGUST 2005

The electricity often ran out when we did not have any cash for the meter. I still remember the embarrassment I felt when Mum sent us out begging the neighbours for ten pence pieces to keep the lights and heating on. **Poverty is no crime,** *nor should it be a matter of shame.*
MAIL ON SUNDAY, 27 NOVEMBER 2005

PRACTICE

practice makes perfect
in order to master any skill you have to repeat it over and over

The importance of putting theory into practice and learning by experience is an ancient one. For Corinthian tyrant Periander *Practice is everything* (APOPHEGM, c. 600 BC); *Practice is the best of all instructors* according to Publilius Syrus (SENTENTIAE, c. 43 BC); and Pliny the Younger tells us that *It is difficult to retain the knowledge one has acquired, without putting it in practice* (LETTERS, c. AD 108).

Thomas Norton, an English lawyer and politician, has *Use maketh Masterie* in his ORDINALL OF ALCHIMY (1477). This was, by the fifteenth century, already a known proverb, having been quoted in Dan Michel's AYENBITE OF INWIT (1340). (See *The cowl does not make the MONK.*) A sixteenth century variant on this is *Use maketh perfection or perfectness*, which persisted until at least the early nineteenth century; Sir Walter Scott uses it in his journal entry for 27 January, 1879.

Thomas Wilson comes very close to the modern proverb as early as 1553 in his ARTS OF RHETORIQUE, where he cites *Before arte was inuented, eloquence was used, and through practise made perfect*, but even so *Practice makes perfect* does not really become the preferred version until around the middle of the eighteenth century.

At this same period, Dr Samuel Johnson communicates the notion of practice making perfect by quoting a Latin proverb in a letter of 16 April 1763: *If at the end of seven years you write good Latin, you will excel most of your contemporaries: Scribendo disces scribere. It is only by writing ill that you can attain to write well.* Johnson is probably continuing a tradition begun over two

centuries before. In ADAGIA (1536) Erasmus lists a number of Latin proverbs, variants of the same idea, which teach that learning comes through practice: *By building learn to build, By singing learn to sing*, etc.

Although 'practice makes perfect,' in some situations physicians' knowledge and performance may decline with the passage of time, suggests Stephen B. Soumerai... Researchers conducted a systematic review of studies from 1966 to June 2004 relating medical knowledge and health care quality to physician age and years in practice. Of 62 published studies, more than half (52%) suggested that physician performance declined over time for all outcomes measured.
NURSING ECONOMICS,
1 SEPTEMBER 2005

Smith says she often hears: 'I can easily flirt with someone I don't like, but when it comes to someone I do, I get all tongue-tied.' Her response to them is 'practice makes perfect'. The more we get used to doing something, the less uncomfortable it becomes.
GUARDIAN, 10 MARCH 2007

PRICE

every man has his price
everyone is open to bribery if the inducement is sufficient

Popular view has it that Sir Robert Walpole, leading Minister of England under George I and II (1676–1745) is the originator of the phrase. Lord Lytton, for example, wrote a blank-verse comedy entitled WALPOLE; OR, EVERY MAN HAS HIS PRICE (1869), in which he made the Minister say both *Every man has his price, I must bribe left and right* and *Every man has his price, my majority's clear*. That Walpole was often unprincipled in his political life is widely acknowledged.

However, there has been a long and detailed debate as to whether it was, in fact, Sir William Wyndham who drew attention to the proverb. Wyndham led the Tory opposition against Walpole in the House of Commons. According to William Cobbett's PARLIAMENTARY HISTORY OF ENGLAND (1806–20), in a debate on a motion to repeal the Septennial Act on 13 March 1734, Sir William spoke before Sir Robert, just before the division that rejected the motion, with these words:

*Let us suppose, sir, a gentleman at the head of the administration, whose only safety depends upon corrupting the members of this House. This may now be only a supposition, but it is certainly such a one as may happen; and if ever it should, let us see whether such a minister might not promise himself more success in a septennial, than he would in a triennial parliament. It is an old maxim, that **every man has his price**, if you can but come up to it. This, I hope, does not hold true of every man; but I am afraid it too generally holds true; and that of a great many it may hold true, is what, I believe, was never doubted of...however, let us suppose this distressed minister applying to one of those men who has a price, and is a member of this House.*

This account comes from a report on the debate in the contemporary publication THE BEE. Wyndham is, in veiled parliamentary fashion, accusing Walpole, of 'buying' support, because he knows that *Every man has his price*.

But, as Wyndham himself says, it is *an old maxim*, not coined by him. And the notion is old indeed, as a remark, made by Epictetus in DISCOURSES (c. AD 100), has: *Different men sell themselves at different prices*.

The attribution to Walpole may have come about because his many vociferous opponents, led by Wyndham, obviously considered that such a cynical adage correctly summed up the Minister's beliefs and his ruthlessness in keeping himself in power. Thus, through political mud-slinging, a maxim about Sir Robert's credo began to be ascribed to him.

Possibly, then, popular opinion may be technically wrong in attributing the saying's origin to Walpole, but it seems to be right in substance, in that it correctly describes his political beliefs and corrupt practice. All men of power face the same issue – differently expressed, it was reiterated on the other side of the Atlantic at a similar period. *Few men*, wrote George Washington to Robert Howe in 1779, *have virtue to withstand the highest bidder.*

*Twenty-first century politicians can't hope to escape the consequences of granting pardons to convicted criminals. Not in any country with a legal system anyway. And not when it involves somebody who owed $48 million in unpaid taxes. Any man with that kind of tax bill must have been good for a heftier bribe than a few hundred thousand. **Every man has his price** – and it seems Bill Clinton's wasn't much.*
MIRROR, 17 FEBRUARY, 2001

*The Pentagon has found another way to deal with the Iraqi resistance. Don't shoot them. Pay them. In the good old tradition that **every man has his price**, the Pentagon is paying Sunni religious scholars to influence their followers in Iraq, according to* The New York Times.
SEATTLE POST-INTELLIGENCER, 6 JANUARY 2006

PRIDE

pride goes before a fall
arrogant people are invariably made to look foolish and ridiculous

Variants: Pride goeth before a fall; Pride comes before a fall

This is from the biblical Old Testament. PROVERBS 16:18 reads: *Pride goeth before destruction, and an haughty spirit before a*

THERE ARE THREE THINGS...

Three things drive a man out of the house: smoke, rain, and a scolding wife. This proverb was probably compiled by Pope Innocent III (DE CONTEMPTU MUNDI, c. 1210) from verses in the biblical book of PROVERBS, chapter 30. The saying came into frequent use, being found in the works of Langland, Chaucer, George Gascoigne and Shakespeare. It is an example of a genre of proverb which collects together either a set of things which share a common feature, or sets of features that are attributed to one subject.

Such proverbs, which became a feature of a number of European languages, enjoyed popularity in the middle ages and, during the Renaissance, collections of these sayings were made, inspiring later imitators:

Dryve fro your herte three thinges that been contrariouse to good conseil, that is to seyn, tre, coveiteise, and hastifnesse (Chaucer, TALE OF MELIBEUS, c. 1386)

Three things are unsatiable, priests, monckes, and the sea (Anon, PHILIP AND MARY, c. 1560)

A ship under sail, a man in complete armour, and a woman with a great belly are three of the handsomest sights (James Howell, ENGLISH PROVERBS, 1659)

Some of the earlier instances of these proverbs are quite complex. One particular example, which is traceable to an eleventh century Arabic text, gives a long list of qualities that a beautiful woman should possess – expressed in multiples of three, of course:

And the maiden said: 'The woman is beautiful who possesses eighteen traits ... she who is long in three, and small in three, and broad in three, and white in three, and black in three, and red in three ... I say long in three, that she be of great estate, and that she have a long neck and long fingers, and white in three, her body white, and her teeth white, and the white of her eyes white, and black in three: black hair and black brows and the black of her eyes black, and red in three: lips, cheeks, gums, and small in three: small mouth, small nose and small feet, and broad in three: broad of hips and broad of back and wide of forehead...

fall. From the early sixteenth century the expression was *Pride will have a fall*, and so it continued for over three centuries. Then in THE ANTIQUARY (1816), Walter Scott has *Pride goeth before destruction* and later writers use *Pride goeth before a fall* or *Pride comes before a fall*.

Down the centuries, writers have striven to put into their own telling words and images the wisdom contained in the proverb:

The lofty pine is oftenest agitated by the winds, high towns rush to the earth with a heavier fall, and the lightning most frequently strikes the highest mountains. (HORACE)

An avenging God closely follows the haughty. (SENECA)

> *Like little wanton boys that swim
> on bladders,
> This many summers in a sea of glory,*

But far beyond my depth: my high-blown
pride
At length broke under me.
(SHAKESPEARE)

To lordlings proud I tune my lay,
Who feast in bower or hall;
Though dukes they be, to dukes I say,
That pride will have a fall.
(GAY)

When pride and presumption walk before,
shame and loss follow very closely.
(LOUIS XI)

What is pride? A whizzing rocket
That would emulate a star.
(WORDSWORTH)

It was a foregone conclusion that we would
*win the war. But **pride goes before a fall**,*
and the all-important question now is
whether we can win the peace. In fact,
we are at serious risk of losing it.
SYRACUSE POST-STANDARD,
18 JULY 2003

Confidence is high in the [Lyon] camp, as
they beat Werder Bremen so comfortably
and are just a few wins away from taking
their fourth consecutive French league title.
*But they say **pride goes before a fall**, and*
I think it is dangerous to underestimate
Guus Hiddink's team, who have been every
bit as dominant in Holland as Lyon have
been in France.
RACING POST, 5 APRIL 2005

PROCRASTINATION

procrastination is the thief of time

putting off taking action wastes time

The proverb is a line from NIGHT THOUGHTS, a poem of 1742 by Edward Young:

Beware, Lorenzo! a slow, sudden death.
Be wise to-day, 'tis madness to defer;
Next day the fatal precedent will plead;
Thus on, till wisdom is pushed out of life.
Procrastination is the thief of time;
Year after year it steals, till all are fled,
And to the mercies of a moment leaves
The vast concerns of an eternal scene.

Warnings against procrastination have sounded for centuries. Firstly, it wastes time. Back in the first century, Seneca wrote that *While we are procrastinating life speeds by* (AD LUCILIUM c. AD 64). Then, it is hazardous. Writers in the sixteenth and seventeenth centuries pointed out the dangers of not doing something that really needed to be accomplished. Erasmus alerts us to the fact that *Procrastination brings loss, delay danger* (COLLOQUIA: ADOLESCENS, 1524), and W D Montagu that *There is no safetie in procrastinating* (AL MONDO, 1633).

Not surprisingly, there is an abundance of proverbs in every language that preaches against time wasting and delay:

Delays are dangerous
When the fool has made up his mind the market has gone by (Spanish)
Stay but a while, you lose a mile (Dutch)
When the horse has been stolen the fool shuts the stable (French)
After death the doctor (French)
A little too late, much too late (Dutch)

And a rich stock of sayings encourages immediate action:

God keep you from 'It is too late'
(Spanish)
Strike while the IRON is hot
Make HAY while the sun shines
Never put off till TOMORROW what you can do today
There's no TIME like the present
Take time by the forelock

For those who find all this insistence on immediate action burdensome, there is another side to the coin. When what needs to be done is nothing but a tedious duty, procrastination might be looked upon as saving one's personal time. This is certainly how Lord Henry Wotton looked upon it, for he was always late on principle, his principle being that *Punctuality is the thief of time* (Oscar Wilde, THE PICTURE OF DORIAN GRAY, 1891).

No matter how much you think about something it's clear nothing changes until you take some action. **Procrastination is the thief of time***, the sooner you get moving on it the sooner you can see some real results.* GLASGOW DAILY RECORD, 4 APRIL 2006

Did life happen and your dreams got put on the back burner? This has occurred to most of us. We have all heard that **procrastination is the thief of time***. I don't think that is entirely the case. Time is constant; we all have the same hours in every single day, it is how we choose to use those hours that steals the time. We all seem to think that things will take longer than they really will, so we talk ourselves out of doing them. Just what have you been procrastinating about lately? Laundry? Getting the car washed? Or is it something much deeper than household chores? Have you gotten in a rut?* SALT LAKE CITY DESERET NEWS, 17 MAY 2007

See also *Never put off till* TOMORROW *what you can do today;* TOMORROW *never comes*

PROPHET

a prophet is not without honour save in his own country

a person's gifts and talents may be recognised by others but rarely appreciated by those close to him

Variants: A prophet is not without honour, except in his own country; A prophet is without honour in his own country

The Bible records how Jesus, after travelling around teaching and healing, returned to Nazareth, and began to teach in the synagogue. The people there wondered who he thought he was, trying to tell them what to do. He was, after all, just the son of the local carpenter. Jesus answered their cynicism with the words *A prophet is not without honour, except in his own country, and in his own house* (MATTHEW 13:58), and was unable to minister to them because of their hostility.

Jesus's words have been used proverbially in literature since the early seventeenth century. Tobias Smollett, for instance, has *The captain, like the prophets of old, is but little honoured in his own country* (THE EXPEDITION OF HUMPHRY CLINKER, 1771).

*However, a '***prophet is not without honour, save in his own country***', and however emphatic the belief in Newman's sanctity was elsewhere in the world, there was a certain wariness in Britain – somehow canonisation has often been looked on as a rather 'un-English' procedure.* INDEPENDENT, 6 DECEMBER 2001

For all their success in a career that spanned more than 40 years, the Andrews Sisters were frustrated by small crowds in their hometown. Minneapolis Star *columnist Cedric Adams puzzled over this in 1951: 'Every stop was pulled out.... Radio stations bent over backwards to plug them; they worked benefit shows 'til they dropped in their tracks. What happened? Nothing. The box office at the theater was strictly on the duddy side...The Bible quotation is, "***A prophet is not without honor save in his own country***."' The sisters admitted that this curious ennui*

hurt their feelings, but it couldn't dim their fondness for their hometown.
MINNEAPOLIS STAR TRIBUNE,
12 APRIL 2002

See also *FAMILIARITY breeds contempt*

PUDDING

the proof of the pudding is in the eating
the wisdom of a course of action is tested out when it is put into practice

Early medieval *puddings* were rather like a black pudding or haggis. A length of pig or sheep intestine would be blown open with a reed and filled with a mixture of oatmeal, minced meat, suet and seasoning, then secured at the ends with thin wooden skewers known as pudding-pricks – hence the sixteenth century proverb *Everything hath an end, and a pudding hath two*. Later, meat or vegetable-based mixtures were encased in a floury dough and boiled or steamed in a cloth, or pudding-poke instead of a gut, and sweet puddings were also eaten.

Recipes for these delicacies were in print at the beginning of the seventeenth century when the proverb was first recorded. One book, HAVEN HEALTH of 1584, had: *Of the inward of beasts are made Puddings, which are best of an hog*. Its author, Cogan, would surely be as much concerned as we are today with what the pudding tasted like. It may have looked and smelt delicious but have been stodgy in the centre or have had too much salt in it. It had to be subjected to the ultimate test: it had to be tasted before it could be judged good. It had to be *proved*. The word *proof* is used here in its old sense, to mean not 'demonstrate' but 'test', as in *the EXCEPTION proves the rule*. The proverb has been current since at least the early seventeenth century.

*The miracles of Lourdes are dismissed as a deliberate deception perpetrated by the Church; but **the proof of the pudding is in the eating**, and if people claim that Marian intervention has worked, the writer of a book such as this should examine those claims closely.*
NEW STATESMAN, 10 DECEMBER 2001

Q My meal out gave me food poisoning. Can I sue?
*A ...**The proof of the pudding may be in the eating**, but proving the pudding poisoned can be very difficult indeed.*
WOMAN AND HOME, FEBRUARY 2004

*That this nasty turn of events may have involved cannibalism is suggested by several things. One is the way the remaining long bones, such as those of the leg, have been broken up, possibly in an attempt to extract their marrow for eating. The other is the pattern of burn marks on the bones, which may have come from their being cooked. But as sceptics point out, while such evidence certainly suggests a violent end, it does not necessarily mean a gastronomic one. The victims of Cowboy Wash may have died in some religious ritual or in a marauder's massacre. To establish cannibalism, **the proof of the pudding really must be in the eating**.*
ECONOMIST, 5 JANUARY 2006

PUNCTUALITY

punctuality is the politeness of kings
good time keeping shows respect for others

Variant: Punctuality is the politeness of princes

This is a translation of the French *L'exactitude est la politesse des rois* and was a favourite saying of Louis XVIII (1755–1824), who founded a constitutional monarchy in France after the defeat of Napoleon. Samuel Smiles, who attributed the maxim to the wrong Louis in his SELF-HELP (1859), considered punctuality to be the duty of gentlemen also:

A proper consideration of the value of time, will also inspire habits of punctuality. 'Punctuality,' said Louis XIV, 'is the politeness of kings.' It is also the duty of gentlemen, and the necessity of men of business. Nothing begets confidence in a man sooner than the practice of this virtue, and nothing shakes confidence sooner than the want of it. He who holds to his appointment and does not keep you waiting for him, shows that he has regard for your time as well as for his own. Thus punctuality is one of the modes by which we testify our personal respect for those whom we are called upon to meet in the business of life.

The French novelist and journalist Émile Gaboriau, on the other hand, considered good timekeeping to be a courtesy to the inner man. *Punctuality,* he wrote in OTHER PEOPLE'S MONEY (1867), *is a politeness which man owes to his stomach.*

L'exactitude est la politesse des rois is French, in case you don't know. It means 'punctuality is the politeness of kings'. What Lou baby was trying to say was that that kings don't have to be on time. Everyone else should be. Or were expected to be in my day. Or have a pretty bloody good excuse.
    It costs nothing to be on time. It's basically a matter of politeness. You are being terribly rude to your friends if you keep them waiting.
AAP GENERAL NEWS, 23 APRIL 2002

Punctuality is the politeness of kings and now, it appears, of professional footballers. It had better be if they want to play for Sunderland while Roy Keane is the manager, anyway. When the Sunderland coach left Wearside on Friday…it did so without three regular members of the squad. The Swedish midfielder Tobias Hysen and striker Anthony Stokes might have started against the Tykes, with reserve goalkeeper Marlon Furlop on the bench, but when they did not turn up on time Keane simply left them behind.
INDEPENDENT, 12 MARCH 2007

PURSE

you can't make a silk purse out of a sow's ear
it is impossible to make something fine out of materials that are rough and basic

While other domestic animals have coats and their ears are covered with shorter silkier hairs, the sow is blessed with bristles, a rough skin and ears just about the right size and shape for a draw-string purse. Unflattering comparisons between the poor sow's coarse complexion and finer materials have been made since at least the beginning of the seventeenth century. Her ears have proved inferior to *cheverel, satin, velvet* and finally, in the eighteenth century, *silk* purses.
    The pig's ears were not the only part of its anatomy to be criticised. In the seventeenth and eighteenth centuries, its curly tail was pronounced unsuitable for arrow shafts and whistles.

*The temptation with the 2001 Infiniti QX4 sport utility vehicle is to invoke the old admonition that **you can't make a silk out of a sow's ear**. It doesn't quite fit, though, because the new QX4 does exhibit many high-society attributes, and it's derived from the Nissan Pathfinder, which nobody would accuse of harboring porcine predilections.*
WASHINGTON TIMES, 11 AUGUST 2000

***You can't make a silk purse out of a sow's ear.** The players that Rafa has at his disposal are simply not good enough.*
LIVERPOOL DAILY POST,
25 OCTOBER 2005

· Q ·

QUART

you can't fit a quart into a pint pot

you can't fit a large amount into a small receptacle

A *quart* is a 'quarter of a gallon', that is 'two pints'. Therefore, it is vain to attempt to pour a quart into a pint pot. This inevitable logic is recorded in THE LIVING OF CHARLOTTE PERKINS GILMAN (1935), written by Gilman herself: *However, one cannot put a quart in a pint cup.*

The proverb is applicable to any context where too much is being attempted with too little space, time or resource. And, in spite of the metric system, people are happy to quote a proverb that retains the old units of capacity.

I had to abandon my train on Friday, before we even departed from London's Kings Cross bound for Edinburgh, on the service run by something called GNER…

*At great expense to the public purse, I had a first-class ticket, a reservation for a comfortable coach, a clutch of reading material – everything seemed in place. Except, that is, for the coach. It had disappeared, leaving dozens of well-heeled and well cheesed-off burghers fuming. One staff member was almost in tears as she tried to explain that **you just can't fit a quart into a pint pot** and that complainers would have to see the management – who were, of course, nowhere to be found.*
MAIL ON SUNDAY, 3 FEBRUARY 2002

Trying to fit a quart into a pint pot is the challenge when children turn into young adults and start to demand space of their own.
NEWCASTLE JOURNAL, 15 APRIL 2006

Usage: Informal

QUESTION

there are two sides to every question

there are two contrasting views to every issue

Variant: There are two sides to every issue

According to Diogenes Laertius (c. AD 200–250), it was Protagoras who, in the fifth century BC, first propounded the idea that there are *two sides to every question, exactly opposite each other*. The Greek philosopher was particularly skilled in promoting the less convincing argument to give it equal weight.

The maxim is cited in Charles Kingsley's THE WATER BABIES (1863), but reference to its wisdom is found in written sources of the previous century. One of these is in THE SPECTATOR (1711–12), a periodical edited and mainly written by Steele and Addison. The magazine claimed to be the work of members of a club who represented various interests in society. In one article (Addison, THE SPECTATOR, No 122, 1711), Sir Roger de Coverley, fictional representative of the country gentry, is asked to settle an argument between the quarrelsome

Tom Touchy and Will Wimble. Having patiently listened and carefully deliberated, Sir Roger tells them *with the air of a man who would not give his judgement rashly, that much might be said on both sides.*

Walsh illustrates the proverb with a moral tale written by the Rev Joseph Spence under the name of Sir Harry Beaumont. A prince erected a statue to the goddess of Victory at a crossroads. The goddess held a magnificent shield, one side of which was gold and the other silver. One day two knights, coming to the crossroads from opposite directions, greeted one another and passed the time of day. Then one knight commented on the golden shield. The other corrected him, declaring that it was silver. Before long the knights were in hot dispute and came to blows, each unseating the other from his horse. A peasant, who happened to have seen the incident, approached, patiently explained their error and pleaded with them *never to enter into any dispute, for the future, till they had fairly considered both sides of the question* (BEAUMONT'S MORALITIES, 1753).

At Brown University, copies of the Daily Herald were seized and dumped somewhere. The action was, of course, both denounced and defended – there are two sides to every question, after all – and faculty members were given the opportunity to make fools of themselves.
MILWAUKEE JOURNAL SENTINEL, 25 MARCH 2001

One obstacle is the journalists' truth-in-the-middle tradition – the idea that there are two sides to every question, and that the truth lies somewhere in the middle.
SOCIAL RESEARCH, 22 SEPTEMBER 2006

· R ·

RACE

slow but sure wins the race
patience and perseverance lead to achievement

Variants: slow but steady wins the race; slow and sure wins the race

Hares epitomise speed but they do not always win the race. The reference is to Aesop's well-known fable of THE HARE AND THE TORTOISE (c. 570 BC). The hare was confident that he could beat the slow old tortoise in a race and set off at a great speed. Judging himself to be so far ahead that he could not be caught, the hare sat down and took his ease but had not rested long before he fell asleep. The patient tortoise plodded on and, some time later, passed first the sleeping hare and then the finishing line. *Slow and sure had won the race.*

The first recorded use is by Robert Lloyd in his poem THE HARE AND THE TORTOISE (1762):

> *The bets were won, the Hare awake,*
> *When thus the victor Tortoise spake.*
> *Puss, tho' I own thy quicker parts,*
> *Things are not always done by starts.*
> *You may deride my awkward pace,*
> *But slow and steady wins the race.*

The saying is taken up again a century later by Samuel Smiles, in the rather moralising tone that it can still retain today: *Provided the dunce has persistency and application, he will inevitably head the cleverer fellow without those qualities. Slow but sure wins the race* (SELF-HELP, 1859).

A shorter form, *Slow but sure,* predates Lloyd's poem by at least 150 years. One saying, then, appears to have been fleshed out to form another. Nevertheless, *slow but sure* has stood the test of time and is still often quoted.

Slow but sure wins the race, as the tortoise famously told the hare. And an experiment in Coventry this week seemed to support the old saying.
As part of Bike2Work Week – during which everyone is encouraged to either cycle or walk to work at least once – two employees from Coventry Primary Care Trust were asked to go head-to-head on the roads. One was asked to use a bike and the other a car. Cyclist Rob Bennett, a 34-year-old resources officer, beat car driver Barbara Hunter, a 53-year-old smoking cessation adviser, by a clear five minutes.
COVENTRY EVENING TELEGRAPH, 19 JUNE 2002

It's amazing how effortlessly the children's fable about the tortoise and the hare translates into the adult world, even into the mercurial realm of publishing. Two contenders in this season's cutthroat chick-lit competition prove the moral of that old story yet again: Slow but steady wins the race. In the contest to win a place in the hands of every woman whose male relatives are watching football, the glib hare is definitely Citizen Girl, by Emma McLaughlin and Nicola Kraus. The careful tortoise and, in our opinion, the clear victor, is Case Histories, by Kate Atkinson.
CHICAGO SUN-TIMES, 7 NOVEMBER 2004

See also *ROME wasn't built in a day*

RAIN

it never rains but it pours

problems do not come singly but in showers

In 1726 IT CANNOT RAIN BUT IT POURS was chosen as a book title by Dr John Arbuthnot and, in the same year, was also taken as a title for a paper written by his friends Swift and Pope for inclusion in their PROSE MISCELLANIES. By the time Thomas Gray quoted it in his LETTER TO DR WHARTON (2 February 1771) the proverb had become *It never rains but it pours* and has remained in this form ever since.

It never rains but it pours. Phil Mickelson added to his last-hole woes at Pebble Beach on Sunday by spending most of Monday in hospital with food poisoning. RACING POST, 8 FEBRUARY 2001

It never rains but it pours for the poor old Mail on Sunday. *Not only has it had to grovel over its misjudged soft-porn Faria Alam interview, but now the Minx hears that the newspaper has lost a cherished prop to its claims to seriousness – its sponsorship of the prestigious John Llewellyn Rhys prize for young writers.* DAILY TELEGRAPH, 25 AUGUST 2004

REAP

you reap what you sow

you will eventually have to face up to the consequences of your behaviour

Variant: As you sow, so shall you reap

References to sowing and reaping are plentiful in ancient Greek and Latin literature but this proverb is from the Bible and can be found in GALATIANS 6:7: *Be not deceived, God is not mocked, for whatever a man soweth, that shall he also reap*. It is a recurrent theme in both the Old and New Testaments that a

person, or even a nation, reaps what is sown and is rewarded, for good or ill, according to whether actions are performed in obedience to God. In English, the proverb is found throughout the centuries after its early use in THE PROVERBS OF ALFRED (c. 1275): *Hwych so the moo soweth, al switch he schal mowe*.

It is hardly surprising that a task as fundamental to the sustenance of life should inspire a crop of proverbial comparisons. The success of any harvest depends on the quality of the seed. Sir Walter Raleigh reminds us that *according to the several seeds that we sow we shall reap several sorts of grain* (HISTORY OF THE WORLD, 1614). Some have sown corn cockle and reaped a disastrous harvest as Shakespeare notes in CORIOLANUS (1607):

The cockle of rebellion, insolence, sedition, Which we ourselves have plough'd for, sow'd and scatter'd.

Others need to be warned about the folly of scattering thistles: *He that sows Thistles, shall reap Prickles* (Thomas Fuller, GNOMOLOGIA, 1732).

Thomas Draxe has the answer, advising that *He that soweth good seed shall reap good corn* (BIBLIOTHECA, 1633). But for a really abundant harvest of blessing this needs to be done plentifully. The New Testament reminds us that *he which soweth sparingly shall reap also sparingly, and he which soweth bountifully shall reap also bountifully* (II CORINTHIANS 4:6), advice which is echoed in British proverbs. Ferguson in his collection of SCOTTISH PROVERBS (1595) tells us *Saw thin, maw thin*, and Randle Cotgrave's DICTIONARY (1611) concurs: *Little sow, little mow*.

Perhaps a Persian proverb should have the last word: *If you sow thorns, you cannot reap jasmine.*

First there was my revelation in Wilson's Week that Scotland and England were at the foot of the European league for investment in schools. Now comes the disturbing – but not surprising – news that the United Kingdom is near the bottom of the table for adult literacy. You reap what you sow. And we are sowing the seeds of long-term problems by failing to invest properly in the education of our young people.
GLASGOW SUNDAY MAIL, 18 JUNE 2000

But Mr Clifford claimed that the couple had only themselves to blame. 'If David Beckham had been intelligent enough to treat [Ms Gibson] with a little bit of respect, none of this would have happened. You reap what you sow.'
GUARDIAN, 27 APRIL 2005

See also *As you make your BED, so you must lie in it*

RECULER

reculer pour mieux sauter

when facing a challenge or problem, it is best first to step back and take stock before launching oneself at it

No athlete competing in the high jump, nor any horse attempting to clear a fence, leaps from the foot of the obstacle; instead he takes several steps back and runs at it, the better to propel himself over it. The proverb, too, advises stepping back to take a fresh look at a project before taking off. *Stop when you have begun, draw back a pace*, advised Ovid (ARS AMATORIA, c. 1 BC).

From this classical start, the proverb was taken into French. The courtly-love poet Jean d'Arras, writing in the late fourteenth century, has *Always wise men go aback for to lepe the further* (L'HISTOIRE DE MÉLUSINE) and, in the late sixteenth century, Montaigne has: *They have gone back only that they may leap the better* (ESSAYS, 1580). Across the Channel, George Herbert in

JACULA PRUDENTUM (1640) cites in English: *We must recoil a little, to the end we may leap the better*. However, during later centuries there is a continuing tendency to quote the original French. In GUESSES AT TRUTH (1827), the erudite nineteenth-century scholar Julius Charles Hare writes: *We must not overlook the numerous examples which history furnishes in proof that, according to the French proverb, il faut reculer pour mieux sauter*. This has persisted to the present: the proverb is still quoted in French.

He has been visited, also, by a manifestation of evil, which comes to him as 'A presence in the waves of sound, like an ageless dark being...it gathered strength and purpose in a series of sickening, irresistible pulses.' He feels something close to despair as he grasps that the withdrawal of this force is only temporary; it's a case of **reculer pour mieux sauter**. *The devil is biding his time.*
GUARDIAN, 2 SEPTEMBER 2006

*It may be in the best long-term interests of a company to adopt strategies that will lead to short- term profit slippage; '***reculer pour mieux sauter***' as the French like to say, though in practice they tend to major on the retreating, followed by a big lunch and nap.*
NEWCASTLE JOURNAL, 7 FEBRUARY 2007

For other proverbs quoted in French, see *Plus ça CHANGE, plus c'est la même chose*; *NOBLESSE oblige*

REMEDY

the remedy is worse than the disease

the steps taken to improve a situation just make it worse

There are some remedies worse than the disease was one of the maxims of Publilius Syrus in SENTENTIAE (c. 43 BC). Gaius Marius would have concurred. According to Plutarch (first century AD), after an operation to have a varicose vein removed, he remarked, *I see the cure is not worth the pain* (PARALLEL LIVES: GAIUS MARIUS). Francis Bacon, in his essay OF SEDITION AND TROUBLES (1597), is perhaps responsible for bringing the proverb *The Remedie is worse than the Disease* into English.

In another of his essays, OF FRIENDSHIP (1597), Bacon writes *Cure the disease and kill the Patient*, a variant drawn from the Latin proverb above. The derived maxim *KILL or cure*, is still commonly found.

*This is not the first Labour government to pick a fight with trade unions. They all do. But Monbiot's **remedy is worse than the disease**. He wants trade unionists to mirror New Labour's market mentality and hawk their votes and cash around for the highest bidder.*
GUARDIAN, 20 FEBRUARY 2002

*But mine was a tin-pot war without invading armies, without gauleiters and Gestapo, a mere taste of Total War. To see just how tin-pot we need only compare the haphazard buzz bombs and rockets that fell here in 1944 with the weaponry that we shall use on Baghdad; we shall indeed wage Total War, terrifying and obliterating, careless of civilians, **the remedy worse than the disease**.*
EVENING STANDARD, 18 MARCH 2003

REVENGE

revenge is a dish best served cold

revenge is more enjoyable and better executed if not delivered immediately in the heat of passion

Variant: Vengeance is a dish best served cold

Revenge in cold blood is the Devil's own Act and Deed, writes Thomas Fuller in GNOMOLOGIA (1732). If so, then it would seem that Otto Von Bismarck was Devil inspired, for Charles Lowe quotes the Chancellor of the new German Empire as saying *Eat the dish of revenge cold instead of hot* (THE TABLETALK OF PRINCE BISMARCK, 1885). Whatever its origin, the proverb is common to other European languages: French, for instance, has *La vengeance est un plat qui se mange froid* and Italian *La vendetta è un piatto che si serve freddo*.

To follow the proverb's advice would be to spend many hours calmly plotting one's revenge but, according to another piece of sixteenth century proverbial wisdom, time thus spent is fruitless. All that is really needed to wrongfoot one's enemy and gain superiority over him is forgiveness for, as William Baldwin writes, *Forgiuenes is a valyaunte kynde of reuengeance* (TREATISE OF MORAL PHILOSOPHY, 1547), or, to give it a more modern twist, *The noblest vengeance is to forgive*.

'The legal profession is remarkable for its freemasonry,' [Anne] Robinson says. '...they all go to their dinners at Lincoln's Inn and dress up in pantomime gear and think they're the dog's bollocks. And no one has ever been on crap-control with them, no one has ever said, how dare you!'
*Well, they have now. Robinson **serves her revenge cold** with extra relish. In the book, she names and shames all the men present in Court Four that awful day in 1973.*
TELEGRAPH MAGAZINE,
6 OCTOBER 2001

Controversial police commander Brian Paddick was dramatically removed from his post today...The move was ordered after a string of claims by Mr Paddick's former boyfriend James Renolleau...The commander and Mr Renolleau lived together for five years but parted acrimoniously. 'His favourite saying was

always, "*Revenge is a dish best served cold*,"' Mr Paddick said. 'Some people might say that is what has happened.'
EVENING STANDARD, 18 MARCH 2002

Revenge, they say, is a dish best served cold. Taunted about her age by broadcaster Anne Robinson, Lynda La Plante waited almost two years to confront her tormentor.
DAILY MAIL, 8 NOVEMBER 2005

See also *An EYE for an eye, and a tooth for a tooth; HELL hath no fury like a woman scorned; REVENGE is sweet*

revenge is sweet
getting one's own back is satisfying

Homer describes revenge as being *sweeter far than flowing honey* (ILIAD, c. 850 BC). William Painter, whose PALACE OF PLEASURE (1566) – translations of ancient and foreign stories into English – influenced English literature by providing contemporary dramatists with a wealth of material upon which to draw, also wrote that *Vengeance is sweet*. The proverb in the form *Revenge is sweet* was later used by Ben Jonson, Milton, Sheridan and Byron, amongst others. Some, like Milton in PARADISE LOST, (1667), temper the sweetness with a warning:

> *Revenge, at first, though sweet,*
> *Bitter 'ere long, back on itself recoils.*

Revenge recoiled on the Vachell family of Berkshire. The old story goes that they would not allow the Abbot of Reading to have hay carried through their yard. The abbot sent many messengers to plead with the family, the last being a monk whom Vachell killed in a fit of fury. As a result, he was forced to flee and, in bitter regret for his hasty action, took the motto 'Better suffer than revenge' for himself and his family.

The desire for revenge is certainly a powerful and consuming passion which, according to an old Italian proverb, does not diminish with time. *Revenge of a hundred years*, it says, *hath still its sucking [milk] teeth*. Psychologists say that it really does seem sweet since it is providing an outlet for pent-up aggression and wounded feelings, and the victim no longer feels helpless. A radio programme reported the (possibly apocryphal) case of a young woman who, upset with her boyfriend for seeing another girl behind her back, filled his curtain pole with prawns. The shellfish rotted, the smell was disgusting but no one could find out where it was coming from. Eventually the boyfriend felt forced to move... doubtless taking his curtain pole with him.

A Los Angeles policeman has been disciplined for hounding his mother-in-law... He booked her 23 times in one year for speeding. Revenge is sweet, isn't it?
SUNDAY MIRROR, 17 MARCH 2002

It is often said that revenge is sweet. Now scientists have shown that we do indeed get a genuine frisson of pleasure by getting our own back.
DAILY MAIL, 27 AUGUST 2004

See also: *An EYE for an eye, and a tooth for a tooth; HELL hath no fury like a woman scorned; REVENGE is a dish best served cold*

RIDICULOUS

from the sublime to the ridiculous is but a step
it takes only a small thing to make the great and important look foolish and absurd

Napoleon Bonaparte, addressing the Abbé du Pradt, used these words to describe his disastrous Russian campaign, which ended in retreat from Moscow in 1812. He is popularly thought to have coined the saying but he was, in fact, condensing a thought from Thomas Paine's THE AGE OF REASON (1793):

The sublime and the ridiculous are often so nearly related that it is difficult to class them separately. One step above the sublime makes the ridiculous, and one step above the ridiculous makes the sublime again.

And again:

When authors and critics talk of the sublime, they see not how nearly it borders on the ridiculous.

Paine (1737–1809), a political radical, was a prominent figure in France during the French Revolution and Bonaparte's ascendancy. He was made an honorary citizen by the republican government and was elected a delegate to the Convention.

Multilateral treaties that weaken the U.S. do not strengthen freedom abroad; uni- is not iso-. In our reluctance to appear imperious, we could all too quickly abdicate leadership by catering to the envious crowd. After his calamitous retreat from Moscow, Napoleon said with rue, 'From the sublime to the ridiculous is but a step.'
MILWAUKEE JOURNAL SENTINEL,
10 APRIL 2001

Then Murdoch launched the 1993 price war and, to defend his papers' sales, he [Black] instituted the cut-price subscription deals. While advertising was booming that loss of income didn't matter so much. Now it does...[Black] might like to ponder on Napoleon's famous remark after pulling back from Moscow: 'There is only one step from the sublime to the ridiculous.' Quite so.
GUARDIAN, 3 SEPTEMBER 2001

Usage: The proverb is now often used more idiomatically as *to go from the sublime to the ridiculous*, when something exalted is juxtaposed with something trivial, such as genuine pathos with bathos

ROME

all roads lead to Rome
there are many different ways of reaching a goal. There are a number of different routes to the same end

The Romans excelled in building roads. Their highways were long, straight and built to last. Together they composed such a network that, no matter where a journey began, it could end in Rome. This road system was essential for communication; without it the empire would have crumbled.

Unsurprisingly, this proverb is an old one. It is found in Latin in the work of French theologian Alain de Lille 'A thousand roads lead men forever to Rome' (LIBER PARABOLARUM, 1175). It is also common to many European languages: Italian, for instance, has *Tutte le strade conducono a Roma*, French *Tous les chemins mènent à Rome* and Portuguese *Todos os caminhos levam a Roma*.

As for English, in 1391 Chaucer wrote a treatise on the astrolabe, an old instrument used for measuring distances in astronomy. In the PROLOGUE we read that *diverse pathes leden diverse folk the righte way to Rome*. This is the earliest English reference we have to the numerous roads leading to the city.

A similar thought is expressed in non-European contexts, but the focal point is different. In China all roads lead to Peking; in Japan to the Mikado's palace.

Kruszelnicki, at his own expense, studied bellybutton lint samples sent to him by 5,000 people. He concluded the lint is a

MEDIEVAL LATIN

When the Roman Empire fell, Latin remained the international language of literature and scholarship in Western Europe until it was gradually supplanted by vernacular languages in the late medieval period.

There is a rich stock of medieval Latin proverbs, many of which are shared by other languages. *A BIRD in the hand is worth two in the bush* is one such, having equivalents in Icelandic, German, Italian, Romanian, Portuguese and Spanish. Indeed, Latin proverbs were often used at that time to teach other languages. Where a proverb was first coined in the vernacular and then shared through Latin, it is often impossible to trace the primary source.

Sometimes, a proverb might have a strong rhyme:

Aqua et panis est vita canis ('A dog's life is water and bread').

Sometimes it would take the form of a jingle:

Campus habet lumen, et habet nemus auris acumen ('Field hath eye and the wood hath the keenness of an ear' – see *WALLS have ears*)

Aegrotavit Daemon, monachus tunc esse volebat; Daemon convaluit, daemon ut ante fuit ('The Devil was sick, then he would be a Monk; The Devil recovered, and was a Devil as before'). This became *the Devil sick would be a monk*, and was said of someone who, in times of illness or difficulty, prays and makes fervent promises which are forgotten the moment pain passes.

See also: *A new BROOM sweeps clean; All that glitters is not GOLD; All roads lead to ROME*

---

combination of clothing fibers and skin cells that are led to the navel, via body hair, *'as all roads lead to Rome.'*
CINCINNATI POST, 4 OCTOBER 2002

Blocker took a more conciliatory tone, promising a closer relationship with state officials. 'All roads lead to Rome,' Blocker said.
ORLANDO SENTINEL, 16 AUGUST 2006

See MEDIEVAL LATIN, above

Rome wasn't built in a day
impressive results are not obtained overnight

Ancient Rome was a great imperial city. *A city greater than any upon earth,* wrote the Latin poet Claudian, *that from one small place extended its power so that upon it the sun never sets* (DE CONSOLATU STILICHONIS, c. AD 400). In the opinion of many, no other city in history has contained so many magnificent buildings. Even today, the Pantheon remains virtually complete; there are substantial remains of the Via Appica Antica (the main road to southern Italy of the third century BC), the Colosseum, the Roman

Forum, the Palatine Hill, the Arches of Titus and Constantine, and many other monuments. No wonder the empire and its buildings were not built in a day!

This truth is widely recognised in proverbial form. The earliest known reference comes from a French text written towards the end of the twelfth century. The saying has been in constant use in England since at least the middle of the sixteenth century; John Heywood includes it in his PROVERBS (1546).

Stevenson notes that the names of other great cities often replace that of Rome in variants of the expression. The French, for instance, also say *Paris n'a pas été fait en un jour* ('Paris was not made in a day'). A great local city is perhaps easier to relate to than an even greater one that is more distant, but nowhere else can compete with *the grandeur that was Rome* (Edgar Allan Poe, TO HELEN, 1836).

'I know **Rome wasn't built in a day***, but why does it take four years to get a positive decision for one, moderately sized, inner city store?' Sir Terry pleaded last November.*
DAILY TELEGRAPH, 11 JANUARY 2002

Rome wasn't built in a day *and you won't lose two stone overnight. Set yourself weekly goals instead, starting by simply dumping any junk that you used to eat in between meals.*
PEOPLE, 18 JANUARY 2004

Usage: Regularly used as an encouragement to persevere

See also *Slow but sure wins the RACE*

when in Rome, do as the Romans do

when you are away from home fit in with other people's customs and ways of doing things and don't expect them to change to accommodate yours

Confucius, Euripides, Sophocles and the rabbis who set down the TALMUD are among the wise who have warned travellers to remain sensitive to the different customs and practices they might meet along their way. The proverb *When in Rome do as the Romans do*, however, has a Christian origin.

When St Monica joined her son St Augustine in Milan, she was surprised to find that the Church there did not fast on a Saturday as the Roman Church was required to do, and was perplexed as to which practice she should then follow. St Augustine in turn consulted the wise St Ambrose, who gave this sound advice: *When I am here [at Milan] I do not fast on a Saturday; when I am at Rome, I fast on a Saturday. Follow the custom of the church where you are* (St Ambrose, ADVICE TO ST AUGUSTINE, AD 387). St Ambrose went on to summarise his good counsel: *If you are at Rome, live after the Roman fashion; if you are elsewhere, live as they do there.*

The proverb and variants of it were certainly in common use in the sixteenth century in both England and Europe. Don Diego, Spanish ambassador to the court of Henry VIII, slightly paraphrased the words of St Ambrose to account for his adoption of Protestantism in England: *When you are abroad, live in the manner of the place.*

More widely, a Nigerian author, Ojoade, has shown that there are many parallel proverbs that express the same idea in Chinese, Malay, Russian and Persian. He quotes a large number of similar sayings from language groups in his own country and from other African countries. Remarkable evidence for the universal nature of the relativity of human behaviour.

Audrey didn't seem to mind being outside.
She was of a pioneering disposition.
They could have put her in a mule wagon
and she'd have made the best of things.
'When in Rome,' she always said.
Well, when in Rome, maybe, but not
when you've been posted to the asshole of
the universe.
LAURIE GRAHAM, THE FUTURE
HOMEMAKERS OF AMERICA, 2001

When in Rome do as the Romans do –
and the same thing applies in China, says
Citroen. The Chinese prefer saloons to
hatchbacks and their market is expanding
at a phenomenal rate so Citroen has been
quick to respond by giving its best-selling
C4 hatchback a boot.
BIRMINGHAM MAIL, 17 MARCH 2006

Usage: Like many proverbs it is not often quoted in its full form, except in literature. Spoken and journalistic English commonly reduces the saying to *When in Rome…*, leaving the rest to be understood by the listener.

ROSE

a rose by any other name would smell as sweet

it is the intrinsic quality of a person or thing that matters, not what they are called

The proverb comes from a passage in Shakespeare's ROMEO AND JULIET (1591). The story revolves around two star-crossed lovers who are thwarted by a bitter feud between the Montagu and Capulet households. When Romeo, a Montagu, and Juliet, a Capulet, fall in love they know their relationship will be forbidden by their families. Juliet considers the value of a name:

Tis but thy name which is my enemy …
What's in a name? that which we call
a rose
By any other name would smell as sweet;
So Romeo would, were he not Romeo called
Retain that dear perfection which he owes
Without that title.

If a rose by any other name would
smell as sweet, then it stands to reason a
tax increase by any other name would be,
well, a tax increase.
SALT LAKE CITY DESERET NEWS,
26 FEBRUARY 2003

A rose by any other name would smell
as sweet. At least that's what Shakespeare
thought. But would calling a builders'
merchant a support services firm boost its
stock market rating?
INVESTORS CHRONICLE,
13 JANUARY 2006

ROSEBUDS

gather ye rosebuds while ye may

youth and love are beyond price, so enjoy them while you can; life is passing by, so make the most of the opportunities it offers while you can

The proverb is a line from a poem by Robert Herrick (1591–1674) who was well known for his love poems and pastoral verses. His poem TO THE VIRGINS, TO MAKE MUCH OF TIME was widely known and loved in the seventeenth century. It is a wistful exploration of the theme of passing time, of aging and of death. It encourages young women to taste and enjoy the gifts life has to offer while they may be had:

Gather ye Rose-buds while ye may,
Old Time is still a-flying.
And this same flower which smiles today,
Tomorrow will be dying…
Then be not coy, but use your time;

And while ye may, goe marry:
For having lost but once your prime,
You may for ever tarry.

The rose as symbol of the fleeting bloom of youth was not a new one in literature, however. Ausonius, the Roman poet of the fourth century, wrote an idyll entreating the virgin to gather fresh roses in her youth, reminding her that life, like the flowers, would quickly fade and pass away. The French poet Ronsard expresses the same idea in LINES TO HIS MISTRESS (1555), as does Spenser in THE FAERIE QUEEN (1596).

Gather ye rosebuds while ye may, even if your arthritis is flaring up. This is the lesson of Paul Cox's Innocence, *an Australian film about romantic love in old age, a subject so uncommon it makes* Innocence *stand out from the crowd.*
BOSTON HERALD, 28 SEPTEMBER 2001

Place this next to George W. Bush's recent statement that since African-Americans die at a younger age, on average, than whites, they should hail the dismantling of Social Security as somehow beneficial because they don't live long enough to reap precisely the same benefit as the composite white person. (Meaning? Grab the money and run? **Gather ye rosebuds while ye may?** *Or don't expect this Administration to come up with measures that might actually extend your life expectancy?)*
NATION, 14 MARCH 2005

Usage: Given its poetic origin and vocabulary, it not surprisingly has an elevated and rather dated flavour

See also CARPE diem; Make HAY while the sun shines; Strike while the IRON'S hot; TIME and tide wait for no man; There's no TIME like the present; Never put off till TOMORROW what you can do today

· S ·

ST SWITHIN

**St Swithin's day, if thou dost
rain, for forty days it will remain**
if it rains on 15 July [St Swithin's day],
it will continue for forty days afterwards

Each year the English await the
weather forecast for St Swithin's Day,
15 July, to determine what the summer
weather will be like. According to the
old rhyme:

*St Swithin's day, gif ye do rain, for forty
days it will remain;
St Swithin's day an ye be fair, for forty
days twill rain nae mair.*

St Swithin or Swithun, the Bishop of
Winchester, was a humble and holy man
who was chaplain and trusted advisor to
Egbert, King of Wessex, and tutor to his
son. He was known for his charitable
works and for his building and repairing
of churches, which he would dedicate
barefoot. When he died in AD 862, he
was buried, according to his wishes, in
the churchyard just outside the north
wall of the Old Minster where his grave
might be trodden on and the sweet rain
might fall upon him. The monks,
however, thought his simple grave
unworthy of so great a saint and,
following a poor labourer's vision of
Swithin, arranged to move his remains
to the inside of the cathedral. The
ceremony was planned for 15 July 971
but was greatly impeded by heavy rain
which, according to tradition, continued
to pour for a further forty days. Even
then, St Swithin was not permitted to

rest in peace. When the Normans
founded a new cathedral church, his
relics were moved again on 15 July
1093, but this time without a stormy
protest from the saint.

Curiously, although the legend dates
back to the tenth century, the earliest
known record in English literature is
in Ben Jonson's play EVERY MAN
OUT OF HIS HUMOUR (1599):
*O, here, 'St. Swithin's, the XV day,
variable weather, for the most part rain,'
good; for the most part rain: why it should
rain forty days after, now, more or less,
it was a rule held afore I was able to hold
a plough.*

In 1752, England eventually fell
into line with her Catholic neighbours
and changed from the Julian to the
Gregorian Calendar, thus moving
the day, if not the date, of St Swithin.
Even so, the good saint continues
to manifest his displeasure at having
his dying wish contradicted as the
DAILY EXPRESS (1 May 1993)
reports: *Saint Swithun – Bishop of
Winchester in AD 852 – did so well with
his rain last year that the cathedral roof is
now leaking.*

Not only that but the curse has also
crossed the Atlantic:

*St. Swithin's Day, if thou dost rain
For forty days it will remain;
St. Swithin's Day, if thou be fair
For forty days 'twill rain nae mair.*

David Austin has named a new rose to celebrate the 900th anniversary of the Cathedral's dedication. Called Saint Swithun, it'll be launched at Chelsea on May 24. It has fragrant pink blooms with all the charm of the old-fashioned rose, plus the modern rose's repeat flowering habit. Ten per cent of receipts go to Winchester Cathedral.

Scotland basks in a rare heatwave, while England is a swamp from **rains that began on St Swithin's Day, lashing the land for 40 days and 40 nights**.
GUARDIAN, 12 NOVEMBER 2001

St Swithin's Day *passed yesterday and with it – just possibly – any hopes of a sunny summer.*
HUDDERSFIELD DAILY EXAMINER,
16 JULY 2004

See also WEATHER WISE, page 220

SEEING

seeing is believing
you can believe something is true when you can see the evidence

There are many references to first seeing and then believing in Latin and Greek texts. *Seeing is believing* has been a proverb in English since at least the seventeenth century, and is also commonly found in other European languages; the Italians, for instance, say *Who sees with the eye believes with the heart*.

The proverb's development was perhaps influenced by a famous Bible story. Thomas was not with the other disciples when the risen Christ appeared to them and refused to believe that this had happened unless he could see Jesus and feel his wounds. When Christ appeared to him, Thomas acknowledged him as God, as recounted in JOHN'S GOSPEL, chapter 20, whereupon Jesus said to him: *Thomas, because thou hast seen me, thou hast believed; blessed are they that have not seen, and yet have believed.*

It has been said that **seeing is believing**, *and that maxim certainly holds true in most personal injury cases. Jurors who can plainly see evidence of a plaintiff's pain, like a missing limb or scarring from burns, usually don't need much convincing that the pain is real. But when the plaintiff's pain is caused by an 'invisible' connective-tissue injury, your task becomes much harder.*
TRIAL, 1 JUNE 2005

Is seeing believing? A series of photographs apparently showing two planes close to collision over east London has created a buzz across the blogosphere. On first viewing, the pictures raise a common internet problem – can you trust what you see and read? Do these photos show a near miss, a trick of perspective or are they fake?
DAILY TELEGRAPH, 31 JANUARY 2006

SHARE

share and share alike
in a joint venture any loss or gain should be divided equally

A fable of Aesop (sixth century BC) illustrates the sharing spirit. Two men were walking down a road when they came upon an axe. One man hurried to pick it up. 'What a piece of luck we've had,' his friend said. 'It's not *we* who have had the luck but *I*,' retorted the other. They had not gone much further when the man who had lost the axe came running along the road to find them. 'We've had it now!' exclaimed the man with the axe. 'It is not *we* who have had it but *you*,' replied his companion, 'since you would not let me share the ownership.'

The proverb is recorded in Cotgrave's DICTIONARY OF THE FRENCH AND ENGLISH TONGUES (1611): *'Escot' Whereat every guest paies his part, or share and share like*. The modern form *Share and share alike* was used by Daniel Defoe in ROBINSON CRUSOE (1719) and by

WEATHER WISE

Traditionally, when the British meet, conversation turns to the weather. This preoccupation, however, is not peculiarly British. Many languages have a fund of proverbs, which before the days of more scientific methods of forecasting, reflected the concern with the weather of those in agriculture and fishing.

Scores of proverbs related to the saints' days observed in past centuries by which the country dweller measured out his year (See *ST SWITHIN'S day, if thou dost rain*). They foretold weather conditions and harvest yields. Here are just a few:

If it does rain on St Michael (29 September) and Gallus (16 October), the following spring will be dry and propitious

If it rains on Corpus Christi Day (Thursday after Trinity Sunday) there will be little rye to put away

> *Remember on St Vincent's Day (22 January)*
> *if that the sun his beams display,*
> *be sure to mark his transient beam*
> *which through the casement sheds a gleam,*
> *for 'tis a token bright and clear*
> *of prosperous weather all the year*

If it's cold on St Peter's Day (22 February), then the cold is here for a lengthy stay

If at Christmas ice hangs on the willow, clover may be cut at Easter

As at St Bartholomew's Day (24 August) so will all the autumn stay

Clear on St Jacob (20 July) plenty of fruit.

According to this fourteenth century rhyme, a fair St Paul's Day (25 January) was crucial to the happiness and stability of the realm:

> *If St Paul's Day be faire and cleae,*
> *It doth betide a happy yeare,*
> *But if by chance it then should raine,*
> *It will make deare all kindes of graine.*
> *And if ye clouds make dark ye skye,*
> *Then meate and fowles this year shall die;*
> *If blustering winds do blow aloft,*
> *Then wars shall trouble ye realme full oft.*

Other weather predictions were made by observing the sky. These were only sometimes reliable. *When clouds appear like rocks and towers, the earth's refreshed by frequent showers,* for instance, is an accurate description of shower-bearing cumulonimbus clouds. But the well-known saying *Red sky at night, shepherd's delight; red sky in the morning, shepherd's warning* is less dependable, although a glowing sunset does indicate clear skies to the west from where many of the weather systems that affect Britain come.

Sometimes, even in our changeable climate, certain prevailing conditions make prediction certain. The saying *Dew in the night, the day will be bright* is reliable since dew forms on still nights when skies are clear, an indication of high pressure which brings sunny weather. The direction of the wind, shown by the weathervane on the church steeple, gave an indication of how cold it would be:

> *When the wind is in the east, it is neither good for man nor beast;*
> *When the wind is in the west, then 'tis at its very best*

An east wind is a lazy wind because…it will go through you before it will go round you
The west wind is a gentleman and goes to bed (that is, it drops in the evening).

Another well-known proverb *Rain before seven, dry before eleven* often proves correct. A band of rain does not usually last longer than a few hours, so if it sets in early a dry spell before eleven is probable.

Observation of plant life was also relied upon. This proverb about the budding of the oak and the ash was found to be *generally correct* by a correspondent with NOTES AND QUERIES (1852):

> *If the oak's before the ash,*
> *Then you'll only get a splash.*
> *But if the ash precedes the oak,*
> *Then you may expect a soak.*

But an article in the TIMES LITERARY SUPPLEMENT (4 August 1911) cast doubt on its reliability, stating that in North Germany the signs are exactly inverted, and also in Cornwall.

Heavy crops of berries foretold a hard winter, the fruit being needed to feed the birds:

> *Holly berries shining red,*
> *Mean a long winter, 'tis said*

> *Mony haws, mony snaws;*
> *Mony slaes, mony cauld taes*
> (Scottish)

cont'd

However, the abundance of any crop depends on weather conditions in its embryonic stage and not those prevailing when it comes to maturity. And the same applies to the humble onion:

> *Onion skin, very thin,*
> *Mild winter coming in;*
> *Onion skin thick and tough,*
> *Winter coming cold and rough.*

The behaviour of animals and birds was also held to be significant:

> *When a cow tries to scratch its ear,*
> *It means a shower be very near.*
> *When it begins to thump its ribs with its tail,*
> *Look out for thunder, lightning and hail.*

Does a cow's ear really only itch when a shower is expected? And, surely, the angry swishing of its tail has more to do with bothersome flies than storms? Here are a few more:

When harvest flies hum, there's warm weather to come

If the birds begin to whistle in January, there are frosts to come

When sheep and lambs do gambol and fight, the weather will change before the night

When the peacock loudly calls, then look out for storms and squalls

When you hear the asses bray, we shall have rain on that day

If bees stay at home, rain will soon come; if they fly away, fine will be the day

Seagull, seagull, sit on the sand. It's never fine weather while you're on the land.

Weather forecasting has come a long way since Aristotle wrote his METEOROLOGICA in the third century BC but, even with the sophisticated help of satellites and computers, weathermen can still get it wrong. They failed, for instance, to warn of the hurricane that hit the south of England in 1987. So perhaps it is unfair to pour too much scorn on our forebears who, by searching for signs and weather patterns in the world about them, attempted to stay one step ahead of the elements.

For those with an academic bent and a command of German, entries in the Bibliography under Helm and Hellmann provide substantial analysis, with an international perspective, of weather proverbs. Hellmann's own bibliography is seven pages long, showing how important climate has been over many centuries. For readers of French, Legros analyses many weather proverbs from Walloon in southern Belgium.

Maria Edgeworth in ORMOND (1817): *The woman...was dividing the prize among the lawful owners, 'share and share alike'.* The expression is often heard on the lips of exasperated parents trying to cajole their bickering offspring into sharing out sweets or toys.

Share and share alike. If you're going to the beach with friends, be prepared: Bring enough sunblock, toys, and snacks for everyone.
GOOD HOUSEKEEPING, 1 AUGUST 2004

Apparently all youngsters have to grasp the idea of mine before they can get to grips with the notion of yours or ours. Which means any call to **share and share alike** *– whether it's dummies, dinner or Dad, falls on deaf ears until they hit the terrible twos.*
GLASGOW DAILY RECORD,
24 OCTOBER 2006

SHEEP

you might as well be hanged for a sheep as for a lamb

if the penalty is the same whatever the offence, you might as well commit the more serious one

Variant: As good be hanged for a sheep as for a lamb

For hundreds of years, death by hanging was the punishment for anyone convicted of stealing. This brutal form of justice was not supported by everyone, however. In the Tudor period, for instance, those with a humanist outlook acknowledged the responsibility of society to provide for the poor. Thomas More shared these views. In UTOPIA (1516) he wrote:

...this punyshment of theves passeth the limites of Justice, and is also very hurtefull to the weale publique. For it is to extreame and cruel a punishment for thefte, and yet not sufficient to refrayne and withhold men

from thefte. For simple thefte is not so great an offense, that it owght to be punished with death. Neither ther is any punishment so horrible, that it can kepe them from stealynge, which have no other craft, wherby to get their living. Therfore in this poynte, not you onlye, but also the most part of the world, be like evyll scholemaisters, which be readyer to beate, then to teache, their scholers. For great and horrible punishmentes be appointed for theves, whereas much rather provision should have ben made, that there were some meanes, whereby they myght get their livyng, so that no man should be dryven to this extreme necessitie, firste to steale, and then to dye.

One way of avoiding the death penalty for certain lesser crimes was to be sentenced under the benefit of clergy, where felons were handed over to be dealt with by the Church. Criminals were branded on the thumb to prevent them from claiming this benefit more than once. During the second half of the seventeenth century, however, some kinds of property theft were removed from the benefit of clergy list due to unease over rising crime levels. Among these were housebreaking, shoplifting goods with a value of five shillings or more and theft of sheep and cattle. Anyone driven by hardship to steal a lamb suffered the same fate as someone who took a sheep and made off with more valuable spoil. Thieves reasoned that, since they were risking their necks whatever they took, they might as well feast on the larger animal. *As good be hang'd for an old sheep as a young lamb* is found in John Ray's English PROVERBS (1678).

Somewhere along the line, Mrs Blair clearly decided that **she might as well be hanged for a sheep as for a lamb.** *She was clearly going to be carped at by the media anyway. Now at least she's being carped at over something useful, worth discussing and*

defining – the role of political spouses in the 21st century – rather than something pointless, useless and over-defined – the role of female figureheads in the media.
INDEPENDENT, 11 JULY 2002

You can scarcely step into a department store to buy a shirt without the clerk trying to flog you a card... And as for such credit-card slogans as '...takes the waiting out of wanting!', isn't the inability to defer gratification one of the hallmarks of a psychopath?
    Authority, and the media are, in some ways, culpable. Student loans, still unthinkable two decades ago, have done much to normalise debt in society. Small wonder if rather too many graduates decide **they might as well be hanged for a sheep as for a lamb***.*
DAILY MAIL, 6 OCTOBER 2005

Usage: Purists insist on *hanged* but common parlance accepts *hung*. The sense has weakened, such that the proverb may now apply to minor misdemeanours, or even be simply a sign of commitment to a project and a willingness to accept any cost, should there be one.

See also *In for a PENNY, in for a pound*

SHIP

don't spoil the ship for a ha'p'orth of tar
don't risk the failure of an enterprise through small economies of time, effort or money

Variant: Don't lose the ship for a hap'orth of tar

This is not a nautical proverb and has nothing to do with caulking seams on wooden vessels. Its origins, in fact, are in farming, where tar smeared on an animal's sores or open wounds would protect them from flies and deeper infection. Neglecting to treat wounds in

order to save on tar was false economy, since the animal might die. This cheap and effective remedy was used on both pigs and sheep. Indeed, in its original form, the proverb was *Ne'er lose a hog for a halfp'north of tar*. Over time, however, either animal found a place in the saying, as John Ray reports: *Ne'er lose a hog for a half-penny-worth of tarre. Some have it, lose not a sheep, &c. Indeed tarre is more used about sheep than swine* (ENGLISH PROVERBS, 1678).

Gradually, then, sheep usurped the hogs in the proverb. But further changes were ahead. The rustic pronunciation in many areas of England made *sheep* sound like *ship*. By the nineteenth century, when the proverb had become widespread and was divorced from its rural roots, its original meaning was no longer understood and so the written form *ship* could be adopted without problem. A further shift in form and step away from the original sense took place when the *ship* was not *lost* for want of tar but *spoiled*, so that by 1886 E J Hardy was writing in HOW TO BE HAPPY THOUGH MARRIED: *People are often saving at the wrong place, and spoil the ship for a halfpenny worth of tar.*

UUP leader David Trimble still did not know whether the IRA would do enough to reverse the decline in unionist confidence. 'I am sure they are getting ready to do something,' he said. 'But, whether it will be enough, we shall have to wait and see. I have appealed to them **not to spoil the ship for a ha'p'orth of tar***', the former First Minister said.*
BELFAST NEWS LETTER, 8 APRIL 2003

Value engineering is a slippery word for reducing the specification. We do not want to **spoil the ship for a ha'p'orth of tar***, Coun Wilkes added.*
BIRMINGHAM POST, 11 FEBRUARY 2006

See also *A STITCH in time saves nine*

SIGHT

out of sight, out of mind

we soon forget about those people or
things we no longer see

The proverb is an ancient Greek one
dating back at least to Homer in the
eighth century BC.

The painter Nathaniel Bacon,
writing to Jane Lady Cornwallis in the
early seventeenth century, rightly calls
the saying an *owlde proverbe* for it
appears in the PROVERBS OF
HENDYNG (c. 1320) almost three
centuries earlier in a slightly different
form: *Fer from eze, fer from herte, Quoth
Hendyng*. And in HIS DE IMITATIONE
CHRISTI (c. 1420), Thomas a Kempis
has: *Whan man is out of sight, some he
passeth oute of minde*. John Heywood
records the proverb exactly as we know
it today in his collection of 1546.

Bacon's mother, Anne, however,
took issue with the wisdom of the
saying. In 1613 she herself wrote to
Lady Cornwallis and had this to say:
*I do perceive that the old proverbis be not
alwaies trew, for I do finde that the absence
of my Nath doth breede in me the more
continuall remembrance of him*. Had it
been current, the contrary expression,
Absence makes the heart grow fonder, might
have proved a more exact maxim for
Lady Bacon.

*Empty desk, empty mind, I always
say...there is a pattern to untidiness which
I have noticed in myself and others. One
guiding principle seems to be 'out of sight,
out of mind'.*
KNOWLEDGE MANAGEMENT, MAY 2001

*When we did our magic show for the
seniors, my father had had to convince me
to do the vanishing act. He explained the
reality to me – out of sight out of mind –
but I still believed that once the black
curtain came down, I'd be gone for good.*
JODI PICOULT, VANISHING ACTS, 2005

SILENCE

speech is silver, silence is golden

speech is a valuable gift but knowing
when to keep quiet is even more so

The MIDRASH ON LEVITICUS (c.
600), rabbinical commentaries on the
Old Testament book, teaches that *If
speech is silvern, then silence is golden*.
Since gold is the more precious of the
two metals, it follows that it is
sometimes better not to speak at all.
George Herbert defines the art thus:
Speak fitly, or be silent wisely (JACULA
PRUDENTUM, 1640). It cannot
always be assumed, however, that one's
silence is creating a good impression.
Even so, Abraham Lincoln recommends it above speech for, as he points
out, *It is better to remain silent and be
thought a fool than to speak out and remove
all doubt* (EPIGRAM, c. 1862). Sadly
there will always be those who are *not
able to speak, but unable to be silent*
(Epicharmus, FRAGMENTS, c. 550
BC). For people thus afflicted there is
both comfort and warning in Benjamin
Franklin's maxim: *Silence is not always a
sign of Wisdom, but Babbling is ever a Folly*
(POOR RICHARD'S ALMANACK,
1758). It seems that the path between
wise speech and wise silence is a
difficult one to tread.

In spite of the early origin, *Speech is
silver, silence is golden* is relatively recent
in English. Thomas Carlyle quotes it as
a *Swiss Inscription* in SARTOR
RESARTUS (1836), which may have
been its introduction into the English
language. Indeed, Carlyle seems to
have had something of a fixation about
the maxim. Critic John Morley,
commenting on a collected edition of
Carlyle's works, says, *The canon is
definitely made up and the whole of the
golden gospel of silence effectively compressed
in thirty-five volumes* (LITERARY
MISCELLANIES, vol i, pub. 1904).

Since then the proverb has often appeared in its full form but, even more frequently, shortened to *Silence is golden*, which gained the ultimate accolade of becoming the title of a pop record in the 1960s.

*Despite his [Wolstenholme's] criticism of some modern broadcasters – 'They don't seem to realise that while **silence in radio is death, in television it can be golden'** – he is revered by those within the business.*
DAILY TELEGRAPH, 27 MARCH 2002

When there's a prolonged pause in an offer, the person speaking first generally loses. **Speech is silver; silence is golden.**
ARLINGTON HEIGHTS DAILY HERALD, 31 JANUARY 2005

SMALL

small is beautiful

greater benefits accrue to units and activities of limited scale

Smallness has always had its champions. Early English proverb collections followed Greek and Latin originals in their renderings:

Vnto lyttle thynges is a certayne grace annexed. (Richard Taverner, PROVERBS, 1539)

Little things are pretty. (John Ray, ENGLISH PROVERBS, 1678)

and, at the same period, Edmund Spenser put the thought into verse in his VISIONS OF THE WORLDS VANITIE (1591):

> *Hereby I learned have, not to despise What ever thing seemes small in common eyes.*

But the virtue of smallness today is acknowledged in a different arena. An influential business book in the second half of the twentieth century was Professor E F Schumacher's SMALL IS BEAUTIFUL (1971). The title became a widespread catchphrase, used to support the burgeoning movement for human scale and human values in big business and government. Interestingly, Schumacher wanted to call his book THE HOMECOMERS. His publisher Anthony Blond came up with SMALLNESS IS BEAUTIFUL, then finally an associate, Desmond Briggs, coined the watchword of a generation.

*After a string of mergers which at long last have given Birmingham and the wider West Midlands press and PR agencies the clout to compete with some of the best in London, it would appear that '**small is beautiful**' has become the vogue once again. Lots of media types are setting up on their own, quite often by taking a business in which they have become fairly knowledgeable off a much bigger agency.*
BIRMINGHAM POST, 28 NOVEMBER 2005

*Because **small is beautiful** probably best explains why it is I never choose to leave Wales for any considerable length of time...*
CARDIFF WESTERN MAIL, 10 DECEMBER 2005

SMOKE

there's no smoke without fire

rumours are never groundless, they all have some truth in them

Variant: Where there's smoke there's fire

In THE TALE OF MELIBEUS (c. 1386), Chaucer attributes this proverb of fire and smoke to the first century philosopher Seneca (c. 4 BC–AD 65): 'It may nat be' seith he [Seneca] 'that, where greet fyr bath longe tyme endured, that ther ne dwellth som vapour of warmnesse.' Stevenson, however, traces the same phrase back still earlier to Publilius

Syrus's SENTENTIAE (c. 43 BC): *Never, where there has been fire for any length of time, is smoke lacking.* In any event, smoke has been a metaphor for gossip, rumour or scandal issuing from at least a spark of truth for over two millennia. The proverb is common to many European languages and is cited in almost all of the great proverb collections in English.

It has also proved a productive image – authors such as George Eliot have reinterpreted it in their own fashion: *Gossip is a sort of smoke that comes from the dirty tobacco-pipes of those who diffuse it; it proves nothing but the bad taste of the smoker* (DANIEL DERONDA, 1574).

'It killed him,' said Toby… 'He couldn't take it. He adored her. Everyone started this "no smoke without fire" stuff…even Aunty Daisy started to ask questions.'
SALLEY VICKERS,
MISS GARNET'S ANGEL, 2000

As recently as May, unbeknown to the public, the showbusiness world was abuzz with rumours that the couple had separated, and that Ross had moved out of the family home to live with comedian friend Frank Skinner… The rumours were never confirmed – or denied – although as another friend said: 'Let's just put it this way, there's no smoke without fire.'
DAILY MAIL, 21 AUGUST 2002

SPEAK

speak when you're spoken to
respond when you are addressed but not otherwise

*A child should always say what's true
And speak when he is spoken to,
And behave mannerly at table,
At least as far as he is able.*
(Robert Louis Stevenson, WHOLE DUTY OF CHILDREN, 1885)

This is another of the maxims by which British children have traditionally been brought up. Model children do not gaze in mute embarrassment at their shoes or glare insolently into the distance when addressed by their elders and betters but *speak when they are spoken to*, answering clearly and politely.

Children have been raised along these lines for many centuries. Thomas Fuller gives two helpful maxims in GNOMOLOGIA (1732): *Speak, when you are spoke to; come, when you are called.* And 72 years later similar advice was repeated by Maria Edgeworth in THE CONTRAST (1804):

> *Come when you're called,
> And do as you're bid;
> Shut the door after you,
> And you'll never be chid.*

This is still your boss and whether it is a meal in a restaurant, a group outing or a quiet drink, it still comes under the category 'work-related'… But there's no need to adopt a 'speak when you're spoken to' attitude.
EVENING STANDARD, 15 JULY 2003

When she returned, Laura informed her that she should talk only to the boss. 'You need to learn that in professional kitchens you speak to the chef and that's it,' she spat…'I used to work in a kitchen. You do your job and you speak when you're spoken to.'
MIRROR, 23 APRIL 2005

Usage: The phrase today could be addressed to anyone, child or adult, where a contributed comment was felt to be completely out of place. However, it would be an aggressive thing to say.

See also *CHILDREN should be seen and not heard*

SPEED

more haste, less speed

the faster you attempt to go, the less progress you will actually make

It was proverbial in ancient Greek that too much haste meant tasks were performed both badly and late: *In my haste to be done I am making less speed* (Plato, REPUBLIC, c. 375 BC). The maxim passed into English, the earliest known record being in the DOUCE MANUSCRIPT (c. 1350). *The more haste, the worse speed* was a common form from the fourteenth to the early twentieth century.

The well-known etymologist W W Skeat points out that the original sense of *speed* in Old English was 'success' rather than 'rapidity' as we understand the word today. Thus, the meaning of the proverb is 'The more haste, the worse success'.

But she was a girl who did things fast...
'More haste less speed' she might have said to Sarah had she been a pupil, in the days when she had some belief in her own precepts.
SALLEY VICKERS,
MISS GARNET'S ANGEL, 2000

*Gemini May 22–Jun 21: Mars, planet of energy and action, moves into your sign. Renewed enthusiasm concerning old problems and fresh incentive involving new projects engulfs you now. Pace business and romantic activities. **More haste less speed** surely applies now!*
BIRMINGHAM SUNDAY MERCURY,
12 FEBRUARY 2006

Usage: Often used as a rather smug and annoying comment to someone in a desperate hurry

See also *FESTINA* lente

SPIRIT

the spirit is willing but the flesh is weak

good intentions are often stifled by one's human inability to fulfil them. It is difficult to overcome one's bodily cravings with good intentions

Chapter 26 of MATTHEW'S GOSPEL tells how, after their last supper together, Jesus takes his disciples out to the garden of Gethsemane. Knowing his death is imminent, Jesus takes Peter, James and John further into the garden, where he explains how heavy his heart is and asks them to watch with him while he goes to pray. When he returns he finds them asleep. Rousing Peter, Jesus says to him: *What, could ye not watch with me one hour? Watch and pray, that ye enter not into temptation; the spirit indeed is willing, but the flesh is weak* (verse 41).

The proverb is used by Walter Scott in his JOURNAL for 23 July 1827. In the twentieth century, Aldous Huxley discusses the instincts of the flesh and the inability of the spirit to stand up to them in THOSE BARREN LEAVES (1925): *The spirit is willing but the flesh is weak. Weak in pain, but weaker still, he thought, more inexcusably weak, in pleasure. For under the torments of pleasure, what cowardices, what betrayals of self and of others will it not commit!*

On a less exalted plane, the proverb is often used as a flippant excuse for submitting to temptation.

*Throughout history we have brought to the fore that '**the spirit is willing but the flesh is weak**'. First a denial, then an admission, followed by apology.*
KENTUCKY POST, 8 OCTOBER 2002

*United resemble a bandy-legged marathon runner reeling towards the finish. **The spirit is willing but the flesh is weak**. But they summoned up the energy to outwit the*

stewards to throw their shirts at their fans, and they may even have the luxury of resting players at Chelsea on Wednesday night.
SUNDAY MIRROR, 6 MAY 2007

SPRAT

throw out a sprat to catch a mackerel

it is worth taking a small risk to make a large profit

Fishing is a risky business; you have to be prepared to *venture a small fish to catch a great one* (John Clarke, PAROEMIOLOGIA, 1639), or perhaps to *lose a fly to catch a trout* (Herbert, JACULA PRUDENTUM, 1640). Even the French are willing to *lose a minnow to catch a salmon*.

Sometimes, however, things don't go as planned. Throughout the seventeenth century, disappointed fishermen *fish'd for a herring and catcht a sprat*. William Hone came along a little late in the day and inverted the existing proverb in order to put them right: *It is but 'giving a Sprat to catch a Herring,' as a body might say* (EVERY-DAY BOOK, 1827). And Captain Marryat seemed to have the right idea, too, when he spoke of a plan as *a sprat to catch a mackerel* (NEWTON FORSTER, 1832). Dickens's characters expected large returns for their small stakes: *It was their custom...never to throw away sprats, but as bait for whales* (MARTIN CHUZZLEWIT, 1844). The idea of such a sizeable haul caught on, and by 1869 W C Hazlitt was listing *Set a herring to catch a whale* amongst his collection of English proverbs. This optimism was short lived, however. It was replaced by realism in the twentieth century when, for most people, the risk of throwing out a sprat was again expected to yield no greater return than Captain Marryat's modest mackerel.

It's a sprat to catch a mackerel, of course, but Sir Richard Branson is on the right tracks to woo disaffected travellers back to the train. Virgin's halving of fares on its West Coast line throughout next month shows goodwill at a time when other train operators appear mean-heartedly penny-pinching with their price hikes.
BIRMINGHAM EVENING MAIL,
11 JANUARY 2001

During our conversation, a bright young woman brings in an elderly couple. They have won a prize on a scratchcard handed to them by the club. 'Congratulations! Well done!' she beams, and fills in a welcome form. This is kept from my view but questions can include 'Are you working?' and 'Do you have a credit card?' All applicants win a prize – a holiday or wine or spirits, which critics say amounts to a sprat to catch a mackerel.
INDEPENDENT ON SUNDAY,
20 JANUARY 2002

See also *NOTHING ventured, nothing gained*

STICKS

sticks and stones may break my bones but names will never hurt me

a defiant chant shouted at school bullies; physical violence may wound a victim but taunts will not

The popular rhyming proverb, probably dating back no further than the nineteenth century, has its roots in an older saying. An unknown fifteenth century writer tells us that *fayre wordis brake neuer bone* (HOW THE GOOD WYF TAUGTE HIS DOUGHTIR, c. 1450), but the same is true of harsher language as Robert Greene points out: *Wordes breake no bones, so we cared the lesse for his scolding* (WORKS, 1584).

The modern rhyme is a show of defensive bravado and its wisdom is unsound; names and harsh criticism may not harm physically but certainly leave deep emotional scars. An old English rhyme from the thirteenth century PROVERBS OF ALFRED, paraphrased in later English by John Skelton (1460?–1529), acknowledges the destructive power of the spoken word:

> *Malicious tunges, though they have no bones,*
> *Are sharper then swordes, sturdier then stones*

Sir Henry Sidney, in a letter (c. 1560) to his son, Sir Philip Sidney, wrote: *A wound given by a word is oftentimes harder to be cured than that which is given with the sword.*

Let John Lyly summarise the whole with this neat analogy: *Nettells haue no prickells yet they sting, and wordes haue no points, yet they pearce* (EUPHUES, 1580).

Remember the days of 'Sticks and stones may break my bones, but names will never hurt me'? That may have worked as a temporary coping mechanism in childhood, but sometimes the damage done by chronic bullying can be severe and long-term.
KANSAS CITY STAR, 9 MARCH 2004

Remember that playground mantra, 'Sticks and stones may break my bones but names will never hurt me.' They shouldn't. But they do. Because we let them.
SOUTH WALES ECHO, 13 MARCH 2006

STONE

a rolling stone gathers no moss

a person who is constantly moving from place to place will never amass wealth (or affection)

In his FIVE HUNDRED POINTS OF GOOD HUSBANDRIE (1573), Thomas Tusser quotes the proverb, still relatively new to English, along with an explanation of its meaning:

> *The stone that is rolling can gather no moss,*
> *For master and servant oft changing is loss.*

The original form of this ancient Greek proverb was *A rolling stone gathers no seaweed* and probably refers to the action of the tides rolling the stones on a Greek seashore in and out with the tide, so that no weed could begin to cling to their surface. According to Stevenson, we owe the change from *seaweed* to *moss* to Erasmus, who recorded his new and definitive rendering in the 1523 edition of his ADAGIA. Twenty-three years later, it had become well known enough to be recorded by John Heywood: *The rollyng stone neuer gatherth mosse* (PROVERBS, 1546).

Not surprisingly, the saying is common to many European languages, where there are direct analogues. There is also a good number of kindred proverbs that express the same idea:

A tree often transplanted does not thrive (Quintilian)
Selden moseth the marble-stone that men often treden (Langland, PIERS PLOWMAN, 1362)
The still hog gets the swill (American)

While he's cagey about his private life (he'll admit under pressure that he's 'a rolling stone that gathers no moss'), his career remains peachy keen.
ELLE, MAY 2001

As the saying goes, a rolling stone gathers no moss. Moving from one company to another without any clear reasons will only hurt your future chances of securing positions.
NEW STRAITS TIMES, 17 JUNE 2006

See CHANGING WITH THE TIMES, page 233

STOOLS

between two stools you fall to the ground

dithering between two courses of action brings disaster or the loss of both opportunities

The proverb 'to sit down between two stools' has ancient origins. Seneca uses it in CONTROVERSIA (c. 60 BC). IL PROVERBE AU VILAIN, a French text from the late twelfth century, has: *Between two stools one falls bum to the ground*, and over three centuries later the French author Rabelais says: *He would sit between two stools with his bum to the ground* (GARGANTUA, 1534). The earliest recorded uses of the saying in English are in John Gower's CONFESSIO AMANTIS (c. 1390):

> Bot it is seid and evere schal,
> Between two stoles lyth the fal

In the intervening centuries, there has been some concentration on the part of the anatomy that actually hits the ground. It was described first as the *arse* and later as the *tail*. The eighteenth century seems to have been surprisingly delicate. Witness first Fielding in TOM THUMB (1730):

> While the two stools her sitting-part
> confound,
> Between 'em both fall squat upon the
> ground

then Jephson: *Between two stools they say a certain part of a man comes to the ground* (TWO STRINGS TO YOUR BOW, 1791).

That people should be described as falling between stools is not strange for, as late as the Stuart era, chairs were rare; people sat on stools, chests or backless benches. The proverb is an apt figurative statement about someone who tries to span more than one area and fails through lack of commitment to any one side. In Anthony Trollope's BARCHESTER TOWERS (1857), the slippery clergyman Obadiah Slope is torn between wooing Mrs Bold for her fortune and the penniless, and still married, Signora Vesey-Neroni, to whom he is attracted and the resulting scandal is, of course, Mr Slope's downfall:

*...[Mr Slope] having written his letter to Mrs Bold... proceeded to call upon the Signora Neroni. Indeed it was hard to say which was the old love and which was the new, Mr Slope having been smitten with both so nearly at the same time. Perhaps he thought it not amiss to have two strings to his bow. But two strings to Cupid's bow are always dangerous to him on whose behalf they are to be used. A man should remember that **between two stools he may fall to the ground**.*

Since the twentieth century, the entire proverb is rarely found. Instead, it has been forged into an idiom *To fall between two stools*, which is very common indeed. The idiom is not restricted to people but can also be applied to things, as the example below from THE RACING POST shows.

*The book **falls uncomfortably between two stools**. On the one hand, a greater sophistication of argument is required to appeal to the serious form student. On the other, the data and conclusions need to be more concise and harder hitting to win over less-experienced gamblers.*
RACING POST, 14 JUNE 2001

*This Bradford band were too pop for true metalheads and too metal for pop fans. They may have **fallen between two stools**, but they didn't give a monkey's.*
MIRROR, 28 JANUARY 2005

STORM

after a storm comes a calm

difficult circumstances will inevitably give way to more peaceful ones

Variant: After the storm comes the calm

As Genevieve Taggard puts it in OF THE PROPERTIES OF NATURE FOR HEALING AN ILLNESS (1894–1948):

> Try tropic for your balm,
> Try storm,
> And after storm, calm.
> Try snow of heaven, heavy soft, and slow,
> Brilliant and warm.
> Nothing will help, and nothing do
> much harm.

The earliest recorded use of the proverb is in the devotional text, ANCREN RIWLE of c. 1200. Later, William Langland used the notion of sunshine after inclement weather in PIERS PLOWMAN (1377): *After sharpe shoures moste shene is the sonne.* Thereafter the weather theme recurred but always differently expressed. Sometimes the metaphor was used to give the pessimist's view: *Calm continueth not long without a storm* (George Pettie, PETITE PALLACE, 1576). In 1605 William Camden used the phrase in the form familiar today: *After black clouds clear weather. After a storm comes a calm* (REMAINS).

A quiet period after a particularly trying experience is often referred to idiomatically as *the calm after the storm*. There is also the similar expression *the calm before the storm*.

A parallel proverb is *After rain comes sunshine*, and one authority gives a French origin for this.

After the storm, the calm. With the cheers growing silent in the distance, Julius Francis returned to the solace of his hotel room to be hit by a force greater than anything unleashed by Mike Tyson. As the door closed behind him the grim reality of defeat descended like a hammer. Feeling he had let himself, his supporters and his country down, this proud man collapsed on his bed and wept.
MIRROR, 31 JANUARY 2000

After the storm comes the calm. Southern family rockers Kings of Leon so enjoyed the success of their first two records that they treated themselves to all sorts of narcotic and carnal pleasures. Because of the Times *is the sound of a band having a close look at the darkness that follows such hedonism.*
EVENING STANDARD, 2 APRIL 2007

See also *The darkest HOUR is that before the dawn*

any port in a storm

in times of want or need any haven will suffice. A last resort

The dangers of a storm at sea are self-evident to any sailor. In such circumstances, it is imperative to find a sheltered anchorage, often in a port, to await better weather. In days gone by, it was common to winter in a port in order to escape the rigours of that season. Wherever you happened to be, provided it offered protection, was better than exposure to the elements.

Because of Britain's sea-faring traditions, many expressions first used onboard ship found their way into the everyday speech of folk who never left dry land. This is one such proverb. An early use is in James Cobb's play THE FIRST FLOOR (c. 1780), since when it has developed much wider applications; help of any kind, even if not normally acceptable, constitutes *any port in a storm*.

CHANGING WITH THE TIMES

The meaning of a proverb is not immutable. It changes in relation to how people understand it, and this is in turn determined in part by the contemporary values of society. An interesting case in point is *A rolling STONE gathers no moss.*

Traditionally this was a caution against excessive mobility. This is very understandable in the settled, agricultural communities of previous centuries, where the wanderer had a generally bad reputation.

However, there has always been at least a small element of ambiguity in its meaning. Horatio Alger (1832–99) fled to Paris from America as a bohemian rebel, ultimately returning to become a minister of the Church and influential author of boys' books. Many of them are on the theme of a footloose youngster who in the end makes good. One in particular is entitled THE ROLLING STONE, in which the hero gains riches and success. So the life of *a rolling stone* could have positive connotations.

Dialectal proverbs were also questioning the wisdom of the adage. In CHESHIRE PROVERBS (1917), J C Bridge notes that over the years two English regional tags had been added to the proverb, and that these tags contradict it. A Cheshire saying is *A rolling stone gathers no moss but a tethered sheep winna get fat,* whilst in Surrey and Sussex the tag is *and a sitting hen never grows fat.*

The twentieth century saw fundamental social changes that sharpened what had previously only been hints of ambiguity of meaning. The rise of urban patterns of life and, especially, the demands for mobility in order to follow jobs and careers became more insistent. Consequently, being *a rolling stone* was a positive virtue, not a handicap.

Another reason for questioning the original meaning of the proverb has a connection with connotations. In the original *moss* is seen as something desirable, a symbol of well-being, a velvety green covering one wants to put on. However, more generally this is not the case. George Bernard Shaw puts it well in his Preface to MISALLIANCE (1914): *We keep repeating the silly proverb that rolling stones gather no moss, as if moss were a desirable parasite. The last thing a gardener wants is moss in his lawn!*

By the second half of the twentieth century the proverb was still extremely common (97 per cent of the 162 respondents in Lundgren's survey knew it), yet there was major uncertainty as to what it meant. Lundgren found in his group of 1957 American undergraduates that two thirds of them believed the expression meant 'If you want to succeed, be on the move, for fear you become an old moss-back.'

For nearly 3,000 years, and across endless cultures and languages, *A rolling stone gathers no moss* has reflected society's view that stability is a virtue. In the last hundred years, mobility is in the ascendant. Language has responded, not by introducing a new proverb for new perceptions but by offering a reinterpretation of the old adage. The two senses now run side by side. The social conditions of the twenty-first century may decide which one will win out.

If he can restrain his glee about a new opinion poll showing the SNP 4 per cent ahead of Labour, Mr Salmond is in with a real chance of snatching victory next May. Evidence is mounting that the electorate really is deserting Labour in droves…This shift in voting intentions is not about Braveheart patriotism. It is a case of **any port in a storm** *for people sickened by Labour's broken promises and diplomatic ineptitude.*
DAILY MAIL, 28 AUGUST 2006

While Labour is campaigning to form a government and has ruled out a coalition with the Tories, Plaid Cymru who can never form a government on their own is frantic to find any potential partner for just a whiff of power. **Any port in a storm**.
CARDIFF WESTERN MAIL,
26 APRIL 2007

See also *Half a loaf is better than no* BREAD

STRAW

a drowning man will clutch at a straw

a person facing overwhelming difficulty will grasp at any fleeting opportunity to save himself

The proverb first appeared in literature at the beginning of the seventeenth century. During the first 130 years or so, various forms had drowning men clutching at *twigs*, *helpless things*, *reeds*, *thorns* and *rushes* before finally settling upon *straws* around the middle of the eighteenth century. The picture of a drowning man hoping against hope that the straw will bear his weight and save him is vivid enough but the Italians take his desperation even further. They have a proverb which says *A drowning man will catch at razors*.

A drowning man will clutch at a straw is an apt proverb that represents the power

brokers at the helm of the so-called Gang of Six. The straw in this scenario is the cash from the Welsh Rugby Union to Caerphilly, Ebbw Vale and Neath. The greedy six clubs merely want to use the cash as a "get out of jail" card to stem their worries of bankruptcy and pay the huge wage bill of less-than-super players.
CARDIFF WESTERN MAIL,
19 DECEMBER 2001

So, British Prime Minister Tony Blair has announced that he will work for peace in Palestine until he leaves office in around 10 months' time, and after that, no doubt will be available for speaking engagements on his efforts in that direction. He has already been off to the region to meet Prime Minister Ehud Olmert of Israel and his Palestinian counterpart Mahmoud Abbas and, for good measure, Fouad Siniora, prime minister of what is left of Lebanon; and they all seem to agree that Tony might be the very man to get the US-sponsored Road Map back on track. But, as they say, **a drowning man will clutch at a straw**.
MIDDLE EAST, 1 OCTOBER 2006

Usage: The proverb is now often shortened to the idiom *to clutch at a straw* or *at straws*

it's the last straw which breaks the camel's back

the final, often insignificant, event which makes hardship too burdensome to endure any further

Variant: It's the final straw which breaks the camel's back

A variety of metaphors in a number of languages has been used to express the idea of total breakdown resulting from a final, tiny stroke: *A chord may be finally broken by the feeblest of pulls* (sixteenth century Spanish); *A cup may overflow with the last tiny drop* (seventeenth century English; French has *glass*); and *A single grain is charged with making the balance heavier* (Arabic). Archbishop John Bramhall, writing in 1677, said that *It is the last feather that breaks the horse's back*, an expression also recorded by Thomas Fuller in his GNOMOLOGIA in 1732. Then, in 1848, Charles Dickens used the proverb in the form we are familiar with today: *The last straw breaks the laden camel's back* (DOMBEY AND SON).

The proverb has been the subject of several examples of humour and light verse. This little ditty is by Harry Graham (MORE RUTHLESS RHYMES FOR HEARTLESS HOMES, 1930):

The Last Straw
Oh, gloomy, gloomy was the day
When poor Aunty Bertha ran away!
But Uncle finds today more black.
Aunty Bertha's threatening to run back!

Congestion on Southern California's freeways – already the nation's worst – will intensify and finally come to a gridlocked halt in just a few years unless dramatic steps are undertaken, traffic experts say… 'Once it gets too much, the system collapses… It's the last straw that breaks the camel's back.'
LOS ANGELES DAILY NEWS,
30 DECEMBER 2003

The huge rise in energy bills hitting many of Britain's 25 million households this month could prove to be the straw which breaks the camel's back for many hard-pressed family budgets.
BIRMINGHAM POST, 11 MARCH 2006

Usage: *The last/final straw* is often used idiomatically without the rest of the proverb

SUN

don't let the sun go down on your anger
deal with anger and disagreements promptly, and don't let them drag on into a new day

Variant: Let not the sun go down on your wrath

The proverb is a biblical one. In his letter to the church at Ephesus, Saint Paul writes: *Be ye angry, and sin not; let not the sun go down upon your wrath* (EPHESIANS 4:26). If believers become angry with one another, they are not to fall into sin by bearing a grudge but are to resolve the matter quickly.

The injunction seems sound. A newspaper article giving advice on how to maintain a good relationship quoted the example of a couple who had been happily married for 60 years: *The reason for their enduring love, they said, was because they both refused to go to bed without making up first* (DAILY MAIL, 14 January 1993).

We agreed that a phone call could have saved us months of bitter feelings toward one another. Don't let the sun go down on your anger. No matter who makes you mad or why, go to the person who angered you and get it straight. If I had just called Mike up when I found out what he had done, we could have worked it out right then.
UNIVERSITY WIRE, 17 MARCH 2000

I believe…that the best aphorism for life is, 'Don't let the sun go down on your anger'. Every day is a new day. If you take life as it comes you're likely to be happier and less frustrated.
INDEPENDENT ON SUNDAY,
16 OCTOBER 2005

SWALLOW

one swallow doesn't make a summer

a single indicator of something is not in itself significant

In ancient Greece the swallow was the herald of spring, and such a welcome sight that schoolchildren in Attica were given a day's holiday when the first one was seen. Aesop (sixth century BC) told a fable about a spendthrift who spied a swallow which had been tempted back from its winter migration by some fine, sunny weather. 'Spring is here, thought the young man, and promptly sold his warm cloak, spending the money on carousing in the town. But when the winter weather returned a few days later, the young man learned to his cost that one swallow does not make a spring.

The ancient Greek proverb was *One swallow does not make a spring* – it still is in Spain and Italy. Strictly, the English saying should be the same since this migratory visitor to Europe appears in April after wintering in Africa. Perhaps the swallow's appearance is associated in the English mind with better weather, which comes later in more northerly climes. Hence the change from *spring* to *summer* since the proverb's first appearance in English in the sixteenth century.

The form of the proverb makes it easy to add on clauses, and the saying has been tampered with considerably over the years. Here are just a few examples:

Nay, soft (said the widow) one swallow makes not a summer, nor one meeting a marriage.
(Thomas Deloney, JACKE OF NEWBERY, 1597)

One Swallow makes ('tis true) no Summer, Yet one Tongue may create a Rumour.
(Thomas D'Urfey, COLLIN'S WALK THROUGH LONDON, 1690)

One swallow does not make a summer, nor one goose a farmyard.
(C F Rogers, VERIFY YOUR REFERENCES, 1938)

And, in THE OXFORD BOOK OF ROYAL ANECDOTES (1989), Elizabeth Longford coins this appealing variant:

*King William III was said to have been too small to offer his arm to his massive wife Queen Mary. Instead he dangled from hers 'like an amulet from a bracelet'. **One simile does not make an anecdote**. The simile about the amulet, however, provides a good analogy for the royal anecdote and its event. The anecdote should hang like an amulet from the arm, so to speak, of the greater event.*

*Just as **one swallow doesn't make a summer**, a handful of early season salmon don't make a spring run.*
GLASGOW DAILY RECORD,
18 FEBRUARY 2000

*Just as **one swallow doesn't make a summer**, so one solid round of golf doesn't signal the return of form to a golfer lost in a winter wasteland of mediocrity.*
EVENING STANDARD, 9 MAY 2003

Usage: This ancient proverb is still applied figuratively to a vast range of contexts, from one good quality not making a good man to one good economic indicator not meaning an end to recession

SWINGS

what you lose on the swings you gain on the roundabouts

gains and losses balance out

Variant: What you lose on the roundabouts you gain on the swings

A Latin proverb tells us that what is lost in one way may be recouped in another. An old sixteenth century English proverb from the fishing industry expressed the same idea: *The hakes... haunted the coast in great abundance; but now, being deprived of their wonted bait, are much diminished; verifying the proverb, 'What we lose in hake, we shall have in herring'* (Richard Carew, THE SURVEY OF CORNWALL, 1602).

The modern proverb is another variant, the allusion being to a fairground where the proprietor might one day make a loss on running the roundabouts but a profit on working the swings. Possibly the development of the saying was influenced by Patrick Chalmers's verse ROUNDABOUTS AND SWINGS (1910), part of which reads: *What's lost upon the roundabouts we pulls up on the swings!'*

The expression has been quoted by Somerset Maugham and Shaw, amongst others. There is some variation as to the word order: sometimes the swings gain and other times the roundabouts are in profit. Since it doesn't alter the sense of the saying then either would seem acceptable.

*'They told me his legs were going,' Hoddle said. 'And OK, he's not as sharp as he was at 21, but that's part of the natural process...With Paul, **what you lose on the swings you gain on the roundabouts** with the sharpness of his mind. I can vouch for that from my own playing career.'*
BIRMINGHAM POST, 18 JANUARY 2005

*Investment returns will be influenced by changes in the exchange rate of the pound versus all of the currencies in which the different overseas stocks are denominated. **What you lose on the 'swings' you might gain on the 'roundabouts'**, but it is not unusual for a currency to decline or appreciate against numerous currencies over the same period.*
INVESTMENT ADVISER, 28 APRIL 2007

Usage: Often abbreviated to the idiom *(It's) swings and roundabouts*, meaning it is 'six of one, half a dozen of the other', so the options open are of equal standing

T

TAKE

you can't take it with you (when you go)

make use of your money while you are alive, you can't spend it when you are dead

St Paul, writing to his disciple Timothy, reminds him that contentment and a blameless life are true riches, reinforcing his argument with the words *for we brought nothing into the world, and it is certain we can carry nothing out* (TIMOTHY 6:7). These words have become familiar through the Church of England funeral rites they are amongst those recited by the priest at the start of the service as he enters the church walking in front of the coffin.

The proverb has been in use in England since the first half of the nineteenth century. During the Great Depression, the song LIFE IS JUST A BOWL OF CHERRIES (lyrics by Lew Brown, 1931) gave the saying an American flavour: *you can't take your dough when you go, go, go.*

When a man told the wealthy American film producer Louis B Mayer (1885–1956) *You can't take it with you when you go*, Mayer's reply is reputed to have been *If I can't take it with me, I won't go*.

*Get a grip, Mr Cummings: it is only money, after all. **You can't take it with you when you go** off to the great Head Office in the sky, you know.*
OBSERVER, 24 OCTOBER 2004

*I know so many people with plenty of money and property who scrimp and save out of habit. I tell them **you can't take it with you**. Enjoy it, you could drop dead tomorrow.*
SAGA MAGAZINE, JULY 2005

TANGO

it takes two to tango

some things just can't be done alone. Sometimes two people must share the blame for something

It takes two to quarrel, two to reach a compromise, two to repair a relationship, two to make a happy marriage, two to make love and two to commit adultery – indeed, the saying is often used in the latter instance to put the blame on both partners in an affair.

The maxim comes from a hit song entitled IT TAKES TWO TO TANGO (1952), written by Al Hoffman and Dick Manning and made popular by the singer Pearl Bailey. Rhythmical, alliterative and true, it bears the hallmarks of a successful proverb.

*'The period of conflict management is over. We have entered an era of conflict resolution,' he added. 'It needs two hands to clap. They say **it takes two to tango**. We may be too old to tango but my hand is extended to clap.'*
DAILY TELEGRAPH, 17 APRIL 2005

*I do not think Alastair would find flat racing trainers any less forthcoming than their jumping brethren. After all, a television interview is a two-way affair of questions and answers. **It takes two to tango**.*
RACING POST, 27 NOVEMBER 2006

THIEF

set a thief to catch a thief
someone with experience of wrongdoing is the best person to catch others at it

No one knows the ins and outs of his business as thoroughly as the thief himself, so who better to arrest or deter another of his kind? When Robert Howard used the proverb in a play in 1665 he called it an *old saying*. And indeed, similar advice has been around for centuries. Cato the Younger worked upon the premise that *The authors of great evils know best how to remove them* (49 BC) when, in spite of stiff opposition, he recommended that Senate business should be entrusted to the Roman general, Pompey. On a more domestic note, in the PHYSICIAN'S TALE (c. 1387) Chaucer reminds us of the old theory that a poacher is the best man to watch over the deer, advice that eventually took the modern form *An old poacher makes the best keeper*. In his CHURCH-HISTORY OF BRITAIN (1655) Thomas Fuller combines the proverbs: *Many were his lime-twigs to this purpose... Always set a thief to catch a thief, and the greatest deer-stealers make the best park-keepers.*

In the twentieth century, the title of the Alfred Hitchcock comedy-thriller TO CATCH A THIEF (1951), a story of a falsely accused cat burglar racing to catch a real cat burglar, was based upon the proverb.

The expression 'set a thief to catch a thief' came to mind when I read with disbelief your front page story Police Recruit Crooks last week.
SUNDAY MIRROR, 19 NOVEMBER 2000

Jamie looked at Isabel, who raised an eyebrow. There was an idea forming in her mind. 'Set a thief to catch a thief,' she said, '...what we need to do is get the message to Johnny Sanderson that we're no longer involved in any way...we could get Minty to tell him that she's fully aware of his visit here. If she gets the message to him that she knows that he's been leaning on me, then he would presumably not try anything further. If I came to any harm, he would have at least one arch enemy who would point the finger at him.
ALEXANDER McCALL SMITH,
THE SUNDAY PHILOSOPHY CLUB, 2004

TIME

a stitch in time saves nine
see to a problem as soon as it starts and you will save yourself a lot of work

It is only since the advent of the throwaway society after the Second World War that clothes and linen are often discarded if they are torn, showing wear or just unfashionable. Before this, garments were carefully mended, shirt collars replaced and sheets turned edges to middle to prolong their useful lives. The proverb, recorded by Thomas Fuller in GNOMOLOGIA (1732) as *A Stitch in Time may save nine*, pointed out that prompt action at the first sign of a tear would make mending it easier and the darn less visible.

Louisa M Alcott, the nineteenth century American writer, lived in genteel poverty and was no stranger to good stewardship and the well-stocked workbox. *A stitch in time saves nine* was one of the proverbs she chose to illustrate in her PROVERB TALES. (See ALCOTT'S MORAL TALES, page 240.)

So why did the Bank move now, rather than wait until there were definite signs that the British economy is catching a chill from America? According to Ciaran Barr, chief UK economist at Deutsche Bank, the MPC's philosophy today was a stitch in time saves nine.
GUARDIAN UNLIMITED,
8 FEBRUARY 2001

ALCOTT'S MORAL TALES

Louisa M Alcott (1832–88) was an American novelist and poet. Her father, Bronson Alcott, kept the family poor by his philanthropic and educational enterprises, so Louisa had to work to help support the family. She wrote her first book in 1818 when she was just 16 but became particularly well known for LITTLE WOMEN, published in 1868. Just one year earlier, she had published LOUISA M ALCOTT'S PROVERB STORIES, in which three stories centre around a different proverb. 'Kitty's Class-Day' is based on *A stitch in TIME saves nine*, 'Psyche's Art' on *HANDSOME is as handsome does*, and 'Aunt Kipp' on *Children and fools speak the truth*. Alcott uses some 30 proverbs in her three stories.

In later editions, the collection expands to include: 'A Country Christmas' – *a handful of good life is worth a bushel of learning*; 'On Picket Duty' – *better LATE than never*; 'The Baron's Gloves or Amy's Romance' – *all is fair in LOVE and war*; 'My Red Cap' – *he who serves well need not fear to ask his wages*; 'What the Bells Saw and Said' – *bells ring others to church but go not in themselves*.

In the brief preface to the final edition, Alcott displays a curious attitude to her work and her readers:

…I have collected various waifs and strays to appease young people who clamor for more, forgetting that mortal brains need rest.

As many girls have asked to see what sort of tales Jo March wrote at the beginning of her career, I have added 'The Baron's Gloves', as a sample of the romantic rubbish which paid so well once upon a time. If it shows what not to write it will not have been preserved from oblivion in vain.

A stitch in time saves nine easily applies to one's health. If you take care of yourself now, you reap the rewards of good health later in life.
ALASKA BUSINESS MONTHLY,
1 AUGUST 2005

there's a time for everything

everything has its appointed time or season to happen

Variant: There's a time and place for everything

The proverb is derived from verses in the Old Testament Book of ECCLESIASTES, chapter 3: *To every thing there is a season, and a time to every purpose under the heaven: A time to be born, and a time to die; a time to plant, and a time to pluck up that which is planted; A time to kill, and a time to heal; a time to break down, and a time to build up; A time to weep, and a time to laugh, a time to mourn, and a time to dance…*

It has been in use in English since at least the fourteenth century. Chaucer makes frequent use of it in his various writings, and William Langland used it in RICHARD THE REDELESS (1399): *But all thinge hath tyme.*

Suddenly, music that has been ignored for decades in Nashville is gaining some high profile attention. Paul Burch, one of the young upstarts enthralled with old-time country music, hopes this is a good omen. 'There's a time for everything,' said Burch, hopefully.
CHICAGO SUN-TIMES, 18 MAY 2001

Cher is coming to the UK and Ireland to perform some of her last shows. The pop superstar will be here in May as part of her Farewell Tour… This will be fans' final chance to see the 57-year-old singer in concert. She has decided to bow out 'before rust sets in' and concentrate on her film

career. 'There's a time for everything and I think this is the right time to stop,' she said. 'This show is the best I've ever done and I want to leave on a high.'
SOUTH WALES ECHO,
13 FEBRUARY 2004

See also *Don't spoil the SHIP for a hap'orth of tar*

there's no time like the present
don't put that task off, do it now while you can

The proverb appeared in the play THE LOST LOVER by Mrs Mary de la Rivière Manley in 1696, and in Tobias Smollett's HUMPHREY CLINKER in 1771, and has been in frequent use ever since.

There's no time like the present to save for the future. Joining a pension scheme is the first step to a comfortable retirement – and the earlier you do it, the better.
THE INDEPENDENT ON SUNDAY,
6 AUGUST 2006

There's no time like the present to join a teaching organisation, says Tim Howe.
DAILY TELEGRAPH, 3 JANUARY 2007

See also *CARPE diem; Make HAY while the sun shines; Strike while the IRON'S hot; Gather ye ROSEBUDS while ye may; TIME and tide wait for no man; Never put off till TOMORROW what you can do today*

time and tide wait for no man
don't hesitate or delay before making a decision or an opportunity might be lost

Variant: Time and tide stay for no man

An early form of the proverb is quoted by Chaucer in his prologue to the Clerk's Tale (1387):

*For though we slepe or wake, or rome or ryde,
Ay fleeth the tyme, it nil no man abyde*

but it is much more in literary evidence from the late sixteenth-century onwards. It is mentioned in Robert Greene's A DISPUTATION BETWEEN A HEE CONNY-CATCHER AND A SHEE CONNY-CATCHER (1592) *Tyde nor time tarrieth no man.* By the end of the eighteenth century, it had settled down to the modern wording.

At first glance, the proverb seems self-evident: no one whose livelihood depends upon the sea can afford to miss the tide, whether a ship's captain wanting to set sail or a vendor of shellfish who searches the sands at low tide. Neither the tide nor time will accommodate any delays, and no one has the power to overcome them. Opportunities must be grasped while the time is ripe.

Tide, however, has another meaning, and it is probably this alternative sense that is meant by the proverb. *Tide* once meant 'season' or 'a time ripe for something', although it is now only extant in words like *Christmastide, Whitsuntide*, etc. Therefore, the proverb means 'Time and season (i.e. opportunity) wait for no man'...so *CARPE diem* and *gather ye ROSEBUDS while ye may.*

Time and tide wait for no man, however, and Lennon – the cornerstone of O'Neill's team construction – knows tonight could be a defining moment for one of Celtic's greatest-ever teams.
DAILY MAIL, 10 DECEMBER 2003

Time and tide wait for no man. Engineers for BT are attempting to bring 21st century communications to Holy Island, but they will have to battle with the seas to do so. They are restricted by the tides that famously cover the causeway, cutting off Lindisfarne from the mainland for up to 10 hours each day.
NEWCASTLE JOURNAL, 27 JUNE 2006

See also *CARPE diem; Make HAY while the sun shines; Strike while the IRON'S hot; Gather ye ROSEBUDS while ye may; TIME and tide wait for no man; There's no TIME like the present; Never put off till TOMORROW what you can do today*

time flies

time passes quickly

This is a translation of a Latin proverb, *Tempus fugit*. Man is much preoccupied by the passing of time, probably because it reminds him of his own mortality.

With the ancients, the relentless passing of time was a recurrent theme. *Alas the years glide swiftly by*, sighs Horace (ODES, 23 BC), while Ovid laments, *Time slips by, and we grow old with the silent years; there is no bridle can curb the flying days* (FASTI, c. AD 8).

Modern writers are no more cheerful. In TIME (c. 1900), Albert Fox Jr has obviously been spending rather too many hours pondering the Latin poets:

Just while we talk the jealous hours
Are bringing near the hearse and flowers

while Sir Osbert Sitwell (in MILORDO INGLESE, 1958) meditates on the fact that Time always manages to have the last laugh:

In reality, killing time
Is only the name for another of the
multifarious ways
By which Time kills us.

Sadly, in the time it has taken to read this entry, the reader will be a minute or so closer to eternity.

Tempus fugit: **time flies**. *Oh, Lord, does it ever. Quickly, let's glance back to the year 1987. That January, I cast forth on a new period of my life. At age 62, after 20 years with the Orlando Sentinel, I resigned from active duty and signed up with the army of retired persons.*
ORLANDO SENTINEL, 14 MARCH 2006

Can you believe it's been almost four years since the last city-wide election in York? **Time flies**.
FISHERGATE CONSERVATIVES,
FISHERGATE UPDATE, NOVEMBER 2006

Usage: The Latin *tempus fugit* is still sometimes quoted.

For other proverbs commonly quoted in Latin or English, see under *CARPE diem; CAVEAT emptor; FESTINA lente; Great OAKS from little acorns grow*

time is a great healer

all emotional hurts heal over with the passing of time

Variant: Time is the great healer

Time will bring healing Euripides tells us (ALCESTIS, c. 438 BC), and Menander concurs, saying that *Time is a healer of all ills* (FRAGMENTS, c. 300 BC). Seneca calls time *Nature's great healer* (AD MARCIAM DE CONSOLATIONE, c. AD 40).

In English literature, Chaucer writes *As tyme hem hurt, a tyme doth hem cure* (TROILUS AND CRESEYDE, c. 1380) and, almost 500 years later, Disraeli mentions that *Time is the great physician* (HENRIETTA TEMPLE, 1836). But it is not until the beginning of the twentieth century that the present-day proverb appears in literature and gains common currency.

They say **time is a great healer**, *but it still pains Jim Mackenzie to remember the day he found the body of his tragic pop star son, Billy.*
GLASGOW SUNDAY MAIL, 18 JUNE 2000

Time is a great healer but a rotten beautician.
MIRROR, 23 JUNE 2000

time is money

time is as much of an asset and resource as money; time is precious

In an age when directors of large companies earn vast salaries and fortunes are made on the exchange markets, this proverb has a very modern ring. It is, in fact, very ancient. As early as 430 BC, the Greek statesman Antiphon informs us that *the most costly outlay is the outlay of time* (MAXIM), a maxim repeated just over a century later by the philosopher Theophrastus (MAXIM, c. 320 BC). The French philosopher Montaigne referred to the proverb as an *old saying* when he quoted it in his ESSAYS of 1580. But it was possibly Benjamin Franklin who drew attention to it in the English language when he used it in ADVICE TO A YOUNG TRADESMAN (1748), and the fact that Dickens twice favoured the maxim that made it stay there.

Time is not money, dammit! Interest does not accrue. Saving time makes no kind of sense unless we use the savings generously, joyously and wisely.
GOOD HOUSEKEEPING, AUGUST 2000

Time is money for truckers, but safety is priceless. A three-day inspection campaign is one way to make sure the rules are being followed. So while it's understandable that trucking companies and their drivers dislike that a nationwide truck-safety campaign will cost them time and money, it's still fair that the crackdown take place.
PORTLAND PRESS HERALD, 7 JUNE 2006

TOMORROW

never put off till tomorrow what you can do today

if a job needs doing, get on and do it straight away

An ancient proverb warns against putting off work until tomorrow. He who does so, it goes on to say, is always grappling with ruin. In Chaucer's day it was not work but welldoing that should not be deferred. In TALE OF MELIBEUS (c. 1386) he writes: *Ther is an old proverbe seith: that 'the goodnesse that thou mayst do this day, do it; and abyde nat ne delaye it nat till to-morwe.*

Addison, writing in the SPECTATOR (1712), pronounces that the maxim *should be inviolable with a man in office, never to think of doing that to-morrow which may be done to-day.* And indeed, the proverb has been the axiom of many men of importance.

According to the diplomat James Howell *Secretary Cecil... would oftimes speak of himself, 'It shall never be said of me that I will defer till to-morrow what I can do to-day'* (LETTER, 5 September 1633). Robert Cecil, Earl of Salisbury, was Secretary of State under Elizabeth and James I, rising to the position of Lord Treasurer in 1608 and remaining James's chief minister until his death in 1612. Lord Chesterfield, the eighteenth century statesman and man of letters, extolled the import of the saying and the proverb was chosen by US president Thomas Jefferson as one of ten *canons of conduct* (1817).

Of course, there is the alternative point of view, as expressed by Matthew Browne in THE CHILD'S WORLD (c. 1866):

> *Never do today what you can*
> *Put off till to-morrow*

and that makes a lot of sense, too.

*Never put off till tomorrow what you
can do today because tomorrow the weeds
will simply be bigger.*
BIRMINGHAM EVENING MAIL,
30 JUNE 2001

*Never put off until tomorrow what you
can do today: By tomorrow, somebody
may have levied a tax on it.*
WASHINGTON POST, 1 MARCH 2005

See also: *CARPE diem; Make HAY while
the sun shines; Strike while the IRON'S
hot; PROCRASTINATION is the thief of
time; Gather ye ROSEBUDS while ye
may; TIME and tide wait for no man;
There's no TIME like the present*

tomorrow is another day
do not allow your present troubles to
defeat you, for tomorrow brings the
hope of better things

This proverb is of Spanish origin. It
probably came into English through LA
TRAGICOMEDIA DE CALISTO Y
MELIBEA (1499), more commonly
known as LA CELESTINA, a dramatic
novel that achieved great success
throughout Europe. The earliest
written record of the saying is found in
an outstanding English adaptation of
part of the novel, CALISTO AND
MELIBOEA (c. 1520): *Well, mother, tomorrow is a new day*. Another significant
Spanish influence was Cervantes's
DON QUIXOTE (1605), which was
widely translated into English.
    Tomorrow is a new day persisted in
English until around the middle of the
nineteenth century, when *Tomorrow is
another day* is found.
    More recently Margaret Mitchell
used the proverb to close her book
GONE WITH THE WIND (1936), as
the wilful heroine Scarlett O'Hara
turns her back on the ruins of her life,
and looks to the future with misplaced
optimism.

*Swallowing his bitter disappointment, Coe
commented moments after the 800m final:
'Tomorrow is another day and there will
be another battle'.*
BIRMINGHAM EVENING MAIL,
3 MARCH 2001

*Don't give up on your dreams. Move
forward one day at a time, keep smiling and
remember that tomorrow is another day.*
NEWCASTLE JOURNAL, 19 JULY 2005

See also *Every CLOUD has a silver
lining; Sufficient unto the DAY is the evil
thereof; HOPE springs eternal in the
human breast; The darkest HOUR is that
before the dawn*

tomorrow never comes
a warning not to put things off till later
or they will never get done/happen

The form of the proverb has changed
over the centuries. Taverner (1539)
says *Tomorrow is never present*, Chamber-
lain (1602) has *Tomorrow comes not yet*
and Ray (1678) records *Tomorrow come
never*, a form still current in the first
half of the nineteenth century.
    The dawn of every new day brings
the dawn of a new tomorrow. It is
impossible to catch up with the future,
as Martial's cryptic epigram shows: *Tell
me, Postumus, when does that tomorrow of
yours come?* (c. AD 90). The proverb
is often used as a retort to those who
put off tasks or plans 'until tomorrow'
for, as Benjamin Franklin noted: *Tomorrow every fault is to be amended; but
that Tomorrow never comes* (POOR
RICHARD'S ALMANACK, 1756) or, as
a Spanish proverb puts it, *Tomorrow is
often the busiest day of the year.*

*As long as most of us can remember, the
UK cable industry has been about jam
tomorrow but, for one reason or another,
tomorrow never comes. There's always
some excuse for failure to reach the
ever-receding horizon of profitability...*
INDEPENDENT, 20 JULY 2001

I'm the same with losing weight as I am with my tax return. It's always something I'll start tomorrow but, of course, **tomorrow never comes.**
BIRMINGHAM SUNDAY MERCURY,
18 JANUARY 2004

See also *Make HAY while the sun shines; PROCRASTINATION is the thief of time; Never put off till TOMORROW what you can do today*

TOUGH

when the going gets tough, the tough get going
when the situation worsens, those who are bold and strong rise to meet the challenge

The modern proverb is generally attributed to Joseph P Kennedy Sr (1888–1969), father of US President John F Kennedy, though it is impossible to be certain of its exact coinage. Joseph Kennedy was a highly ambitious businessman and politician. He made his fortune through canny investment and playing the stock market in ways that, nowadays, would be judged illegal: insider dealing and market manipulation. His support for Franklin D. Roosevelt's presidential campaign in 1932 also brought political rewards, including the appointment as US Ambassador to Great Britain.

During the Second World War, Kennedy favoured appeasement and sought to meet with Hitler, a move that eventually forced his resignation when Roosevelt began to adopt a more forceful anti-German policy. Denied further political advancement for himself, Kennedy channelled his energies into preparing his son Joseph Jr for the presidency. However, when he was killed in the war Joseph Kennedy Sr transferred his efforts to his next son, John F Kennedy, who became

President in 1961. The axiom dates from this period. According to J H Cutler in HONEY FITZ (1962), a biography of Joseph P Kennedy's friend and fellow politician John F Fitzgerald, *Joe made his children stay on their toes... He would bear down on them and tell them, 'When the going gets tough, the tough get going.'*

Joseph Kennedy knew what he was talking about. Apart from his own ruthless ambition, there were plenty of challenges in his private life, too. Of his nine children, four predeceased him, none of whom died of natural causes. Another daughter was mentally retarded following an ill-advised operation on her brain.

The proverb is now widely used. In 1986, a song with that title was written for the Michael Douglas film THE JEWEL OF THE NILE. Sung by Billy Ocean, it became a big hit in Britain and the US.

When the going gets tough, the tough get going, even when they're facing 60. On Wednesday, DC Comics is releasing a new comic book starring Wonder Woman as she celebrates her 60th anniversary.
SEATTLE POST-INTELLIGENCER,
12 NOVEMBER 2001

When the going gets tough, the tough get going. Except that in Barbara Amiel's case, she didn't. Or rather she hasn't so far. Derided as the ultimate hard-nosed gold-digger, Lady Black has yet to give her critics what they desperately want by leaving her husband as his fortunes take a dramatic dive.
DAILY TELEGRAPH, 13 JULY 2007

TRUTH

truth is stranger than fiction
real-life happenings are more unbelievable than the wildest imaginings of writers of fiction

The close relationship between truth and fiction has been a source of comment for over two millennia. Horace insisted that to be convincing, fiction should be close to truth: *Fictions meant to please should be very close to truth* (DE ARTE POETICA, c. 20 BC); James Russell Lowell emphasised the paradox that fiction might be more true than fact: *There is a truth of fiction more veracious than the truth of fact* (THE BIGLOW PAPERS, 1848). Byron quoted the proverb in his DON JUAN (1823):

*Tis strange – but true; for truth is always strange –
Stranger than fiction*

and references to the saying can be found throughout nineteenth century literature.

At times, as the proverb claims, true stories seem so improbable as to stretch one's credulity. One such is told about Dr Thomas Young who was amongst those attempting to decipher the Rosetta Stone. He had been given an ancient Egyptian papyrus manuscript, which he was struggling to make sense of. Amongst the hieroglyphics he made out three names written in Greek characters, Apollonius, Antigonus and Antimachus. A short time afterwards a friend gave him a number of papyrus documents which he had just procured. Dr Young turned with interest to one of these, a manuscript in Greek. Suddenly he noticed with excitement the words Antimachus, Antigensis and then Portis Apollonii. He was looking at nothing other than a Greek translation of the very document which was causing him so much difficulty and frustration. *A most extraordinary chance,* Dr Young said, *had brought into my possession a document which was not very likely, in the first place, ever to have existed, still less to have been preserved uninjured, for my information, through a period of near two thousand years; but that this very extraordinary translation should have been brought safely to Europe, to England, and to me, at the very moment when it was most of all desirable to me to possess it, as the illustration of an original which I was then studying, but without any other reasonable hope of comprehending it, – this combination would, in other times, have been considered as affording ample evidence of my having become an Egyptian sorcerer.* The strange coincidence proved a key to unlocking the whole mystery of hieroglyphics.

Remarkable as this incident is, it is not exceptional. Yet who, on coming across such a story in a work of fiction, would not accuse the author of an unlikely and contrived plot – a thought expressed by Shakespeare in TWELFTH NIGHT (1601): *If this were played upon a stage now, I could condemn it as an improbable fiction.*

Truth is stranger than fiction, or so the saying goes. This is the real-life saga of Viv Nicholson's downfall from rags to riches to rags again after winning the pools.
LIVERPOOL ECHO, 30 NOVEMBER 2001

*It's often said that **truth is stranger than fiction**, and it couldn't get much more strange than a 1940s Boone County murder case and its aftermath.*
CINCINNATI POST, 9 NOVEMBER 2006

· U ·

UNITED

united we stand, divided we fall

strength lies in unity, division causes weakness

This is an American maxim which became the motto of the state of Kentucky in 1942. It comes from the patriotic LIBERTY SONG, written by John Dickinson and published in the BOSTON GAZETTE on 18 July 1768:

> Then join hand in hand, brave
> Americans all.
> By uniting we stand, by dividing we fall!

The line became a rallying cry in the American War of Independence (1775–83), a fact acknowledged by George Pope Morris in THE FLAG OF OUR UNION (1849):

> A song for our banner!
> The watchword recall
> Which gave the Republic her station:
> 'United we stand, divided we fall!'
> It made and preserved us a nation!

There is nothing American about the idea behind the maxim, however. It was expressed centuries earlier in Aesop's fables and in the Bible. (See *a HOUSE divided against itself cannot stand*.) Nor is the saying limited to American politics and revolution; it has been used as a rallying cry throughout the English-speaking world in trade unions, churches and armies.

Shore said the story carries a message for today about the strength of people who stick together, whether they're in Syracuse, New York City, Washington, D.C., or anywhere in the world. Then, in one clear voice, all the pupils said: 'United we stand, divided we fall.'
SYRACUSE POST-STANDARD,
20 SEPTEMBER 2002

As Women's History Month begins, I feel I need to remind feminists around the world that **United We Stand, Divided We Fall** *is not just a cute catch phrase. It's the only way to get anything accomplished.*
UNIVERSITY WIRE, 1 MARCH 2002

See also *A HOUSE divided against itself cannot stand*

· V ·

VARIETY

variety is the spice of life
what makes life interesting is constant variation and change

The proverb comes from Book II of THE TASK (1784), a poem by William Cowper. Among lines about dress, where Cowper mocks all the excesses and caprices of ever-changing fashion, we find:

> *Variety's the very spice of life,*
> *That gives it all its flavour. We have run*
> *Through every change that fancy at the loom,*
> *Exhausted, has had genius to supply.*

The line has been cited as a proverb since at least the early twentieth century.

Variety is the spice of life, so why should you stick to the same club week in week out? In response to members' suggestions, Esporta has developed the Freeway scheme which allows you to try out different clubs in your area, or while you're on holiday.
ESPORTA, SUMMER 2001

*They say **variety is the spice of life** – and I certainly get plenty of it over the course of a working week at the Examiner. As third man behind John Gledhill and Mel Booth I have responsibility for laying out pages and sub-editing. But any journalist worth their salt would say the best part of the job is gathering and writing stories – and I get plenty of opportunity to do that too.*
HUDDERSFIELD DAILY EXAMINER, 17 MAY 2005

See also *All work and no play makes JACK a dull boy*

VIRTUE

virtue is its own reward
The satisfaction of having acted properly is sufficient recompense in itself

Stoicism was an important and widespread school of philosophy in the ancient world. It was founded by Zeno around 310 BC and its influence is felt in the works of Seneca, Epictetus and others. One of its tenets was that *Virtue is its own reward*, a view that was expounded by many classical writers.

English writers later debated the belief. Sir Thomas Browne took issue with it: *Ipsa sui pretium virtus sibi, that Vertue is her own reward, is but a cold principle and not able to maintain our variable resolutions in a constant and settled way of goodness* (RELIGIO MEDICI, 1643). While Thomas Carlyle, in his MISCELLANIES (1857), pointed out that *To propose a reward for virtue is to render virtue impossible*. The proverb has been current in English since at least the mid-seventeenth century.

*I read with dismay that Kenneth Behring's generous donation to the National Museum of American History will be rewarded by his having his name prominently added to the museum's and that he will have input into Smithsonian programs... Mr. Behring is to be commended for his largess, but he should be told that **virtue is its own reward**.*
WASHINGTON POST, 30 SEPTEMBER 2000

*Gradually, Anne becomes more sensible,
and also beautiful and brainy and popular.
Marilla gets kinder and happier, and even
Matthew starts to perk up.* **Virtue is its
own reward**, *you see, and something more
than that: the truly virtuous have the
power to infect the world around them for
the better. And so, in the long run, the truly
virtuous will win.*
NEW STATESMAN, 3 DECEMBER 2001

WALLS

walls have ears

be careful how and where you disclose your private affairs for, even when it is not apparent, someone may be listening

The proverb advises that, though people may think they are alone when they share their secrets, there may well be someone concealed behind a nearby wall listening to every word. The notion was expressed in the BABYLONIAN TALMUD: BERACHOT (c. 450). In England, in the Middle Ages, it was the countryside which conspired not only to eavesdrop but also to spy. A medieval Latin proverb from at least the turn of the thirteenth century warns that *Field hath eye and the wood hath the keenness of an ear*. Chaucer used it in THE KNIGHTES TALE (c. 1387), and there are several references to it in sixteenth century literature. Ray recorded the expression in his proverb collection of 1670. In the following centuries, Swift and Scott were amongst those writers who used the saying.

Walls have ears appears in French around the turn of the sixteenth century, and in English in the following century. Swift mixes all sorts of proverb variants to good effect in A PASTORAL DIALOGUE (1727): *Walls have Tongues and Hedges, Ears*.

Precautions against being overheard are obviously important during wartime. *Walls have ears* gained a new lease of life during the Second World War when it was a slogan of government propaganda to make people aware that *Enemy ears are listening* and *Careless talk costs lives*.

*'Obviously we can win the title. We're in a great situation.' But Portakabin **walls have ears** and he suddenly corrects himself. 'We can't celebrate too much. The Bradford game is a big one, just as big as the Roma one. The Premiership is bigger than anything.'*
SUNDAY MIRROR, 12 MARCH 2000

*'I do believe you get a rebellious pleasure from saying the word out loud. Though I would suggest you expunge it from your vocabulary. **Walls have ears**.'*
SARAH DUNANT,
THE BIRTH OF VENUS, 2003

See MEDIEVAL LATIN, page 214

WASTE

waste not, want not

if you do not squander your money or resources, you will never be in need

This makes an apt proverb for the age of consumerism. The current proverb is found in literature from the end of the eighteenth century but its use by Maria Edgeworth makes it evident that the saying was already well known: *The following words were written...over the mantelpiece in his uncle's spacious kitchen, Waste not, want not.'* (THE PARENT'S ASSISTANT, 1796).

Indeed, the notion of squandering resources was discussed by ancient writers, amongst them Plautus: *He shall come to want who wastes his substance*

(MERCATOR, c. 200 BC). The theme was picked up in English by the unknown author of PROVERBS OF WYSDOM (c. 1450), who wrote:

Who of plente wyll take no hede,
Shal fynde defawte yn tyme of need.

And the Tudor playwright and poet Richard Edwards, who wrote a great deal on the theme of the virtuous life and whose work is peppered with proverbs, cited *Want is next to waste* in his PARADISE OF DAINTY DEVICES (1576). By the early eighteenth century, the alliterative proverb *Wilful waste makes woeful want* was current, and remained so until well into the nineteenth century. The present-day saying *Waste not, want not* is a variant from this proverbial trail.

Eventually the skin behind the old head splits and the caterpillar crawls out.For about an hour afterwards the caterpillar stands still while its new skin hardens. Many species at this stage eat their old skin – waste not, want not!
TIMES EDUCATIONAL SUPPLEMENT,
31 MARCH 2006

The other day I did something so fabulously stupid that even I can't quite believe I actually did it. I was in a shoe shop buying a pair of trainers…and when the assistant brought out a pair I liked, I said I'd have them, despite the fact that they were a bit too small. Why didn't I ask for the next size up? Um, well, I'm quite self-conscious about my feet and I didn't want the assistant to know that I needed a larger size…my journey to and from work is now marred by a slight pinching around the toes and will continue to be until I've worn the damn things out ('waste not, want not' being another of my annoying self-imposed mantras).
GOOD HOUSEKEEPING, APRIL 2006

WATERS

still waters run deep

a quiet and composed manner may hide knowledge, deep emotion, talent, etc

Variant: Silent waters run deep

Still waters are deep. No ripple on the surface betrays what lurks beneath. The notion is found in DISTICHA (c. 175 BC), which some attribute to Cato: *Though the stream is placid, perchance it hides the deeper wave.* An early English reference to this comes in the CURSOR MUNDI, an anonymous poem of the early fourteenth century written in northern Middle English: *Ther the flode is deppist the water standis stillist.* Those who brood in silence without betraying their emotion are to be feared, for *the stillest humours are the worst* (John Ray, ENGLISH PROVERBS, 1670).

Still waters are silent. Another Latin writer, Quintus Curtius, says: *The deepest rivers run with the least sound* (DE REBUS ALEXANDRI MAGNI, c. AD 50), a statement echoed in Seneca's HIPPOLYTUS: *Light griefs are loquacious, but the great are dumb.* Sir Walter Raleigh found inspiration in both in a poem he wrote for Queen Elizabeth I (1599):

Our passions are most like to floods
and streams,
The shallow murmur but the deep are dumb.

Still water is almost motionless. Shallow water is swift; grudges are noisily expressed and quickly over. The brooding resentment symbolised by deep water scarcely slides by: *Take heed of still waters, the quick pass away* (George Herbert, JACULA PRUDENTUM, 1640).

Still waters run deep indeed, causing Thomas Fuller to cry *God defend me from the still Water, and I'll leap myself from the Rough* (GNOMOLOGIA, 1732).

The saying still waters run deep
sums you up – you're more complex
and introspective than you may appear.
You also tend to get overemotional.
MARIE CLAIRE, 1 JULY 2006

George is an intensely private man, not one
for talk (he thinks it is 'over-rated')… But,
as the old saying goes, still waters run
deep. And underneath the calm there is a
tide of emotions that threatens to burst forth.
BIRMINGHAM POST, 16 SEPTEMBER 2006

Usage: Silence in others may hide
meditation and reflection and hidden
depths. It may hide unforeseen skills,
even dubious practices. It may arouse
emotions from admiration through
to fear. The proverb is used as a
comment in situations such as these,
and many others.

WEAR

it is better to wear out than to rust out
it is better to die from being too busy
than from sitting about all day

This proverb is usually the retort of a
vigorous elderly person upon being told
to take things more slowly. Plutarch
shared this attitude. Speaking of the
elderly he says that their worth is
extinguished by idleness as iron is destroyed
by rust (MORALIA: OLD MEN IN
PUBLIC AFFAIRS, c. AD 95). A
favourite maxim of Martin Luther
(1483–1546) was *If I rest, I rust*, and
German has other proverbs linking rust
and inactivity.

The English proverb comes from a
remark made by Bishop Cumberland
(1632–1718) who, upon being told by
a concerned friend that he was
overworking and would wear himself
out, replied *It is better to wear out than to*
rust out. This anecdote has been given
several airings, one of them in Horne's
SERMON ON THE DUTY OF

CONTENDING FOR THE TRUTH
(1786). It impressed the fiery
evangelical George Whitefield, who
quoted Cumberland as he toiled for the
gospel: *I had rather wear out than rust out*
(remark c. 1770, cited in Southey's
LIFE OF WESLEY, c. 1820).

Some people who are getting on in
years, however, feel justified in winding
down a little. Shakespeare's Falstaff
(HENRY IV PART II, 1597) has a word
for those who would really rather just
rust out in peace:

If ye will needs say I am an old man, you
should give me rest. I would to God my
name were not so terrible to the enemy as it
is. I were better to be eaten to death with a
rust than to be scoured to nothing with
perpetual motion.

Adopting his grandmother's maxim that it
was 'better to wear out than rust
away', Maurice traded his family's large
Victorian house on the Somerset coast for a
desolate settlement on the northern tip of
Baffin Island.
DAILY TELEGRAPH, 2 MAY 2004

At 95, the Californian still has an
athlete's body… When he's back home,
Clentzos says, he goes to the Pasadena
Athletic Club every day to work out, lifting
weights, doing calisthenics and swimming…
'If you sit around like an old car, your tires
will start to crack and you'll fall apart,' he
says. 'It's better to wear out than to
rust out.'
OAKLAND TRIBUNE, 26 AUGUST 2004

WIND

it's an ill wind that blows nobody any good
in every difficulty or loss there is
usually someone who benefits by it

The proverb was already known in the
sixteenth century, being recorded by
John Heywood in his PROVERBS

(1546). The expression is a nautical one and refers to sailing ships. Where sailors travelling east would have to work hard to tack against an easterly wind, the same wind would be advantageous to a ship travelling in the opposite direction, with the wind behind it filling the sails. Somebody will benefit, whatever the direction of the wind. Tusser makes this point in his 'Description of the Properties of Wind' in FIVE HUNDRED POINTS OF GOOD HUSBANDRY (1573):

> Except wind stands as never it stood,
> It is an ill wind turns none to good.

The expression figures in many of the proverb collections and in the work of major authors such as Shakespeare: *Ill blows the wind that profits nobody* (HENRY VI, PART III, 1593).

*They say **it's an ill wind that blows no good**, but one charity hopes to benefit from falling share prices. Now that many telecommunications and technology stocks are worth a fraction of what investors paid for them, some may be eager to wash their hands of them and do somebody else a good turn at the same time.*
DAILY TELEGRAPH, 6 OCTOBER 2001

***It's an ill wind that blows nobody any good**, and the ill winds of April, May and most of June have finally blown in one benefit. Namely, that the summer sales have more unsold stock than usual. If you went shopping at the weekend you have my sympathy because, had you waited a couple of days, you would have saved yourself a packet.*
EVENING STANDARD, 20 JUNE 2005

Usage: The proverb is often shortened to *It's an ill wind*, the rest being understood.

WORD

there's many a true word spoken in jest

a humorous, joking remark may hide a profound insight or a serious criticism/ a light-hearted comment may turn out to be true

The cook and the monk in Chaucer's CANTERBURY TALES (c. 1387) both testify to the truth behind the proverb. The cook says that *A man may seye full sooth in game and pley* (PROLOGUE TO THE COOK'S TALE), and the monk that *Ful oft in game a sooth I have herd saye* (PROLOGUE TO THE MONK'S TALE).

At the end of the sixteenth century David Fergusson recorded a Scottish saying which, although expressed in archaic vocabulary, is identical in word order and meaning to the modern expression: *There are many sooth words spoken in bourding* (SCOTTISH PROVERBS, c. 1595, pub 1641). The proverb is frequently found thereafter. Both French and Italian have equivalent adages.

International wits have over centuries taken advantage of punching home their point – with a smile:

The Romans would never have had time to conquer the world if they had been obliged first to learn Latin (Heinrich Heine).

If the art of conversation stood a little higher, we would have a lower birthrate (Stanislaw Lee).

One more word out of you and I'll paint you as you are (Berlin artist Max Liebermann to a talkative sitter).

Very nice, though there are dull stretches (Antoine de Rivarol, on reading a couplet).

You have Van Gogh's ear for music (Billy Wilder on hearing Cliff Osmond sing).

These particular examples are taken from Brandreth's excellent THE JOY OF LEX (1980), though the list could be endlessly extended.

*Joe Royle insisted he was only joking when he suggested his Manchester City side were 'in freefall', but, as the saying goes, **there's many a true word spoken in jest**. It's now five games without a victory for City, the early-season front-runners…*
INDEPENDENT, 12 MARCH 2000

*Match of the Day host Gary Lineker cheekily suggested the BBC won't bother to cover the Premiership next season because it has become so predictable. It was a tongue-in-cheek remark to herald the imminent end of the BBC deal to cover Premiership football. But **there's many a true word spoken in jest** and beneath the smile Lineker had a point.*
MIRROR, 16 APRIL 2001

Usage: There are two currently different senses. The first is in appreciation of a home truth or particularly apposite remark that has been made, sometimes on purpose and sometimes not, as a joke. The second is when a humorous remark that was never intended to be taken seriously turns out to be prophetic and comes true.

WORDS

fine words butter no parsnips
fine words (such as flattery or lavish but empty promises) are powerless to change things

Variant: Fair words butter no parsnips

Over the centuries, one way to make a dish of plain food more palatable has been to add a knob of butter to it. Since the proverb was coined during the seventeenth century, fair words have been unable to lend appeal to *fish*, *cabbage* or *turnips*, as well as the humble *parsnip*. The phrase finally settled into its present-day form in the second half of the eighteenth century.

Not everyone subscribes to the theory that fine words are ineffective, however. The nineteenth century novelist William Makepeace Thackeray puts up a robust argument to the contrary: *Who…said that fine words butter no parsnips? Half the parsnips of society are served and rendered palatable with no other sauce* (VANITY FAIR, 1847). But for Ogden Nash, once a parsnip, always a parsnip: *Parsnips are unbutterable* (MY DEAR, HOW EVER DID YOU THINK UP THIS DELICIOUS SALAD? 1935).

*Isn't it sad that even one of New Labour's finest is as addicted as they all are to double talk? He should remember what my mum used to say: '**fine words butter no parsnips**'.*
THE PEOPLE, 29 JUNE 2003

***Fine words butter no parsnips**. In spite of all Labour's promises on funding, sixth-form teachers dine on asparagus, grown in the garden of middle England's schools, while lecturers tuck into plates of root veg.*
TIMES EDUCATIONAL SUPPLEMENT, 11 MARCH 2005

See also *ACTIONS speak louder than words*

WORKMAN

a bad workman blames his tools
someone who has produced a shoddy piece of work will not admit that he is at fault but will seek to lay the blame elsewhere

Variant: An ill workman quarrels with his tools

Every workman needs the tools appropriate to his trade to do his work. According to Rabelais in GARGANTUA (1534) *A good workman can use any kind of tools*. In spite of this, there is the class of workman who seems unable to find tools to his liking and who blames the poor standard of his finished work upon this fact. He is the *bundler* whom we have all had the misfortune to hire at one time or another. *A bundler*, says Randle Cotgrave, *cannot find good tooles* (DICTIONARY, 1611).

The old form of the proverb was *An ill workman quarrels with his tools*. It is found in literature from the first half of the seventeenth century and is still occasionally heard today, although the twentieth century variant *A bad workman blames his tools* is the current form.

*Holidaymakers often tell me they don't consider themselves good enough skiers to appreciate the difference in skis... In Britain, we have it ingrained from a tender age that **a bad workman blames his tools**. This is a false belief that makes us reluctant to exploit all the tools available. And if you have not taken advantage of the craze for short skis yet, it is not just a case of being out of fashion, but of missing out on the chance to enjoy yourself.*
GUARDIAN, 1 DECEMBER 2001

*On his frequent raised eyebrows at the behaviour of the [snooker] table, Williams added, 'I did not play well but it does not help when you're trying to fight the table as well as your own form. A **bad workman blames his tools** but that table was an absolute joke, really, and Stuart agreed with me in the interval. The ball was sometimes coming off the cushion three times the speed it hit it – but not every time so it's impossible to judge your position.'*
CARDIFF WESTERN MAIL,
22 JANUARY 2004

WORLD

half the world doesn't know how the other half lives
one half of society cannot begin to imagine the problems, or pleasures, that occupy the other half daily

Variant: Half the world don't know how the other half live

The proverb is found in the work of Philippe de Commines, courtier of Louis XI of France, who was acclaimed as the first historian since ancient times to present his subject critically and philosophically. In his MEMOIRES (1509) de Commines writes: *This confirms the old saying, One half the world does not know what the other half is doing.* Twenty-three years later, Rablelais quotes the proverb in the form with which we are familiar in his PANTAGRUEL (1532). Its first appearance in English is to be found in George Herbert's collection JACULA PRUDENTUM (1640).

The saying can be applied to those who, from their position of social advantage, are unable to imagine the misery of the disadvantaged. James Kelly explains the proverb thus: *One half of the world kens not how the other lives. Men bred to ease and luxury are not sensible of the mean condition of a great many* (SCOTTISH PROVERBS, 1721). But today it can equally describe those on low income who get a glimpse of a more glamorous or socially superior lifestyle.

'Half the world doesn't know how the other half lives,' said Evelyn McPherson, sitting on their small sofa decorated in lion faces and framed by stuffed animals.
'When I was a boy,' Horace McPherson said, 'I didn't know we was poor. Everyone around us had what we had.'
VIRGINIAN PILOT, 3 MARCH 2001

*Finals day provided an interesting insight into **how the other half lives**, particularly the mega-rich tennis stars to whom £7,000 is little more than a laughing matter.*
BIRMINGHAM POST, 18 JUNE 2007

Usage: The full proverb is now more commonly reduced to the idiomatic expression *how the other half live*

it takes all sorts to make a world

the vast variety of humankind entails the need for tolerance

Variant: It takes all sorts to make the world

The adage was brought into English in 1620 by Thomas Shelton in his much acclaimed translation of Miguel Cervantes's DON QUIXOTE (1615): *In the world there must be of all sorts.* Philosopher John Locke, writing early in the eighteenth century, echoed Cervantes's thought, and was later credited with its coinage by Samuel Johnson in Boswell's LIFE OF JOHNSON (17 November 1767): *Some lady surely might be found…in whose fidelity you might repose. The World, says Locke, has people of all sorts.* Sometime during the first half of the nineteenth century, the proverb was moulded into the present-day form *It takes all sorts to make a world*, and has been in constant use ever since.

*They say **it takes all sorts to make a world**. But none quite so strange as the ones photographer Drew Gardner discovered for a new exhibition… he has just finished photographing a selection of British eccentrics who have found their fame through the pages of Guinness World Records.*
DAILY MAIL, 18 SEPTEMBER 2001

*I watched with amazement Janet Street-Porter on Tuesday night on Channel 4. I could not believe her attack on North Wales people and their language… **It takes all sorts to make a world** and I would have thought with her background in journalism she would be of the attitude of 'live and let live'.*
LIVERPOOL DAILY POST,
2 DECEMBER 2003

Usage: Can be said as an appeal for tolerance in the face of diversity, or as a resigned comment when faced with behaviour that goes beyond the normal

See also *LIVE and let live*

WORM

even a worm will turn

even the meekest or humblest person will eventually be goaded into retaliation

Variant: A worm will turn; every worm will turn

A correspondent in NOTES AND QUERIES (1853) denied that a worm would turn in anger when stepped upon. He preferred to think that the proverb was coined in the days when the word *worm* could be applied equally to a viper, a creature much better equipped to round upon its enemy. What the proverb meant, he argued, was that those who had the ability to fight back would certainly do so, and so people should take care how they treated them.

The proverb, however, means just what it says and draws the lesson that even the meekest person can be roused to retaliate from the keenly observed natural fact that, when a lowly earthworm is dug up or its tail trodden on, it instinctively writhes, turning back upon itself and appearing to threaten its attacker. This was certainly how Shakespeare understood the already current analogy when he wrote: *The smallest worm will turn, being trodden on* (HENRY VI, PART III, 1593).

The proverb is alluded to extensively in English literature from the sixteenth century onwards, thanks to the influence of Shakespeare. It is not, however, exclusive to English; the French, for instance, say *un ver se recoquille quand on marche dessus* ('A worm recoils when you step on it'). The figurative use of *worm* to mean 'a lowly, despised person' was current even in Old English. Wycliffe, the great Christian reformer, was described as one in 1402 for introducing the seeds of schism in the earth. The term certainly pre-dates the proverb itself.

The worm is turning. Teachers are fed up with being insulted and regimented and made to do government paperwork... In Britain today, properly qualified teachers are gold-dust. Everyone wants them. Only it doesn't feel that way, does it? Teachers feel just as fed up and put-upon as they always have done, and are hell-bent on making themselves even rarer by taking early retirement at, say, 33.
TIMES EDUCATIONAL SUPPLEMENT,
14 SEPTEMBER 2001

Why do children who are being bullied and abused keep silent for so long? I suppose my self-esteem was so low that I assumed I deserved the treatment I received, but every worm turns eventually. One day I came out of school and found Otty waiting in her little car to meet me. The unexpected joy of this treat was just too much and I suddenly blurted out: 'I'm sorry but I just can't go back – ever!'
JENNIFER REES LARCOMBE,
JOURNEY INTO GOD'S HEART, 2006

WRONGS

two wrongs don't make a right
avenging oneself by paying someone back in kind does not justify the unkind action

Two blacks do not make a white was a proverb current in the early eighteenth century. In his SCOTTISH PROVERBS (1721) James Kelly defined it thus: *Two blacks make no white. An answer to them who, being blam'd, say others have done as ill or worse.* This proverb was in common use until the early twentieth century. Indeed, it is still heard occasionally but has been largely replaced by an alternative adage of parallel construction and meaning *Two wrongs don't make a right.* This proverb was cited as *Two wrongs will not make a right* by Alan B Cheales in his PROVERBIAL FOLK-LORE (1875), and has been in frequent use ever since.

But while companies have every right to trace errant customers to get their money back, and of course tracing agents have every right to act on their behalf, the cost when they do so illegally – both to individual privacy and to the taxpayer – can be immense. 'The information commissioner's position is that two wrongs don't make a right,' says Alec Owens.
BIG ISSUE, 6 JANUARY 2002

'I was aiming for the body. I didn't plan to hit Floyd low,' Judah said later. But he fuelled the controversy by adding that 'Roger was choking me.' For his part Mayweather said he had been fouled but declared: 'I didn't return it because two wrongs don't make a right.'
GUARDIAN, 10 APRIL 2006

YOUNG

you're only young once

youthful behaviour is only tolerated in the young; be young and act young while you can

This is an American proverb, in use since at least the early 1940s. It is said when overlooking a youthful misdemeanour or permitting an activity no sensible adult would engage in. The Australian feminist, writer and broadcaster Germaine Greer is credited with the further insight *You're only young once, but you can be immature forever*.

*Remember that top-to-toe beige is fashion suicide. Boring clothes attract boring people. **You're only young once**, and in your 30s you should still be experimenting with colours and trends; you can still wear twentysomething clothes...*
DAILY MAIL, 10 JANUARY 2005

Queues formed early today as hundreds of wannabe stars flocked to St James' Park in Newcastle for the auditions of the sixth series of the reality show...
*At the front of the queue was 19-year-old Chris Redford who arrived at 4am to beat the rush. The Gateshead student said: 'I want to be on the programme because it's a laugh. **You're only young once.**'*
NEWCASTLE EVENING CHRONICLE, 12 FEBRUARY 2005

• bibliography •

This is a selective list of some of the books to which reference has been made. Details of major historical proverb collections can be found in An accumulation of wisdom (page 120) and Erasmas's Adagia (page 34). For an extremely valuable and comprehensive bibliography of proverbs, Mieder (1982) and (1990) are incomparable.

(1849–1935), *Notes and Queries for readers and writers, collectors and librarians*, London: Oxford University Press

The Phrase Finder at www.phrases.org.uk

Apperson, G. L. (1929), *English Proverbs and Proverbial Phrases: A Historical Dictionary*, London: J M Dent

Bartlett, J. (1992), *Familiar Quotations* (16th ed.), Boston: Little, Brown

Benham, W. G. (1948), *Denham's Book of Quotations, Proverbs and Household Words* (3rd ed.), London: Ward, Lock

Bombaugh, C. C. (1905), *Facts and Fancies for the Curious from the Harvest Fields of Literature: A Melange of Excerpta*, Philadelphia & London

Bonser, W. (1930), *A Bibliography of Works relating to Proverbs*

Brewer, E. C. (1991), *Brewer's Dictionary of 20th Century Phrase and Fable*, London: Cassell

Brewer, E. C. (1993), *Brewer's Dictionary of Phrase and Fable* (14th revised ed.), London: Cassell

Browning, D. C. (1951), *Everyman's Dictionary of Quotations and Proverbs*, London: Dent

Cahoon, D., & Edmonds, E. M. (1980), The Watched Pot Still Won't Boil:

Expectancy as a Variable in Estimating the Passage of Time, *Bulletin of Psychonomic Society, 16* (No. 2), (pp 115–116)

Dent, R. W. (1981), *Shakespeare's Proverbial Languages: An Index*, Berkeley: University of California Press

Dournons, J. Y. (1986), *Dictionnaire des Proverbes et Dictons de France*

Ewart, N. (1983), *Everyday Phrases*, Poole: Blandford

Fergusson, R. (1983), *Penguin Dictionary of Proverbs*, London: Penguin

Halliwell, J. O. (1850), *Dictionary of Archaic Words*, London: John Russell Smith

Hellmann, G. (1923), Über den Ursprung der volkstülichen Wetteregeln (Bauernregeln), *Sitzungsberichte der Preussischen Akademie der Wissenschaften*, (pp 148–170)

Helm, K. (1939), Bauernregeln, *Hessische Blatter fur Volkskunde, 38*, (pp 114–132)

Houghton, P. (1982), *A World of Proverbs*, Poole: Blandford

Jente, R. (1931–32), The American Proverb, *American Speech, 7*, (pp 342–348)

Jorgensen, P. A. (1976), Valor's Better Parts: Backgrounds and Meanings of Shakespeare's Most Difficult Proverb, *Shakespeare Studies, 9*, (pp 141–158)

Kabbaj, M. & Cherradi, El Fadili (1988, 2nd ed.), *Un Bouquet de Proverbes Marocains*, Casablanca: l'Imprimerie Idéale

Kirshenblatt-Gimblett, B. (1973a), A Playful Note: The Good Old Game of Proverbs, *Proverbium, 22*, (pp 860–861)

Kirshenblatt-Gimblett, B. (1937b), Toward a Theory of Proverb Meaning. *Proverbium, 22*, (pp 821–827)

Krueger, D. W. (1978), The Differential Diagnosis of Proverb Interpretation, in W. E. Fann, I. Karacan, A. D. Pokorny, & R. L. Williams (eds.), *Phenomenology and Treatment of Schizophrenia* (pp 193–201), New York: Spectrum

Lean, V.S. (1902–4), *Collecteana*, Bristol

Lehman, E. (1960), The Monster Test, *Archives of General Psychiatry, 3*, (pp 535–544)

Lundberg, G. A. (1958), The Semantics of Proverbs, *ETC: A Review of General Semantics, 15*, (pp 215–217)

Maloux, M. (1971), *Dictionnaire des Proverbes, Sentences et Maximes* (2nd ed.), Paris: Larousse

Maw, W. H., 6c Maw, E. W. (1975), Contrasting Proverbs as a Measure of Attitudes of College Students Towards Curiosity-Related Behaviours, *Psychological Reports, 37*, (pp 1085–1086)

Mieder, W. (1982), *International Proverb Scholarship: An Annotated Bibliography*, New York: Garland

Mieder, W. (1990), *International Proverb Scholarship: An Annotated Bibliography, Supplement 1 (1800–1981)*, New York: Garland

Meider, W., *De Proverbio* – Electronic Journal

Nares, R. (1822), *Glossary of Words, Phrases, Names and Allusions, particularly of Shakespeare*, London: Routledge

Ojoade, J. O. (1978–79), When in Rome do as the Romans do: African Parallels, *Midwestern Language & Folklore Newsletter, 1–2*, (pp 13–18)

Reich, J. H. (1981), Proverbs and the Modern Mental Status Examination, *Comprehensive Psychiatry, 22*, (pp 528–531)

Rees, N. (2004), *A Word in Your Shell-Like*, Glasgow: Harper Collins

Reisner, R. (1971), *Graffiti, Two Thousand Years of Wall Writing*, New York: Cowles Book Company

Ridout, R., & Witting, C. (1967), *English Proverbs Explained*, London: Heinemaiut

Simpson, J. (1992), *The Concise Oxford Dictionary of Proverbs* (2nd ed.), London: Oxford University Press

Smith, W.G. (1966), *The Oxford Dictionary of English Proverbs* (2nd ed.), London: Oxford

Skeat, W. W. (1910), *Early English proverbs ... of the 13th and 14th Centuries with illustrative quotations*

Stevenson, B. (1947), *Book of Proverbs, Maxims and Familiar Phrases*

Taylor, A. (1931), *The Proverb*, Cambridge, Massachusetts: Harvard University Press

Taylor, A. (1958), 'All is Not Gold that Glitters' and 'Rolandslied', *Romance Philology, 11*, (pp 370–371)

Taylor, A. (1965–66), The Road to 'An Englishman's House...', *Romance Philology, 19*, (pp 279–285)

Taylor, A. (1967a), The Collection and Study of Proverbs, *Proverbium, 8*, (pp 161–177)

Taylor, A. (1967b), Stolen Fruit is Always the Sweetest, *Proverbium, 7*, (pp 145–149)

Taylor, A. (1968), A Place for Everything and Everything in Its Place, *Proverbium, 10*, (pp 235–238)

Titleman, G.Y. (1996), *Random House Dictionary of Popular Proverbs and Sayings*

Trench, R. C. (1853), *Proverbs and their Lessons: being the substance of lectures delivered to young men's societies*, London: Kegan Paul

Vinken, P. J. (1958), Some Observations on the Symbolism of 'The Broken Pot' in Art and Literature, *American Imago, 15*, (pp 149–174)

Walsh, W. S. (1892), *Handy-Book of Literary Curiosities*, Philadelphia: Lippincott

Wright, T. (1846), On Proverbs and Popular Sayings, In T. Wright (eds.), *Essays on Subjects Connected with the Literature, Popular Superstitions, and History of England in the Middle Ages* (pp 124–175), London: John Russell Smith

• index •

C

S

Dictionary of Idioms
and their Origins

Linda and Roger Flavell

What is an idiom? Among other things, it is an expression whose words do not mean what they say. Someone *spilling the beans all over the table* may make a mess, but *spilling the beans all over town* means something else entirely. Idioms are also inflexible – you can't *beat about the shrub* or say that *the bush was beaten about*. English contains a great store of idioms that can be used in creative and forceful ways.

Dictionary of Idioms – first published in 1992, reprinted 17 times and now fully revised and expanded – examines over 500 of these expressions, tracing each one's source and history. New entries include *to play fast and loose* (from a 16th-century fairground game) and *head over heels* (an illogical variation on the more sensible 'heels over head').

'This *curate's egg* is *just the ticket* for the interested browser.' THE HERALD

'The authors present their eclectic material in a relaxed and speculative way, supported by a fascinating diversity of well-chosen quotations.'
INDEPENDENT ON SUNDAY

ISBN 978-1-85626-664-2/£9.99

Dictionary of Word Origins

Linda and Roger Flavell

Words are the building blocks of language, but their derivations are often stories in themselves. Have you ever wondered why we wear *perfume*, read *magazines*, vote for *candidates*, speak in *jargon*? With entries from *accolade* to *zoo* and including such disparate items as *blackmail, fiasco, influence* and *rigmarole, Dictionary of Word Origins* explains the origins and development of 300 commonly used words. Essays scattered throughout the book deal with more general topics such as *'A Taste of India'*, *'Days of the Week'* and *'Precise Timing'*.

In selecting words for inclusion, Linda and Roger Flavell have chosen those with a story to tell. The result is a fascinating guide to the richness and diversity of the English language. It boasts both sufficient scholarly accuracy to satisfy the serious student and much to the delight the browser motivated by a quest for knowledge and the love of words.

'A light-hearted trip through the fascinating byways of the English language.'
GOOD BOOK GUIDE

ISBN 978-1-85626-564-5/£7.99

The Dictionary Series Box Set

Linda and Roger Flavell

- Contains the four titles *Dictionary of Idioms*, *Dictionary of Proverbs*, *Dictionary of Word Origins* and *Dictionary of English Down the Ages*

- Over 1200 pages to delight the word lover and satisfy the scholar

If you've ever wondered why we wear perfume, read magazines, talk in jargon, behave lewdly or lackadaiscally, turn to *Dictionary of Word Origins*. For the origins of 'two wrongs don't make a right' or 'absence makes the heart grow fonder', try *Dictionary of Proverbs*. *Dictionary of Idioms* explains why we 'pull the wool over someone's eyes' or drink a 'hair of the dog', while *Dictionary of English Down the Ages* looks at a thousand years of historical events and the words that grew out of them – from the Norman Conquest that brought us dungeons and curfews to the twentieth-century movement that changed the meaning of the word green.

ISBN 978-1-85626-656-7/£29.95